W9-DAI-711

Christianity

Christianity

Roland H. Bainton

Foreword by Jaroslav Pelikan

A MARINER BOOK
HOUGHTON MIFFLIN COMPANY
BOSTON · NEW YORK

First Mariner Books edition 2000

Foreword copyright © 2000 by Jaroslav Pelikan
Copyright © 1964, 1992 by American Heritage Inc.

All rights reserved

An American Heritage Book

For information about permission to repro-
duce selections from this book, write to Text
Permissions, American Heritage Inc., Forbes
Building, 60 Fifth Avenue, New York, New
York 10011.

AMERICAN HERITAGE is a registered
trademark of American Heritage Inc. Its use
is pursuant to a license agreement.

Library of Congress Cataloging-in-
Publication Data is available.

ISBN 0-618-05687-4

Printed in the United States of America

QUF 10 9 8 7 6 5 4 3 2 1

Contents

Foreword

More than a third of a century ago Marshall B. Davidson, who was one of the editors of *Horizon Magazine,* invited me to review and evaluate (anonymously) a commissioned manuscript that he had under consideration as a book: *Christianity,* by Roland H. Bainton. The book was subsequently published by the American Heritage Publishing Company in 1964. The invitation made sense, despite the delicacy of the situation into which it placed me, for in 1962 I had succeeded the author of the manuscript in his chair of church history at Yale (which I held until 1972, when President Kingman Brewster, Jr., made me a Sterling Professor). Since the publication of Bainton's *Christianity,* many books on that subject have come and gone, but Bainton's account has turned out to be a hardy perennial. I have met people casually on a plane or train or after a guest lecture who, upon learning that I was a professor at Yale, asked me if I had known Roland Bainton and then spoke warmly about how they had been enlightened by this narrative of Christian history. As the textbook in a college course, as the basis for an adult discussion group at a church, or as personal summertime reading, it has become a classic; and now it promises to continue its ministry for another generation of readers, and more.

As a Latin proverb observes, "Every book has its own special destiny, *Habent sua fata libelli.*" One of the interesting destinies of this particular book—interesting because it tells us something not only about the book and its author but also about our own time— is that a recital of Christian history written more for readers outside the churches than for professed believers has become a standard item on Christian reading lists. Because of the "secular" audience that he had in view, Roland Bainton felt obliged (or was asked by his editors) to explain terms, concepts, practices, and doctrines that the average Christian might have been expected to know very well already, and to identify saints and sinners from the history of Christianity who would have been, or should have been, household names in any Christian church or family. But in fact such an acquaintance with the leading figures and the basic elements of the Christian tradition can probably no longer be taken for granted (if indeed it ever could), either in those who have grown up in the church or in those who have gone to college, or even in those who have done both. Whatever this situation may portend for the future state of the American soul and for the health of the churches—and I know I am not the only one in whom it arouses some deep concern—it does go a considerable way toward explaining why this book, among the many that have taken on a similar assignment, has managed to "keep going and going."

At the scholarly level, one of the reasons for this success must surely be Bainton's steadfast refusal to let himself be typecast as a narrow specialist in only one period or only one dimension of the history of Christianity. He is certainly best known today for his sprightly biographies of several Reformation figures—Michael Servetus (*Hunted Heretic,* 1953), Desiderius Erasmus (*Erasmus of Christendom,* 1969), and above all Martin Luther (the prizewinning *Here I Stand,* 1950); I have always wished that he had added one on Ignatius of Loyola, who was a kind of doppelgänger to the others. But even his fellow church historians were often unaware that his first publication had been in the field of the early church: *Basilidian Chronology and New Testament Interpretation* (1923). In 1960, moreover, he published both his monograph, *Constantine and Religious Liberty,* and his collection of studies, *Early Christianity.* Thereby he was living up to the stipulation that had been laid down in September 1888 (six years before Bainton was born) by the greatest of all modern scholars in church history, Professor Adolf von Harnack of the University of Berlin: that anyone who wants to study any period in the history of Christianity—be it the Middle Ages, or the Reformation, or the church in the Byzantine Empire, or even, though Harnack did not mention it, the history of American Christianity—must first of all acquire a more than superficial grasp of the early centuries, where the successes were achieved, the mistakes were made, and the patterns were set that later centuries would follow or reform or reject. Without such a grasp, the historian of a later period will have nothing better to go on than what Harnack (employing the English phrase) called "a certain common sense," rather than a genuine and firsthand understanding of the real issues. I am afraid that in all the fields I have enumerated, Harnack's judgment has repeatedly been vindicated during the intervening century. But Roland Bainton—most strikingly perhaps in his concentration on the issues of peace and war at different times in Christian history, as well as in his narrative of the Christian campaigns against slavery—could draw upon his knowledge of the ancient church to illuminate later developments.

That attention to slavery and war aptly illustrates another feature of this book, indeed of most of his books, that I always admired even though (or perhaps even because) I could not emulate it. Although I did go on for several years giving the lecture series in general church history at the Yale Divinity School that had been Professor Bainton's bread-and-butter course for so many decades, my real interest, my only genuine claim to scholarly expertise, and eventually my own bread-and-butter course (and a five-volume book) have been in the history of the development of Christian doctrine, or "historical theology" (*Dogmengeschichte* in German), as it was labeled when I taught it at the University of Chicago before coming to Yale. Therefore I had to rely on the work of other scholars (including Bainton) when I lectured on the relations between church and state or on the mission and expansion of Christianity or on the American Protestant churches. And because the complex interrelation between continuity and change has long been my special shtick, I have concentrated on relating the doctrinal development in one period to the doctrinal development in another period, idea to idea and system to system, rather than on relating it to the institutional, political, social, or biographical contexts of its own period. By contrast, when this book treats the controversies over the doctrine of the Trinity or the origins of monasticism or the impact of the Christian gospel on art and literature, it persistently emphasizes the total context. Roland Bainton was, in other words, an ambidextrous historian of Christianity.

He was ambidextrous (or, perhaps better, Janus-faced) in another sense as well, for both as a scholar and as a man, he was always able to look both ways, to see the world and the church and their history with the eyes of faith and yet to know, as though from the inside, the mind of the gainsayer and the skeptic. The skeptical French man of letters and historian Ernest Renan (1823–1892) prefaced his heavily romanticized *Life of Jesus* of 1863 with this job description: "To write the history of a religion, it is necessary, firstly, to have believed it (otherwise we should not be able to understand how it has charmed and satisfied the human conscience); in the second place, to believe it no longer, for absolute faith is incompatible with sincere history." The lifework of Roland Bainton, and in a special sense this history of Christianity from the very beginning in the Christmas story to the second half of the twentieth century, can stand as a vigorous refutation of that false dichotomy. He did "understand how it has charmed and satisfied the human conscience," and in some of the most moving passages of this book—for example, in the three or four pages about Saint Francis of Assisi—he waxes lyrical about how the dedication of Francis to poverty "was indeed an emancipation from care, but basically it was in the very spirit of Christ himself." But he understood just as well how the name and "spirit" of Christ have served as a cloak for hypocrisy and oppression and as a pretext for war and persecution. Whenever his account comes to the sectarian champions of toleration and religious liberty, or to the militant pacifists of Anabaptist and Quaker history, and to the unchristian treatment of such sectarians at the hands of the official churches and their political accomplices, his sympathies become obvious, as does his basic alienation from much of what in some circles still passes for conventional Christianity. In interpreting the great creative intellects who have arisen in the history of the church—Athanasius, Augustine, Thomas Aquinas, Martin Luther, or Jonathan Edwards—he manifests a far deeper empathy with their existential and personal stories than with "all the theological squabbling" and metaphysical speculation in which they let themselves become involved or with the authoritarian dogmas that they defended. Therefore one of the most trenchant and telling portraits in the entire book is his one-sentence account of Dante Alighieri: "In theology he was a Thomist, in politics an imperialist, in piety a Franciscan who portrayed Christ on the cross abandoned by all save Lady Poverty, and in his excoriation of evil popes almost a sectarian."

Throughout this book Professor Bainton reveals an awareness, which is sensitive to the point of sometimes being painful, that believing the Christian faith and living according to the Christian way of life cannot avoid ambiguity. One by one, the forces that have shaped the distinctively modern understanding of reality have produced an outlook that has contradicted the Christian worldview. The Enlightenment, which helped to establish religious toleration and human rights and thus to lay the philosophical foundations for modern democracy, did so at the expense of the historic

Judaeo-Christian belief in a transcendent revelation. Karl Marx brilliantly diagnosed the class struggle as the moving force in human history, but in the process he dethroned divine providence and dismissed religion as an "opium of the people." Charles Darwin traced the origin of animal species, including ultimately the human species, to the long processes of evolution rather than to an instantaneous fiat of the Creator "in the beginning"; therefore, "in an age when scientific discovery was making religion increasingly difficult for educated people to accept, Darwin's *On the Origin of Species* may have delivered the greatest blow." For a growing number, Christianity has become not only "increasingly difficult" to believe; it is, worse yet, unnecessary and uninteresting, and therefore irrelevant. Yet in spite of his sobering awareness of the realism of this situation in all its grimness, Roland Bainton the critical modern historian ever remained Roland Bainton the man of faith, as in his final paragraph: "What of the future? No man knows. . . . Yet the shadow of the cross is cast across the years, and faith in the Resurrection has quickened myriad hearts. . . . Like the Christian himself, the Church must in faith step forward boldly into darkness, leaving the outcome to God."

The declaration of a faith stepping boldly into the darkness of the future was, of course, written before the tumultuous events of the final third of the twentieth century, both in the church and in the world. Professor Bainton does not seem to have foreseen, for example, that the most vibrant geographical area for Christian growth at the end of the century would be sub-Saharan Africa. In Africa and many other regions (including especially Southeast Asia, the Middle East, the Caucasus, and the Balkans), the tensions and conflicts of Christianity with Islam—which go back to the expansion of the religion of the Prophet into the historic centers of Christendom in the Near East and in Africa, and were punctuated climactically by the history of the Crusades—have demonstrated how much unfinished business there is for Christianity to address in the new century. Closely related to this problem, and at the same time fundamentally different from it, is the altered relation of Christianity to Judaism: with the Nazi Holocaust, the creation of the State of Israel, and then the radial reformulation by the Second Vatican Council of the Christian doctrine of the permanence of the covenant of God with the people of Israel—this book was originally published in 1964 and has only one paragraph on the council—there is a new polarity in the relation of Christianity to other faiths. In addition, I hope that I am not reflecting only my personal and confessional position when I find here a strikingly Western slant and a corresponding underemphasis on the Eastern Orthodox Church. Despite occasional hints, moreover, the narrative in this book does not lead a reader to anticipate the revolution in the role of women in the church, which must surely continue to be a major focus of activism, and a major point of controversy, as far into the future as anyone can look. The "preferential option for the poor," which has become a dominant leitmotif in the social ethic of many churches, especially of the Roman Catholic Church, is a development that Bainton would have hailed with enthusiasm; but he does not touch on it except in passing. Yet all of these and other drastic changes, largely overlooked though they are in these chapters, do stand in a recognizable continuity with the centuries that are so graphically described in Bainton's volume.

In 1985, the year after his death, Beacon Press decided to reprint Professor Bainton's *The Reformation of the Sixteenth Century* and asked me for a foreword. Some of what I said there bears repeating here:

> Almost twenty-five years ago, in the autumn of 1960, I was invited to open conversations with the faculty and administration of Yale about the possibility of my becoming Titus Street Professor of Ecclesiastical History, to succeed Roland H. Bainton, who was nearing the statutory age of retirement and was therefore, legally speaking, "too old to teach."
>
> "Too old to teach," indeed! Roland Bainton went on teaching—not Yale students alone, but the world—for another two decades plus. And even now, when he cannot teach in person anymore, he goes on doing so through the remarkable library of volumes that he produced, both before and after his retirement.

The reissue of Roland H. Bainton's *Christianity* guarantees that he will go on doing so, well into the twenty-first century.

Jaroslav Pelikan
Sterling Professor of History Emeritus
Yale University
April 2000

Christianity

I
Backgrounds of Christianity

**This Byzantine relief shows a central event in
the religious history of the Hebrews: the giving
of the Law to Moses from the hand of God.**

In those days a decree went out from Caesar Augustus that all the world should be enrolled. This was the first enrollment, when Quirinius was governor of Syria. And all went to be enrolled, each to his own city. And Joseph also went up from Galilee, from the city of Nazareth, to Judea, to the city of David, which is called Bethlehem, because he was of the house and lineage of David, to be enrolled with Mary, his betrothed, who was with child. And while they were there, the time came for her to be delivered. And she gave birth to her first-born son and wrapped him in swaddling cloths, and laid him in a manger, because there was no place for them in the inn.

"And in that region there were shepherds out in the field, keeping watch over their flock by night. And an angel of the Lord appeared to them, and the glory of the Lord shone around them, and they were filled with fear. And the angel said to them, 'Be not afraid; for behold, I bring you good news of a great joy which will come to all the people; for to you is born this day in the city of David a Saviour, who is Christ the Lord.'"

In these words the historian Luke records that event which in the western world divides all history. Our chronology is reckoned before and after the birth of Christ. All the years prior to his coming are tallied in descending order, those thereafter in ascending order. How incredible it would have appeared to the ancient Sumerians and Assyrians, the Babylonians and Persians, the Greeks and Romans, had they been told that the days of their years would come to be reckoned in terms of an event to occur in a village too insignificant to be mentioned on their monuments or in their annals! How amazing it would have been to Augustus to be informed that he would be famed less as the founder of the Roman Empire than as that emperor under whose rule this child was born! And as for Quirinius, what surprise it would have caused him to foresee that he, of all the governors of Syria, should be remembered best, and solely because of his connection with that event.

Augustus and Quirinius would have been not only amazed but shocked had they been told that the child who would make them memorable was a Jew, for the Jews alone would do no homage to the emperor as divine. Jesus was a Jew who went up to Jerusalem for the great religious feasts of his people and on the

Sabbath regularly attended the synagogue. He declared that he had not come to destroy but to fulfill the Jewish Law and the mission of the Hebrew prophets. If we would understand Jesus, we must understand the religion in which he was reared, and if we would understand Christianity, we must begin with Judaism, for the one religion is the daughter of the other.

The Jews began as an agglomeration of small tribes who later attained political independence only in the interludes between the fall and rise of great empires. They have bequeathed no monuments testifying to magnificence. They built no pyramids like the Egyptians, no ziggurats like the Sumerians. There are no tombs of the Hebrew kings with chaplets of finely wrought gold and chariots studded with jewels, no palaces and fortresses like those of Crete and Mycenae. Palestinian archaeology has unearthed no statues of David and Solomon but only water pots like the one from which Rebecca watered the camels of Abraham's servants or the sickle like that with which Boaz reaped while Ruth gleaned.

But the ancient Hebrews, contemptible in the eyes of their contemporaries, created something more enduring than palaces and pyramids. They created a literature, traditionally classified as law, prophecy, and writings, comprising twenty-eight books that in the century before Christ were canonized as Holy Scripture. (*Canon* is derived from the Latin word for a measuring stick; the writings canonized were those that measured up.) Some of the works thus gathered together deal with the events of the writers' own times; others record traditions that were transmitted orally for quite possibly a thousand years, often with amazing accuracy.

This body of literature, called by Christians the Old Testament, is unique. Even in its earliest portions it sets forth a philosophy of history such as the empires of the Levant never envisioned and the Greeks only later approximated. History was for the Hebrews the plan of God, focused on his chosen people, whose very weakness served all the more to display his power. Through all their vicissitudes he was leading them. In all their disasters he was chastening them. In all their sufferings he was using them that they might be a light to the Gentiles who someday would come to the House of the Lord and receive the Law from Mount Zion. History to the Hebrews was a drama investing the future with a mighty hope.

Judaism is a religion of history and as such may be contrasted with both religions of nature and religions of contemplation. Religions of nature discover God in the surrounding universe; for example, in the orderly course of the heavenly bodies, or more frequently in the recurring cycle of the withering and resurgence of vegetation. This cycle is interpreted as the dying and rising of a god in whose experience the devotee can share through various ritual acts, and thus also become divine and immortal. For such a religion the past is not important, since the cycle of the seasons is the same one year as the next.

Religions of contemplation, at the other pole, regard the physical world as an impediment to the spirit, which, abstracted from the things of sense, must rise by contemplation to union with the divine. The sense of time itself is to be transcended, so that here again history is of no import. But religions of history, like Judaism, discover God "in his mighty acts among the children of men." Such a religion is a compound of memory and hope. It looks backward to what God has already done. The feasts of Judaism are chiefly commemorative: Passover recalls the deliverance of the Jews from bondage in Egypt; Purim, Esther's triumph over Haman, who sought to destroy the Jews in the days of King Ahasuerus; and Hanukkah, the purification of the Temple after its desecration by Antiochus Epiphanes. And this religion looks forward with faith; remembrance is a reminder that God will not forsake his own.

The faith of Judaism was anchored in the belief that God was related to his people by covenant—he as Lord and they as vassals—that at times had been renewed and enlarged. The first covenant was with Abraham, the traditional father of the Hebrews. The Bible relates that he migrated to Palestine from Ur of the Chaldees (in the land between the Tigris and Euphrates rivers, later known as Babylonia) sometime between 2000 and 1700 B.C. That the Hebrews had close cultural relations with this region is likely: the accounts of the creation, the flood, and other traditional stories in the Old Testament are clearly related to Babylonian myths; the Ten Commandments are reminiscent of the Code of Hammurabi; the Tower of Babel recalls the ziggurat at Ur.

But how marvelously the Hebrews transformed these ancient materials! In their version of the creation we find no union of earth god and sky goddess, no mere analogy with procreation.

God, the unutterable majesty, spoke from out of the shroud of mystery and said, "Let there be light," and before ever there was a sun or a moon there was light. Out of sheer nothing, by the fiat of divine will, all that is began to be. In the Hebrew version the flood was occasioned by the vileness of man. But from out of the mass of the wicked, God chose one righteous man and all his house that by these few the divine purpose for the ages might be fulfilled. And if one compares the Code of Hammurabi with the Ten Commandments, one passes from the conditional—"If a man steal . . . then . . ."—to the imperative—"Thou shalt not steal."

The God of Abraham—he was called El, and his name survives in such compounds as Beth-El and Israel—commanded Abraham to leave his father's house and to journey to a country that should be shown him. The Bible relates that he and his descendants journeyed to the land of Canaan, to be known as Palestine. They were probably semi-nomads, migrating annually with their flocks for pasturage and not settled on the farms or in the cities of Canaan. With this Abraham God made a covenant, by a promise that he and his descendants would possess the land of Canaan and that they should be blessed with prosperity and progeny, in number like the stars of heaven or the sands of the sea. Abraham begat Isaac, and Isaac Jacob, and Jacob in turn twelve sons from whom stemmed the twelve tribes of Israel. The name *Israel*, meaning "he that strives with God," was given to Jacob after he had wrestled all night with an angel and had received a blessing. In later history that name came to be applied to the ten northern tribes, while the name *Judah* (whence the word *Jew*) was applied to those in the south of Palestine. But after the ten tribes were deported in the eighth century B.C. and lost to history, the name *Israel* was again extended, and now *Israelite*, *Hebrew*, and *Jew* are virtually synonymous.

All Palestine in the age of the patriarchs was under the suzerainty of Egypt, and when a famine afflicted the land, as it periodically did, the inhabitants sought the verdant valley of the Nile—not only the Hebrews, but their neighbors as well. The Hebrews interpreted their own migration as a part of God's plan, for he had earlier arranged that Joseph should be sold as a slave into Egypt by his brothers, and that once there he should

This Egyptian relief shows a bound Semitic
captive. Throughout most of their history
the Hebrews were at the mercy of the
powerful empires that succeeded each other
as rulers of the East: Egypt and Assyria,
Babylon, Persia, Greece, and Rome.

rise to be prime minister of Pharaoh and should be in charge of the supplies of grain at the very moment of the famine. Thus he was in a position to save his father's house.

The fugitives from drought stayed on in Egypt until there came a Pharaoh, possibly Rameses II (1304–1237 B.C.), with a passion for building, who impressed the Hebrews into forced labor so excessive that their leader in exile, Moses, came before Pharaoh with the demand, "Let my people go." Not until God had smitten Egypt with ten plagues would the ruler consent. In the last plague, the death of the first-born in the homes of the Egyptians, God spared—"passed over"—the children of the Hebrews. The commemoration of this event, called Passover, remains probably the oldest of the religious festivals celebrated today. Then, when Pharaoh capitulated, Moses led his people into the wilderness. How many they were cannot be determined. The biblical account cannot be corroborated from Egyptian annals, which do not refer to the Sojourn or the Exodus, but the number cannot have been large, since not all the Hebrews came down into Egypt and not all those in Egypt went back to Palestine. Perhaps the band did not exceed a thousand.

But for these, whether few or many, the religion of Israel took on a new quality when Moses conducted them to the foot of Mount Sinai, and there, from out the cloud brooding over the brow of the mountain, the God of Abraham, Isaac, and Jacob disclosed himself with a new name. Henceforth he is called Jehovah, or in a more exact transliteration, Yahweh. And he there made with Israel a new covenant, not simply a promise of prosperity and progeny, but a covenant of commitment that they should observe the Law, including the Ten Commandments, given to Israel by the hand of Moses. Yahweh said: "You have seen what I did to the Egyptians and how I bore you on eagles' wings . . . Now therefore, if you will obey my voice and keep my covenant, you shall be my own possession among all peoples . . . and you shall be to me a kingdom of priests and a holy nation." This concept of the covenant related the Hebrews to their God in a manner that was unique in history. He had chosen them, not by reason of their merit, but through his sheer grace, to be the instruments of his purpose.

After the escape from Egypt the Bible tells of the wandering in the desert wilderness, and then, after these forty years of trial and discipline, of the conquest of Canaan—the "promised land" of Abraham's covenant—under Joshua in the late thirteenth or early twelfth century B.C. This is portrayed in the Books of Joshua and Judges as swift, gory, and drastic. The walls of Jericho collapsed miraculously at the blowing of the trumpet. When the cities of the Canaanites were stormed the inhabitants were put to the sword by the victorious Hebrew soldiers.

At some points the biblical account is not accurate. The Canaanites were obviously not exterminated since, as told elsewhere in the Bible, they remained for centuries as an irritant to Israel. Indeed, whether this was in fact a military conquest or rather a process of gradual infiltration of the land by the Israelites cannot be fully determined. Jericho had been destroyed before Joshua's time, and he may have only had to occupy the ruins of the city. Also, it has been argued that the Israelites were not sufficiently advanced in the art of war to capture the Canaanite cities, defended as they were by chariots drawn by horses, of which the Israelites had none. Even much later, in David's day, when horses were captured from the Philistines they were not used for military purposes.

From the point of view of Christian history the question does not need to be resolved. In any event, the Hebrews did settle in Palestine, and what is related in the Book of Joshua to have happened there is more significant to later Christian history than what may actually have occurred. For here is pictured a war of aggression, deemed just and even holy simply because commanded by God as a part of his historic plan. The enemy who resisted his will was accursed and therefore to be attacked with unflagging zeal, with no humanitarian softness, and with less reliance on military efficiency than on God's miraculous assistance. God was believed to be present on the field of battle in a chest called the Ark of the Covenant. This view of war was to be revived with direct appeal to the Old Testament in the Christian crusades about two millenniums later.

At the outset the Hebrews certainly did not have Palestine to themselves. The Canaanites remained, and there were other invading peoples with whom the Hebrews had to contend: Moabites, Edomites, and Ammonites, who established kingdoms east of the Jordan that in some cases lasted into the Christian era. Into northern Syria came the Aramaeans, and to the south, bordering on Arabia, were the Midianites, who confounded the Hebrews as much with their camels as did the Canaanites with their horses and chariots. Probably only after centuries of slow penetration did the tribes of Israel assume their ascendancy over this land and its many and mixed peoples.

In the Old Testament the Canaanites are often called the Amorites, a people also of many tribes: the Hivites, the Girgashites, the Jebusites (who held the fenced town of Jerusalem), and so on. From the Canaanites the Hebrews learned much, both of the arts of agriculture and of city dwelling. In this period the Hebrews adapted their Aramaic speech to a dialect of the Canaanites and produced the classical Hebrew tongue, in which the larger portion of the Old Testament is written. They later returned to Aramaic and some of the Testament is in this language, which was to be the language of Jesus. The Hebrews also took from the Phoenicians—a group of Canaanites along the north coast of Palestine—their most brilliant invention, the alphabet, which also passed to the Greeks, to the Romans, and to the rest of the western world.

But one aspect of Canaanite culture the Hebrews would not assimilate, namely, religion. For the Canaanites were addicted to the fertility cults of a god called Baal, appearing in many local forms, and a goddess Astarte, whose rites included child sacrifice and sacred prostitution. The story in the Old Testament of how God arrested Abraham's hand when he was about to sacrifice his son Isaac may indicate that the Hebrews had never practiced child sacrifice, or had come to reject it. And to inject sex into religion was to them utterly abhorrent. The gravest danger to Israel was not that her sons would apostatize, as some did, but rather that they might transform Yahweh into a Baal. Lest this should happen, the Baalim (the plural of Baal) were to be exterminated from the land.

If the Hebrews had rivals for the conquest of Canaan to north, east, and south, a more formidable rivalry threatened from the west, where the Philistines, a people perhaps of Illyrian origin, invaded the coastal plain toward the end of the thirteenth century B.C. It was they who gave their name to the land: *Palestine* is a modification of *Philistia*. They were pushing farther inland and acquiring control over the land of the Hebrews. This assault could not be met by a loose confederation of tribes who came together only when the spirit of Yahweh inspired some leader to summon them to conflict. Such a procedure was altogether too casual. Therefore, the seer Samuel agreed to anoint Saul, an inspired captain, as king. But Samuel himself had grave misgivings over this course and warned the people that the monarchy would impose on them exacting burdens.

Even more serious was the foreboding that the rule of a king would compete with the rule of God. Israel up to this point was a theocracy. The very word *theocracy* was later coined by the Jew Josephus to describe this people ruled by God, whose will was made known to them by seers and prophets. In matters of war God's will was executed by inspired bands of warriors, like the band of Gideon, which was deliberately reduced in size to prove that God, not human prowess, had given the victory. In place of this system would come standing armies, taxes, and, worst of all in the eyes of the purists, foreign alliances, principally because they entailed religious alliances. Those who made military covenants were expected to recognize each others' gods. The resolve on the part of Israel not to pay tribute to alien gods was to be for them a source of both inner division and outward isolation. The unbroken loyalty of the Jews to Yahweh throughout the centuries has been both their glory and their tragedy.

The anointing of Saul by Samuel toward the close of the second millennium B.C. is very important for later political theory in western Europe. This anointing meant the institution of a sacral rather than secular kingship; however, it involved a point of ambiguity. Was royal authority conferred directly by God or through the mediation of a priest or prophet as his earthly representative? By anointing Saul did Samuel confer upon him kingship, or did he merely ratify what God had already done by sending upon him his spirit? These two theories of kingship occasioned much controversy in the Christian Middle Ages.

Saul did not vanquish the Philistines; that was the work of David, who had been the leader of a mercenary band serving under the Philistines. They were willing that he should become the king of Judah, believing that the tribes would thus be divided. But instead David went on to become king of all the tribes (1005–970 B.C.), and he succeeded in decisively breaking the power of the Philistines. His kingdom reached to the north past Galilee. In the south he took Jerusalem from the Jebusites and made this city the religious center for all the Hebrew tribes. The choice was very wise, because a shrine located in the existing territory of any single Hebrew tribe would have been unacceptable to the others. To Jerusalem David brought the Ark of

This Byzantine silver plate shows David being anointed as king by the prophet Samuel. David's kingdom became the most powerful state of the Levant. His conquests extended as far as the river Euphrates; the most important of them was Jerusalem, which was to become the Jews' holy city.

the Covenant, which was simply an empty chest. Yahweh was merely localized in space, never incarnated or depicted in any form.

David was succeeded by Solomon (970–930), whose name in Hebrew contains the root *shalom*, meaning peace—an appropriate appellation, since Solomon eschewed war and did not seek to extend his boundaries, but rather to glorify his holdings with such costly structures as the great Temple at Jerusalem. But as war was waged, so peace was conserved by alliances, and these alliances meant foreign marriages, which in turn involved the importation of other gods than Yahweh. Solomon married a daughter of Pharaoh and also a daughter of the king of Tyre, and many other princesses. For the gods of his numerous foreign wives this builder of the Temple of Yahweh constructed shrines on the Mount of Olives. More sumptuous than any other structure, however, was Solomon's own palace, which took thirteen years to build. The two builders of magnificent temples at Jerusalem were essentially secular spirits. The first was Solomon and the second Herod the Great. Little wonder that to Solomon should have been ascribed the least religious books in the Jewish Scriptures: Proverbs, Ecclesiastes, and the Song of Songs, and the Book of Wisdom in the Apocrypha!

Such sumptuous building required money which must be raised by taxation. Under Solomon the people groaned beneath their burden; when he died their grievances became outspoken. Solomon's son Rehoboam was accepted as his successor in Judah, which had come to believe that the monarchy was divinely vested in the dynasty of David. But the ten tribes of Israel still had much of the ideology of the old confederation. They applied the principle of covenant to the kingship, thus subjecting it to conditions, and demanded that Rehoboam lighten the financial burden and relieve them of the forced labor under which they had been suffering. He replied that whereas his father had beaten them with rods, he would beat them with scorpions. In consequence they called Jeroboam to be their king, and thereby the northern and southern kingdoms were divided.

In the early centuries of the first millennium B.C. the rising "world" power was Assyria, in Mesopotamia, a nation of ruthless, warlike people who threatened their neighbors on all sides. The menace to the Hebrews became acute when Tiglath-pileser III came to the throne in 745 B.C. The northern kingdom of Israel united with Damascus to resist the Assyrian hordes. When King Ahaz of Judah refused to join the coalition he was besieged by the other two, and when he appealed to the Assyrians for help they overran Israel. Then, in 721 B.C., when Israel rebelled, the Assyrians under the great Sargon deported the ruling aristocracy of the ten tribes and replaced them with people from Mesopotamia. The peasants of Israel remained, and the mingling of these peoples produced those later known as Samaritans. In time the Mesopotamian immigrants accepted Yahweh as their god. Judah was allowed to continue as a vassal state, after paying ransom that stripped the very gold from the Temple doors. But this meant that an altar to the god of the Assyrians had to be erected near the altar of Yahweh in Jerusalem. King Hezekiah destroyed the pagan shrine, but when Sennacherib the Assyrian "swept down like a wolf on the fold" the altar removed by Hezekiah had to be restored.

In the seventh century B.C. a new power, Babylonia, arose to threaten Assyria, and Egypt, although long the enemy of Assyria, now rallied to her help in order to preserve the balance of power. With this division among his towering neighbors, King Josiah of Judah seized the chance to shake off Assyrian dominance. He swept Jerusalem clean of idolatrous abominations and issued the biblical Book of Deuteronomy, the "Book of the Law" that had recently been discovered in the Temple. As Pharaoh Necho proceeded across Palestine to help Assyria, Josiah stood in his way. A historic battle was fought at Megiddo in 609 B.C., and Josiah, the reforming king, was "carried . . . dead in a chariot . . . to Jerusalem."

But Necho failed to restore the balance; he was himself crushed by Nebuchadnezzar, king of the Babylonians. Then came Judah's turn. Jerusalem fell before the Babylonians in 587 B.C. King Zedekiah, the last king of Judah, was spared having his eyes put out only long enough to see his son slain. The Judean aristocracy was carried off to its long captivity in Babylon, the Temple of Solomon was razed, and the Ark of the Covenant forever disappeared. The monarchy in the united kingdoms had lasted two and a half centuries; Judah as a vassal state had had a king of the House of David for another one a half centuries. For the next four centuries there was to be no native king at all.

The captive Jews sat by the waters of Babylon and wept. Why had Yahweh abandoned his people; as the psalmist sang, "My

God, my God, why hast thou forsaken me?" When the Assyrian had just begun his oppressions, the prophet Isaiah answered this lament by asserting that the calamity was a chastisement for Israel's sins and that the Assyrian was the rod of God's anger. To propose that God was using this great empire to discipline a few tribes who had been faithless to his covenant was an audacious assumption. Israel put herself at the center of world history, and by so doing she made her God the God of all the world, and the mightiest empires of the world but devices in his plan for his chosen people.

Isaiah's explanation was persuasive in those days when Israel had gone whoring after foreign gods. But what was to be said when the good king Josiah, who put away the abominations, was brought back dead in a chariot? Was it chastisement that Jerusalem should be a heap and that the Ark of the Lord have disappeared? Could it be that Yahweh allowed the righteous to suffer? Job confronted the problem on an individual level, and his only answer in his sore affliction was to bow before the inscrutable will of the Almighty. In Babylon another prophet, known as the Second Isaiah, spoke of the trials of the whole nation of Jews: "Comfort, comfort my people, says your God. Speak tenderly to Jerusalem, and cry to her that her warfare is ended, that her iniquity is pardoned, that she has received from the Lord's hand double for all her sins." Double! What is the meaning of suffering which exceeds chastisement? This same prophet spoke of the servant who was smitten and afflicted and upon whom, despite his innocence, had been laid "the iniquity of us all" and "by [whose] stripes we are healed." The suffering of the innocent thus might minister to the redemption of the guilty. The "servant" may well have been meant by the prophet to be a personification of Israel, but Christians have always seen in this figure a foreshadowing of Christ.

But in any event, what of the fate of the guilty? Must they forever expiate their crime? The answer here was the proclamation of divine forgiveness that sounds throughout the Old Testament: "Though your sins are like scarlet, they shall be as white as snow; though they are red like crimson, they shall become like wool"; "Let the wicked forsake his way, and . . . return to the Lord, that he may have mercy on him, and to our God, for he will abundantly pardon."

Besides precipitating such questions and answers the Babylonian captivity gave a new quality to Judaism. Since the Temple was destroyed, Jerusalem inaccessible to the exiles, and the priesthood scattered, they focused their piety upon the Torah, the Law, which was to be comprised in the first five books of the Old Testament, called the Pentateuch. The Law was now elucidated and amplified, and religion consisted of obeying its precepts. This great body of exegesis eventually became the Talmud, the civil and canonical law of the Jews for ages to come.

Two points in the Law were especially stressed. The first was the keeping of the Sabbath. The redactor of the creation story in Genesis represented God himself as observing the Sabbath, for he created the world in six days and rested on the seventh. The other point was a new emphasis on the importance of circumcision as a sign of the covenant. This rite had not distinguished the Jews from their earlier Semitic and Egyptian neighbors, but it did differentiate them at the outset from the "uncircumcised Philistines," as it now did from the Babylonians, and as it would later from the Greeks and the Romans. Such emphasis on the Law and the remoteness from the Temple necessitated some other place for public worship and instruction in the Law. The synagogue was the answer, though whether it actually was instituted within this period the extant evidence does not permit us to say.

The duration of the Babylonian captivity has traditionally been reckoned as seventy years (more precisely, it was seventy-two) dating from the destruction to the rebuilding of the Temple in Jerusalem. But the turning point in the fate of the exiles came with the rise of the Persians and the capture of Babylon by their king, Cyrus, in 538 B.C. The Jews regarded the Persians as liberators, and as a matter of fact the conquerors were comparatively liberal. They respected the languages of the subjugated and were not disposed, in this period at least, to encroach upon their religions. Cyrus decreed that the Jewish exiles might return to Palestine and that the Temple there might be rebuilt. The reconstruction, promptly commenced, was completed under his successor, Darius, in the year 515 B.C. Not all the exiles went back to Palestine: a colony of them remained in Babylon into the Middle Ages. Nehemiah became the leader of those who did return, and under him the people rebuilt the walls of Jerusalem. Ezra, another leader, imposed upon the Jews in Palestine the rigorous devotion to the Torah that had developed in Babylon. To preserve religious purity, those who thus adhered to the Law were not to marry with those who did not.

Persian ascendancy ended with the victory of Alexander the Great at the Battle of Issus in 333 B.C., which introduced a new era in the relation of the Jews to the world about them. Alexander envisioned the unity of mankind. He certainly proposed to blend at least the cultures of the Greeks and the Persians. This meant orientalizing the West and Hellenizing the East; inevitably the Jews were involved.

Alexander had been the pupil of Aristotle and knew Hellenism in all its aspects. One of the characteristics of the Hellenic spirit was curiosity. The Greeks were interested in everything in the world about—the stars, the plants, and the human body, in physics and medicine. They were interested in more than appearance; they sought to discern the relations of things. The Greeks developed geometry; the Romans simply built roads. The Greeks inquired as to the nature of things, the nature of nature, the nature of God. The Hebrews desired to know only his will. Among the Greeks there were philosophers who saw in the cosmos a principle of order and who defined beauty in terms of harmonious proportions.

Little wonder that Greek philosophers discovered a rationale for the ideal of the unity of mankind! The Stoics taught that there is already such a unity. Men, endowed with reason, participate in the rational order of the universe and are capable of resolving their differences in a reasonable way by the concourse of minds rather than the clash of arms. Men, being rational, are able to perceive that there is a moral order in the cosmos, the law of nature, the norm for all the laws of men. According to this philosophy the gift of reason has been conferred upon all men regardless of race; the distinction between the Hellenes and the barbarians had come to be that between the cultivated and the uncouth, not that between the Greeks and other peoples. Social status was a matter of indifference, for all men were created equal. There was once a golden age with no slavery, property, or war. The existence of these institutions is due to a fall of man, which did not, however, obfuscate his reasoning capacity. Since man participates in the order of the cosmos, he should be considered a citizen of the cosmos, a cosmopolite. Such ideas were later to have a profound effect on Christian thinking.

For the cultivation of another Greek ideal, that of the good life in which enlightened men converse together, there was need for the polis, a city like Athens, in which to gather. For the Greeks the city was not so much a fort as a forum, a place of beauty, whose high places were not capped by ramparts, but crowned by temples of incomparable grace. Such cities were introduced into the Levant, cities adorned not only with temples and gardens, but also with gymnasiums, theatres, and hippodromes. When cities of this type arose in Palestine they created a problem for the orthodox Jew, who looked askance at the gymnasiums where athletes ran naked.

But Hellenistic culture and Judaic culture were so complex that there were many points of convergence as well as of divergence between them. The Stoic picture of the golden age from which man had fallen comported well with the story in Genesis of the fall of Adam and Eve. The Stoics, thinking in pantheistic terms, equated the divine with the principle of rationality in the cosmos. Their assumption of a law of nature, valid among all men, was easy to reconcile with the ethical demands of the Ten Commandments and to translate into the law of God. Aristotle, interested in natural science and causality, considered God to be the first cause of whatever is and the prime mover of whatever moves. The Platonists called God the ultimate intelligence ordering the universe. Such descriptions are not alien to the picture of the Hebrew God who wills, acts, and speaks. The Stoic belief that all men were created equal was remote from Hebrew speculation, but no people had such a burning sense of indignation against injustice to the common man as had the Jews. For example, when King David, in order to marry Bathsheba, placed her husband in the forefront of the battle where he was slain, the prophet Nathan told the king the story of a rich man, who to feed his guests took not from his own abundant herd, but seized the one ewe lamb of a poor man. David adjudged this rich man deserving of death, and the prophet thundered, "You are the man!" There is no scene comparable to this in the literature of antiquity.

The discrepancy between Hellenic and Hebraic attitudes was indeed sometimes less than the discrepancy between varieties within the separate cultures. Among the Greeks, for example, the Epicureans denied immortality, the Stoics believed that at death the individual soul is absorbed into the world soul, and the

The recently discovered Dead Sea scrolls, a
fragment of which is shown here, are relics
of a Jewish community that dwelt by the sea
at the time of Christ. The group may have
been Essenes, members of an ascetic sect
thought to have influenced John the Baptist.

Platonists believed in the immortality of the soul as distinct from the body, which perishes. Among the Hebrews we shall later meet the Pharisees, who affirmed the immortality alike of the soul and the body, and the Sadducees, who denied both.

Hellenic and Hebraic views as to property and poverty differed, but together they had an important subsequent influence on Christian concepts. The Greeks had much sympathy for communism. Plato set forth the ideal in *The Republic*, and the Stoics believed communism to have prevailed in the golden age. Aristotle recognized private property. The Cynics had a cult of poverty, chiefly as a device for insuring peace of mind. In those turbulent times the man of wealth never knew whether he might not die a slave; he could attain composure by stripping himself in advance of all that he might lose. The ideal was to live simply, like a dog. The name *Cynic* came from the Greek word for dog. Tools should be reduced to the strictly utilitarian. A knife needs no jeweled handle, nor does a table require ivory legs. Among the ancient Hebrews we find the holding of property by the tribe but never a cult of poverty. For them prosperity was a mark of divine favor; and poverty was either a chastisement or a trial of faith.

The religion of the Greek philosophers rejected all the anthropomorphisms and immoralities of the gods of Homer's pantheon, but retained the gods as allegorical figures. Homer's gods were moralized by converting their stories into symbolic myths. For example, the god Kronos was alleged to have devoured his own children. The philosophers said that Kronos was to be equated with Chronos, the god of time, who does obliterate that which he has brought into being. Not only Homer was retained by Greek philosophers, through allegory, but also the various cults of the Greek religion, which were invested with a spiritual meaning.

In the case of war we have noted that the Hebrews introduced the idea of the crusade fought for God, under God, and without giving quarter. The Greeks fashioned the concept of the just war, whose purpose is to vindicate justice and restore peace, and in which violence should be minimal. Plato protested against the ruining of wells and orchards and made a distinction among the enemy between the innocent and the guilty.

Greek and Jewish traditions and ideas had, in fact, so much in common that they could be fused at certain levels. The fusion with philosophic Hellenism took place most naturally among those Jews who had long lived in a gentile environment, and there were many. The Diaspora, the dispersion of the Jews from Judea, had begun centuries before Christ. We have noted the continuing colony of Jews at Babylon. At Elephantine in Egypt there was a colony in the fifth century B.C. which died out in the following century, but others were established. When he took Jerusalem, Pompey sold thousands of Jews into slavery at Rome. They proved to be poor slaves because they would not work on the Sabbath nor eat certain foods. But they made such excellent associates that many soon acquired their freedom and became an influential group in the capital. By the time of the Christian era the Jews had dispersed throughout much of Asia Minor and the Mediterranean world, where Paul met them in the course of his travels. It is said they numbered about a million in Egypt, with a heavy concentration in Alexandria. These Jews spoke Greek. Some of them still knew Hebrew, but for the majority the Scriptures were translated into Greek somewhere around 200 B.C. This version of the Bible is called the Septuagint, because it is supposedly the work of some seventy scholars.

Among the Alexandrian Jews there flourished in the first century of the Christian era a cultivated scholar named Philo, who Hellenized the Old Testament by the same device that the philosophers had applied to Homer, namely, allegory. In the Old Testament he found much of Greek philosophy. Philo saw no danger to Judaism in this, for he believed that Plato, having lived later than Moses, had derived from him all his ideas, and Philo continued to observe the Jewish law. His attempts to reconcile Greek thought with Jewish teachings later helped to shape Christian theology.

The great clash between Judaism and Hellenism occurred when Hellenistic kings claimed divinity for themselves. This was a phase of the orientalizing of the West, which had assimilated many eastern ideas. It was later to return them in altered form to the East. The Romans of the republican period looked upon the elevation of man to divinity as presumption. The Greeks called it *hybris*—meaning, very roughly, arrogance or insolence. Yet the Greeks did regard the founders of their city-states, long since dead, as having been gods on earth. In Egypt the living Pharaohs claimed to be gods, and the Persians developed an elaborate ritual of prostration in the presence of their rulers. These elements were fused by the successors of Alexander into a form of emperor worship, which was eventually adopted by the Romans and then required of all in the empire. Here is the root of the clash between Christ and Caesar. The Jews confronted the problem even before the Romans invaded Palestine.

The conflict came with the successors of Alexander in the East, the Seleucids, who became the rulers of Syria and, in time, of Palestine. Under Antiochus Epiphanes (his very name means "God made manifest") a determined effort was made to Hellenize Judea. The gymnasium was introduced in Jerusalem. Although the orthodox among the Jews scowled, others were willing to accommodate themselves to Greek practices. Even some priests would first officiate in their robes in the Temple and then run naked in the gymnasium. Then Antiochus began interfering with the priesthood and in 167 B.C., meeting opposition, defiled the sanctuary at Jerusalem by sacrificing a pig on the altar. The Jewish religion was interdicted on pain of death and pagan sacrifices were required of the Jews. Following this development, a certain Jew who was on the point of complying with the new regulations, together with an officer of the king, was cut down by another Jew; and out of this conflict developed a war between the Jews and their Seleucid oppressors. The slayer was of the clan of Hasmon, whose members were known as Hasmoneans. It was they who led the revolt. These warrior clansmen are also known as the Maccabees, after Judah, called Maccabeus ("the hammer"), one of their leaders. Ill-armed though they were, these bands of passionate Jewish warriors, in the spirit of Joshua and Gideon, drove the Seleucid forces from Jerusalem and eventually recovered the kingdom of David.

The power of the Seleucids had already been declining, but the valor of the Maccabees is not to be discounted. They were nerved by a book purportedly written during the Babylonian captivity, but actually written following the desecration of the Temple by Antiochus' order. It relates the experiences of Daniel, who was cast into a den of lions because of his religious intransigence, and of three Hebrew youths, who were thrown into a fiery furnace because they defied an order of Nebuchadnezzar to bow down before his image. They had maintained that their God could deliver them (as indeed he did), but even if he did not, they would in no case bow down. The Maccabees well knew that in this cryptic story Nebuchadnezzar signified Antiochus Epiphanes, and that the deliverance of Daniel and the three youths foretold the deliverance of the Jews from his power. This Book of Daniel was the first in the apocalyptic literature that, with its disguised messages of hope and salvation, strongly colored the spiritual life of the Jews and early Christians when they suffered persecution.

With Jerusalem freed, the Temple was purified and rededicated in the year 165 B.C. on the twenty-fifth of Kislev, which usually falls in December according to our calendar and which date the Jews still celebrate as the first day of Hanukkah. The religious objective had been achieved. The Hasmoneans were now not content but sought to extend and maintain a monarchical state. This involved, again, foreign alliances. The purists among the Jews who recoiled from Hasmonean policy and who felt that the monarchy itself conflicted with the lordship of Yahweh became known as the Pharisees. The party of the priests, who were Hellenizers and allied with the Hasmoneans, were the Sadducees. When in 103 B.C. Alexander Jannaeus, a Sadducee high priest of profligate and barbarous character, declared himself king, the Pharisees clamored for his death. He retaliated by crucifying eight hundred of them at a public banquet which he attended with his concubines.

A bloody civil war ensued, which was checked only when Pompey ended the Seleucid kingdom and established Roman rule over Syria and Palestine in 63 B.C. After twenty-three years of continued political turmoil the area of the old Maccabean kingdom was entrusted to a vassal king called Herod the Great, an Edomite. He was charming, astute, magnificent, and brutal. Although he was half Jewish and had a Hasmonean wife, throughout Palestine he constructed Hellenistic cities with temples to the pagan gods. At Caesarea he built a city with an artificial harbor, later to be the Roman capital for the area. A string of fortresses within signaling distance of each other guarded the approach to Jerusalem.

But of all Herod's works none exceeded in magnificence the rebuilding of the Temple in Jerusalem. All that the art of Hellas could supply was lavished on the sanctuary of the Jews. One thousand priests were trained as stone-cutters, carpenters, and decorators, lest any impure hand sully the Holy Place. Because

The Menorah, the seven-branched
candelabrum, is one of the most ancient
symbols of the Jews. It continues to be at the
center of the Jewish celebration of Hanukkah.

Herod was not of the priestly house he refrained from entering the most sacred precinct; because he respected Jewish scruples he refrained from stamping his own image on coins. When the Temple was completed, after Herod's death, eighteen thousand men were out of employment. Its adornment was sumptuous, with golden doors, a figured Babylonian curtain before it, and a huge golden vine above the lintel. From the altar of incense, from the seven-branched candlestick, and from burnt offerings rose clouds of smoke. Animal sacrifices were daily performed, and the sacrificial altar was covered with reeking blood and guts and with flies. Removed alike from the splendor and the squalor was a room, empty and dark—the Holy of Holies, the dwelling place of the Most High, the successor to the lost Ark of the Covenant—into which only the high priest entered once a year on the Day of Atonement. This monument Herod had built less for the glory of God than for his own eternal renown, but within little more than a half century hardly one stone was left upon another.

Higher than the Temple Herod constructed a palace and at a still greater eminence a citadel. Such was his scale of values—a temple, a palace, and a fort. But Herod is chiefly remembered for the slaughter of the babies of Bethlehem in his effort to eliminate a scion of the House of David who might contest his throne. The account is not incredible. Herod was a ruthless man who executed one of his ten wives, his mother-in-law, and three of his sons. (Augustus said that it were better to be Herod's sow than his son.) But it should be said in Herod's favor that by his respect for the religion of the Jews he prevented an insurrection and, as a consequence, an invasion by Roman forces.

But through the extravagance of his building he left the land impoverished and even more seething with disaffection than at his accession. Prior to his time the Jews had been sucked into Rome's civil wars, and one hundred thousand of them had fallen in conflicts not their own. The death of Herod brought struggles for the succession. In the uncertainty that followed, riots in Jerusalem led to a massacre of three thousand. In Galilee, where Jesus was growing up, a certain Judas, mentioned in the Book of the Acts of the Apostles, headed an insurrection against the authorities, killing not only Gentiles but also neutralist Jews. The Roman governor of Syria suppressed the uprising and crucified two thousand. Guerrillas, who infested the mountain fastnesses and the caves of the desert, emerged as the party of the Zealots, who cried, "Yahweh alone is king." Among the other parties of Judaism were the Sadducees, who fraternized with any rulers; the Pharisees, who kept the Law and awaited divine vindication; and even stricter than the Pharisees, the Essenes, some of whom are presumably identical with the members of the Qumran community disclosed through the finding of the Dead Sea scrolls. In the interests of purity the members withdrew to the wilderness, like ancient Israel, and established themselves in caves on the banks of the Dead Sea, there to await the triumph of God through the victory of the Sons of Light over the Sons of Darkness.

Rome dealt with the political problem of succession in several ways. In the northern portion of Herod's domain two of his sons were established as vassal rulers with the title of tetrarch. One of them was Herod Antipas in Galilee. But in the south Judea and adjoining areas were made into a Roman province under a procurator with headquarters at Caesarea. In Jerusalem the high priest enjoyed practical autonomy in conjunction with an assembly of the aristocracy called the Sanhedrin, which could pronounce a fellow Jew deserving of death but had to refer his actual execution to Rome. The procurators from time to time came to Jerusalem, but they did not display as much understanding for Judaism as Herod had done. The best-known of them, Pontius Pilate, at one time sent Roman troops into Jerusalem bearing the image of the deified Caesar on their ensigns. A concourse of Jews rushed down to Pilate's headquarters at Caesarea to protest this desecration of the holy city. Pilate threatened them with massacre, but when the Jews fell on their faces awaiting the sword, he gave in.

Many solaced themselves with the expectation of a national deliverer. This might be either an earthly figure, a king of the seed of David, a Messiah (an anointed one), or a heavenly being. As the latter he appears in the Book of Daniel, where he is called a Son of Man. In later Jewish apocalypses he is depicted also as a preexistent heavenly deliverer. Throughout the entire history of Israel, when her fortunes on earth were most bleak, the hope for deliverance from heaven waxed strong. When the ancient prophets thundered doom at an unrepentant people, either they or their redactors tempered denunciation with the comforting assurance that God would forgive and restore. After centuries of blasted hopes, when the land was occupied by the unbelievers, the struggle took on cosmic proportions. The enemy on earth was viewed as the instrument of sinister forces in the heavenly places. The outcome would be that Yahweh would triumph over all foes, and having cast the demonic assailants into the abyss, would break the teeth of sinners, consign mighty kings to a valley of fire, and give the carcasses of their minions to the vultures. Such was the mood of the people of Israel at the time that Jesus was born.

II

The Ministry of Christ

This Gothic statue of Christ welcomes the
faithful at a transept of Chartres Cathedral.

The death of Herod caused mourning at Rome, for he had been a loyal administrator. The birth of Jesus went unnoticed. For more than a hundred years no Roman historian mentioned him. Our information about his life comes from the four Gospels of Matthew, Mark, Luke, and John, together with a few other references in the New Testament and a few inconsequential sayings called *agrapha*, culled from early documents. We do not even know the precise date of Jesus' birth. According to Matthew it was some time before the death of Herod the Great in 4 B.C. Luke records that it was at the time of the census of Quirinius, which was in A.D. 6. But again according to Luke, Jesus was thirty years old in the fifteenth year of Tiberius' reign—from August, A.D. 28, to August, A.D. 29. That would place his birth very close to the traditional beginning of the Christian era.

The details of his birth are given only in the Gospels of Matthew and Luke. They agree that he was of the lineage of David and was born in Bethlehem, the native town of David, though Mary and Joseph lived in Nazareth. They happened to be in Bethlehem at the time Mary was delivered because the census required that each man be enrolled in his own city, and Joseph had come from Bethlehem.

In the Gospel accounts only Matthew and Luke mention the virgin birth of Jesus. Paul's writings give no indication that he had ever heard of it. Mark's Gospel commences only with the baptism of Jesus. According to John, Jesus pre-existed as the Word—the Greek *Logos*—the immanent reason of the Stoics made incarnate in Christ.

Whether fact, legend, or myth, the birth stories enshrine two themes, celebration in heaven and rejection on earth. The angels sang, but because "there was no room for them in the inn" the Saviour had to be born in a stable and cradled in the feedbox of a donkey. To be sure, according to the Scriptures, wise men came from the East to do homage to the new-born King of the Jews, but none came from among the rulers at Jerusalem. Indeed, King Herod "sought the young child's life." Of his own people only shepherds gathered about the crib. As the Gospel of John says, "He came to his own home, and his own people received him not." The birth presaged the Passion.

Jesus' childhood was spent in the midst of poverty. The parables of Jesus portray sparse living, where the loss of a coin, or of clothes by moths or tools by rust, was a household calamity. Joseph, the head of the household, was a carpenter, and Jesus may have learned this trade. The Apocryphal Gospels relate that Jesus was able, when a board was too short, to lengthen it miraculously, but the genuine Gospels record no divine interventions to alleviate the lot of the small artisan. Jesus' early proficiency in the Law is indicated by the story in Luke that when only twelve he astonished the rabbis in the Temple at Jerusalem with his questions and answers. Of his youth nothing more is known.

What lay behind his resolve to embark upon the ministry of an itinerant rabbi we do not know. This began when in his thirtieth year Jesus was baptized by his cousin John, called the Baptist, in the River Jordan. John was a desert ascetic, perhaps from the Qumran community. He announced the coming day of God's wrath upon the Israelites, "a brood of vipers," who to be saved should mend their lives rather than rely upon their descent from Abraham. John predicted that one greater than he would come after him as the agent of God's judgment, and he saw that figure in Jesus.

The first preaching of Jesus was indeed very much like that of John. Returning to his native Galilee, Jesus traveled about the countryside speaking to throngs on the hilltops or at the lakeside, in synagogues and in homes, saying to them, "the kingdom of God is at hand; repent." The kingdom of God meant the rule or lordship of God. Of course, God is always Lord, but Jesus meant that God's lordship was not only present but would in the near future be made manifest by his dramatic intervention into history.

In preparation for this event Jesus, like John, declared that Israel should mend her ways and accept God's lordship here and now. Jesus demanded absolute loyalty to God: "Seek first his kingdom and his righteousness." With an absolute loyalty went an absolute trust: "Take no thought for the morrow. Be not anxious for food and raiment. Look at the birds of the air: they neither sow nor reap nor gather into barns, and yet your heavenly Father feeds them. Are you not of more value than they? And why are you anxious about clothing? Consider the lilies of the field, how they grow; they neither toil nor spin; yet I tell you, even Solomon in all his glory was not arrayed like one of these. But if God so clothes the grass of the field, which today is alive and tomorrow is thrown into the oven, will he not much more clothe you, O men of little faith?"

These were amazing words in such a time and in a land of such poverty. Of all this Jesus was certainly not unaware. Yet to those who had little more security than the birds and the lilies he counseled trust in God and readiness to forsake even what little they had in response to the demands of his kingdom.

This did not mean that they should withdraw into desert caves. It did not necessarily mean giving up family life. Jesus gave his sanction to marriage, both by his attendance at the wedding at Cana in Galilee and by his direct word. He did not condemn all possessions. He excoriated the rich who "devoured widows' houses." But to only one person did he say, "sell what you possess and give to the poor," because this man inordinately treasured his worldly goods. Jesus feared wealth because it might divert the owner from devotion to the kingdom of heaven. "Truly," he said, "it will be hard for a rich man to enter the kingdom of heaven." He decried striving for wealth as indicating a lack of trust. He deplored the hoarding of wealth by man, whose soul, any night, might be required of him. That was no Cynic cult of poverty, no ascetic rejection of creature comforts, but the forgoing of the easy life because of an exacting obligation. There was no demand for universal and absolute renunciation; however, since loyalty to the kingdom of God was considered to be the primary loyalty, it might possibly entail the forsaking of goods and kin, of father, mother, wife, and child.

Jesus did call upon some to leave all and to follow him as traveling evangelists. According to tradition his initial band of disciples, called the apostles, numbered twelve. They were a motley group. Peter, the fisherman, the first to be called, was mercurial. James and John, sons of Zebedee, likewise fishermen, were called "sons of thunder," perhaps because they proposed to call down fire from heaven to consume a Samaritan village which denied hospitality to them and their Master. These two were ambitious and pressed upon Jesus the request that they should sit at his right hand and at his left when he came into his kingdom. The apostle Nathanael had a contemptuous spirit, and when first told of Jesus asked whether any good thing could come out of Nazareth. Thomas was a doubter and Judas Iscariot a traitor. Andrew and Bartholomew were scarcely impressive, and Matthew, the publican—a Jewish collector of taxes for the Romans—had the most despised occupation in Palestine. Probably among them all Matthew was the only one who could read and write. He had to in order to record the taxes. He and John are the only apostles to whom Gospels have been ascribed. Peter may have been illiterate, since his memoirs allegedly were taken down by Mark and made into the Gospel bearing Mark's name. The members of this band, far from prepossessing, were in time so inflamed by love, by loyalty, and by faith that they—the "offscouring of all things"—overcame the world.

The twelve were not the only disciples. On one occasion Jesus sent out seventy. There were also a number of women among his followers. One was a woman of the streets, who washed the Master's feet with her tears and wiped them with her hair. She is commonly identified with a woman from Galilee who was present at the Crucifixion and to whom the risen Christ appeared in the garden. Her name was Mary Magdalene.

But although Jesus had a following, in the main he was rejected by men. The majority of his contemporaries were alienated by his teachings. The Zealots, who sought to foment a violent revolution against Rome, scorned Jesus' spirit of nonresistance when he said: "You have heard that it was said, 'An eye for an eye and a tooth for a tooth.' But I say to you, Do not resist one who is evil. But if any one strikes you on the right cheek, turn to him the other also; and if any one would sue you and take your coat, let him have your cloak as well." "You have heard that it was said, 'You shall love your neighbor and hate your enemy.' But I say to you, Love your enemies and pray for those who persecute you."

At the same time Jesus alienated the Sadducees, who, as already observed, denied the immortality of body and soul alike. They were Hellenists and condoned fraternization with their Greek and Roman masters; they were among the partisans of Herod Antipas, the tetrarch of Galilee, whom Jesus once referred to as "that fox."

The Pharisees were the party with whom Jesus had the most in common, yet conflict is often most acute between those most nearly akin. Jesus agreed with the Pharisees that Israel should keep the Jewish Law and leave vindication to God, but differed from them radically as to what was involved in the keeping of the law. The Pharisees were the party devoted to observance of

In this fifteenth-century German engraving,
Christ is being tempted by a devil whose
body is composed of parts of noxious beasts,
both real and imaginary. According to the
synoptic Gospels, the devil tried to tempt
Christ for forty days in the barren hills
above the Jordan Valley.

all the accretions to the Law that had been made over the years by zealous scribes and elders, such as the prohibition of eating an egg laid on the Sabbath. When criticized for healing a man on the Sabbath, Jesus retorted, "The sabbath was made for man, not man for the sabbath. . . ." The Law, he said, that allows a son by giving to the Temple to evade responsibility for his parents is in flat contradiction to the commandment to honor father and mother. All the kosher regulations about the washing of hands, pots, cups, and vessels he branded as the traditions of men, not the commandments of God. For man is not defiled by anything from without, but only by thoughts that proceed from within. Jesus, therefore, did not dissociate himself from those deemed unclean; least of all did he withdraw to preserve his purity in the isolation of the Qumran community.

At the same time he insisted that he had not come to destroy the Law and the prophets but rather to fulfill them through the demands of a higher righteousness. He went beyond the injunction not to murder and taught men to reject even anger, not only to refrain from adultery but to eschew even lust. Positively, he enjoined love for all men, including enemies, personal and national. The motive behind this higher righteousness was simply loyalty to God rather than the hope of delivering Israel or of ensuring a personal reward.

The concept of reward is not absent from the Gospels, to be sure, but there is no neat equation between deeds and recompense, and no mention of a conscious accumulation of merits. All depends on God's grace. Those to whom reward is announced at the judgment will be taken by surprise and will exclaim, "Lord, when did we see thee hungry and feed thee?" The laborer who is hired at the eleventh hour will receive the same reward as those who have borne the heat of the day. Even so, God's mercy is incalculable; it is not measured out in accordance with the canons of a rigid equity. He gives to one his due, to another unmerited bounty. Such concepts went counter to popular piety.

All the good people were scandalized because Jesus consorted with publicans, who increased their wages by extortion, and because he associated with prostitutes, even presuming to forgive their sins. When asked by what authority he did this he pointed to the example of God, who does not withhold his benefits from the bad but sends his sun and rain upon the just and the unjust.

Once, on a visit to his native Nazareth, Jesus explained to a congregation why he had healed the sick at Capernaum, a predominantly gentile city, and not in his own home town. He called to mind that there were many widows in Israel during a famine in the days of Elijah, but the prophet helped only a widow in the heathen city of Sidon, and there were many lepers in Israel in the time of Elisha, but the only one cured was Naaman the Syrian. Thus, from the evidence of the Old Testament he illustrated the fact that God's mercy was not confined to Israel, that sometimes God had shown greater favor to the Gentiles than to those who followed the Law; and he concluded, "no prophet is acceptable in his own country." The Nazarenes were so incensed by his words that they attempted to throw Jesus over a cliff. Somehow, he escaped.

An affront to Jewish national pride offended even the people of no strong religious conviction, and every party in Palestine was outraged by Jesus' prediction that the day would come when not one stone of Herod's Temple would remain upon another. There were some, to be sure, who would have made him king, but only because they misconstrued his aims; when they realized their mistake they were ready to cry, "Crucify him!"

Rejected by men, did Jesus expect to be vindicated by God? Jesus had proclaimed that the kingdom of God was at hand. This meant, as has been observed, that the rule of God, already present and demanding immediate loyalty, was soon to be displayed in power. There would be a great manifestation, preluded by wars and rumors of wars, earthquakes and famines. The sun would be turned into darkness and the moon into blood, and the stars would fall from heaven. Then the Son of Man would come on the clouds with great power and glory to gather his elect. All this would happen within that generation, though God alone knew precisely when.

What did Jesus mean when he said that some then living would see the kingdom of God? The disciples certainly thought he had in mind the expulsion of the Romans and the restoration of the kingdom of David and of the Maccabees. After the Crucifixion the disciples on the way to Emmaus felt their hopes had been utterly blasted. As Luke recounted, "we had hoped that he was the one to redeem Israel." Again, when Jesus appeared to his disciples after the Resurrection they asked, "Lord, will you at this time restore the kingdom to Israel?"

They obviously believed him to be the Messiah, but did he think of himself in that role? When Simon Peter confessed that Jesus was the Christ (the Greek word for Messiah), Jesus commended him, yet strictly enjoined him and all the disciples to keep this a secret. What sort of Messiahship was it that could not be proclaimed? Was the point to wait until the great day when the Son of Man would come on the clouds of heaven? Did Jesus believe that he was not only the earthly Messiah of the seed of David but also the heavenly Son of Man? The disciples did, and there are sayings attributed to Jesus in which the title plainly refers to himself: "the Son of Man has nowhere to lay his head"; "the Son of Man came not to be served but to serve." But again there are passages in which the term seems to refer to another: "every one who acknowledges me before men, the Son of Man also will acknowledge"; and, "whoever says a word against the Son of Man will be forgiven. And whoever speaks against the Holy Spirit will not be forgiven." Jesus may actually have identified himself with the Son of Man. But it is also possible that the disciples, having made this identification by the time they composed the Gospels some decades later, attributed the expression to Jesus. Such questions elude historical solution.

But much more important is it to know what kind of Messiah, what kind of Son of Man, what kind of kingdom of God Jesus envisaged. The Zealots looked for a Messiah who would break the invader with a rod of iron. In the Book of Daniel and in other Jewish apocalypses the Son of Man was to reign after the enemy had been given to the burning flames. How utterly foreign is all this to the spirit of Jesus! Would loving one's enemies restore the kingdom to Israel? Might it not destroy any kingdom that ever was? When his followers sought by force to make Jesus a king he fled from them to the hills. He reproved the spirit of those who sought domination: "You know that those who are supposed to rule over the Gentiles lord it over them . . . It shall not be so among you; but whoever would be great among you must be your servant, and whoever would be first among you must be your slave . . ."

Jesus may have thought of his role as unique in the redemption of Israel but feared the traditional titles for a redeemer, which were certain to be misconstrued. The total image that emerges from the sayings and deeds of Jesus conforms best with the picture portrayed by the prophet Isaiah of the Suffering Servant, "despised and rejected by men . . . with whose stripes we are healed," and with the prediction of the prophet Zechariah of a king who would be "humble and riding on an ass," who would "command peace to the nations."

Already rejected by many and not yet vindicated by God, what course had Jesus to pursue? He might have withdrawn to gentile territory; he did, in fact, make an excursion to Tyre and Sidon. But then he came back and went to Jerusalem, perhaps simply because as a loyal Jew he would not omit the Passover pilgrimage. But there are indications that he intended to precipitate a crisis. On the Sunday before Passover he rode into Jerusalem on a donkey in reminiscence of Zechariah's prediction. Palm branches were strewed in his path by throngs shouting, "Hosanna! Blessed is he who comes in the name of the Lord."

The next day Jesus went into the Temple. He saw there the money-changers who replaced the currency brought by the Jews from abroad with the Temple coinage which alone was valid for the purchase of animals for sacrifice. In blazing indignation against those who profaned the Holy Place Jesus overturned the tables and dispersed the traffickers in sacrifice. The excitement in Jerusalem must have been intense, for such an act might well have been interpreted as Messianic, as a prelude to the great day of the Lord. But the priests, who practically ruled Jerusalem, could hardly view this gesture save as an affront to their authority. And the jubilant throngs of the first day of the week must have been chilled when nothing more happened on the second or the third day. Instead of calling down legions of angels to drive out the Romans, Jesus did nothing more dramatic than to sit in the Temple and teach.

Still, for the moment, Jesus enjoyed such popular support that the Jewish authorities feared to seize him without having a specific accusation against him. The Herodians and the Pharisees thereupon contrived a plot. Only a common hatred could have united those two parties. They well knew that by Roman law Jesus could not be put to death by the Sanhedrin, and the only offenses that the Roman government would punish were civil and political crimes. No civil crime could be proved. There remained, therefore, the charge of sedition. The plotters came to Jesus with the incriminating question, "Is it lawful to pay taxes to Caesar, or not?" If Jesus answered Yes, the Zealots would be alienated. If, on the other hand, he answered No, he could be

An illumination from an eleventh–century
manuscript shows, at top, a sleeping Jesus.
Awakened by the frightened apostles, He
"rose and rebuked the wind and the sea; and
there was a great calm." Below, Jesus aids a
possessed man, turning his demons over to
swine who cast themselves into the sea.

charged before the Roman procurator, Pontius Pilate, with sedition.

Jesus' reply was unequivocal. He asked to be shown a denarius, a silver coin minted outside Palestine and bearing the head of the emperor Tiberius and an inscription declaring him the son of the divine Augustus. Strict Jews would not touch these coins. When, then, his questioners produced one, it was quite plain that to this extent they were themselves guilty of apostasy. Jesus asked, "Whose likeness and inscription is this?" They answered, "Caesar's." Jesus then replied, "Render therefore to Caesar the things that are Caesar's and to God the things that are God's." His point was that if they compromised by carrying the coins, they should pay the tribute, but their supreme duty lay in unqualified loyalty to God. It was an embarrassing retort for the questioners, but at the same time it was incriminating for Jesus. It would both enrage the Zealots and displease the Romans and their party.

On Thursday night Jesus dined with his disciples. He foresaw that on one pretext or another he would be condemned. He predicted that one disciple would betray him and all would fail him. Simon Peter asserted that though it meant death, he would not desert his Master, but Jesus predicted that before the cock crowed Peter would three times deny knowing him.

The first three Gospels have accounts of the Lord's Supper, but the version given by the apostle Paul is that which has served as the basis of the liturgy. These are his words: "For I received from the Lord what I also delivered to you, that the Lord Jesus on the night when he was betrayed took bread, and when he had given thanks, he broke it, and said, 'This is my body which is for you. Do this in remembrance of me.' In the same way also the cup, after supper, saying, 'This cup is the new covenant in my blood. Do this, as often as you drink it, in remembrance of me.' For as often as you eat this bread and drink the cup, you proclaim the Lord's death until he comes."

After the supper they went out to the Garden of Gethsemane, at the foot of the Mount of Olives. While the disciples slept, Jesus withdrew to pray: "Abba, Father, all things are possible to thee; remove this cup from me, yet not what I will, but what thou wilt." Then came an armed band from the priests, led by the traitor Judas, to arrest Jesus.

What secret did Judas betray? The usual assumption is that he disclosed the whereabouts of Jesus, but that should not have been necessary because he taught daily in the Temple. Judas may have disclosed the Messianic secret and thus have provided a ground for the accusation of sedition. The first hearing was before the high priest. When Jesus was taken in the garden, all the disciples fled; but Peter, the boldest, followed and stood in the courtyard of the priest's palace. Presumably he could hear the examination. Caiaphas, the high priest, asked Jesus, "Are you the Christ?" He answered, "I am." Caiaphas tore his mantle, declaring this to be blasphemy, and Jesus was pronounced deserving of death.

In the meantime, by the light of a fire someone recognized Peter as a follower of Jesus. He denied it. A second and a third time the point was made and he swore that he never knew the man. At once the cock crowed and Peter went out and wept bitterly. The account of this episode in the Gospels is unique in the literature of antiquity. The Greeks and the Romans would have treated the remorse of a rustic as a joke. Christianity had introduced a new sensitivity.

Since the priests could not pass sentence of death, they delivered Jesus to Pilate. We read that Pilate asked Jesus, "Are you the King of the Jews?" Jesus answered enigmatically, "You have said so," and would say no more. Pilate is represented as seeing through the guile of the accusers and of trying to save Jesus by utilizing a favor annually accorded the Jews at Passover: the release of one prisoner of their choice. He offered them either Barabbas, who in an insurrection had killed a guard, or Jesus, and they cried out for Barabbas. As for Jesus, they clamored "Crucify him!" When Pilate sought to dissuade them, they pointed out that he who showed leniency to one claiming kingship was not Caesar's friend. Pilate wilted and condemned Jesus to death by crucifixion, an ignominious form of punishment, preceded by scourging, and usually reserved in Roman times for slaves, common criminals, and revolutionaries.

Jesus was scourged, crowned in mockery with thorns, and compelled to carry his own cross until, when he sank beneath the weight of his burden, another was impressed to take over. The place of execution was a hill outside Jerusalem called Golgotha, which means the place of a skull. And they crucified him between two thieves. The passersby railed at him, and the chief priests mocked him, saying, "Let the Christ, the King of Israel, come down now from the cross that we may see and believe." And Jesus prayed, "Father, forgive them, for they know not what they do." He was offered wine mixed with myrrh as a sedative, but he did not take it. Quoting the first verse of the twenty-second Psalm, he cried out, "My God, my God, why hast thou forsaken me?" thus identifying himself with the age-old agony of his people. Then, with a loud cry, he yielded up his spirit.

Late Friday afternoon he was laid in a tomb. Early on Sunday morning, according to Mark's Gospel, certain women, including Mary Magdalene, came to the tomb and found it empty. There are several differing accounts of the reappearances of Jesus after the Crucifixion. In one strand of the tradition he is said to have appeared first to the women at the empty tomb; in another it was at the shore of the Lake of Galilee. The apostle Paul said that the Lord appeared first to Peter; the place is not mentioned. Subsequently, according to Paul, the Lord showed himself to the twelve apostles, then to five hundred brethren at once, to James, the Lord's brother, and finally to Paul himself. The accounts of the Gospels describe the risen Christ as able to speak, eat, and to be touched. Paul, in reference to his own experience of the risen Christ, says only this: "He who had . . . called me through his grace was pleased to reveal his Son to me. . . ."

But whatever the variations in the accounts, one point is plain. The disciples were sure that Christ crucified was Christ risen from the dead. Without this certainty there would probably have been no Christian Church. Heartbroken that their Master had been put to death as a common criminal, their hope shattered that he would restore the kingdom to Israel, his closest followers had dispersed. But faith in his resurrection and the consciousness of his living presence brought the disciples of Jesus together again and averted the dissolution of the fellowship.

III

The Church in An Alien World

Portraits of the deceased as an orant, a figure with arms outstretched in prayer, were common in the art of the catacombs.

During the first few centuries following the death of Jesus the Christian faith spread with phenomenal rapidity throughout most of the ancient world. What had been a small, local movement within Judaism was transformed into a far-reaching fellowship of many different peoples, well organized and with a distinctive worship. Less than three hundred years after the Crucifixion, Christianity had become the officially favored religion of the great Roman Empire.

The beginning of the infant Church, which was to grow with such remarkable vigor, is usually dated from Pentecost (the fiftieth day after Passover) following the death of Christ. On this occasion the disciples were gathered in an upper room when an exaltation of spirit seized them, as if tongues of fire had descended upon their heads. To date the rise of the Church from this experience is somewhat arbitrary, for on this subject there can be no precision. However, the Church certainly then began to win converts. That day Peter preached the first Christian sermon; his message was to believe in the Lord Jesus, crucified, risen, and exalted to the right hand of God. The seal of admission to the new fellowship was baptism, accompanied by an intense emotional experience called the descent of the Spirit. In response to Peter's preaching that day, according to the Acts of the Apostles, three thousand were converted.

After the withdrawal of Christ from the earthly scene, the situation of the disciples was naturally changed. They had regarded Jesus as the Messiah who would restore the kingdom to Israel. Now he was considered to be the heavenly Son of Man who would come again in the very near future to inaugurate the kingdom of God. With joyous expectancy they awaited his coming, in the meantime sharing their possessions according to need, observing the Law and attending the Temple daily, and breaking bread together "with glad and generous hearts." "Breaking bread" refers to a common meal called the agape, or love feast, which included a celebration called the Eucharist, meaning a thanksgiving. These occasions looked backward in commemoration of the Last Supper and forward in anticipation of the returning Christ; they marked a fellowship of believers holding communion with the risen Christ. The meetings were held in private homes which for many years to come continued to serve as churches. A particular room might be arranged to serve as a baptistery.

Although the followers of Christ professed to be faithful Jews and continued to observe the basic Mosaic law, they nevertheless held beliefs and engaged in practices that were repudiated by the orthodox. Reports of successful preaching by the disciples and of dramatic miracles performed in the name of Jesus deeply concerned the authorities of Jerusalem. Shortly after Pentecost, Peter and John were arrested and charged to be silent; but they answered, "Whether it is right in the sight of God to listen to you rather than to God, you must judge." The blow next fell on Stephen. He was charged with blasphemy because he was alleged to have said that Jesus would come again and destroy the Temple and abolish the Law. When he refuted his accusers, "stiff-necked people, uncircumcised in heart and ears" who resisted the Holy Spirit, Stephen was condemned and stoned to death. He was the first Christian martyr.

This sudden tragedy had far-reaching effects. In the face of the ensuing persecution many of the disciples fled, and wherever they went, north toward Antioch or south toward Egypt, they preached the Gospel. (*Gospel* is the Old English form of the Greek word *evangelion*, meaning "good news.") The evangelist Philip moved into Samaria and was followed by Peter and John. Mark, Peter's amanuensis, is traditionally credited with the evangelization of Egypt and the disciple Thomas with that of India.

But the great sphere of missionary expansion was to be the gentile world to the west, and the apostle to this region was preeminently Paul. Paul had been a Jew of the tribe of Benjamin (*Paul* is the Greek form of his original name, Saul), a zealous Pharisee and a persecutor of Christians, who, when Stephen was stoned, had stood by consenting to his death. After ferreting out suspects in Jerusalem, Saul received authority from the high priest to go to Damascus to see whether there had been any Christian infiltration into that synagogue. But as he approached Damascus, "suddenly a light flashed from heaven about him. And . . . a voice [said], 'Saul, Saul, why do you persecute me?'" That vision of Christ made Saul the persecutor into Paul the apostle; the encounter, he later insisted, made him as much as the others a witness to the resurrection of Christ.

Paul was to be the greatest theologian of the early Church—

and one of the few epochal figures in all history; a figure second only to Jesus in the history of Christianity. He was admirably suited for the role of apostle. Although a Jew, he had been reared in the Greek city of Tarsus in Cilicia, in Asia Minor. He was able to address a mob in Jerusalem in Aramaic, the language of Christ, and he could address the Gentiles in Greek, in which language alone his letters survive. He was also a Roman citizen, which meant that he could not be scourged without trial and that he enjoyed the right of appeal to Rome. It also meant that he could be executed only by the axe and not by crucifixion.

For Paul, Christ stood at the apex of history. In Christ, Paul claimed, culminated the covenants God had made with Noah, Abraham, and Moses. As the prophet Jeremiah had promised, there was a new covenant, not graven on stone like the Ten Commandments, but on the hearts of men; not a stricter law like that of the Pharisees, but rather a new dispensation superseding the Law altogether and embracing Jew and Gentile alike. For Paul this new covenant—this new testament—was realized in Christ.

Paul recognized that the Gentiles had a law of their own, the law of nature; but he saw also that they failed to obey it, just as the Jews had failed to keep the Law of Moses. Man is incapable of fulfilling such laws and thereby gaining God's favor, because all men have been corrupted by the fall of Adam. Salvation cannot be achieved through the works of any law, but only through the mercy of God. This mercy is vouchsafed through Christ, who, being God's Son, renounced his equality with the Father and suffered himself to be born of a woman and die upon the cross, that men might be reconciled to God and, through faith in Christ, share in his death and rise "to walk in newness of life." But why then do not all men respond? Because God has pre-destined only some to be saved. Paul thus introduced the doctrine of predestination, which was to be of vast import in later Christian thought.

Paul was the greatest of all missionaries. When the early Christian evangelists confronted the gentile world a very serious problem arose. Should observance of the Jewish Law be imposed upon Gentiles who were converted to faith in Christ? Judaism itself was missionary but had not made great gains among the Gentiles, because it required them to accept circumcision and dietary regulations. For Paul this was no problem, because to his mind the Law was no longer binding, even upon Jews. But the original disciples, including Peter, had not passed through the inner struggle by which Paul had emancipated himself from the strictures of the Law. At first they were of no mind even to consort with the Gentiles. However, Peter's prejudices were broken down by a vision. He had objected to eating anything deemed unclean by kosher standards. But in his vision a voice told him that what God had made clean he should not consider impure.

Peter understood this to mean not only that no meat but that no man was unclean in the eyes of God; and when, the next day, a Roman centurion called him, asking him to explain the Gospel, Peter went and received this Gentile into the faith. When Peter returned to Jerusalem, he was taken to task by the circle of James, brother of Jesus and leader of the Church there, for breaking bread with the uncircumcised; but he defended his course so persuasively that his questioners exclaimed, "Then to the Gentiles also God has granted repentance unto life." When ritual regulations and circumcision were no longer imposed, Christianity was relieved of a great handicap in its appeal to Gentiles of the Roman world.

But by the same token, the breach with Judaism became irreparable, a situation that only worsened when the Christians abandoned the seventh day of the week as the Sabbath in favor of the first day, the day on which Jesus rose from the dead. Precisely when this change was made we do not know, but in the Book of Revelation, the last in the New Testament, there is a reference to "the Lord's Day." The Sanhedrin pronounced a curse upon the Nazarenes, as the followers of Christ were contemptuously called. The term suggested that Christianity had its rise not at Bethlehem in Judea, but at Nazareth in half-pagan Galilee.

The Christian Church survived precariously in Palestine until the great insurrection of the Jews that led the emperor Titus in A.D. 70 to besiege Jerusalem and destroy the Temple. Of Herod's great structure only part of the foundations remained standing. The Menorah, the holy candelabrum with its seven candlesticks, was carried off to Rome, where it is portrayed on the triumphal Arch of Titus. A second rebellion, which was headed by Bar Kochba in A.D. 132–35 during the reign of the emperor Hadrian, resulted in the end of the Jewish state until the modern revival of Israel.

There were several factors that assisted the spread of Christianity throughout the Roman Empire. The synagogues, long since widely distributed in various parts of the empire, afforded Paul a port of entry in every city he visited. Although he was invariably rejected by the majority of the congregation he almost surely made converts among those Hellenized Jews. The conquests of Alexander had introduced a new cosmopolitanism into the ancient world. Among other things a common language, Hellenistic Greek called the Koine, was used from Italy to India. It was the language used by Paul in his Epistles. Following the consolidation of Rome's conquests by Caesar and Octavian, the vast empire enjoyed a period of peace—the *pax romana*—that lasted for three hundred years. Cleared of pirates by Pompey, the Mediterranean became a Roman lake. The superb roads that bound the empire together were relatively free of brigands. Paul suffered shipwreck, exposure, cold, hunger, and "peril of robbers" on his journeys, but still was able to travel and preach through Asia Minor, Thrace, Greece, and Italy; had he not been put to death he might well have realized his wish to go to Spain. Wherever he went, whether in the synagogue or the forum, Paul, thanks to the tolerance of Roman rule, was free to debate the cause of Christianity, provided he said nothing subversive of Rome's political authority.

Although this gentile world which Paul addressed rejoiced in the benefits of the Roman peace, it was subject to deep malaise. Political independence was gone. The city-states with their local loyalties were losing their political and economic autonomy, and no longer commanded the passionate devotion of their inhabitants. Men felt themselves adrift in a world grown too large, and they consequently craved such intimate fellowship as might be found in religious cults.

Worse than loneliness was ennui. For many life had lost its allure. The Roman peace may have contributed to this feeling, for peace as well as war has its vices. The capital battened on the exploitation of the provinces. Rome witnessed the rise of an aristocracy that was idle, pampered, luxurious, and lascivious. The capital city also attracted a motley horde that included the dregs of the populace of the empire. The mob clamored for bread and circuses, for staged combats of beasts with beasts—lions from Africa, tigers from India—of men with beasts, and of men with men. Artificial lakes were constructed large enough to float navies which engaged in actual combat. It is strange that there was so little protest from cultivated men. Seneca did protest that "man sacred to man" should be killed for sport, but nothing was done to arrest the madness, which spread to the provinces. The Greeks, who had been content with their Olympian games, came also to have arenas, and a number were constructed in the provincial cities of Gaul and elsewhere. Freed from war, men let blood for amusement.

Such avid pursuit of excitement witnesses to a profound malady of spirit. There were those who explained the vicissitudes of life in terms of malign supernatural influences. The swift dislocations of the civil wars of Rome that preceded the great peace led many to wonder whether life was not subject to the whims of the goddess Fortuna, who disposes capriciously of men. The Greeks had long had the concept of Moira, fate, and Tyche, caprice, which can thwart even the gods. In the classical period, however, this fate did not destroy freedom. Man could react to fate. This is the very essence of Greek tragedy. Fate determined that Oedipus should unwittingly kill his father and marry his mother, but of his own volition he pursued every clue until the ghastly truth was established and then took the guilt upon himself and spared the citizens of his city, Thebes, the vengeance of the gods.

But in the later period the Greek Moira came to be combined with Babylonian astral determinism. Man's fate was believed to be ruled by the conjunctions of the stars; he must therefore seek to discover lucky days for such events as marriage, and in all undertakings to take account of his horoscope. Juvenal tells of a woman who would not rub a salve on an itching eye until she had checked the position of the stars. To ward off possible malign influences on their lives men also resorted to magic by means of charms and amulets.

But merely to fend off evil is not so reassuring as to lay hold of life; hence the great appeal of the religions of redemption. Probably many of those who assuaged their disquiet through the games reflected little on the meaning of life, but some certainly began to be convinced that understanding and hope lay only in the beyond. Those so minded were hospitable to the messages of the oriental cults, including Christianity, with their promises of salvation.

At one point or another on his journeys Paul met the whole

gamut of contemporary paganism. At Lystra in Lycaonia in Asia Minor Paul, accompanied by Barnabas, cured a cripple. Immediately the populace assumed that Paul and Barnabas were gods in the guise of men. Barnabas was identified with Zeus, and Paul, who did the talking, with Hermes, the messenger of the gods. The priest of Zeus brought oxen to sacrifice to these divinities. At Ephesus, the capital of the Roman province of "Asia," Paul came into conflict with the fertility cult of Artemis, who was portrayed in silver statuettes with what appear to be many breasts. Paul asserted that these idols were nothing because the god was nothing. The silversmiths, whose trade was threatened, thereupon stirred up a riot.

In Galatia Paul had to deal with a type of religion which sought to avoid malign elements of the cosmos by observing special days, months, seasons, and years. At Athens he faced audiences avid for new ideas. Stoic and Epicurean philosophers who questioned him listened attentively until Paul proclaimed the resurrection of Jesus; then some mocked him, as might have been expected, for they did not believe in immortality. He might have had a different reception from Platonists, who believed in the continued life of the spirit.

Paul's journeys took him through Asia Minor and Macedonia to Greece. He desired to reach Rome, where there was a Christian congregation, by whom founded we do not know; not by Paul, obviously, and there is no evidence in the New Testament that it was founded by Peter. However, about A.D. 51–52 the emperor Claudius expelled the Jews from Rome because of rioting occasioned by one "Chrestus," presumably Christus—a vague but evocative reference to the uproar caused by the intrusion of Christianity among Jews in the capital. Probably in consequence of that expulsion a Christian-Jewish couple, Priscilla and Aquila by name, migrated to Corinth where Paul met them. Perhaps they were the founders of the Roman Christian congregation.

Before continuing his westward course toward Rome Paul went to Jerusalem to bring money he had raised among the Gentiles as a contribution to the Christian congregation there, which had not done too well with its experiment in communism. While in Jerusalem Paul was accused by the Jews of bringing Gentiles into the Temple, and in the ensuing riot he was arrested by the Roman authorities. As they were about to "examine" him by scourging, Paul insisted on his rights as a Roman citizen. As a security measure, he was then taken under guard to the Roman capital at Caesarea. The procurator of the province, Festus, might have released him had not Paul taken the case out of his hands by appealing to Rome.

Paul had confidence in Roman justice and had every reason to expect that Caesar's court would dismiss the charges, because hitherto Roman rulers had looked upon Christianity as a Jewish sect and had intervened in disputes between the two factions only to protect the weaker party from violence. Yet Paul's case at Rome, after long delays, ended in his execution under Nero.

What had happened that changed Rome's attitude? Nero, to be sure, was not a rational man. Yet he apparently saw what wiser men had failed to observe, that Christianity was a new religion. Writing some fifty years after the event, Tacitus tells us that to divert the odium arising from the general belief that he had set fire to Rome, Nero "blamed and savagely punished people popularly hated for their crimes and called Christians. The name was derived from Christ, who was executed under Tiberius the emperor and the procurator, Pontius Pilate. Suppressed for a moment, this execrable superstition broke out again not only in Judea, where it began, but even in the city of Rome where all things base and shameful flow together and enjoy a vogue. Therefore, those first were taken who confessed, then on their testimony a vast multitude was convicted, not so much on the charge of arson as of hatred of the human race. A sport was made of their execution. Some, sewn in the skins of animals, were torn apart by dogs. Others were crucified or burned, and still others, as darkness drew on, were used as torches. Nero devoted his gardens to the spectacle, provided a circus, and himself, in the costume of a charioteer, rode around among the crowd, until compassion began to arise for the victims, who though deserving of the severest penalties were actually suffering not for the public good but to glut the cruelty of one man."

Although the account refers to Judea as its place of origin, there is otherwise no hint that Christianity was an outgrowth of Judaism. This recital raises other questions. What did the Christians confess? That they had burned the city? Under torture men will confess anything. Or simply that they were Christians? In that case, they must have been recognized as distinct from Jews

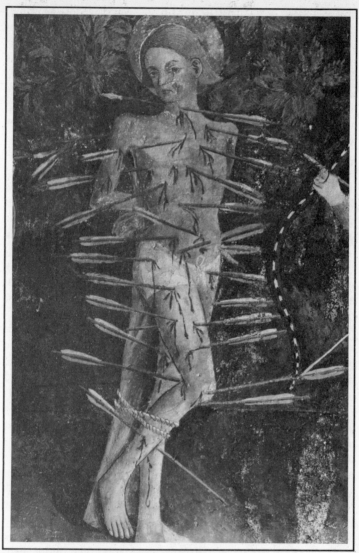

This twelfth-century fresco shows Saint
Sebastian, one of Diocletian's victims, being
used as a target by bowmen. The cult of the
martyrs flourished in the early Middle Ages,
when believers took a special interest in the
martyrs' ability to work wonders and
triumph over suffering.

and merely to be a Christian must have been considered a crime.

But what is meant by saying that they were convicted of *odium humani generis*, hatred of the human race? With the emergence of Christianity in the pagan world, two intensely religious cultures came in conflict. The more religions embrace the whole of life, the more numerous are the points of conflict. The Greeks and Romans had deities for every aspect of living—for sowing and reaping, for rain, wind, and every weather, for volcanoes and rivers, for birth, marriage, and death—and they showed reverence for ancestors, for hearth and home. But to the Christians these gods were nothing, and their denial of them was deemed atheism by the pagans. By such blasphemy the gods would be incensed and would visit their resentment not only on the offender but on the entire community. Consequently, those who denied the gods were not only atheists but enemies of the human race.

The Jews also denied the pagan gods, and they occasionally suffered severe persecutions. But whereas the Christians were everywhere and were much more actively converting Gentiles, the Jews lived largely by themselves; their dietary laws and practice of circumcision further separated them from gentile life and, as we have seen, discouraged proselytism. More important, the Jews were tacitly exempt from participating in the cult of the deified emperor. If Christians claimed not to be Jews they would forfeit this exemption.

Again, the privilege of unrestricted expansion was accorded to Judaism and other selected religions. The Roman government made a distinction between recognized and unrecognized religions, *religiones licitae* and *illicitae*. All the religions in the empire were tolerated in the lands of their origin; and the government intervened only to suppress criminal rites, such as those of the Druids, who practiced human sacrifice, and of the Phoenicians, who cast children into the fires of Moloch. Rome even invited the introduction of the worship of Magna Mater from the East in 204 B.C,. in order to enlist her divine help against Hannibal. But the indiscriminate spread of religions was not permitted. Rome resisted the orientalizing of the West by eastern cults, which nevertheless infiltrated and one by one became *religiones licitae*. Judaism enjoyed this status, but if Christianity was to be considered a new religion, it would have to be numbered among the *religiones illicitae*.

Another point of even greater moment was emerging. Although the Roman government was disinclined to impose a religion upon its subjects, the need was acutely felt for one common religion that, in addition to all local cults, would be practiced throughout the empire and thus act as a cohesive force. This common religion was found in the cult of the deified ruler. Under Augustus the worship of the emperor became the religious bond of the empire. Although Augustus took pains not to claim divine status for himself, during his lifetime the worship of his *genius*, his divine spirit, became an established cult—a cult that for many actually did involve the worship of the emperor's person as a divinity. Upon his death the Senate proclaimed Augustus a state god.

Succeeding emperors varied greatly in their personal attitude to the cult. Tiberius wanted no deification for the emperor unless the Senate also were deified, though, as we have seen, on his denarius he called himself the son of the divine Augustus. But Caligula took the imperial cult very seriously and had the temerity to order setting up his statue for worship in the Temple at Jerusalem. This was in the year A.D. 40. Philo, the Jewish philosopher of Alexandria, who happened to be in Rome at the moment, remonstrated. Petronius, the Roman governor of the Palestinian area, sent word that he would not enforce the order calling for worship of the emperor. He was ordered to commit suicide, but luckily before the instruction reached him the news arrived that the emperor had been assassinated. After that no attempt was ever again made to require emperor worship of the Jews. They were the only people in the empire to enjoy this immunity.

One can understand, therefore, why the Christians were eager to be accounted Jews by the Roman government, and why the evangelist Luke should insist that Christians were preaching nothing but Moses and the prophets, as if to say that those who believed in the risen Christ were the only true Jews. None but Christians, however, accepted this view. In the eyes of Rome Christianity was a new religion, and now the fight that Judaism had waged against the deification of a human being, whether before or after death, was taken up by the Christians, though in different form. For Judaism the confrontation was between Yahweh and any "divine" ruler; for the Christian it was between

Christ, in whom the one God became man, and Caesar, a man on the way, at least, to becoming a pagan god.

That this issue had become apparent by the time of Nero is very doubtful. Tacitus, who must surely have known that it was crucial in his own day, does not mention it for Nero's time. The emperors immediately succeeding Nero did not insist upon universal acknowledgment of their divine status. Vespasian made a joke of posthumous deification, and when asked on his death bed about his condition, replied that he felt as if he were about to become a god. At the end of the first century, however, Domitian went beyond all his predecessors and referred to himself as *dominus et deus*, lord and god. Christians could not, of course, accept such pretensions and flatly rejected the imperial cult. In consequence Domitian struck at the nonconformists and Rome became "drunk with the blood of the saints." Our information on this score is derived to a large extent from the book that now stands last in our New Testament, the Book of Revelation, written about A.D. 95. Written in the midst of persecution, like the Book of Daniel, Revelation could employ only veiled imagery. Rome is there described as the new Babylon, the great whore seated upon the seven hills. Before she can be overthrown, the Lamb that was slain (a reference to Jesus) must cast the great beast into the abyss. Then will the new Jerusalem descend "out of heaven . . . as a bride adorned for her husband." Before the first century was finished the issue between Christ and Caesar had become crucial.

The relation of the Church to the state naturally varied with circumstance. Whereas at the end of the first century, during the persecutions under Domitian, the Book of Revelation equated Rome with all the demonic powers, the Book of the Acts of the Apostles, written before Paul's death, played up Rome's protective attitude toward Christians. In the Epistle to the Romans, Paul took a median position, asserting that government was instituted by God and entrusted with the sword to protect the good and punish the bad. He instructed Christians to obey the laws and pay taxes out of conscience rather than from fear. In other words, Paul endorsed the police power of the state. But Christians refused to concede the state absolute power if its commands contravened those of God, and they applied to Rome the words Peter had addressed to the Jewish authorities: "We must obey God rather than men."

But in other respects the early Christians accepted many of the current political and social institutions, in part because of the belief that with the imminent return of the Lord Jesus the whole order of society would be changed. Consequently Paul advised no one to seek to alter his status, whether rich or poor, free or slave, married or unmarried. Paul regarded marriage as honorable. Although he thought that unions should be contracted only within the faith, he advised that unions already contracted should not be dissolved if one partner became a convert and the other remained a pagan. And although the unmarried might better remain unencumbered and free wholly to serve the Lord in the short interval before his return, they might marry if they could not control their desires. Paul thus countenanced marriage, but favored celibacy because of the particular circumstances.

The organization of the early Church was at the outset somewhat informal. The various church functions were exercised by those endowed through the Holy Spirit with suitable qualifications, such as prophets (preachers), apostles (traveling evangelists), healers, teachers, administrators, and so on. Fortunately there were those who had the gift of telling who were so endowed. In practice this amounted to self-government by each local church, or congregationalism, since the congregation endorsed the sagacity of its weightier members. Some persons were simply appointed. The Jerusalem church thus selected seven men to administer poor relief; presumably they were identical with those later called deacons. Pastoral care might be exercised by several persons, and there are indications that in certain churches a collegiate government was administered by men who were known as presbyters, or elders, because of their age and as bishops, or overseers, because of their function. But presiding at the Lord's Supper could be performed only by one person at a time, and perhaps out of this need arose the institution of a single bishop in one community.

Although as self-governing units local churches were congregational, still a conference of leaders meeting at Jerusalem issued decrees regarding the freedom of Christians from the Jewish Law. This procedure suggests a presbyterian polity in which a collegiate body has a measure of jurisdiction over several local congregations. Paul's supervision of all the churches of his foundation, in turn, corresponded functionally with the role of a modern bishop and thus suggests an episcopal polity. Thus, elements of the three main systems of government as they are practiced today in Christian churches may be traced back to the apostolic age.

The relation of Christianity to the Roman government in the early years of the second century is made abundantly clear in a document written by Pliny, the Roman governor of Bithynia in Asia Minor, to the emperor Trajan between the years A.D. 111 and A.D. 113. He wrote: "I have never been present at the trial of Christians, and I do not know what to ask or how to punish. I have been very much at a loss to know whether to make any distinction for age or strength, whether to excuse those who have renounced Christianity, whether the name itself, lacking other offense, or the crimes associated with the name should be punished. In the meantime this is what I have done. I have asked the accused whether they were Christians. If they confessed, I asked a second and a third time, threatening penalty. Those who persisted I ordered to be executed, for I did not doubt that whatever it was they professed they deserved to be punished for their inflexible obstinacy. There were others of equal madness who, because they were Roman citizens, I sent to Rome. Presently . . . more cases came to light. An anonymous document came in with many names. I dismissed those who said they were not or never had been Christians, and who in my presence supplicated the gods and placed wine and incense before your image, and especially cursed Christ, which I hear no true Christians will do."

Pliny continued with further details but admitted that he could discover nothing worse than a depraved superstition. The emperor Trajan replied that Christians were not to be hunted out but if brought to public attention were to be handled as Pliny had indicated. Anonymous accusations—"the curse of the age"—were not to be considered.

Pliny's letter does not sound as if he were inaugurating a new policy. We may assume that the main lines of procedure date at least from the time of Domitian. Whatever its beginning, this policy determined the handling of Christians by Rome throughout the second century. Though Christianity itself was deemed a crime, suspects were not to be ferreted out and prosecution was to be instituted only when the existence of Christians came to public attention, presumably through popular denunciation.

This the populace was quite ready to provide. Sometimes Jews instigated persecution, because, although there were some Jewish converts to Christianity, the majority in the Diaspora observed the anathema pronounced by the Sanhedrin against the Nazarenes. Among pagans the old charge of atheism was never dropped, and the conviction that Christians were guilty of hatred for the human race was reinforced by the increasingly apparent aloofness of the Christians from many aspects of the common life, so much so that Christians came to be called the "third race," neither pagan nor Jewish, but a race apart. The Christians gave some handle to the charge by their admission that they did not regard themselves as citizens of any country because their citizenship was in heaven. "They live in their fatherlands as transients," wrote one unidentified Christian to a correspondent in the second or third century. "Every foreign country is their fatherland and every fatherland a foreign country."

Yet, as a matter of fact, they did in the main share in community life. They did not withdraw to isolated retreats, as the Essenes did to the caves of the Dead Sea; but since they remained in the midst of society, their abstention from certain common customs and activities became all the more conspicuous.

For Christians in the Greco-Roman world the friction was increased by their immersion in an urban culture. In the Hellenistic and Roman world the Christians were so much associated with cities that the word for a man of the country, *paganus*, came eventually to mean pagan. Cities require contacts. Farmers slaughter their own livestock for meat, but urbanites must go to market for theirs. So for the Christian came the question whether he might eat meat that had first been sacrificed to idols and afterward offered for sale in the public stalls. Paul had ruled that since the idol was nothing, the meat had not been contaminated. Yet he said that they who had scruples should refrain, and if they had none, they might still refrain out of regard for the conscience of another. One can imagine the effect on the pagans if Christians refused to purchase these meats.

Not only must the Christian not practice idolatry, he must not contribute to idolatry by assisting in any way in the making of idols. He might be a sculptor, but he must not carve images of the gods. He was restricted, therefore, to the decorative aspects of tombs or monuments, but even here might not carve a lion, a

Mystery religions attracted many who were
dissatisfied with the sterility of pagan ritual.
The votive offering above was dedicated to
Jupiter Heliopolitan. The hand holds an
image of that god, whose cult fused the cults
of Jupiter and the sun god.

whale, or a bull—or gild any figure—if it represented a god. Placing incense on the altar of the emperor was, of course, forbidden, but even celebrating his birthday was compromising because this implied recognition of his divinity.

The schools presented a difficulty because they used as textbooks the works of Homer and Virgil with their stories of the pagan gods; and the ordinary teachers did not allegorize these stories after the manner of the philosophers. Hence, early in the history of Christianity the need arose for parochial schools. Hospitals as such were unobjectionable, but pagan hospitals were dedicated to Aesculapius, the god of healing. Could the Christian lie in a hospital bed while the priest went down the corridors chanting to a god whom the Christian denied? Also, the Church discouraged interfaith marriages, and although Paul had advised against separation because of a difference in faith, after death the individual partners might be buried in different cemeteries.

Other current practices were rejected by Christians on ethical grounds. Gladiatorial combats, for example, were absolutely forbidden, although their seduction continued to be felt; as late as the early fifth century Augustine tells the story of his friend Alypius, who to please a companion agreed to attend a spectacle, but resolved to keep his eyes shut. When the shouting began his eyes popped open, and he was yelling above the rest. Any shedding of blood (*effusio sanguinis*) was abhorrent even in civil justice. The Christian could not assume the office of a judge who would have to pass sentence of death.

The taking of life in war was unanimously condemned by all Christian writers of the period prior to Constantine whose works are extant. They felt that war was incompatible with the injunction of the Lord to love one's enemies. There were other reasons as well. Late in the second century Tertullian of Carthage, the first Christian theologian to write in Latin, took the legalistic stand that Christ, when he told Peter to put up his sword, had thereby disarmed every soldier. Tertullian did not concern himself with what would happen if the state renounced the sword. The outcome should be left to God; in any case, according to Tertullian, the consequences, whatever they might be, would be of only short duration, for he still believed in the imminent return of the Lord. Marcion, an influential if unorthodox Christian of whom we shall hear more presently, regarded anything physical as repulsive, especially the gore of battle. Origen, a leader of the Christians at Alexandria in the early third century, believed that triumphant Christianity would so change the quality of society that war would vanish.

However, some Christians did serve in the army, regardless of the injunctions of Church leaders. Yet whatever the exceptions, Christian abstention from military service was so notorious that Celsus, a pagan critic writing about A.D. 180, averred that if all men were like the Christians, the empire would be overrun by lawless barbarians.

The Christians seemed strange to others also because, like the Cynics, they rejected luxury and personal adornment. Christian leaders admonished their flocks to refrain from attention to personal appearance. Women should not blacken their eyelids, rouge their cheeks, or perfume their persons. Men should not pull out any hairs. Clothes should be undyed, for if God had wished there to be purple clothes, he would have made purple sheep. Nor should there be any great distinction in costume for male and female. A simple white robe would do for both. Wigs should not be worn. If the presbyter laid his hand in blessing on a wig, whose hair would he bless? Delicate sheets do not induce sleep; tables require no ivory legs; nor do knives need jeweled handles. The Lord Jesus did not come down from heaven with a silver foot bath to wash the disciples' feet.

These various injunctions directly follow Cynic themes, but their point was different. The Christian was not seeking to outwit fate by renouncing everything before fate could take it away. He was denying the world, the more freely to follow the Lord. And, as Tertullian observed, he was in training for martyrdom. Tertullian demanded whether a foot that wore an anklet would bear the gyve of the torturer, whether the neck adorned with a necklace would submit to the axe of the executioner. To the pagan such behavior made the Christians all the more appear to be a "third race." The impression was not dispelled by the fact that Christians led normal, even exemplary, family lives, and practiced agriculture and the handicrafts like the others in their communities. Despite their hospitality and philanthropy, despite their devotion to plague victims when pagans fled, despite so many proofs of Christian love for mankind, the belief persisted that they were haters of the human race. And herein lies the deepest reason for popular persecution.

During the second century the persecutions were sporadic and erratic. The first instance was under the emperor Trajan, whose otherwise moderate policy has been noted. One of the victims was Ignatius, the bishop of Antioch in Syria, who was brought to Rome to die in the arena. On the way his guards permitted him to visit Christian congregations whose members and bishops had not been arrested. One can easily surmise why Ignatius should have been taken and others left. He was certainly an aggressive Christian leader, and although extravagant craving for martyrdom was discouraged by the Church—whose counsel was "neither flee nor provoke"—Ignatius desired to be martyred in order that he might the more speedily be with Christ. He declared that if the wild beasts were not hungry, he would urge them on.

As Ignatius passed through Smyrna he was received with honor by Polycarp, bishop of the congregation there. Not until some forty years later, when a mob clamored for his death, did Polycarp suffer a like martyrdom. An account of the event survives in a letter written by his own congregation immediately following the execution. In the arena, Polycarp was given an opportunity to save himself by recantation. The proconsul, following the procedure outlined by Pliny, told Polycarp to say, "Away with the atheists," meaning the Christians. But Polycarp pointed to the heathen in the stadium instead and shouted, "Away with the atheists." One might suppose that this would have settled the matter, but the proconsul began again, saying, "Curse Christ." Polycarp answered, "I have served him eighty-six years, and he has done me no wrong; how can I blaspheme the king who saved me?" The proconsul tried once more: "Swear by the genius of Caesar." Polycarp replied simply, "I am a Christian." The proconsul threatened to throw him to the beasts. Polycarp answered, "Bring them in." The magistrate menaced him with fire, but Polycarp counseled him that the fire which burns for an hour is not to be compared to the fire of eternal punishment; and he was then burned to death. This was in A.D. 156. In his long life Polycarp had served as an important link between the age of the apostles and that of the great Christian writers of the second century.

The greatest persecutors were not the worst emperors, but rather the better ones. Although he was a Stoic philosopher, the noble Marcus Aurelius took very seriously the popular rites performed for the welfare of the state. As a propitiation to the gods he compelled criminals sentenced to death to slaughter each other in the amphitheatre. Before starting out to fight the Marcomanni he called upon the priests of Rome to sacrifice oxen for the safety of his arms. Christians, who refused to subscribe to such practices, appeared to Marcus Aurelius as obstinate fanatics, dangerous to the public security.

A wave of persecution struck the churches of Lyons and nearby Vienne in southern France in the year A.D. 177. Mobs accused the Christians of incest and cannibalism. The accusation of sexual irregularity may easily arise against any disliked group that holds meetings in secret, and the Christians did not admit non-Christians to the celebration of the Lord's Supper. The charge of cannibalism was also connected with this rite because the pagans heard that the Christians consumed somebody's flesh and blood. Under torture some of the accused recanted, but they were then punished as criminals rather than as Christians. Yet some among those at the last recovered their courage and died for the faith. The fury was soon past and the congregation was able to reassemble.

Such haphazard persecution advanced that which it sought to destroy. As Tertullian said, "The blood of the martyrs is seed." The Church grew and growth brought new problems. In the first half of the second century we meet a phenomenon recurrent in the expansion of Christianity. First the Church must accommodate itself to the culture in which it takes root and in which it seeks to win converts; the Gospel must be couched in images intelligible to the heathen. The next stage is one of assimilation. The convert who is taken into the Christian community thereupon blends the old in his outlook with the new, perhaps to the enrichment, but almost invariably to the perversion of Christianity.

This pattern was strikingly illustrated by the rise of Christian Gnosticism. Gnosticism was one of the religions of contemplation, which despised the world of matter and sought salvation by way of emancipation from the flesh. There was a great variety of Gnostic systems and ideas, but the core of the Gnostic myth was this: the ultimate is the great abyss of being, describable only by negatives—the unknown, the incomprehensible, the incommensurable, the unfathomable. This abyss is dynamic, and within its fullness (*pleroma*) differentiations arise by way of emanations. One of the emanations is Wisdom. She was filled with inordinate curiosity to understand the secret of the pleroma and in her distress gave off matter, which with the aid of the demiurge was shaped into our visible world.

Here is the reverse of the Hebrew myth of creation, in which the world was created good and evil appeared later with the fall of man. In the Gnostic account the fall of Wisdom came first, and the creation followed in consequence. Hence the material world was the result of the fall and therefore bad. Man is a composite being consisting of spirit imprisoned in matter, from which release is sought. At this point the role of Wisdom was reversed. Apparently penitent for her mischief, she became a redeeming principle, aiding man in his liberation by communicating to him the illumination, or gnosis, which enabled him to detach his spirit from the flesh so that it might ascend until reunited with the pleroma. Not only is matter an impediment to salvation, but time is also; salvation means deliverance from its weary, recurrent cycles.

As an amalgam of popular Near Eastern beliefs and Greek philosophy, Gnosticism was quite ready to combine with existing religious systems, but it always conferred upon their mythology its own meaning. For example, Gnosticism absorbed Hebrew myths but completely reversed their values. Since the world is evil, Yahweh, who created the world, must be the evil demiurge. The serpent, who told Eve to eat of the tree of knowledge of good and evil, was a redeemer, for the knowledge of good and evil is precisely the saving gnosis. All those persons commended in the Old Testament were evil servants of the evil Yahweh, and those reproved, like Cain, belonged to the illumined.

When Gnosticism was combined with Christianity the result was no less a distortion. Gnostic Christians believed in Christ as the Redeemer, but since his function was to deliver man from the thralldom of the flesh, he could not have had any flesh. It merely appeared that he had. His body was a phantom which only seemed to exist. Plainly, this view subverted the whole Christian doctrine of the Incarnation and the Crucifixion. The greatest fight in the early Church was to establish not the divinity, but the humanity of Christ. Again, the Incarnation was an event in time, but what the Gnostics sought was release from time; Gnosticism thus stripped history of all significance.

In the early decades of the second century Gnosticism and

Christianity were blended by some distinguished intellectuals who felt that they were simply making a synthesis of all truth. The Christian Gnostics were Christian in that they gave Christ the supreme place of honor, even above Wisdom. But what happened to the Hebrew background of Christianity in such thinking is apparent in the case of Marcion, the son of a bishop. Marcion was a Gnostic in his attitude toward the created world. It is bad, said he, and full of flies, fleas, and fevers. The God who made it, the creator God, could not have been the father of our Lord Jesus Christ, but was rather a malevolent demiurge. Marcion's contention meant that Christianity would have to sever itself from all its Hebrew antecedents and that the Old Testament must be rejected.

The spread of Gnosticism faced the still weakly organized Church with a grave crisis. What the Church believed to be the real truth had to be formulated, and what it did not believe had to be refuted; and those who were to be received in baptism must first be instructed in these matters. At baptism new converts were required to make a confession of their faith. The earliest version of this formal confession, called the Old Roman Symbol, developed later into what we know as the Apostles' Creed, which reads as follows: "I believe in God the Father Almighty; Maker of heaven and earth. And in Jesus Christ his only Son our Lord; who was conceived by the Holy Ghost, born of the Virgin Mary; suffered under Pontius Pilate, was crucified, died, and was buried; he descended into hell; the third day he rose from the dead; he ascended into heaven; and sitteth at the right hand of God the Father Almighty; from thence he shall come to judge the quick and the dead. I believe in the Holy Ghost; the holy Catholic Church; the communion of saints; the forgiveness of sins; the resurrection of the body; and the life everlasting. Amen."

Here, in direct contradiction to Gnostic precepts, it is asserted that God did create the physical world; that Christ was actually physically born; that he truly suffered; that this was at a definite point in history (under Pontius Pilate); and that he died a real death. By such affirmations the Church guarded the faith against perversions. This is by no means all that was believed, but this much had to be believed and its contrary rejected by those who professed Christianity.

On what authority did Christians base such definitions of

their faith? First of all they appealed to the authority of the Scripture, meaning at this point the Old Testament, which contains the doctrine of God's creation of the world *as good*. But Marcion could not be convinced by the testimony of a book that the world is good. He argued that since the world is bad, the book is not good, and he collected all the passages in the Old Testament about the vindictiveness of God to prove that Yahweh's acts were contrary to Christian ethics. The churchmen replied that Marcion had made the dichotomy too sharp. In the Old Testament Yahweh was not only wrathful but also "abundant in steadfast love," and in the New Testament Jesus was not always tender, for he promised at the Judgment to send sinners into everlasting fire. The Church Fathers—this is the term used for the major Christian writers up to about A.D. 600—could not, of course, deny that elements of the Old Testament were incompatible with Christianity. The apparent contradictions were explained by allegory, after the manner of Philo. For example, the polygamy of the patriarchs meant that they were married to more than one virtue, and the slaughter of the Amalekites indicated the eradication of vices.

But though the Old Testament gave support to certain Christian doctrines, there were others that it did not teach, and for these a Christian literature was necessary. Most of what was later included in the canon of the New Testament had been written during the first century: the four Gospels, the Acts of the Apostles, the letters of Paul to the various churches and to individuals—Timothy, Titus, and Philemon. Two letters also bore the name of Peter, three the name of John, and one each the names of James and Jude. The Epistle to the Hebrews was anonymous. The Book of Revelation, which we have noted, was written by a man named John. Which portions of this material were written by the persons to whom they have been ascribed cannot always be ascertained; there is little question that virtually all of it came from the Christian community of the first century, with a few portions possibly dating from the second century.

Was all this, and only this, worthy to be placed on a par with, or above, the Old Testament? The first man to address himself to that question was Marcion. His favorite apostle was Paul because he had so decisively rejected the Law of the Old Testament. Therefore Marcion made his canon include Paul's letters to the churches and the letter to Philemon, but not those to Timothy and Titus, and, as for the rest, only the Gospel of Luke. Why he chose that particular Gospel we do not know; perhaps it was more familiar in his native Pontus than were the others.

Christian leaders also drew up lists of what they considered authoritative writings, including the works in Marcion's canon, as well as the other books mentioned above. By about the middle of the third century the collection represented in our New Testament was commonly recognized as the canon or rule of faith. There was controversy for a time only over a few books. John's Gospel made trouble because its dates for the death and resurrection of Christ differed from those in the other Gospels. In John's Gospel Jesus died on the fourteenth of the Jewish months of Nisan, the day the Passover lamb was slain. He did not live to eat the Passover supper, and this Gospel has no account of the Lord's Supper. But in the other three Gospels he did share with his disciples in the Passover meal and therefore must have suffered on the following day, which was the fifteenth.

Beyond that arose the question as to whether the Crucifixion or the Resurrection should be celebrated. The churches of Asia Minor, which followed the chronology of John's Gospel and which were called Quartodecimans (fourteenthers), commemorated the Crucifixion. The Roman church, which followed the first three Gospels, celebrated the Resurrection. All four Gospels agreed that Jesus had died on a Friday and had risen on a Sunday; but should the day of the week or the date of the month be observed? Romans and Asians disagreed, and as a consequence some Christians were feasting while others were fasting. The Roman church established the practice of observing a fixed day of the week rather than a fixed day of the month, the first Sunday after the first full moon after the vernal equinox. The Asians demurred, and about A.D. 190 Bishop Victor of Rome excommunicated their churches. The dispute eventually subsided and the Roman practice came to prevail in all churches.

While the controversy raged there was a disposition to undercut the Asians by rejecting their gospel, but Irenaeus of Lyons, himself an émigré from Asia Minor to Gaul, preached peace and defended John's Gospel. There must be four Gospels, he asserted, just as there were four faces in the vision of Ezekiel, those of a man, a lion, an ox, and an eagle. This amusing argument became the basis for the symbolic representation of the four

One of the most frequently portrayed saints
was Martin of Tours, the Roman legionary
in Gaul who cut his cloak in half to share
with a beggar, as shown in this Catalan
painting. The beggar later appeared to him
in a vision, revealing himself to be Christ.
When Martin became bishop of Tours, in
372, he refused to change his simple life and
lived in a monastery outside the city.

evangelists: a winged man for Matthew, a winged lion for Mark, a winged ox for Luke, and an eagle for John.

The Book of Revelation was accepted only slowly in the East, as was the Epistle to the Hebrews in the West. Athanasius, the bishop of Alexandria, who had lived in exile in Rome in the period after Constantine and who enjoyed the support of the Roman church, served as a mediator. His Festal Epistle of A.D. 367 is commonly regarded as the first to define the canon of the New Testament as consisting of those twenty-seven books that now make up its content.

The acceptance of these books meant the rejection of others, which are now called the New Testament Apocrypha. They consist of several gospels of Jesus' childhood, an account of his descent into Hades to release the spirits imprisoned by Satan, accounts of the travels of Peter, Paul, and other apostles, and reports of contests in miracles between Simon Peter and Simon Magus. In the last, Simon Peter caused a dried sardine to swim and a child at the breast to pronounce a pompous anathema on the other Simon, who displayed his powers by cavorting in the air.

This literature enjoyed a wide vogue, but the discriminating judgment of the Church Fathers prevailed over popular taste and excluded it from the canon. Nevertheless, during the Middle Ages scenes from the apocryphal gospels continued to be illustrated along with those from the genuine Gospels.

The authority of the books that were considered the canon of the New Testament depended in good part upon their having been written either by an apostle or by one of his companions. But the authenticity of such writings might be questioned. About the opening of the third century Serapion, the bishop of Antioch, was asked by his congregation whether they might read in their church services the Gospel of Peter. He supposed, of course, that anything by Peter would be satisfactory, and consented, not yet having read the book. On doing so, however, he discovered that it was Gnostic, and he retracted his permission, informing his congregation that it could not possibly have been written by Peter.

If, then, the books of themselves did not establish the truth of doctrine, recourse must be had to the underlying oral traditions. These, in turn, did not in themselves provide an infallible guide. The Gnostics claimed an oral tradition of their own, consisting of an esoteric wisdom which they asserted Jesus had privately committed to certain of his disciples and which they in turn had transmitted to their successors. Irenaeus replied that if Jesus did have any such special wisdom to communicate, he would have entrusted it to those disciples whom he most trusted, and they in turn to their especial confidants. And surely those whom Jesus most trusted were those to whom he had entrusted the churches. By the same token, those in whom the disciples reposed the greatest confidence would have been those to whom they had passed on the churches. Therefore, to discover the true tradition one should turn to churches of apostolic foundation in which there had been an unbroken succession of appointed bishops. Irenaeus pointed to the Church of Rome as the preeminent example, founded by the two martyred apostles, Peter and Paul, and presided over by a continuous succession of bishops, each of whom was known by name.

By the end of the second century three sources of authority had emerged: the canon, the creed, and the oral tradition. The first two were interpreted in terms of the third. The Church was developing in its role as custodian of all, and thus as the living source of authority. This development in turn had two aspects: the growth of the authority of the bishop as head of a local congregation or district, and the growing preeminence of the Church of Rome over other churches. As to the bishop, by the beginning of the second century his position had become more clearly defined, and the system of a single bishop in charge of a single congregation prevailed in Syria and Asia Minor. Ignatius and Polycarp were bishops in this sense. A maxim of Ignatius was, "Do nothing without the bishop."

The early organization of the Church in Rome—which was to become the very seat of authority—is obscure. Although Clement of Rome is called in subsequent tradition the third bishop of Rome, in his letter to the Corinthians (written about A.D. 95) he makes no reference whatever to his own authority, nor does he clearly indicate that Rome had a single bishop. However, Clement is the first to enunciate the idea of the apostolic succession of church officers. By A.D. 185 the ideas of a single bishop in a church and of his apostolic succession were combined in Irenaeus' argument. He traced the Roman succession down to his own time: Linus, Anacletus, Clement, Evaristus, Alexander, Sixtus, Telesphorus, Hyginus, Pius, Anicetus, Soter, Eleutherus. But if Sixtus was the sixth bishop, Peter could not have been the first. This has been explained by placing Peter, as an apostle, in a special category; but by this line of reasoning Paul could have been the first bishop. Peter is not definitely named as the first bishop of Rome until the Liberian Catalogue, compiled in Rome about A.D. 354. But this ascription rests on an earlier tradition. A letter spuriously attributed to Clement of Rome and dating from the third century has Peter say to the Roman congregation: "I ordain this Clement to be your bishop: and to him alone I entrust my chair of preaching and instruction. I bestow on him the power of binding and loosing which the Lord bestowed on me, so that whatever he shall decree on earth shall be decreed in the heavens."

Interestingly, this document does not mention either Linus or Anacletus. The lists of the Roman bishops emanating from the East make Peter a founder of the Roman church, but not its first bishop. That Peter was in Rome and suffered in Rome is as strongly attested as in the case of Paul. That he was the first bishop is rather a matter of faith than of historical demonstration. However, from the time of Nero's persecutions the Church of Rome was bound to be venerated as the church of the two apostolic martyrs. (Peter was placed above Paul because of the words of Jesus, that on Peter the Rock he would found the church.) By A.D. 185, as indicated by Irenaeus, the Church of Rome had attained preeminence as the custodian of the apostolic tradition.

The formulation of Christian doctrines and the strengthening of Church organization had provided Christianity with necessary safeguards against such threats as Gnosticism had posed. But the attendant growth of the Church further altered its relations with the Roman government. In the first half of the third century the emperors of the house of Severus, to further unity among peoples of the empire, pursued a policy of mingling the different religions, with a strong stress upon the oriental cults. Septimius Severus, the first emperor of the house, who came to the throne in A.D. 193, married the daughter of the priest of the sun god of Emesa, in Syria. Alexander Severus was said to have in his private chapel statues of Abraham, Orpheus, and Christ (representing Judaism, the mystery religions, and Christianity). Septimius' successor, who was born in Emesa, had taken the name Elagabalus (Heliogabalus), as he was the high priest of the sun god Elagabal. With his accession, the cult of the deified emperor was divested of all the restrictions imposed by the emperor Augustus and became unabashedly oriental. Christians could never accept this. The Severi did not try to compel them to do so, although in A.D. 202 Septimius Severus thought to check expansion of the two intransigent religions by prohibiting conversions to Judaism and to Christianity on pain of death.

We have a very moving account of a martyrdom in North Africa that resulted from this edict, as it was described by Perpetua, one of the victims. Perpetua was of the nobility, twenty-two years old, with a child at the breast, whom she was allowed to suckle in prison. Associated with her was Felicitas, a slave girl, who was with child and feared that she would not be able to die with the others because Rome did not execute pregnant women. As the day of the examination drew near, Perpetua's father came to undermine her resolution to die for her faith, saying, "Daughter, pity my white hairs! Pity your father, if I am worthy to be called your father. . . . Give me not over to the reproach of men! Consider . . . your son, who cannot live without you. Lay aside your pride and do not ruin us all." And Perpetua grieved for his sake. At the trial the procurator said to her, "Spare your father's white hairs. Spare the tender years of your child. Offer a sacrifice for the safety of the emperors." She answered, "No." "Are you a Christian?" "I am."

The jailer was kindly disposed and admitted friends to see the prisoners. "Now when the games approached, my father came to me worn with trouble and began to pluck out his beard and throw himself on his face and curse his years, and . . . I sorrowed for the unhappiness of his old age." All the condemned prisoners prayed that Felicitas might not be left behind on the road to the same hope, and her pangs came upon her and she cried out. Then one of the jailers said to her, "If you cry out at this, what will it be when you are thrown to the beasts?" She answered, "Now I suffer what I suffer, but then another will be in me who will suffer for me, because I, too, am to suffer for him." She gave birth to a girl, whom one of the sisters reared as her own. When, later, the martyrs passed by the procurator's stand, they said, "You are judging us. God will judge you." They were then executed in the arena at Carthage before the populace of the city.

This wave of persecution was of short duration and not widespread. From the accession of Septimius Severus in A.D. 193

down to the persecution of Decius in A.D. 250 the Church in fact enjoyed an almost unbroken peace. During this time the oriental cults, particularly the Mysteries, flourished as well. It appears that in the third century they became the chief rivals of Christianity, so much so that in the latter part of the century the emperor Aurelian attempted to establish the cult of the sun god as the state religion.

Judging from the writings of the early Church Fathers, Christians were more concerned with the menace to their religion from Gnosticism and the older paganism than from the mystery cults; perhaps they did not see where the greatest danger lay. These mystery religions were so called because their rites were not disclosed to the uninitiated. Most of them had in common the dying and rising of a god. The chief deities were frequently in pairs, a male and a female, the one dying and the other aiding the resurrection.

In Palestine, the deity Baal had a female partner called Ashtoreth. The Eleusinian myth diverged from this pattern in that the principal pair consisted of a mother and a daughter. The usual scheme was found in Babylon with Tammuz and Ishtar; in Syria with Adonis and Astarte; and in Asia Minor with Attis and Magna Mater, the Great Mother. In the Orphic cult the dying female Eurydice was restored by the male Orpheus. In the ancient Egyptian religion the god Osiris was dismembered by his brother but, except for his reproductive organs, was reassembled by his wife and sister Isis. Thus resurrected, Osiris became the god of the dead and the judge of souls. The goddess Isis was portrayed in terms of poetic beauty as the radiantly fair queen of heaven.

The dying and rising of the god usually coincided with the fall and spring equinoxes. All the cults had fertility elements, and even in Mithraism, which had no female deity, sculptures of Mithra slaying the bull show, not blood spurting, but stalks of grain sprouting from the wounded flank. But such cults were more than devices for securing good harvests. In the performance of their rites men were assured that like nature, they, too, would be reborn after death, and that through union with the risen god they would themselves be made divine and thereby immortal.

Such union might be accomplished in various ways. In the Dionysian cult the devotee killed and consumed with the utmost haste an animal supposedly inhabited by the god, who on the death of the animal would soon depart. In other cases, as in the religion of Magna Mater and in Mithraism, there might be a baptism in the life-containing blood of a goat or a bull. Inebriation and sexual stimulation might excite a state of ecstasy interpreted as being filled with the god. More refined methods of accomplishing the union included sacred meals of bread and wine or of fish; the witnessing of a dramatic enactment of the myth of the god; or sometimes, as in the Orphic cult, the employment of music.

Great as the conflict was between Christianity and the Mysteries, they did have in common certain aspirations and certain practices: the quest for redemption from mortality and evil, the closeness of association in intimate gathering-places, the social fellowship in which slave and free, male and female were equal. Certain concepts could easily be refashioned and adapted to Christian belief and practice. Blessedness in the fields of Osiris could be transferred to the new Jerusalem, and security under the tutelage of Isis, the beneficent queen of heaven, could be transmuted into refuge beneath the folds of the robe of the *Regina Coeli*, the Virgin Mary, the Mother of God.

But there were some respects in which those who came to Christianity from the Mysteries threatened to subvert the faith. They might destroy faith in God the Father, since their rites centered on a dying and rising saviour, with no higher god. A greater danger was that Christ might be regarded as a fertility god, dying and rising with the seasons, since indisputably he did rise in the spring. For a time some Christians in Asia Minor celebrated Easter on the twenty-fifth of March, the vernal equinox on the old calendar, the day on which Attis rose from the dead. The Church discouraged this practice, but in the fourth century it permitted the transferring of the celebration of Jesus' birth from the sixth of January to the twenty-fifth of December, the winter solstice and the birthday of the solar deity. The reason for the change was to institute a counter-attraction on this day when Christian converts were joining their pagan neighbors for the celebration. The danger was that the Christian festival would be too much like the one it sought to counter. In general the Church was flexible at the periphery but adamant at the core. For instance, certain fertility symbols were allowed to become

This eleventh-century ivory carving
portrays Peter dictating the Gospel to Mark,
with an angel watching over them. Mark,
who wrote of the royal lineage of Christ, has
been portrayed symbolically as a winged
lion in other works of the Renaissance.

associated with Easter—eggs and rabbits—but the Church strongly insisted that Jesus be worshiped as a historical figure and not as the god of a vernal myth.

The sacraments also had to be carefully defined. It was a view among the mystery cults that to be immortal man must be united with the god; sometimes the union was effected through a sacred meal. In Christianity the Eucharist served this end, not in any crude and magical fashion, but by a life-transforming union with Christ, so that man became a new creature. But it might be interpreted as an actual eating of the god, as it was in the Mysteries. John's Gospel appears to have been combating such a view when it reports Jesus as saying that one must eat the flesh and drink the blood, but then adds, "It is the spirit that gives life, the flesh is of no avail. . . ."

The period of comparative relaxation under the Severi enabled the Christian leaders to devote greater attention to the intellectual problems of Christianity. There were, naturally, differences of emphasis among the Christian thinkers concerning the relation of Christian teaching to the current philosophical traditions. Tertullian, who lived in Carthage, was the thinker least disposed to any blending of the classical philosophy with Christian traditions. "What," he exclaimed, "has Athens to do with Jerusalem?"

Despite his disclaimer of any indebtedness to Athens, Tertullian was the heir and transmitter of the Greek intellectual tradition in that he had an acutely speculative mind and strove to systematize and define Christian beliefs. It was he who first coined the word *Trinity* and formulated the doctrine of three persons held together in the unity of one substance. He also introduced the word consubstantial, describing the relationship of the Son to the Father. In more common terminology one might say that the Son participates in the being of the Father.

The primary center of the fusion of Christianity and classical culture was not Carthage, however, but rather Alexandria, long a major center of Greek intellectual activity. The two great Christian leaders there in the first half of the third century were Clement of Alexandria and Origen. They were not embarrassed by their debt to Greek philosophy. Clement was notably ready to appropriate the language of the classical tradition and to baptize the ideas of all the contemporary -*isms*. For him Christianity was the true philosophy and the true gnosis, in the sense of knowledge or illumination. He classified Christians according to the stages of their illumination. At the same time Clement was no Gnostic, for he did not turn the story of Jesus into a cosmic myth. He used the poetic language of the mystery religions, but for him Christianity was the true poem and his description of the work of the Lord Jesus was itself poetic creation.

The comparative peace and security enjoyed by Christians in the first half of the third century brought changes within the body of the Church membership. As the religion spread among the population of the empire it attracted as converts people of means. The Church Fathers continued to inveigh against wealth, pointing out that a life of riches offered more temptations to sin than did a life of poverty. But by the third century such rigor was relaxed, and Clement of Alexandria could contend that since continuing philanthropy depends on wealth, a rich man might be saved.

Quite possibly there is some correlation between this type of liberalism and a growing laxity, or at least relaxation of discipline generally. During the first two centuries the Church had looked upon three sins as forgivable indeed by God, but never by the Church—the denial of the faith, sexual immorality, and the taking of life. The penalty for their commission was exclusion from the fellowship of the Church and deprivation of that sacrament which was the peculiar channel of divine grace, the Eucharist. Ignatius had called it "the medicine of immortality and the antidote of death," and Irenaeus had claimed that such a change took place in the elements after their consecration, that they were no longer to be regarded as common elements, and that "our bodies when they receive the Eucharist are no longer corruptible."

Exclusion from the Eucharist thus imperiled salvation, and offenders so penalized craved a relaxation of such rigor. But should the Church run the risk of sullying her purity by permitting the goats to resume fellowship with the sheep?

The first to accept repentant sinners as a matter of official church policy was a bishop of Rome, Callistus, who readmitted penitent fornicators on several grounds: the Church is like the ark of Noah in which there were unclean as well as clean beasts; the Church is like a field in which the tares were to be left to grow with the wheat; and finally, the Church of Rome is the heir of Peter, to whom Jesus had given keys both to bind and to loose. (This is the first recorded reference to this passage by a bishop of Rome.) Tertullian was aghast and exclaimed, "We do not forgive apostates, and shall we forgive adulterers?" But the ruling of Callistus won general acceptance.

Once those guilty of fornication and adultery were readmitted to the Church the question arose whether apostates should not also be readmitted; apostasy had become especially widespread when the Roman government suddenly abandoned its policy of tolerance of Christians for one of systematic, universal persecution. The new policy was due to the result of changing conditions within the empire. The stable administration carried over from the second century was disintegrating, so much so that some historians date the fall of Rome not from the fifth century, but from the third. Anarchy threatened. The Roman legions gained increasing power and set up one military emperor after another. The cause of the trouble was in part economic. Taxation had become ruinous to trade and industry. In the republican period the Romans had sustained themselves by their own labor on small farms, but the wars of expansion had brought hordes of slaves. During these wars and early in the empire the Romans lived on the spoils from the provinces. But these were eventually exhausted and there were no new conquests.

The emperors chosen by the legions were generals who had spent much of their lives defending the frontiers, rough fellows who settled problems of dissension or disagreement within the state not by pleas for tolerance, but by the sword. Like their contemporaries, they were religious and ascribed the ills of the empire not to bankruptcy or bad administration, but to the neglect of the old religion under which Rome had grown great. Hence without dropping the imperial cult they stressed rather the worship of the ancient gods. So deep was the faith that increased religiosity would restore Rome to its ancient glory that in A.D. 212 the emperor Caracalla had conferred Roman citizenship on all free men throughout the empire, in order that there might be more persons qualified to offer acceptable prayers to the gods of the empire.

Decius was the first emperor to demand universal worship of the old Roman gods. He was a general from the Danubian frontier, resolved to have no nonsense; the obstinate Christians appeared to him as enemies of the empire, which because of their atheism had been abandoned by the gods. In A.D. 249 Decius decreed that all citizens of the empire, male and female, Christian and pagan, prove their loyalty by offering public sacrifices to the gods; they would then be given certificates signed by local officials testifying to their compliance. Some Christians, with the connivance of officials, bought certificates without making the proper sacrifices. Some capitulated and ran to the altars. Some were stalwart, and many perished. The fury ended in A.D. 251, when Decius, deserted by his gods, was killed in a battle with the Goths.

There then arose in even more acute form the question of readmitting to the Church those who had been guilty of apostasy. They were numerous, sometimes as many as three-quarters of a congregation. During the long peace, as we have observed, many Christians had relaxed those disciplines that would have better enabled them to hold to the ideals of their faith. Without adequate spiritual preparation they had been caught unexpectedly; like Peter in the courtyard of the high priest, they had denied the Lord and now wept bitterly. They were more eager for restoration since the implications of exclusion from the Church were being even more clearly spelled out. Callistus, we observed, compared the Church to Noah's Ark, outside of which no souls were saved. Bishop Cyprian of Carthage said flatly, "Outside the Church there is no salvation"; and again, "He cannot have God as a Father who has not the Church as his mother." Therefore arose a clamor for readmission.

Cyprian pleaded for leniency toward the backsliders. Reversing Tertullian's question, "We do not forgive apostates, and shall we forgive adulterers?" he asked, "We forgive adulterers, and shall we not forgive apostates?" At the same time Cyprian insisted on discrimination. Those who had bought certificates without having actually sacrificed were certainly guilty of dishonesty; nevertheless they had made plain to the magistrates that they were Christians. Leniency should be extended to them, as well as to those who had sacrificed only after excruciating torture and who well might plead that their bodies, not their spirits, had given way. Those who had gone willingly to make sacrifices must receive the severest treatment.

To deal with these degrees of guilt a graded system of penance evolved, in which the number of years of exclusion from the rites of the Church depended on the gravity of the offense. The concept of penance was developed as a sequel to baptism, which was believed to wash away all previous sins. Since baptism could not be repeated, martyrdom was regarded as a second baptism, a baptism of blood, remitting all sins committed since the first baptism. This was why some, like Ignatius, even desired and invited a martyr's death. For those who had sinned after their original baptism and who might not suffer martyrdom, penance was available. The idea that forgiveness of sins at least once after baptism was possible through penance was first proposed in a work called *The Shepherd of Hermas*, written in Rome around the middle of the second century. The concept gradually evolved until by the Middle Ages penitential acts were considered to be more than evidence of contrition; they were held to be actually meritorious and could be checked off against offenses. How remote was this view from Paul's insistence that salvation is the sheer gift of God's unmerited grace!

Decius' attempt to exterminate Christianity was revived by his successors, particularly by Valerian. In A.D. 258 this emperor made a frantic effort to induce the gods to protect the empire from its various foreign foes, but to no avail. He was captured during a campaign against the Persians in A.D. 260. The next emperor, Gallienus, abandoned the policy of persecution and in A.D. 261 issued what was in effect an edict of toleration. A plausible explanation of this move is that Gallienus' attitude was not that of a frontier general like Decius, but rather that of a cultured patron of philosophy, which was resurgent in his day in the form of Neoplatonism.

Plotinus, the leading figure in this school, flourished in Rome about A.D. 244 to A.D. 270. For him religion was a means of emancipating the soul from the things of sense, that the soul might ultimately be united in ecstasy with the ineffable intelligence (*nous*). Yet though he deprecated the physical world, he nevertheless did not reject sacrifices to the gods. He did repudiate Christianity and even Gnostic Christianity. His pupil Porphyry rejected the entire biblical drama of creation, fall, incarnation, redemption, and judgment and wrote one of the most formidable criticisms to be directed at Christianity during the period of persecution. But the Neoplatonists were averse to using the arm of the state to compel religious compliance; as reasonable men, they felt it better to show by arguments and refutations how preposterous were Christian teachings, thereby to persuade people to reject them. The toleration during the reign of Gallienus was apparently part of the shift to this new mode of attack.

The anti-Christian literature of this period was fairly extensive, though only fragments remain. The Christians, involved in a struggle for survival, were not interested in conferring immortality upon the arguments of their opponents. Still, Christians could not reply to attacks against them without stating what these were; the Christian apologies therefore contain many quotations from pagan critics. We have only fragments of Porphyry's many writings against the Church, but they are enough to show that he was well informed, acute, and a gentleman. He made no vulgar charges, but pointed rather to contradictions in the Scriptures; as, for example, how God could have made the light before he created the sun and the moon, or how Christ could say to his disciples that they would see him no more and at the same time that he would be with them always.

The oldest of such literary attacks upon Christianity of which details survive was by Celsus, whose book *True Discourse* (written about A.D. 180) has been very largely preserved in Origen's refutation of it, published some seventy years later. Celsus was drastic and caustic, though not so credulous as to repeat the popular charges of incest and cannibalism against the Christians. Yet he ridiculed and vilified every article of the Christian creed. God, he said, did not create the world. If he had done so he would have made a better world, which would not have gone wrong. If it had gone wrong, however, God would not have been concerned to set it right. If he had been concerned, he would certainly not have selected Palestine as the locus; nor would he have saved the world through an illegitimate child, who gathered about him some of the worst rascals in the land and told them if they got into trouble in one town to run to the next. (The reference is to the words of Jesus, "When they persecute you in one town, flee to the next . . .") What God would have selected as a disciple a man who would betray him? A robber chief would have had more insight. Jesus was crucified as a felon. He is said to have risen, but who saw him risen? Only a crazy woman and some other deluded persons. (Here the reference is to Jesus' appearance before Mary Magdalene in the garden and before the disciples.) The Christians claimed that Christ must have risen because he predicted his resurrection, but Celsus pointed out that the disciples could easily have inserted the prediction into the record.

The Christian claim that God would send fire to consume the heathen and leave the Christians unburned was silly, wrote Celsus. He repeated the usual charges that Christians stayed aloof from social and political life. We have noted his charge that no Christian would serve in the army, as well as his claim that if all were like the Christians, the empire would be overrun by the barbarians. If Christians would not assume political obligation, said Celsus, then they should withdraw from society and have no families.

Christian writers produced extensive refutations of the charges made against them, whether by mobs, emperors, or philosophers. They replied that Christians were atheists only in the same sense as Socrates, who denied the gods but not God. Immoral the Christians were not, and their congregations stood out against the pagan world as beacons against a dark sky. Seditious they were not, though quite obviously they were guilty of civil disobedience. Their loyalty was to a higher law.

Answering Celsus' accusation that the disciples had falsified the records, Origen pointed out, among other things, that they would scarcely have been willing to die for a lie. Even more acutely he noted that forgers do not manufacture that which is to their discredit. Would Christians have recorded the betrayal by Judas and the denial of Peter had they been seeking merely to ingratiate themselves with the pagan world? Deceivers they were not; deceived they might have been. A century later Athanasius, Bishop of Alexandria, addressed himself to this latter possibility, specifically with regard to the Resurrection. He argued not from the credibility of the witnesses, but from the experience of the Church. "Is he a dead Christ, who even now is revolutionizing the lives of men?"

IV

The Christian Roman Empire

The bas-relief shown here is a symbol of Christ. The early Church did not use the cross as a symbol, and the crucifix did not appear until the end of the fourth century.

The attempt to dispel Christianity by propaganda was no more successful than was the plan to liquidate it by persecution. As the third century waned the religious issue was becoming an ever more crucial concern of the empire. To consolidate the power of the government a universal religion was deemed essential, but Christians remained recalcitrant. Thus the alternatives had come to be: the secularization of the state, which was unthinkable; the extermination of Christianity, which had so far failed; the adoption of Christianity by the ruler, in hope that it would become the religion of the bulk of the population. Early in the fourth century the emperor Diocletian initiated a further attempt at extermination. He was another of those frontier generals like Decius, and associated with him were two men of the same provenance, his subordinates Galerius and Maximian. Also like Decius they sought to restore the glory of the empire by re-enlisting the favor of the gods under whom Rome had attained greatness. Diocletian believed he was personally under the patronage of Jupiter, Maximian under that of Hercules.

The persecution of the Christians began in the year 303 with an edict requiring that church buildings be destroyed and all copies of the Scriptures be consigned to be publicly burned. Christians lost their civil status and legal rights. Next, an edict was issued against the officials of the Church. A third edict was in effect an invitation to repent, but a fourth decreed death for all Christians. The roster of martyrs was so swollen that the days of the year do not suffice for their commemoration. Diocletian retired as emperor in 305, but the persecutions in the East—spurred by Galerius, Maximinus Daza, and others—continued with only short respites until they were stayed in 324.

Diocletian's voluntary withdrawal was part of his valorous and imaginative attempt to avert civil war and stabilize the administration by decentralizing the government and setting up an orderly succession to the imperial office. The empire was divided into two great districts, East and West, each to be administered by an official called an Augustus with the aid of a subordinate called a Caesar. Correspondingly there were two main imperial headquarters: Trèves (Trier) in the West near the Rhine, and Nicomedia in the East at the border between Europe and Asia. There were also two lesser headquarters: Milan in the West just south of the Alps, and Sirmium on the Danube to guard the most menaced frontier. The empire was further subdivided into about ninety-six provinces so that no provincial commander could control too large a military force. Diocletian in the East and Maximian in the West were the first Augusti; they were to retire voluntarily at a given time and to be succeeded by their respective Caesars, Galerius and Constantius Chlorus, father of Constantine. The only dynastic element in the scheme was that Galerius and Constantius Chlorus were obliged to marry the daughters of the Augusti.

The Augusti did not have equal power; Diocletian retained supreme control from his headquarters in the East. When Diocletian retired, Maximian did likewise. The two Caesars became Augusti, Constantius Chlorus in the West, Galerius in the East. New Caesars were appointed, in the West Severus and in the East Maximinus Daza. The scheme seemed to be operating to perfection. However, on the death of his father, Constantine took command of the troops in Britain and Gaul and demanded recognition as his successor, reintroducing the dynastic principle. Galerius consented. Then Maxentius, the son of Maximian, undertook to succeed his retired father, killed Severus, ensconced himself in Rome, and demanded recognition. Galerius refused and instead appointed Licinius, who could find nowhere to exercise his authority save in Illyricum, in what is now western Yugoslavia. To complicate matters Maximian had reclaimed the title of Augustus. Now there were six men undertaking to rule the empire. The very disaster that Diocletian had sought to avert had actually come to pass. Intermittent civil war followed for a period of about twenty years.

The contenders in the East and in the West were reduced to one for each area by a series of elimination contests. The first of these took place in the West between Constantine and Maxentius. At the outset the religious issue was not paramount. Although Constantine and Maxentius both were pagans, neither was a persecutor of the Christians. Maxentius, in accord with the policy of Diocletian and his coterie, took as his patron Hercules, while Constantine placed himself under the tutelage of Apollo, or Helios, the sun god, and thenceforth placed the image of the sun upon his coins. Then Constantine took the as-tounding step of announcing his conversion to the Christian religion.

Thereupon, contrary to the advice of his military strategists, Constantine invaded Italy from Gaul and descended upon Rome. This could have been a rash move, for had Maxentius stayed inside the walls of Rome, he might have withstood a lengthy siege. However, he sallied forth instead, was attacked while crossing the Tiber over the Milvian Bridge, and was drowned. Maximian, having conspired against Constantine, had been apprehended and was granted his preferred mode of suicide. Thus in the year 312 Constantine became the master of the West. He began at once to exercise paternal supervision over the affairs of the Church in that area.

In the East the religious issue persisted. Diocletian, to be sure, did not meddle with it any more. He was tending his cabbages on his farm on the Dalmatian coast. But Galerius, shortly before his death in 311, admitted the failure of the policy of extermination. He issued an edict declaring that since they could not be recalled to the gods of their pagan ancestors, Christians might be permitted to worship their own God. He hoped that the empire might gain some benefit even from the prayers to the Christian deity. Then Galerius died. Constantine had to deal next with Licinius.

The two met at Milan in 313 and agreed on a policy that placed all religions in the empire on a par; each person might worship as he would, so that whatever gods there were might be propitious to the empire. The edict embodying this decision did not give Christianity a preferred position and was not couched in Christian terminology; Licinius was still pagan. Yet a year later in his victorious struggle with Maximinus Daza, who was still persecuting Christians in the East, Licinius appeared as their champion, only again to change and renew the persecutions in the final contest with Constantine a decade later. This struggle was terminated in 324 with the victory that made Constantine the sole ruler of the empire. Under the standard of the cross he had conquered.

Why did Constantine embrace Christianity, and how fully did he understand what he had done? Politically speaking, his course must have appeared sheer folly, since Christianity can scarcely at this time have been the religion of more than one-tenth of the population in the West. A quarter of a century later Bishop Eusebius recalled that Constantine mentioned a vision he had had of a cross in the sky bearing the legend "By this conquer." Another Christian author, writing earlier, said that Constantine had had a dream. The emperor himself testified to an experience of conversion, without mentioning either vision or dream.

However, there must be some truth in the story that Constantine believed the Christian God would guide him to ultimate victory. One might take him at his word and assume simply that he was converted, though one would have to add that evidently he considered Jesus to be a more powerful god than Hercules or Apollo. But how deep was this conversion? Some have assumed that Constantine's faith sat lightly upon him, since he was not baptized until he lay on his death bed. But this was not unusual: the Church taught that baptism washes away all previous sins, and in Constantine's time the prudent usually postponed receiving the sacrament until all their sins had been committed. What makes the nature and depth of his conversion more difficult to evaluate are the ambiguities of his subsequent acts. He attributed his victory over Licinius, for example, to divine impulse: *instinctu divinitatis* were the words carved on his triumphal arch at Rome. But which *divinitas*—Christ or Apollo? The symbol of Apollo remained on Constantine's coins even after the victory over Licinius, perhaps because it could be interpreted either as the actual sun or "as the Sun of Righteousness with healing in his wings." Definitely the emperor gave up the claim to divinity, for when he was called upon to adjudicate in a Church dispute, he inquired why judgment should be asked of him, who also awaited the judgment of Christ.

Yet he stood in a peculiar relationship to God, calling himself "God's man," the instrument of the divine purpose. He believed God to be the Lord of history, who had revealed himself in Christ especially through the Resurrection. Constantine described Christianity as "the struggle for deathlessness," that is, for that immortality assured to men by the resurrection of Christ. God's providential care for humanity, resisted by wicked men, had been vindicated by the martyrs, to whom Constantine now regarded himself as the successor. They by dying, he by fighting had earned the title of *victor*, which he now added to that of emperor.

His legislation gave to the Church privileges previously enjoyed by the pagan cults. Christian houses of worship, of course, were to be restored, and the Church was empowered to hold property as a legally constituted corporation. Manumission of slaves might take place in a church, as hitherto it had in a temple. The clergy, like the pagan priests, were exempted from municipal duties. The laws of Augustus penalizing the unmarried were repealed, reflecting, no doubt, the Christians' high regard for celibacy. The first day of the week was made a holiday. It was called, however, the Sun's Day, rather than the Lord's Day. (Curiously, this remnant of the solar cult survived among the Nordic peoples, including our own Anglo-Saxon forebears; we speak of Sunday, whereas Latin peoples call it the Lord's Day: *dimanche, domenica, domingo.*) Constantine's piety led to the abolition of crucifixion, but the laws against gladitorial combat were not enforced and slavery was not abolished. Constantine effected no drastic change in the structure of classical civilization.

As to the Church, he definitely acknowledged his adherence to it, and called himself "a bishop, ordained by God to oversee whatever is external to the Church." Presumably he meant that he was not a priest and could not administer the sacraments; but there was little else ecclesiastical that he was not ready to do. Constantine did not impose his new-found faith as a state religion. Christianity was not the religion of the majority of his subjects, and Constantine was of no mind to force it upon the pagans; indeed he himself for some time retained the title *pontifex maximus* of the pagan cults. "The struggle for deathlessness," he said, "must be free." What Constantine really did was to recognize a provisional religious pluralism; in the army, for instance, the pagan soldiers were allowed to use a vague prayer devoid of any Christian reference. Yet Constantine definitely announced himself as an adherent of the Christian faith and thus set the course for the development of the Byzantine Empire.

Constantine certainly hoped that the Church would prove to be a politically integrating force. He may not have been fully aware that Christianity was a factor that would correct cultural imbalances within the empire. During the first three centuries after Christ three unbalancing influences had been at work within the Roman world: the infiltration of barbarians into the army, the militarization of the state, and the orientalizing of the court. As to the first, Christianity had not been identified with the barbarian newcomers; its strength lay in the centers of the old Roman population. Constantine, therefore, marching under the standard of the cross against the pagan Licinius, could pose as the champion of *Romanitas*, the heritage of Greco-Roman civilization. Christianity worked against military dominance in government; Christians were concentrated in the most peaceful section of the empire, remote from the threatened frontiers, and on principle had long objected to participation in welfare. Finally, by denying the emperor's divinity, Christians eliminated the imperial cult with its oriental associations. In favoring Christianity Constantine—perhaps unwittingly—was favoring the old Roman, peaceful, republican elements in the body politic of the empire.

For the Christians the Constantinian era brought a radical change of attitude toward the empire and toward their role as citizens. During the two decades of civil war in which the persecution of their religion was an issue, even those who would not fight could scarcely refrain from praying for the success of the arms of the contestant who promised them toleration or favor; and when Constantine emerged victorious under the banner of the cross, Christians hailed him as the Lord's anointed. Their prevailing political philosophy in the new era was voiced by Bishop Eusebius of Caesarea, who picked up the theme voiced earlier only by a few bishops of Asia Minor: that the empire and the Church, founded coincidentally, were two works conjointly designed by God for the redemption of mankind. The Church reconciled man with his Creator; the empire achieved political unification by terminating the diverse kingdoms incited to war by demonic gods. Now Christians could confess one God, one Lord, one faith, one baptism, one empire, and one emperor. By his victory, they averred, Constantine had fulfilled the promise of Isaiah that henceforth swords should be beaten into plowshares and the nations should learn war no more.

Immediately after his victory over Maxentius, however, Constantine discovered that the Church, far from being the cement of the empire, seemed likely to widen the existing cracks in its social structure. For Christianity was often bitterly divided within itself.

The first dispute after Constantine's victory in the West oc-

The embracing rulers represented here are
thought to be Diocletian and Maximian,
co-emperors from 286 to 305. With the
patronage of the gods under whom Rome
had flourished, Diocletian in the East and
Maximian in the West attempted to restore
the glory of the empire. They cruelly and
systematically persecuted the Christians.

curred in North Africa and centered on the problem of discipline for those who had lapsed in the time of persecution. Following the persecution by Decius the laity had been restored to the Church, after due penance. The question after the persecution by Diocletian had to do with the clergy, who in order not to imperil the lives of their flocks had complied with the edict to deliver up the Scriptures to be burned. The rigorists retorted that these *traditores*, "handers over" of the Scriptures (whence our word *traitor*), had abetted the destruction of the Holy Word and could never be restored to communion, let alone to office. This rigorist party acquired the name Donatist, after Donatus, whom they supported against the regularly appointed bishop of Carthage.

The rift was not confined to the religious sphere. In North Africa there were three social strata. At the top were the landholding Latin aristocrats, often purer in their Latinity than the heterogeneous populace of Rome. Below them were the Punics, who, when Carthage had been demolished, were compelled to serve their new Roman masters on the land. They had their own churches and bishops, especially in Numidia. The third group were the Berbers, who antedated both the Punics and the Romans and lived on the steppes. The two submerged elements united to support the Donatists, precisely because the opposite, less rigorous policy was espoused by the local Latin aristocracy and by the Latins in Rome. The Berbers especially were anti-Roman. They had become Christian when Rome was persecuting the Christians; now they supported that branch of Christianity that was disapproved by Rome.

The case was brought to the attention of Constantine because a claim to property was involved. He had decreed the restitution of church buildings confiscated in the persecution. Which party had the rightful claim? Constantine referred the matter to the bishop of Rome, who decided against the Donatists. They would not submit. Constantine thereupon summoned a council of western bishops, who met at Arles in Gaul in 314. This also decided against the Donatists, but still they would not submit; they appealed to the emperor himself. Violence flared. Constantine tried force without avail and then let events take their course. By the time of Augustine, a century later, the Donatists outnumbered the orthodox in North Africa. To reach a solution three methods had been tried: reference to the bishop of Rome, to the emperor, and to the council of bishops. Though none had succeeded, Constantine was committed thenceforth to the conciliar approach.

Then in the East erupted the Arian controversy, a dispute about the relationship of Christ to God. It arose at Alexandria in Egypt, where an aged presbyter named Arius contended that Christ the Son, although the highest of all creatures, was still a creature. He had a beginning of existence: "There was when he was not." He had been made out of nothing; consequently he had changed and was subject to change. The opposing party, led subsequently by Athanasius—then only a deacon and secretary to the bishop of Alexandria—affirmed that man's eternal salvation is imperiled if the relationship of the Son to the Father is not eternal and unchangeable. Behind the view of Athanasius lay the belief, held earlier by Irenaeus, that humanity and divinity are not so disparate as to be incapable of conjunction; the incarnation of God in Christ is the proof. If, then, God became man, man in a measure is able to become God. Christ is the forerunner and the mediator of this relationship; but this he can be only if while fully human he is fully, eternally, and unchangeably divine. If he were a creature he would be a subordinate god, and in that case why should there not be more such gods, as there are in pagan polytheism?

Constantine was aghast. Clearly he did not understand what all the theological squabbling was about, but he did know that it was disturbing the peace, for Arius stirred up even the dock hands in turbulent Alexandria. Moreover, a divided Christianity could not be the cement of the empire. Constantine remonstrated with the bickering Alexandrians in a letter entrusted to his ecclesiastical adviser and emissary, Bishop Hosius of Cordova in Spain. The emperor declared that he had embraced the Christian faith in order to consolidate the empire. How grievously he had been disappointed by the earlier Donatist dispute in the West! In the East, whence the light of Christ arose, he had expected to find healing, but "O most merciful providence of God, what a wound did my ears receive when I learned that you were contending about mere words, points difficult to understand, and unprofitable in any case—squabbles, the fruit of a misused leisure." So, in effect, Constantine wrote to the contending Alexandrians.

The Alexandrians were not in the least quieted by being informed that their contention was "unworthy of men of sense," for they perceived that man's assurance of salvation depends on his relationship with Christ and on Christ's unaltered and unalterable relationship to God. The dispute could not be settled by an appeal to Scripture and tradition because in both each party could find support. The Athanasians could adduce the opening chapter of the Gospel of John, where Christ was declared to have been in the beginning with God and to be he through whom all things were made. The Arians could cite the statement from the Epistle to the Colossians that Christ was "the first-born of all creation." Did that not imply that he was himself created? Among the earlier Christian writers, the Arians could refer to Tertullian, who had given the Son a beginning in time; and the Athanasians looked to Origen, who declared Christ's generation to have been timeless.

It then became necessary to appeal to the consensus of the Church. Constantine therefore summoned a council, which met at Nicaea in Asia Minor in 325. It is called the First Ecumenical, or universal, Council because it included bishops from the East and from the West. To celebrate the twentieth anniversary of his reign, Constantine invited the assembled bishops to dine with him. When those who had survived the great persecution filed between ranks of Roman soldiers to sit down with the emperor, one of their number wondered whether the kingdom of God had come or whether he dreamed. Here was another of those historic moments that was filled with hope. But hope is seldom realized precisely as it is conceived. The council did not resolve Constantine's problems with the Church or the Church's own inner disputes. It rejected any subordination of the Son to the Father. The Greek word used to express their full equality was *homoousios*, meaning "of the same substance or being." The English equivalent (derived from the Latin) is "consubstantial." The Father and the Son were described as two persons sharing in one being or substance. With the Holy Spirit they constitute the Trinity.

The doctrine of the Trinity, as it was developed, is a formula that embraces a concept of great richness. It ascribes to God both unity and plurality: he is one and three. It ascribes to him both being and becoming: as the ultimate ground of being, he is static and changeless; yet there is in him an eternal, timeless process of generation, for the Son is begotten by the Father alone (according to the Orthodox Church) or from the Father and the Son (according to the Roman Church). God is above time and in time; in the Incarnation and throughout the whole history of Israel and of the Christian Church, eternity impinges upon time. God is ultimate being, indescribable save by negatives, yet he has the personal characteristics of the God of Moses, the God who speaks. Christ is the very godhead become flesh, suffering and dying for the redemption of mankind. The doctrine of the Trinity was unifying, as indeed all orthodox Christian thought was unifying. The heretics were commonly dualists. In the second century the Gnostics had separated body and spirit. Now the Arians separated the creature from the creator. Later, as we shall see, the Nestorians tended to split the divine and the human natures in Christ.

But although the Athanasians were able, as it were, to unite God, they could not unite the Church. The council of Nicaea pronounced in their favor. Constantine banished five dissidents, including Arius, and threatened with death any who did not deliver up his books to be burned. (The emperor would not coerce pagans but felt differently about dissident Christians.) But after the council had disbanded, Constantine discovered that the bulk of the population in the heavily Christianized area of Asia Minor had Arian leanings. He was mainly interested in concord and was willing to have the question reopened. Ten years later, in 335, a synod met at Tyre, and this time the Arians won: Arius was restored (though death cheated him of his victory) and Athanasius was exiled. But still the struggle was far from over.

In the year 330 Constantine had transferred the capital of the empire from Rome to the mouth of the Bosporus at the site of the ancient fortress town of Byzantium, which he consecrated to Christ and which became Constantinople. There were good reasons for the move. The new capital stood close to the main focus of the empire's trade; here might be established a bulwark to withstand enemies from the East and to check the inroads of migratory tribes from the steppes; and it was in the East that Christianity was developing strength to displace the moribund ideologies of the ancient world. Although the move was not meant to affect the Church directly, it did in fact leave the bishop of Rome heir to the mantle of the Caesars in the West.

Constantine died in 337, and the empire was divided among his three sons. Constantine II received the provinces of the West; Constans held the middle—Africa, Greece, and Italy, including

This sixteenth-century Russian icon depicts
Syrian Simeon Stylites on his pillar, where
he stood for thirty years. Egyptian hermits
gave impetus to Christian asceticism, which
at times degenerated into a self-denial that
seemed to be practiced more for its own
sake than for the sake of serving God.

Rome; Constantius had the East. Each ruler adopted the religious view prevalent in his own district. The West was Nicene, the East predominantly Arian. Constantine II and Constans were of the Nicene party; but as their domains were separate, the Arians gained ascendancy over the Nicenes. In 340 Constantine II died in a war with his brother Constans, who by uniting the Nicene areas gave this party predominance. However, when Constans in turn was assassinated in 350, Constantius, the Arian, ruled over the whole empire. Then, as Saint Jerome was to observe later, "The world woke up to find itself Arian."

Whichever contending party was victorious in the continuing Nicene controversy would banish the opposing bishops. Under Constantius the banished included Liberius, the bishop of Rome; Hosius of Cordova, who had been the ecclesiastical adviser of Constantine the Great; Hilary, the bishop of Poitiers in Gaul; and Athanasius of Alexandria. Pressures were exerted to break them down. Liberius at one moment assented to the Arian position. Hosius, who was quite old, would never say a word against Athanasius, but became rather muddled over the creed. Hilary and Athanasius remained adamant. All of them, however, protested vigorously against imperial interference. "The purple," they claimed, "makes emperors, not priests."

Then, with the death of Constantius in 361, the empire reverted briefly to pagan rule under his cousin Julian, who has come down in history under the name Julian the Apostate. Although he had Christian training as a youth, his religion was a curious blend of Neoplatonism and popular paganism in which the gods were conceived as emanations from the ultimate One. At first Julian went back to the policy of religious neutrality promulgated in the Edict of Milan and allowed all the banished to return. (Thereby he unwittingly aided the eventual victory of the Nicene position, since the orthodox resumed their sees.)

Julian believed that Constantine had made a great mistake in adopting Christianity as the cement of the empire, not merely because of its theological quarrels, but because Julian considered the faith to be on all counts incompatible with empire. Writing to the Alexandrians, he asked them whether their city had grown great on the precepts of the Galilean, who counseled turning the other cheek, rather than by the mighty deeds of their founder, Alexander the Conqueror. Moreover, Julian found Christianity incompatible with classical culture. Thus he forbade the Christians to teach the pagan classics and advised them to confine themselves to the exposition of the Gospels. It is curious that although Julian denigrated Christianity in any form, he reproached its adherents in his own day with having corrupted the primitive version. The divinity of Christ, the exaltation of Mary—now called the Mother of God—and the cult of the bones of the saints were, he claimed, innovations and corruptions. Inadvertently he paid the Church a high tribute, however: he exhorted his pagan priests to imitate the sober deportment, the hospitality, and the philanthropy he had observed among Christians.

Julian lasted as emperor only two years, from 361 to 363. The Arian-Athanasian controversy was then resumed until it was definitively resolved by the accession to the imperial dignity of the Spaniard Theodosius I, who was responsible for the final victory of the Nicene view. It was he who summoned the Second Ecumenical Council, at Constantinople in 381, where with slight modification the Creed of Nicaea was reaffirmed. Theodosius did much more. He established what even Constantine had never envisaged: the Christian state. Heretics of every sort were forbidden to assemble and their churches were confiscated; they even lost the right to inherit property. As for paganism, once the official religion of the empire, its rituals were proscribed, though its adherents were not treated violently or deprived of their civil rights. Half a century later, in 438, Theodosius II issued the Theodosian Code, which inflicted the penalty of death on those who denied the Trinity (the Arians) and on those who repeated baptism (the Donatists, who would not recognize Catholic baptism); in addition it decreed that no pagans could serve in the army, lest their gods injure the Roman state.

What a change in the two and a half centuries since Celsus had charged that no Christian would serve in the army! What a change even in a century and a half, since the day when Origen accepted the charge and defended Christian pacifism! What an even greater change on the score of religious constraint! Tertullian in the days of persecution had asserted that religion admits of no constraint, and Constantine had declined to coerce the pagans. Yet he started those measures against the heretics that culminated in the Christian state of Theodosius I and eventually in the Theodosian Code.

As a state religion Christianity became to a degree secularized;

the protest against this development led to the great monastic movement. The roots of monasticism, to be sure, reach back into the pre-Constantinian period. In Asia Minor the first hermit of whom we have record came from the sect of the Novatianists; this sect, even before the Donatists, had separated from the Church in opposition to what they considered the Church's laxity toward those who had weakened during the persecution under Decius. There is thus a connection between monasticism and sectarian rigorism. In the cities during the persecutions there had been cells of those dedicated to virginity and schooled for martyrdom. The whole penitential system encouraged heroic deeds of exceptional virtue to expiate sins. Above all, the threat of persecution kept alive the concept of the Church as a *militia christi* fighting against the powers of darkness. When persecution ceased these concepts were carried over into the monastic idea.

Still, the great exodus from society that laid the foundations of monasticism coincided with the era of Constantine: when the masses entered the Church, the monks went to the desert. The desert was chosen because of the belief that the waterless places were the abode of demons and therefore the places where the battle was to be joined. Anthony, generally regarded as the father of monasticism, withdrew into the Egyptian desert in 285 and remained there battling demons for twenty years.

The word *hermit* is derived from the Greek word meaning "desert"; the word *monk* comes from the Greek meaning "alone." But the term *monk* has come to be applied as well to those living in a community. Whether alone or in groups, however, those who thus withdrew from the world did not do so on a family basis; they did not wish to bring children into so disordered a world because it seemed to them to be irresponsible, and more importantly because the duties of raising a family would have come between them and God.

Initially, monasticism was extravagant. The extravagances took the form of extreme castigations of the flesh intended to reduce the body to such enervation that sexual temptation would not arise. Another cause of spectacular asceticism was the spirit of competition: some of the early eastern monks vied with one another to see who could stand longest on one leg without food or sleep, or who could remain the greatest time on the highest pillar. But one should not let such extreme practices obscure the genuine holiness of the many. The significance of monasticism is not to be found in its penchant for sleeplessness and flagellation or in its utter obliviousness to filth and vermin, but rather in its reaching for the infinite and its scorn for all those mundane pursuits on which men dissipate their days. Monasticism quickly passed from the eremitical to the cenobitic, so called from the Greek words *koinos bios*, meaning "the life in common." Pachomius, an Egyptian contemporary of Anthony, is credited with having been the first to introduce community living on an organized pattern. Codification of monastic practice in the East was the work of Saint Basil, between 358 and 364, and in the West, a century and a half later, of Saint Benedict.

Monasticism soon came to have its impact on the world. Bishops began to be recruited, at times against their desires, from among those who had received monastic training. Saint John Chrysostom, for example, who became first a priest at Antioch and later a bishop at Constantinople, had served his apprenticeship as a hermit-monk. When monks were thus transferred to episcopal sees they tended to bring with them into the secular priesthood some of their monastic mores, particularly celibacy, though this became obligatory in the West only in the eleventh century and never in the East for the lower clergy. While monks thus went out into the service of the Church, bishops went on retreats to monasteries to replenish their spiritual energies.

Once the early extravagances had subsided and monks began to live under stable and sensible rules, the monastery began to assume tasks of enormous benefit to the Church and the world. The cell became the study and the monks became scholars. The pioneer in this regard was Saint Jerome (340–420), who began his monastic career as a hermit in the Syrian desert but found that he could exorcise his sexual temptations only by occupying his mind with a tough intellectual discipline. He took up the study of Hebrew and found it so effective that he could even venture to return to the world. At Rome he became a teacher to Bishop Damasus, and to a circle of high-born ladies, on the problems of Biblical exegesis. Hostility toward monks in Christian Rome—which still, to Jerome's mind, in a measure resembled Babylon—led him to withdraw to a monastery at Bethlehem, where he put his linguistic skills to use in translating the Old and the New Testaments from the original tongues into literary Latin. The result was the so-called Vulgate, still in standard use in the Catholic breviary. Jerome illustrates once more the tension between the classical traditions and Christian culture. Once, many years before, in a dream, the Supreme Judge had reproached him with being a Ciceronian rather than a Christian. He resolved to abjure the paganism inherent in ancient classicism but never, fortunately, divested himself of its elegant diction. He was to become the patron saint of the early Renaissance humanists.

Jerome's monastery was called upon quite unexpectedly to assume a new obligation. In the West ever since Constantine's time the empire had been holding off the encroaching hordes of barbarians. Gaul was periodically threatened by the Franks and the Alamanni and Britain by the Picts and the Scots, while Saxon pirates infested the surrounding seas. The provinces along the Danube too were harassed—and more than once overrun—by the Goths. Bickering between the eastern and western emperors weakened the empire, and ruinous taxes sapped the strength and loyalty of the provinces. As the fifth century began, it became apparent that Rome was gravely threatened. Finally, in 410, a force of Visigoths under the leadership of Alaric laid siege to the city and sacked it.

For Jerome the news was heralded by the stream of refugees heading eastward, who crowded into his cloister at Bethlehem in such numbers that only by stealing time from sleep was he able to continue his work on the Gospels. More than Rome itself was lost. The barbarians had also taken the Rhone cities, had pressed into the south of Gaul, into Aquitaine, and were poised for the assault on Spain when Jerome wrote a dirge bemoaning their attacks. Had he written but a few years later he would have been forced to add that Spain, North Africa, and northern Italy too had succumbed to the invaders.

When Rome fell Jerome was desolate. He who had fled from Rome as Babylon now lamented the rape of Rome the fair. The fall of the ancient seat of the Caesars affected the mind of the Mediterranean world quite out of proportion to the military significance of the event, for strategically the loss at the same time of the fortresses on the Rhine and the Danube was as crucial. But the sack of Rome shattered a dream. Since Virgil's *Aeneid* men had believed that Rome would be eternal; the Christians of the fifth century could not know that her eternity would be achieved through the Church.

The enormous losses meant, of course, the fall of the Roman Empire in the West. The imperial name was retained by the rulers of Byzantium at Constantinople, the second Rome. (Centuries later, at the time of the Crusades, the Byzantines still called themselves Romans; the Westerners they called the Franks.) This second Rome would hold out for centuries against the assaults of the barbarians. Then Byzantium itself was battered by new barbarians—the Avars, the Bulgars, and the Serbs—as well as by old enemies, the Persians. Finally, her sway even in the East was to be reduced: a new foe, the Arabs, arose, whom she was unable to hold in leash—in part because her strength had been sapped by internal dissensions caused by theological disputes.

The East never had fulfilled the dream of Alexander that all her peoples should be indistinguishably blended in the unity of mankind. In addition to Greeks, the eastern empire comprised among others Syrians and Copts. They, along with the Georgians and Armenians, with their divers tongues, were to be alienated from the orthodox faith and from the Greeks of the Byzantine empire. In addition a rivalry of cities undermined the unity of the empire. Usually Constantinople, supported by Antioch and Asia Minor, was ranged against Alexandria in religious controversies; when the two were deadlocked, Rome generally cast the deciding vote.

The controversy that embroiled the empire soon after Nestorius became bishop of Constantinople in 428 concerned the relationship of the human and divine natures in Christ. The Council of Nicaea had declared him to be of one substance with God. While affirming Christ's divinity the Apostles' Creed emphasized his humanity. If, then, Christ was both God and man, how were the human and the divine related in him? The tendency on the part of those whose thinking about God and man was dualistic—and who therefore had difficulty in conceiving of humanity and divinity as conjoined—was so to emphasize the distinction between the human and divine natures in Christ as to make him virtually a split personality. This was the general trend of the thought of Nestorius. Specifically, he objected to calling Mary the Mother of God, for it would never do to think of God at the breast. Nestorius would call Mary only the Mother of Christ. His position, stoutly repudiated by Cyril, the bishop of Alexandria, was condemned with the concurrence of

This sixth-century icon, like so much of
Coptic art, was created in a monastery. In a
typically naive and frontal representation,
Christ is shown with his arm on the shoulder
of Saint Menas, an early Christian martyr
whose history, fused with that of a soldier,
has become a popular Egyptian legend. Saint
Menas's image often appears in Coptic carvings.

the bishop of Rome at the Third Ecumenical Council, meeting at Ephesus in the year 431.

Another solution to the problem was to unify Christ's person in such a way as practically to eliminate his human nature. This was the view of the Monophysites (from the Greek meaning "one nature"). Their concern was to ensure that the Son could never be at variance with the Father; and they therefore posited only a divine nature. This view—first propounded by Eutyches, a monk of Constantinople in opposition to his bishop but supported by the see of Alexandria—was repudiated by the Fourth Ecumenical Council, which met at Chalcedon in 451. There it was asserted that Christ was in two natures, inseparable and unconfused. He is of one substance with the Father as to his divinity and of one substance with man as to his humanity. From Rome the pope concurred, and this has ever since been the position accepted by all the Orthodox Churches.

Nevertheless it was not and never has been accepted universally. The Monophysite position was espoused by the Copts in Egypt and transmitted by them to the Ethiopians. In Syria the Jacobite Church was Monophysite. However, Syria had also a Nestorian branch, which obtained a considerable following in Persia and still persists in modern Iran. (Persia, being in constant rivalry with the Greek empire, preferred a form of Christianity unacceptable to the Greeks.) It sent missionaries to India and influenced the Mar Thoma Church, so called because of the supposition that India had been converted by the apostle Thomas. At any rate, the connections of the Mar Thoma Church with Syria are undeniable, since its liturgical language is Syriac and its theology was akin to that of the Nestorians.

The Nestorians pushed as far as China and left as their memorial (about 781) the Nestorian stone, with inscriptions in Chinese and Syriac. Nestorianism enjoyed favor at first in the Mongol Empire. The mothers of several khans were Christians; as late as the year 1277 the leader of a Mongol embassy sent to England was a Nestorian Christian. Naturally these eastern heretics did not accept papal claims. One of the khans inquired how many horsemen and camelmen were in the pope's army. When Tamerlane (1336–1405) embraced Islam, the Nestorian Christians were annihilated. The Church in the Kingdom of Armenia, caught between the Byzantine and Persian empires, preferred a form of Christianity unacceptable to both and became Monophysite. Their neighbors the Georgians, however, remained loyal to the Greek Orthodox Church. The Armenians and the Georgians were thereby so divided religiously that they were unable to unite in a common struggle for independence from the Turks.

Religious rifts coinciding with regional and linguistic cleavages gravely imperiled the stability of the empire after the middle of the fifth century. A solid front in the East against the Persians was indispensable to the emperors at Constantinople. Consequently the imperial policy was oriented toward the conciliation of the eastern dissidents, the Monophysites, rather than the Nestorians, who had moved into Persia. The bishops of Rome resisted all concessions to the heretics and disavowed the attempt of the emperor to conciliate them with an ambiguous formula.

Such was the situation that confronted Justinian when he ascended the imperial throne in 527: the West had been lost to the barbarians, and much of the East—Egypt, Syria, Armenia—was disaffected by religious strife. He set out to mend both rents in the garment of empire.

In the first endeavor he came close to his goal. He brought down the Vandal kingdom in Africa, drove the Visigoths out of Andalusia in southern Spain, and expelled the Ostrogoths from northern Italy. For a brief time the Mediterranean could once again be called *mare nostrum*, "our sea."

Then Justinian applied himself to wooing the more moderate Monophysites, summoning a Fifth Ecumenical Council at Constantinople in 553. The emperor sought to make peace with the Monophysites by hurling anathemas at the memories of three undistinguished Nestorians who had been overlooked in the curses pronounced by the Council of Chalcedon. Vigilius, the bishop of Rome, made a strong remonstrance but was cowed by violence. Then the western provinces of Istria and Illyricum, both in present-day Yugoslavia, foreswore communion with the Eastern Church. The attempt to unite the East religiously only divided the West within itself and failed to pacify the East. The Monophysite heresy still raged.

But the greatness of Justinian lies neither in his western victories nor in his eastern diplomacy, but rather in this: that he gave definitive form to Byzantine culture. It was an amalgam of Roman law, the Christian faith, and Hellenic philosophy channeled into theological speculation, in addition to an admixture of oriental elements. Justinian codified the Roman law in the great *Codex Justinianus*, the Justinian Code, which in the East and West alike survived for centuries as the Roman law. The Christian element is very much manifest in the Code. It began with a section on the Holy Trinity and included rules governing the qualifications of bishops. Moreover, it penalized religious dissenters. Against heretics it repeated the penalties of the Theodosian Code. Pagans were forbidden under pain of death to offer sacrifices to the gods, and any convert to Christianity who lapsed into paganism was to be beheaded; the pagan university of Athens was closed. Jews, too, came under the Code's restrictions: they were forbidden to convert Christians and prevented from holding Christian slaves. The heretics were suppressed and the pagans died out. The Jews survived, to assume their difficult role as aliens in a Christian society.

This whole system has been called Caesaropapism. Contemporaries did not call it that, and modern historians of the Byzantine empire resent the term. They point out that the emperor was not a priest, that he was obligated by oath to introduce no innovations into the life and thought of the Church, and that he might be excommunicated by the patriarch. Time and again emperors were excommunicated, and sometimes driven to submission. The characteristic mark of the Byzantine Church-state pattern, we are told, was harmony, *symphonia*, in which the spiritual and the civil authorities each supported the other. Yet it must not be forgotten that the emperor controlled the election of the patriarch, and that even the decision of a church council was not binding without his consent. Moreover, if he did not think of himself as God, he aspired to be the visible icon of the invisible King, and the ceremonies of the court still had something of the aura of emperor worship.

As the system developed, the *symphonia* was generally achieved by a division of function. The Church felt she could leave political administration to the Christian rulers of state and devote herself to theology and enrichment of the liturgy in the sanctuaries and to the contemplative life in the monasteries. The whole of Byzantine society believed itself to be under the patronage of God and the Mother of God. The Virgin, like a Homeric goddess, would even enter into the fray to throw a lance or sink an enemy ship. The emperor was the Lord's anointed, after the manner of David and Solomon. The temporal achievements of the empire were never attributed to sound finance, efficient administration, or military skill, but only to the favor of Heaven.

Nowhere is the unique quality of the Byzantine amalgam more manifest than in its art and architecture. Here the naturalism of classical art, the pure spirituality that Christianity inherited from Judaism, and an oriental tradition of rich, nonfigurative decoration were fused into one of the most sumptuous arts of all time. It was in Byzantine art that Christianity first developed a characteristic style, in which representation of the familiar, physical world of human experience was sublimated into a suggestion of the world supernal, everlasting, and transcendental. Deliberately stylized figures set against glittering gold backgrounds of mosaic do not re-create a sensible image so much as they evoke a spiritual presence in an other-worldly atmosphere of resplendent grandeur.

When Justinian rebuilt Constantine's Church of Holy Wisdom, Hagia Sophia, and consecrated it in 538, he exclaimed that he had outdone Solomon, and perhaps he had. The dome, as the contemporary historian Procopius described it, hung as it were by a golden chain from heaven, a link in the hierarchy rising from the finite to the infinite and descending from the Creator to the creature. The mosaics, plastered over by the Turks in 1453 and uncovered in our own day, shone with dazzling brilliance. In them Constantine and Justinian were portrayed, the one offering to the Mother of God a model of Constantinople, the new Rome, and the other a model of the Church of Holy Wisdom. Against the unfathomable heights of the dome, where space though contained appears as illimitable as the sky, the Virgin Mother stands lifting her children into the presence of her Son and of God, the Pantocrator, emperor of the universe.

But the reign of Justinian was only a golden interlude for the Roman Empire. When his grip was loosened the Visigoths repossessed the whole of Spain, the Vandals resumed sway in Africa, and the Lombards took over large portions of Italy (though not Rome or Ravenna, the seat of the emperor's exarch). In the East Constantinople was besieged by the Avars, while the Persians overran Syria, Palestine, and Egypt. Jerusalem was sacked in 614. A solid front composed of Greeks, Copts, Syrians, and Armenians was never more essential, but theology—ostensibly,

"It abounds exceedingly in sunlight,"
Procopius wrote of the basilica Hagia
Sophia, "and in the reflection of the sun's
rays on the marble. Indeed one might say
. . . the radiance comes into being within it."
Hagia Sophia still displays medallions left
by the Turks, who changed it into a mosque.

at any rate—stood in the way. A formula had to be found to satisfy the Monophysites without simply conceding their entire position. Since their main interest was to exclude the possibility of divergence between the Son and the Father, the bishop of Rome, Honorius by name (625–638), gave his support to the view that Christ, having two natures, yet had only one will. This view is called Monothelite, from the Greek words meaning "one" and "will."

The gesture was futile and soon became politically irrelevant, for a great storm was swirling in from the Arabian desert that in little more than a century would sweep across the southern shore of the Mediterranean and up to the very Pyrenees. It centered about the figure of Mohammed, who appeared about the year 610 as the prophet of Allah. Profoundly influenced by Hebraism, he had no penchant for sophisticated theological speculation. Like the Jewish sect known as the Rechabites, who would touch no wine, he forbade the use of alcoholic beverages, but at the same time so far reacted against Christian asceticism as to revive the polygamy of the Old Testament patriarchs. The Jewish concept of the chosen people was now transferred to the Moslems, the sons of the prophet. Confidence that Allah would deliver the unbelievers into their hands launched them on an astonishing career of conquest and conversion.

Their way was facilitated by divisions among the Christians. Quite possibly the dissenters from the Eastern Church were the readier to accept the rule of Islam because it appeared to them to be so closely related to Christianity: Mohammed accepted the virgin birth and the role of Christ at the Last Judgment. More inducive to submission was the comparative religious liberty the Moslems accorded to Jews and Christians alike, upon the payment of taxes. Whatever the reasons, the sons of the prophet overran Syria, Palestine, Egypt, North Africa, Spain, and at length Armenia. Southern Italy and Sicily were to be at times in their hands. In all these Christian areas the Church survived— except in North Africa, where the old Punic and Berber elements may have renounced the Christian faith for the same reason that they had earlier embraced heresy, out of opposition to Rome; the diocese of Saint Augustine in what is now Algeria was wholly lost to the faith. In the lands where Christianity had arisen the Church found itself under the heel of the infidel.

When the effort to win back the Monophysites had lost its

political significance, since they were already conquered by their foe, the Monothelite concession was repudiated by the Sixth Ecumenical Council, held at Constantinople in 680 and 681. Bishop Honorius of Rome, who had sponsored the view, was anathematized as a heretic. (This action does not invalidate the modern claim that the popes are infallible; they are preserved from error by the Holy Spirit only when they speak *ex cathedra*, that is, officially and to the entire Church. Honorius had spoken only privately.)

But the Moslems attacked again, and it was under the emperor Leo III, called the Isaurian, that Islam's threat was beaten back again. Constantinople was besieged in 718, but the Moslems were defeated on both land and sea. But if Leo helped restore political peace, he was responsible for another cataclysm, which shook the empire. This was internal, and like so many that had preceded it, it was basically religious, although social, economic, and political factors were also involved. Specifically, it concerned the veneration of sacred images or icons, by then an established practice in the Eastern Church. When Leo launched an attack against the images in an edict of 726, he may have been influenced by the somewhat puritanical Isaurian bishops who strictly interpreted the second of the Ten Commandments. The bishops of Isauria advocated iconoclasm—the breaking of images, including the crucifix. Early Christian practice could be adduced for their position; as we have already noted the early Church had not used the cross as a symbol, and the crucifix does not appear in Christian art till toward the close of the fourth century. Leo must have been moved by conviction, for to stir up another theological controversy in an empire already rent by religious dissension was highly impolitic. And a full-blown controversy it became: riots broke out in Constantinople, and unrest spread as far as Greece and Italy. Leo and the succeeding iconoclastic emperors had the support of the army, but were vigorously resisted by the populace and especially by the monks. The iconoclasts stigmatized the icons as pagan idols, but their deepest aversion was not so much to paganism as to the use of physical forms to represent spiritual concepts.

The reply to those who favored the images was formulated most clearly by John of Damascus, a great theologian who lived under Moslem rule, which left him in a position to speak freely with no fear of being silenced by the emperor. John, of course, appealed to the images mentioned in the Bible—the brazen serpent in the wilderness, the lions in Solomon's Temple—but his primary argument was from the Incarnation and the Eucharist. If God himself in Christ became flesh, then the flesh cannot be evil, and if Christ is bodily present in the bread and wine, then sensory aids to religion are not to be rejected. John then moved to educational considerations. The images, said he, are the books of the unlearned, lifting them up from the symbol to that which is signified. At the Seventh Ecumenical Council, meeting at Nicaea in 787, the images were restored, but with the qualification that the icons must be paintings or sculptures in low relief, not in the round. If the thumb and forefinger could be held on the nose of an image it was unacceptable. For the Byzantine Church as well as for her daughter, the Russian, such sculpture as was to ornament Chartres and the other great churches in the West thus became impossible.

The Byzantine Empire was to continue as a bulwark against Asiatic hordes for another six centuries. The Church contributed alike to its weakness and its strength. Certainly the theological controversies precipitated the splintering-off of the non-Greek elements from the Greek core. In the conflict with Islam this debilitated the empire. On the other hand, the Greek nucleus, after being divested of all alien elements, developed a remarkable toughness and resilience, not least because this people considered itself to be the custodian of the true orthodox faith and of a Christian classical culture. And if the Byzantines did not convert the Arabs, they did, in the course of time, transmit to them the classical heritage that they in turn were to pass on via Spain to the whole of the Christian West.

V
Conversion of The Barbarians

In this illumination from a twelfth-century
manuscript, the influential Saint Augustine
is shown holding one of his works beside the
towers of Hippo.

Although the sack of Rome by Alaric in the year 410 was only an episode in centuries of disorder, the emotional impact of the event throughout the roman world, as noted earlier, was devastating. To endure the shocks of history man must have a philosophy of history, and almost every philosophy of history in that age was cast in religious terms. For the pagans the natural explanation of the disaster was that it resulted from the displeasure of their gods over the Christianization of Rome. In the late fourth century, prior to the catastrophe, the Christians had explained the barbarian invasion of the Danubian provinces by the same type of reasoning. The inhabitants of those provinces were Arians who had adopted Christianity when Arianism was dominant in the empire. When the Arians' territory was ravaged, the orthodox members of the Church saw in this the displeasure of the Christian God over the spread of heresy.

Such was the explanation offered by Saint Ambrose, who was the bishop of Milan from 374 to 397 and a slightly older contemporary of Saint Jerome and Saint John Chrysostom. But when Rome, the capital of Christian orthodoxy as well as the ancient capital of the empire, fell, his explanation of why God suffered the barbarian inroads also collapsed.

A new explanation was needed, and Saint Augustine (354–430), the bishop of Hippo, a small town in North Africa, attempted to provide one. His was a rich and seminal mind. He gathered together strands from Christian thought and from classical philosophy and wove them into a new fabric which was to have a profound influence on the thought of the Church, both in the Middle Ages and in the period of the Reformation. He had no simple answer for anything. The problem of history was set by him in the context of nature and the destiny of man, the character and the purpose of God, the redemptive work of Christ, and the function of Church and state.

Augustine's view of the nature of man was expounded in his *Confessions*. This is the first full-length autobiography in Christian history and the first spiritual autobiography in all history— at any rate in the western world. In classical antiquity autobiography was used as an apologia by public figures like Isocrates, Demosthenes, and Cicero to justify their careers; and though Marcus Aurelius concerned himself with the inner life he did not cast his *Meditations* in the form of a life story. Christianity for the first time made the pilgrimage of the soul more important than the conquest of a province. The *Confessions* of Saint Augustine exceed the personal dimension, however, for in describing his own tortuous course he analyzed all mankind. He was himself an illustration of man's corruption, redemption, and continuing imperfection.

Augustine was born to a pagan father and a Christian mother, Monica. He was reared as a Christian but was not baptized. The account he gives of his youth provides the most penetrating probing of the nature of sin since the New Testament. As a grown man, Augustine inferred from observing babies that even before he could speak he was probably capable of envy of other children. As a boy he robbed the pantry. This was surviving infantilism—feeding on demand. As a youth he was guilty of sexual irregularity. This was surviving animalism. The next sin was vastly more troublesome to explain. With some friends he raided an orchard of green pears. Why pluck unripe fruit? He says he would not have done it had he been alone. This was the bravado of the gang. The boys chuckled over the chagrin of the owner. This was glee over wanton destruction, of which not even an animal would be guilty. Then Augustine records his pleasure in going to a theatre to enjoy weeping over an unreal situation. This was flight into illusion. How different is all this from the earlier Christian rating of the chief sins as idolatry, adultery, and homicide!

As a young man Augustine became a teacher of pagan rhetoric at Carthage. He had contracted a union with a girl whom he could not marry because she was beneath him in status, and by her had one child whom they called Adeodatus, "the gift of God." During these years of his youth in Carthage Augustine went through great spiritual turmoil. In the course of his studies he fell upon a book of the writings of Cicero which reawakened in him an intense desire for truth; but the truth did not appear to him to rest in Christianity and he stoutly resisted his mother's persistent attempts to draw him into the Church. Instead he embraced the creed of the Manichaeans, a sect emanating from Persia. The Manichaeans were even more extreme than the Gnostics in condemning matter as evil. They considered it so evil, in fact, that they deemed it a crime to give birth to children and thus to imprison new souls in bodies; having sexual relations was bad, but having children was worse.

In time the Manichaean explanation of evil in terms of the material came to appear unsatisfactory to Augustine. (In future years he reproached himself that during the fifteen years he had lived with his concubine they had had but one son, uninvited but loved for his own sake.) When his students at Carthage proved unruly Augustine fled from the situation. He decided to go to Rome, against his mother's wishes, and set sail surreptitiously. However, at Rome he had difficulty in collecting student fees, and instead of vindicating his rights, withdrew to a post in Milan. Here he was joined by his mother and some former African students.

Augustine was still groping for a solution to his spiritual problem. Neoplatonism, which he studied through the Latin translations of Plotinus by Victorinus, now attracted him with its doctrine that evil is simply the absence of good; he was even more attracted by the experience of intense spiritual exaltation which it induced. While at Rome he underwent a brief period of skepticism, though he says he never doubted God and immortality. Yet evidently he doubted himself, since he was helped by the argument that the very fact that one could doubt one's existence presupposed one's existence.

Ambrose was at this time in Milan, and Monica, ever determined to see her son baptized, sent Augustine to the famous bishop. Ambrose was a remarkable figure whose qualities were the very reverse of Augustine's; whereas Augustine retreated from embarrassing situations, Ambrose was audacious. Ambrose was no subtle thinker, no analyst of man's inner states. His apprenticeship had been in the public service of northern Italy. When an episcopal election was pending at Milan he sought to keep the peace, lest the Arian and the Nicene factions should break each other's skulls. As he walked down the aisle of the church a child's voice cried out, "Ambrose for bishop." He was a Christian, though he had not yet been baptized, and he protested his unfitness for the office; but the congregation advanced him from baptism to the bishopric in a week.

Ambrose was bolder and more influential as bishop than he had been as a civil administrator. In the year 385, when the dowager empress Justina demanded that one basilica in Milan be placed at the service of the Arian Goths among her troops, Ambrose and his congregation ensconced themselves in the basilica and withstood a siege, maintaining their morale by singing hymns composed by Ambrose. In the face of such earnest resistance the empress capitulated.

On another, later occasion Ambrose defied the authority of the emperor, Theodosius I, who although the vindicator of orthodoxy, had been guilty of a barbarous act. An imperial officer had been killed during a riot at the hippodrome in Thessalonika. In revenge, Theodosius had seven thousand of the populace assembled in the ampitheatre and then ordered his troops to massacre them all. When thereafter the emperor presented himself at Ambrose's church, the bishop refused to celebrate Mass in the presence of the man whose hands were thus imbrued with human blood, and the emperor was driven to do penance. By these forthright actions Ambrose set important precedents for the development of an independent Church in the West.

Such a man was Ambrose. But he was more than a dauntless guardian of the faith; his eloquence was celebrated, and Augustine, professor of rhetoric, went to church to observe his technique in oratory. As he listened he was smitten by something that exceeded eloquence. Here was a man who grappled with the problems of faith and who showed that one could be an intellectual and a Christian.

In the meantime, his mother had prevailed on Augustine to dismiss his concubine. The son now could no longer stand up to his mother and sent the faithful companion of so many years back to Africa. Monica had in addition arranged a marriage for him with a girl two years too young for wedlock; while waiting Augustine formed another irregular union. At this time he heard of the Egyptian monks and was amazed that these illiterate men had such control of their passions, and he became ashamed of his own incontinence. Coincidentally, his confidence in Neoplatonism was shaken by the discovery that the Neoplatonist Victorinus had joined the Church and made a public confession.

Augustine now turned seriously to the New Testament. The "sickness unto death" invaded him and one day he went alone into a garden. He tore his hair and beat his breast, reflecting as he did so that his hand thus obeyed his will whereas his heart would not. (Even in such a crisis he was an inveterate analyst.) From next door he heard the voice of a child at play, crooning *Tolle lege*, "Take up and read." He went to a bench where lay a copy of the New Testament and opening to the thirteenth chapter of Romans read: "Not in reveling and drunkenness, not in debauchery and licentiousness, not in quarreling and jealousy. But put on the Lord Jesus Christ and make no provision for the flesh, to gratify its desires." There and then Augustine realized the peace of spirit he had been searching for. Some time thereafter, together with his son, Adeodatus, he was baptized by Ambrose.

Soon after, with his mother, his son, and others, Augustine set out to return to Africa. Monica died en route, Adeodatus shortly after arriving in Africa. Severed thus from all family ties, Augustine became first a monk and then, in 396, the bishop of Hippo, where he commenced his mighty career as administrator, pastor, and theologian.

Augustine's self-analysis enabled him to revive the thinking of the apostle Paul as no one had done in the preceding centuries. But every revival tends to be an exaggeration, and Augustine spelled out more sharply the implications of Pauline thought. Man, said Augustine, has been so corrupted by the fall of Adam that he is bound at some point to sin. Even his virtues are tainted by his desire for self-aggrandizement. And sin is not merely the absence of good, as the Neoplatonists said, but rather, as with the Hebrews, rebellion against the majesty of God. The only cure lies through the miracle of God's grace, vouchsafed through Christ and conferring upon man forgiveness, restoration, and healing. Yet this healing is never complete. Sin remains to the portals of the grave. Perfection in this life is impossible. Augustine had once thought otherwise, but the years had erased every vestige of illusion. In consequence the hope for a perfect society and a warless world inevitably had to vanish also.

Augustine developed also Paul's teaching on predestination, which is not the view that man is predetermined to do wrong but that he is predestined in his life to come either to blessedness or to punishment merited by his sins. Augustine saw no way of distinguishing the chosen from the rejected. The Church itself he recognized as a mixed company of tares and wheat, which means that the Church is much less distinguishable from the world at large than if it were a community of saints. The line of demarcation is further diminished since, as the Church is not wholly good, so the world is not wholly bad. The pagans are capable of virtues of a sort: discipline, industry, courage, fidelity, magnanimity. Augustine recognized natural law, and when he was asked whether a Christian might accept an oath of fidelity from a pagan retainer who swore by his own gods, he answered yes, on the ground that the principle of fidelity is valid even though the gods be false.

With this body of presuppositions Augustine confronted the problem of the fall of Rome. For him there were two major questions: first, why had God suffered this to happen? and second, should Christians have recourse to war to repulse the barbarians? In his *City of God* Augustine dealt with both.

Why had God allowed this to happen? Certainly not because of the spread of the Christian religion. Rome had been subject to calamities before the advent of Christianity. Rather, Rome's calamities were retribution for her crimes. As the classical authors had themselves admitted, there was a virus of corruption in the Roman bloodstream, manifest in the murder of Remus by Romulus and in the demolition of Carthage. From the pages of a pagan historian Augustine lifted the Greeks' excoriations of Rome and quoted the remark of a Briton, "The Romans make a desert and they call it peace." With the Jews, he saw Rome destined for apocalyptic woes. To be sure, Rome had conferred great benefits upon the conquered, but, Augustine observed, at what price in blood? A century earlier Eusebius had thought that God approved the Roman Empire, since he sent his Son to be born at the time it was founded. But Augustine was not as lyrical as Eusebius over the empire and Christianity as conjoint works of God for mankind's redemption; for, said he, what are great empires without justice if not robber bands on a large scale? To his mind the link with corruption was broken only by the conversion of Constantine, and only if the rulers of the state were Christian would he then agree that their sway should be increased.

In all this argumentation Augustine seems to be saying that Rome fell because of the sins by which she had risen to greatness. But the argument would appear to break down, since the disaster had been so long deferred that not pagan but Christian Rome was paying the penalty. Augustine then set the entire question into a wider frame, from which all moralism was removed. After all, said he, every empire deserves destruction because it is dominated by the lust for power; but God according to his sovereign will allows empires to rise through their own

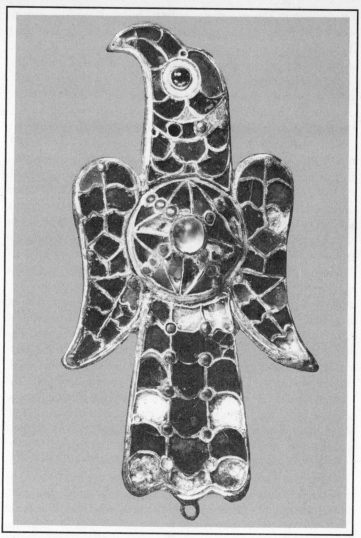

This bird-shaped fibula shows the
accomplishment of Visigoth craftsmen.
Their decoration of precious stones and
colored pastes recalls the vivid art of the
nomads of the steppes.

self-discipline and arrogance, only to bring them down in his own good time. As the prophets of Israel had seen, God may allow the Assyrian to swagger and may even use him as the rod of his anger, only in the end to inflict chastisement upon him.

But if God brings down nations because of their crimes, ought they not in that case to be brought down, and should one try to save them? Should the barbarians be resisted? Yes, wrote Augustine, because, after all, Rome's empire enshrined a certain good. The Roman peace had facilitated the spread of the Gospel, and the Roman order did afford the possibility of the administration of justice. Even though Rome had been reared by blood, she was not to be relinquished to bloody barbarians. When Boniface, the Roman general in Africa, having lost his wife, wanted to become a monk, Augustine exclaimed, "For God's sake not now!" With the Vandals on the point of crossing the Straits of Gibraltar the general must fight.

Was it right then for a Christian to take arms? Here Augustine adapted to Christian ends the classical code of war as finally formulated by Cicero, who had stipulated that war is legitimate only under the auspices of the state. Its object is to vindicate justice and restore peace. Violence must not be wanton. The justice of war is to be determined by the ruler. The code of humanity is to be observed. Good faith is to be kept with the enemy. Prisoners and hostages are to be respected. Such was the view of Cicero. Augustine added two points: the motive for war must be love, and this was possible, he believed, because killing of the body does not entail the death of the soul; and, if the war is to be just, one side must be unjust. Augustine was thus the father of the war-guilt theory.

Finally, he had three codes for three classes. First were the rulers, who should determine the justice and assume the direction of the war. Second were the subjects, who should fight at the behest of rulers but never otherwise; in private relations there should be no self-defense. Third came those dedicated to religion, who should abstain entirely—the priests because they served at the altar, the monks because non-resistance was one of the counsels of perfection.

By thus counseling heads of the Roman empire against barbarian anarchy, Augustine made quite clear that he envisaged a society embodying, to a certain degree, Christian ideals. This society was focused on two institutions, the state and the

Church. The purpose of the state was to maintain justice, defined as giving to each his due, which for Augustine meant primarily the rights of life and property. The state itself, however, need not be just in its external relations in order to be a state, which is a community bound together by a common object of love. From that point of view a robber band could be a state, and to Augustine's mind great states commonly were in effect magnified robber bands. Yet the state may be at least an approximate instrument of justice, particularly if administered by Christian rulers; and those rulers need the direction of the Church—a point of view which suggests the social role the papacy sought to play in the Middle Ages. He was the more ready to assign a role to the Church in society because he envisaged for mankind a long span of time on earth; unlike the early Christians, who expected the speedy termination of the historical process through the return of Christ, Augustine projected the end indefinitely into the future. The role of the saints as judges of the world in the great assize on the last day was then transferred to the Church on earth.

Church and state were the more closely associated because each was thought of as a mixed society, embracing saints and sinners. If the Church was to direct the state, the state was to uphold the Church, even to the point of using coercion in the interests of the true faith. A particular problem confronting the orthodox Church in Augustine's day was its conflict with the Donatist sect. In North Africa its members had become more numerous than the Catholics and often violently attacked Church buildings and priests. Augustine was at first strongly opposed to any use of coercion, until the state stepped in and by fines and imprisonment constrained the Donatists to attend the Catholic churches. Many declared that they were voluntarily converted by what they then heard. Hitherto, they explained, they had been forcibly restrained by their own leaders from hearing the truth of the Catholic faith; now that force had countered force the scales were removed from their eyes. Augustine declared that he could not resist such testimony and proceeded to justify constraint as a work of love, like the saving of a life by the amputation of a limb. He did not personify the state or the Church and did not equate the heretic with the gangrenous limb. He did not approve of the death penalty. However, that analogy was to be utilized centuries later in order to justify the Inquisition.

On another great ethical problem Augustine gave virtually definitive shape to Catholic teaching. His views of sex and marriage were profoundly affected by his revulsion against the Manichaean avoidance of procreation. This is precisely the primary purpose of marriage, said he. Ideally, he believed, there should be no sexual relation save for propagation, though he knew of no married couple that practiced such restraint. The physical act of sex, he held, is not sinful; yet even though the intent is propagation, there is a sinful concomitant in that under the excitement of passion man loses his rational control. This sin, when within the marriage bond, is, however, venial. Augustine came close to wishing that God had devised some other expedient for procreation, yet recognized that marriage is ordained by God. Here one sees elaborated the view of the apostle Paul that marriage is approved by God, yet continence is superior. His attitude was developed in opposition to those who sought to enjoy sex without progeny at all. His position, originating in opposition to the Manichaeans, has profoundly affected the modern Catholic view.

Augustine drew richly from the past. On the classical side he took over from Cicero his love of truth and his concept of the just war, and emulated Cicero's cultivated style of presentation; from the Stoics their teachings on the law of nature and the harmony of the cosmos; and from the Neoplatonists their ecstatic vision of God. On the Judeo-Christian side he gave the Hebrew philosophy of history greater depth. He espoused the teaching of the apostle Paul on grace and predestination and wrote a profound exposition of the Sermon on the Mount, manifesting a deep appreciation for its advocacy of pacifism in private life. His views on Church and state, war and peace, sex and marriage, tolerance and constraint have made their impact afresh on each succeeding generation in the Western Church, whether Catholic or Protestant.

Augustine died in 430 while the Vandals were besieging Hippo. Catastrophic and sudden as this assault may have seemed to the members of Augustine's bishopric, it was just one episode in a long chain of inexorable developments. The barbarians had been infiltrating the empire for centuries. They were not nomads but agricultural folk seeking new lands, partly because of pressures put upon them by other barbarians from farther north and east. Throughout the imperial period they had been received into the Roman armies, and by the fourth century there were barbarian factions at court. Eudoxia, the empress in the days of Chrysostom, was the daughter of a Frankish chieftain, and Alaric, who sacked Rome, was opposed by the Vandal Stilicho, serving as a Roman general. More significantly, whole "nations" of barbarians were settled within the empire and granted a good measure of local autonomy. Constantine, for example, provided land for some three hundred thousand Sarmatians. By such means the relentless pressure of barbarian migrations was for a time brought under government control. When the Romans could no longer maintain such controls the barbarian migrations developed into barbarian invasions.

These invaders were not savages. They possessed ancient and deeply rooted traditions, and their arts were far from primitive. The personal and military trappings dug from the graves of Goths, Franks, and other barbarians are richly ornamented with designs and by techniques in part inherited from the Scythians, Sarmatians, and other tribes with whom they had come in contact during earlier migrations: abstract, geometric forms and fantastic, simplified animal shapes often bejeweled and executed in cloisonné enamels. The barbarians were not slow or inept in appropriating classical and Byzantine art. Roman glassware, bronzes, and coins were early imported into barbarian lands, and classical design motifs can be found in early barbarian ornament. When Theodoric, the Ostrogoth ruler, took over the western capital of Ravenna in 493, he had built there a palace and the Church of S. Apollinare Nuovo, which survives with some of its original mosaics still intact. Others of these gorgeous decorations that may have represented Theodoric and his queen were replaced with different subjects by Justinian when he recovered Ravenna in 540.

Various laws of the Germanic peoples were based on the principle of compensation rather than on that of punishment. For each offense a sum was fixed for the guilty to pay and the injured party to receive, thus averting further strife within the tribal community. Detailed lists of possible injuries and corresponding compensations were drawn up. A murderer paid the family of the deceased an amount in proportion to the victim's rank and importance. Mutilations were paid for according to a detailed graded scale; the highest price was for the loss of an eye or a foot, the next highest for an ear. This whole system of commutations is important historically; centuries later it provided a basis for the ecclesiastical practice of granting indulgences.

The morals of the barbarians were probably no better or worse than those of the Romans. In the fifth century the Christian monk Salvian claimed that the barbarians were more chaste than the Romans; he lauded the Vandal Gaiseric for closing the brothels of Carthage. But Salvian probably knew more about the bad behavior of the Romans than about the good behavior of the Vandals. As for cruelty there was little to choose between the two. Did not the Roman Constantine in his pagan days cast captive German kings to the lions? The Franks themselves reproached the Romans with cruelty, and the prologue to the law of the Franks declared that they were decorating with gold and precious stones the reliquaries of the martyrs whom "the Romans burned with fire, bored through with iron, and gave to the beasts."

Certain barbarian tribes—of which the largest were the Goths—had embraced Christianity in the form of Arianism, at a time when this heresy, as earlier noted, prevailed in the eastern part of the empire, a region these barbarians inhabited in the early fourth century. Their conversion, a colossal achievement, is attributed to the missionary Ulfilas, a Cappadocian raised among the Goths. Other barbarians—among whom were Franks and Saxons—were still pagan in the early fifth century. The task of converting these northern people from their heresy on the one hand and from their paganism on the other was a formidable one. To bring them to a nominal acceptance of orthodoxy was not difficult, for they desired to share the grandeur of Rome, and orthodox Christianity was now the state religion of Rome. But to civilize, refine, and educate these people; to disabuse them of any notion that Christianity was to be esteemed because it had made Rome an empire; and, above all, to induce in them even a modicum of Christian deportment was a colossal undertaking.

The barbarians had been disposed to equate their gods with those of ancient Rome. Thus the Teutons could believe that Woden, to whom they assigned the fourth day of the week as Woden's day—that is, Wednesday—was the same as Mercury, whose day the Latins called *mercredi* and *mercoledi*. Similarly, among the northern peoples the next day of the week was Thor's day, or Thursday; for the Latins it was Jove's day, or *jeudi* and *giovedì*. The barbarians were equally prepared to combine their religion with Christianity; but this combination, when it compromised the unique and particular quality of Christian revelation, was precisely what Christianity—at any rate, Christian leaders—could never tolerate. Among the populace, nevertheless, the saints became the successors of the pagan gods.

Those Arians among the barbarians were not interested in all the niceties of such theological problems as the consubstantiality of the Father and Son. The Arian view that Christ was a creature, albeit the first-born of all creation, did, however, make it possible to think of him as a glorified chieftain.

But the main difference in the West between the Arians and the orthodox lay in the structure of the Church. The Arians had no ecclesiastical center. They did not recognize orthodox Rome, and they had no counterpart to it of their own. The churches belonged to the clan or nation and were subject to the various secular rulers; Christian priests had taken the place of the pagan priests as chaplains to kings. After these barbarians were converted to orthodoxy, they were still loath to accept Roman leadership. The system of local proprietary churches dependent on the king or patron was so entrenched that its conflict with the centralizing tendencies of the Church became a persistent theme of medieval Church history. For a time, however, the establishment of Arian kingdoms in Spain, southern France, Burgundy, Italy, and North Africa aided the centralization of orthodox Christianity under Rome, because the Arian kings usually tolerated the orthodox and did not intervene in their internal affairs. The connection that the Roman Church had once had with the empire was weakened, and in none of the new kingdoms was it subject to the ruling power. For that reason it was able to maintain its universal character throughout all these kingdoms. The orthodox Romans now living under the rule of various barbarians continued to look to Christian Rome as the focus of their faith—as *Roma aeterna*.

The first of the barbarian lands to be effectively evangelized by orthodox Christianity was Ireland. Ireland had never been part of the Roman Empire, but early relations with Roman Britain had probably introduced Christianity by the fourth century. The conversion of the whole country, however, early in the fifth

127

century, is attributed to Patrick, a Briton, although there as elsewhere conversion must have been the work of many men. We are fortunate to have a brief autobiography from the pen of Patrick. When the Roman legions were withdrawn from Britain for the defense of the Continent, the Irish, then called Scots, began swooping down on the British coast, carrying off plunder and inhabitants whom they enslaved. Among the captives was Patrick. He had been reared a Christian, and his father was a deacon, but Patrick's religion sat lightly upon him. However, when he was shipped to Ireland and was forced to be a swineherd, he prayed ardently for his release.

After six years he managed to escape and found his way to the coast where a ship carrying a cargo of hounds was about to sail for Gaul. Patrick was taken aboard to look after the dogs. On the Continent the company traveled without meeting anyone for days, until food ran out. The commander of the company suggested that the Christian among them supplicate his God. This Patrick did, and a drove of pigs appeared. Patrick felt that he had earned his passage; he slipped away, and wandered until he came to a monastery. After spending several years there he somehow managed to make his way to England. The joy of his family at his homecoming turned to dismay when in a dream he was summoned to return to Ireland with the good news of the Gospel. He went, first, however, to the Continent for training, probably at a monastery, and was detained there for fourteen years as unsuited to the task he had set himself because he was too much of a rustic. His persistence won, and in 432 he was able to go to Ireland with papal authorization and with the status of bishop.

At this point his account ends; as to what happened in Ireland over the next century we have only legends. From our knowledge of later events we can make some inferences as to what must have preceded them. Patrick went as a bishop. By the mid-sixth century the entire structure of the Church in Ireland was monastic. Presumably, the monastic community, maintaining itself on the land, better fitted a rural society and a tribal culture than the parish-church system. Another point of great significance is that Patrick brought to Ireland the Latin language for Church usage, and with it some measure of the classical heritage. This expansion of Latinity had much to do with the ultimate survival of Latin in relatively pure form. On the Continent

Latin was in the process of being transformed into the Romance tongues and was preserved from complete submergence only because the Church retained it for liturgical and official documents and the state followed suit. Yet the danger was always present that even this Latin would be corrupted into the emergent vernacular. There was no such danger in Ireland, where there had been no Latin-speaking population and where the native speech was solely Gaelic. Here Latin continued separate from the common tongue and undefiled; when the Continent was ravaged by subsequent invasions the Irish monks were to go to western Europe and return the gift of pure Latinity.

In the conversion of Europe monasticism played a most vital role. The earliest monasteries in the West, such as the ones at Marseilles and Lérins and the islands off the Ligurian coast, were modeled after those of the East. But conditions in Italy and lands to the north did not favor the oriental type of monasticism, and within a relatively brief time new ideals were formulated that gave a lasting character to the institution in Europe. Saint Benedict, a contemporary of Justinian, has been called the patriarch of western monasticism. Early in the sixth century, after a period during which he lived as a hermit in an almost inaccessible cave, he established a monastic community at Monte Cassino, between Rome and Naples, looking down on the valley of the Garigliano. For his spiritual sons Benedict devised a rule that was temperate, sensible, and liveable—a rule that was to provide the basic program for western monasticism. He encouraged no contests in austerity, no spectacular macerations of the flesh, so familiar in eastern monasticism. To the vows of poverty, chastity, and obedience he added the principle of stability. He would not allow monks to be either hermits or holy vagabonds. They were to live in community and under strict discipline. Only on urgent business might the monks leave the monastic enclosure, and upon their return they were not to relate what they had seen.

The monastery had to be self-sustaining, with its own tillable soil, well, buildings, and in later times fishpond, rabbitry, and poultry yard. In the earliest period the monks provided most of the essential labor. Meals were frugal, consisting of bread, wine, vegetables, and fish or occasionally poultry. Meat was only for the sick. Bathing was deemed a luxury and was discouraged. The life was austere but scarcely ascetic.

However, the purpose of the monastery was not to ensure

The barbarians followed Germanic law but
allowed their new subjects to continue living
under Roman law, codified by the Visigoth
king Alaric II. This illustration from a
manuscript of his code shows the leaders of
society: a barbarian king at top left, a
bishop top right, a duke and a count below.

comfort, but to honor God by praise and to benefit the monastic community by prayer. The Benedictine Rule called for the chanting of the entire psalter every week. In winter the monks rose about two-thirty in the morning and immediately went to the chapel to chant the first office of the day. During the day they engaged in meditation or individual study and in labor in the fields and the monastic house, pausing every three hours for the communal chanting of prayers. The one meal came at *nona*, the ninth hour following the start of the day at six A.M. Since the monks could not wait until three P.M., the meal was advanced to midday; the hour was still called *nona*, from which our word *noon* was derived. The monks retired for sleep about five-thirty after the final prayers of the day. In summer they rose somewhat earlier, worked longer hours, and went to bed later; they were permitted an hour of rest and a second light meal. Throughout the seasons on Sundays there was no manual labor and prayer services were longer.

Benedictine monasticism was designed neither for missionary work nor for the promotion of scholarship, although eventually it made enormous contributions to both. Like other early monasteries, Monte Cassino was established on a site removed from the distractions of worldly interests, a retreat where the monk might practice the Christian virtues according to the counsels of perfection. The first members of the community were recruited from the Roman population rather than from the barbarians. The single Goth in Monte Cassino was a phenomenon, especially because despite being a Goth he was so meek.

Just when the barbarians entered the monasteries in any number is not known. At first they viewed the monks with whom they came in contact with incredulity and contempt. However, monks who cleared and planted wilderness tracts by their self-sustaining labor created stable and productive communities about which laymen settled for their own advantage. Monasteries became outposts of Christian civilization whose influence spread to surrounding heathen territory. Monks became the Church's militia in winning the West for Christianity.

The role of the monastery as a center for scholarship developed gradually. Benedict wished his monks to be literate, but only so that they could peruse the sacred texts and the works of the holy Fathers. That they should become renowned as copiers of manuscripts and as transmitters of ancient culture would have seemed to him a distortion of his purpose. The new development came nevertheless. Cassiodorus, a well-born Roman prefect and author turned monk and a contemporary of Benedict, envisaged the two monasteries he founded as schools for the acquisition and transmission of learning. Two centuries later, during the Carolingian period, monastic institutions were to give added impetus to this objective by relieving monks of manual labor in order to afford them more time for scholarship. Over the centuries following the collapse of the western Roman Empire, when other educational institutions had vanished with the barbarian intrusions and urban culture had died away, it was the monasteries that kept alive the classical tradition as well as the propagation of Christianity.

But another and ultimately a greater institution than monasticism in the Christianizing of Europe was the papacy. It began to assume its medieval form in the late sixth century, a time when Rome was in ruin. Following the sack of the city by Alaric had come other invasions by Vandals and Ostrogoths. Marble statues were smashed, and their heads, limbs, and torsos strewed the weed-clogged cobblestone streets. More serious, the barbarians had severed the aqueducts, and the higher sections of the city were deprived of water; the Campagna, flooded by water streaming through breaches in the conduits, was filled with malarial swamps. Disease infested the city.

Refugees were pouring into Rome from territories occupied by the barbarians. Following the death of Justinian the sway of the Byzantine emperors had again receded. They had not formally renounced suzerainty over the western parts of the empire and had committed the rule of the portions of the Italian peninsula unoccupied by the barbarians to an official called an exarch, whose seat was at Ravenna. But the Lombards had replaced the Ostrogoths as a power in the north and in several other parts of Italy, and they were continually extending their rule to other areas.

For centuries the government had provided the residents of Rome with bread and circuses. Now neither the emperor at Constantinople nor his exarch at Ravenna could bring grain ships from Africa or the islands. Also, Lombards frequently captured Romans and held them for ransom, and the emperor had no funds with which to redeem them.

At this point the Church stepped in. Its resources were as-tounding and available for use in areas where transport was not impeded by enemies or by natural barriers like the Alps, and where currency was viable. The Church had grainlands in Sicily and Sardinia, forests in Brutium and Calabria, and possessions even in Istria. It was able to charter vessels to bring grain to Rome from the islands, to ship lumber to churches in Egypt and blankets to the monks at Mount Sinai, to provide money to ransom prisoners from the Lombards.

How did the Church come to have such enormous possessions? In general it received them through donations by the faithful. Philanthropy had come to be regarded as a good work, contributory to salvation. Further, since Constantine had permitted the Church to own property, it received some fixed revenues from its holdings. In the administration of this wealth the papacy developed an organization as extensive as and more efficient than that of the imperial officials in Italy, an organization built and directed on the same principles, the same law, and the same structure as the civil administration of the empire.

The title of pope was not reserved for the bishop of Rome in the West until the eleventh century and was never recognized as his exclusive right in the East. But in common parlance today it is used for the bishops of Rome since the beginning of the office. Twenty-five years after the death of Justinian the See of Peter was occupied by Gregory I. Like Cassiodorus, Gregory was a well-born Roman who became a monk. During the plague of 589–90, shortly before the confirmation of his election to the papacy, Gregory had led a penitential procession through the streets of the city. As the dirgeful suppliants approached the bridge before the mausoleum of Hadrian, it is said, Gregory saw above the tomb the archangel Michael sheathing his flaming sword to indicate that the plague was stayed. The sepulcher was later called il Castello di Sant'Angelo, the Castle of the Holy Angel. In the Middle Ages it became a fortress of the popes.

The pope had died in the plague, and Gregory—a papal deacon and the pope's secretary—was chosen as successor to the office. He accepted the election only after a serious inner struggle, for he would have preferred to return to his monastery. It was during his pontificate, when the exarch at Ravenna was unable to feed the Roman populace or ransom prisoners, that the Church actively took over these and other functions traditionally exercised by temporal rulers. The assumption of these burdens by the Church led to political negotiations and treaties with the Lombards. The emperor at Constantinople fulminated against the usurpation of power, but the pope paid the bills. The papacy was, in fact, on its way to becoming a sovereign power in Italy and a director of sovereigns in the lands beyond. Although the rise of the temporal power of the papacy is commonly assigned to the middle of the eighth century, Gregory had in fact established that power to a degree a century and a half earlier. He is often called the first medieval pope, and he is remembered as Gregory the Great.

Gregory was well educated and, again like Cassiodorus, he had earlier experience in the Roman civil service. He was trained as a lawyer and had been a prefect of Rome. He had under him a large bureaucracy to supervise, check, and coordinate. The old Roman concept of justice determined all his ways in adjudicating disputes. In collecting revenue no false weights were to be tolerated; neither would any inhumanity to slaves be permitted, nor pressures by the Church to insure her rights in testamentary disputes with laymen.

Gregory's letters of instruction crackle with commands and reprimands. Here are examples of questions submitted by subordinates to the pope, and his answers: A man has bequeathed to the Church an amber cup and a boy slave to cover his funeral expenses. But the cup was not his. What then? Answer: In civil law a bequest is inalienable. If it was not owned by the deceased, his legal heir must recompense the owner. But since the Church does not operate according to civil law, the cup must be returned; in any case, no charge should be made for funerals. A second case: Inasmuch as a Christian slave cannot be held by a non-Christian, what shall be done in the case of a certain slave whose master was a Samaritan? The slave had been emancipated when it was discovered that he had been baptized. However, the Samaritan then became a Christian and claimed him back. Answer: The master might by no means reclaim his slave. A third case: Money has been borrowed to redeem captives and cannot be repaid. May the sacred vessels of the Church be sold to meet the debt? Answer: They may.

Another of the many reasons why this pope is remembered as Gregory the Great is that during his papacy monasticism was brought into the active and important service of the Church. In 596 he sent forth the prior of a Roman monastery, Saint Augustine—called Augustine of Canterbury to distinguish him from Augustine of Hippo—to regain England for the Church. Following the withdrawal of the Roman troops England had been invaded by Angles, Saxons, and Jutes, and Christianity had been largely superseded by paganism. Some missionary activity had already been directed to the British Isles. In 563 Saint Columba, a Celtic abbot, had gone from Ireland to Scotland, where he established a monastery on the island of Iona. After converting the king, the saint and his disciples won the inhabitants of Scotland, then called the Picts. The Celtic Irish were ready to convert the Anglo-Saxons. Unlike the barbarians who invaded other parts of Europe, these barbarians were brutal in their conquest of Britain; consequently those native Britons that survived the invasion were driven west into Wales and Cornwall. It was left to the Irish monks settled in Scotland to begin the conversion of the Anglo-Saxons of northern England, just shortly after Augustine undertook the conversion of the south.

Augustine commenced in Kent under the favor of Queen Bertha, a Christian queen eager to convert her pagan husband. King Ethelbert was willing to grant Augustine an audience but only out of doors, where Augustine would be less able to exercise what the king supposed were his magical powers; for he was reputed to be able to make tails grow on the backs of those with whom he was displeased. The king was so far persuaded that he granted land for the foundation of a monastery at Canterbury, ever after to be the seat of the English primate. Successors of Augustine worked farther north, in particular Paulinus in Northumbria. By the time of King Oswy, in the mid-seventh century, the two missionary thrusts converged, the followers of Columba working toward the south and those of Augustine toward the north. Oswy's queen was from the south and followed Roman practice for calculating the celebration of Easter; but Oswy had received his Christianity from the north via the Irish monks settled there and observed an old practice of celebrating the date that had been in vogue in Patrick's day. Thus the discrepancy invaded the king's very household; as during the controversy of the second century over the date for celebrating Easter, one faction feasted while the other fasted.

There were other points also in dispute. The monks of the Roman observance shaved their heads on top, leaving a rim of hair above the ears in token of the crown of thorns, whereas the

Irish, perhaps in imitation of the Druids, shaved up to a tuft on the crown. Such trivial distinctions symbolized the independence of Celtic Christianity from Rome. Oswy brought the matter to a decision at the Synod of Whitby in the year 664. The Celtic advocate appealed to the authority of Columba, the Romans to that of Peter, to whom Christ had given the keys. Oswy asked the Celtic defender if the Gospel account of Christ's gift to Peter were true; and the defendant admitted it was. Oswy promptly resolved to take no chances of alienating the doorkeeper of heaven and accepted the Roman custom. All differences did not automatically cease, but the trend was toward unification. Christianity in the British Isles moved back into the main current of Continental affairs.

Europe was for the most part won to orthodox Christianity by the mass conversion of peoples. A century before Gregory had dispatched Augustine on his epic missionary journey, at the time when the non-Greek elements in the East were splintering from the orthodox empire, an entire barbarian kingdom in the West embraced the faith, led by Clovis, king of the Salian Franks, and his queen, Clotilda. The story of Clovis's conversion, narrated almost one hundred years later by Gregory of Tours, ascribes the initiative to the queen. Clotilda, a Christian Burgundian princess, had long reasoned with her husband, telling him that his gods were mere idols and the stories about them most indecent. Clotilda pointed him to the God who, out of nothing, created heaven and earth, who adorned the firmament with stars, who caused the air, the earth, and the waters to teem with life, who bedecked the land with verdure, who created man and sustains him as his own. Clovis replied that this was nonsense; yet he allowed their first son to be baptized. The babe died in his baptismal robes, and Clovis blamed the baptism. Another son was born, baptized, and fell sick. Clovis claimed that baptism would kill him, too, but the mother prayed and the child recovered.

About 496 Clovis was engaged in a battle with the Alamanni. In danger of being defeated, he cried: "Jesus Christ, Clotilda says thou art the Son of the living God, and thou canst give victory to those who hope in thee. Give me victory and I will be baptized. I have tried my gods and they have deserted me. I call on thee. Only save me." The king of the Alamanni fell and his army fled. Clovis returned and told Clotilda what had occurred.

An eighth-century Irish monk created this
bronze plaque of the crucified Christ, with
soldiers and attendant angels. The monks of
the Middle Ages devoted themselves to
religious works of art and writing as well as
to the cultivation of the land around them.
In prayer and labor the monks' aim was to
lead a perfect Christian life.

She then summoned Bishop Remigius (Saint Remi) of Reims, who exhorted the king to renounce his gods. "Yes," said Clovis, "but, holy father, my people will not consent. However, I will speak to them." Before he spoke, however, they with one accord renounced the pagan gods. The Church was then bedecked with hangings, fragrant candles flared, the aroma of incense filled the shrine with divine fragrance so that many thought they were in paradise. Gregory related that Clovis advanced like another Constantine to the baptismal font; the bishop said, "Bend your neck. Worship what you burn and burn what you worship." Then the king was baptized in the name of the Father and of the Son and of the Holy Ghost and anointed with the holy oil, the oil of Clovis, which over centuries to come was to give divine sanction to the monarchy of France. And with Clovis were baptized three thousand of his army.

Did Clovis embrace Christianity for its own sake, or were his motives ulterior? Some think that Clovis made an astute political move, for he was not yet master of Gaul. The other kingdoms, such as those of the Burgundians and the Visigoths, were largely Arian. Clovis had passed directly from paganism to Nicene orthodoxy, which eliminated the possibility of an Arian confederation; but Clovis did not want a confederation. He wanted a conquest. "I cannot endure that these Arians should possess any part of Gaul," he is reported to have said. "With God's aid we will go against them and conquer their lands." In the conflict he would have the support of his Roman Christian subjects, who probably constituted 80 percent of the population; in the territories he aspired to conquer he would have the sympathy of those of the Nicene faith. On the whole, it would appear that for the conquest of Gaul his conversion was strategic, and it did succeed.

The conversion of Clovis had far-reaching consequences. Gaul thereby became the highway for the Church's militia to the north. If the king of the Franks had been hostile, missionaries from Rome would have had great difficulty in passing to Britain, Germany, and Scandinavia. On the other hand, the mass conversion of the Franks meant that they carried elements of their former paganism into their Christianity. Missions have two options. One is by way of individual conversion, with an adequate period of instruction prior to baptism. This was in general the technique of Protestant missions in the great revivalist movements of the eighteenth century, with their emphasis upon individual change of heart. The disadvantage of this method is that persons in a pagan culture, thus converted, become by reason of their change in faith alienated from their own culture and are compelled to move into a foreign enclave. The other method is mass conversion such as converted Europe. Kings like Clovis embraced the faith. Their people followed by acclamation. This meant that individuals were not dislocated, but it also meant that they brought with them into the Church the body of their old beliefs and mores.

For Clovis himself Jesus was a tribal war god, a new Yahweh of hosts. The Franks militarized Saint Peter, who was noble in their eyes because he had wielded his sword and sliced off the ear of the high priest's servant, in order to protect the Lord Jesus. The archangel Michael of the flaming sword became a heavenly champion and his name was given to the Norman citadel Mont St. Michel. Similarly, in other lands and in other times Saint George, a military saint, became the patron of England and Saint James the patron of Spain.

The mores of the Frankish aristocracy, lay and clerical, after the nominal conversion remained appallingly short of Christian standards. The behavior of kings and queens, and of bishops and their wives, would have shamed the gods of Olympus, not only for sexual irregularity but for stark brutality. One queen requested that if her two physicians failed to cure her they be executed. She died and the king fulfilled her request. A duke buried alive a servant and a maid because they had married without his consent. One priest who had obdurately refused to surrender some property to the bishop of Clermont was buried by him together with a corpse. The bishop of Le Mans thought it ridiculous that because he was a cleric he should not avenge himself. The laity did not regard the clergy as sacrosanct; some of the parishioners of the bishop of Rouen murdered him while he was saying Mass. Yet all this was not without criticism from more sensitive souls. Gregory of Tours, the narrator of these events, was once standing before the palace of King Chilperic, grandson of Clovis, with the bishop of Albi, who asked him what he saw on top of the palace. Gregory, who had become inured to atrocities, answered, "A roof." The other replied, "I see the naked sword of the wrath of God."

However, there was widespread ostensible piety. Churches

and monasteries were constructed in great numbers; unhappily, most of them were destroyed in the troubled centuries to come. The church was the focus of many important activities of community life. Mass was said daily and was attended by the populace in large numbers, especially on Sundays and holy days. The throngs in the churches were such that King Guntram feared to attend without a guard lest an assassin lurk amid the mob.

Vast possessions came into the hands of the Church. In the Merovingian period—that is, very roughly, from about 500 to about 750—the churches and the monasteries held from a quarter to a third of all the land in the kingdom. Now, as earlier in Italy, rulers made use of churchmen in governmental administration because they were the only learned men in the land. Bishops and abbots resembled the counts and dukes in their status, functions, and behavior, the more so because ecclesiastical property was no longer vested in the Church as a corporation, but personally in the hands of the bishop or the abbot. In extremities, kings confiscated the lands of the Church to finance the needs of the state; thus Charles Martel used income from Church lands to equip the cavalry which repulsed the invading Saracens near Tours in 732. However, new donations replenished the holdings of the Church; although the king used the lands of the Church to reward services by the nobles, they in turn gave to the Church.

The faith of the populace centered more on Christ as the heavenly ruler than as the suffering redeemer. The barbarian converts were oppressed by no deep sense of sin and the consequent need for redemption. They required rather to be ruled and defended. The saints, with their particular assignments, may well have meant more to the people than Christ the universal redeemer; certainly at this time the cult of the saints first achieved broad popularity. Saint Anthony took care of pigs nd Saint Saturninus of sheep, Saint Gall looked after hens, and Saint Medardus protected vines from frost. Saint Apollonia, whose teeth had all been pulled out by her persecutors, cured toothache, Saint Hubert hydrophobia, Saint Genevieve fever, and Saint Blaise sore throats. A ribbon inscribed with the name of Saint Amable tied around a child's wrist prevented nightmares. And so on.

Many tales were circulated about the miraculous powers of saints. A story was told of a bishop whose church had caught fire. He went to the altar and wept so copiously that the fire was extinguished. The powers of saints were often considered to be greater after their death than while they lived; hence the great concern to possess relics, even to a wisp of a beard or the parings of fingernails. Two beggars, one lame, one blind, it was said, happened to be caught in a procession carrying the relics of Saint Martin and were fearful that they would be cured and deprived of their occupation. The one who could see but not walk mounted the shoulders of the one who could walk and not see, and they hurried to get beyond the range of the saint's miraculous power, but they failed to make it.

In the late sixth century Ireland repaid her debt to the Continent when some of her monks came to arrest the anemia of this half-pagan Christianity by a transfusion of fresh spiritual zeal. They came to this ostensibly Christian land not so much as missionaries as to make what was for Irishmen the supreme sacrifice of living and dying away from home. But men of such dedication, by their very deportment, were a rebuke to bishops who did not hesitate to commit murder. The most notable among these monks was Columbanus, who in 590 founded a monastery at Luxeuil. He speedily infuriated the Gallic clergy, who looked upon a divergence in liturgy as more serious than a lapse in morals. As in England, the Celtic Christians on the Continent disagreed with the Roman Christians over the proper date for celebrating Easter. In this matter Columbanus' views were anachronistic. But he was on firmer ground when he scathingly denounced the conduct of the son of Queen Brunhilde. In consequence, he was driven out of the Frankish kingdom and went eventually to Italy, where he founded the monastery of Bobbio. His disciple, Saint Gall, established a monastery in Switzerland that still carries his name.

However superficial, the conversion of the Franks directly from paganism to Nicene orthodoxy led to a very close rapport between this people and the papacy, which resulted in a religio-political alliance of the two in the eighth century. The development was quite different in the case of the Vandals in Africa, the Lombards in Italy, and the Visigoths in Spain. The Vandals remained Arian until their power in North Africa was destroyed by Justinian in 533. The Arian Lombards accepted Catholicism more than a century later than the conversion of the Franks, after Queen Theodelinda, prompted by Pope Gregory I, had induced her husband Agilulf to make this change. But unity in the faith, in this instance, did not lead to friendly collaboration, for the Lombards continued to harass papal lands until their kingdom was absorbed by the Franks late in the eighth century.

After the conversion of their king Recared from Arianism to orthodoxy in 587 the Visigoths in Spain speedily established a pattern, intermittently recurrent in Spanish history, of fanatical orthodoxy, close association of Church and state, and great independence of Rome. All three of these aspects are related to the earlier Arianism, though in different senses. The fanatical orthodoxy was a reaction against the previous heresy; also, perhaps to vindicate their own theological rectitude, the Visigoths were much harsher toward the Jews than were the Merovingians. But the other two points show a continuance of the Arian pattern. As earlier noted, among the Arian tribes the priest had been attached to the ruler and the Church to the crown; neither depended upon a universal ecclesiastical authority. The Visigoths' adherence to orthodoxy did not alter the alliance of their religious establishment with the state, nor did it induce a disposition to take directives from Rome.

In the year 711 Tarik led the hosts of Allah across the Straits of Gibraltar, and before him fell Roderick, the last of the Visigothic kings. In accord with the general Moslem practice the native inhabitants were not forced to give up their religion. Jews and Christians might worship as they would, but they had to pay heavy taxes. The Jews found such burdens less onerous than the persecution they had endured under the fanatical Visigoths. For the Christians, of course, there was a complete reversal in status. Some in consequence renounced their faith and then entered into all the privileges of the Moslem. They were known as *renegados*. Those who remained faithful were known as Mozarabs.

The Arabic, or Moorish, government of Spain was changed in the mid-eighth century, when the Omayyad dynasty in Baghdad was supplanted by the Abbasids. A prince of the Omayyads, escaping, went to Spain and there overturned the government. Under the new dynasty the culture of the Moors reached a pinnacle far loftier than any in contemporary Christian Europe. The relations of Moslems, Christians, and Jews were intermittently hostile and friendly. There were wars in plenty, but sometimes Christians and Moslems united to fight on one side against Christians and Moslems on another. The Christians, however, were never entirely subjugated. They maintained themselves in mountain fastnesses in the northern provinces of Asturias, Navarre, and Aragon and soon began to push out in the *Reconquista*, a process of wresting Spain from Moslem control that was not completed until 1492, when the Moors were expelled from Granada. Not even in the period when the force of the crusading spirit was driving the unbelievers either to Africa or to the Christian faith were cultural relations between Christians and Moslems altogether severed.

VI

The Search for Order

A Carolingian monarch, probably Charles
II, is shown at his coronation.

By the mid-eighth century the Saracen advance in the West had been arrested, and the momentum of the barbarian invasions had temporarily slowed. During an interval of relative freedom from external pressures Europe began its struggle to recover order from the political and cultural confusion of the previous several centuries. The initial phases of this long struggle involved two forces concerned with the restoration of order—Church and state—allied for their mutual benefit. Then fresh inroads of barbarians from north and east again shattered the structure of society, and the stormy centuries that followed saw the development of direct conflict between Church and state over the exercise of authority.

In the first phase of the consolidation of a new order the central figures were the Frankish king Pepin and the Anglo-Saxon missionary Saint Boniface. In his own tongue called Winfrith, meaning "the lover of peace," the missionary preferred Boniface, the Latin name meaning "the doer of good," by which he is better known. In his person the newly converted Saxons in England were undertaking, with approval of but without prompting from Rome, to convert the peoples of what is now Germany. Boniface traveled far, beginning in Frisia and reaching Saxony, Bavaria, and Hesse. Whatever variety there may have been in the speech of the Continental Germans, the biographer of Boniface records that he addressed thousands in the vernacular, and never once mentions an interpreter. In spite of political division, all the Germans had one basic tongue, and the Gothic Bible of Ulfilas, like Boniface's spoken words, could serve them all. The fact that it was the work of an Arian did not disqualify it as a translation. Boniface became known as the apostle of Germany, although he was not the first to undertake Christian missions in German lands; he might better be called the organizer than the originator of Christianity in that region.

Boniface was a great integrating force. His missionary work brought together England and the Continent. It brought together France and Germany, for the Frankish kings gladly gave him their protection and support, and it brought together Rome and the churches of the North. We have already noted how the proprietary churches of the North looked rather to their patrons than to the pope. Boniface himself took an oath of allegiance to the pope and called upon the churches of Gaul to profess their fidelity too. Boniface also combined in his own person the secular and the regular forms of the ministry. The term *secular* was applied to the clergy who served in the world (*saeculum*), whether as priests, bishops, archbishops, or popes. The term *regular* was applied to those who observed the monastic rule (*regula*). Boniface was made archbishop of Mainz and was thus a secular; he founded the monastery of Fulda and was thus also a regular.

Finally, Boniface had a great influence on the relations of Church and state. It was he who cemented the alliance of the papacy with the kingdom of the Franks. The popes needed some strong defender. They were still menaced by the Lombards, but their most persistent threat came from the populace of Rome itself. Now that the papacy had come to represent wealth and prestige, the great Roman families desired to have their own members elected to the office. Papal elections were often attended by riots resulting from family feuds. The pope had no armies of his own with which to suppress them. Where could he turn for a defender of Saint Peter, if not to some political power? The Lombard king obviously could not assume the role, for he himself was threatening to seize Rome. Africa and Spain had both succumbed to Islam. The emperor at Constantinople was not only busy fighting the Avars and the Turks, but was also quarreling with the popes, who resisted iconoclasm and were infuriated by the threat that imperial troops would come and smash the image of Saint Peter. Help might be expected only from Gaul, the land of Clovis, the oldest of the orthodox kingdoms, and the only important Christian power in western Europe. The popes looked to Gaul in times of molestation.

Gaul had troubles of its own. Although the decadent Merovingian kings had papal sanction—they were anointed with the oil of Clovis—the actual administration of the kingdom was assumed by the mayors of the palace. Charles Martel, who had repulsed the Saracens near Tours in 732, was one of this able line of palace administrators. Nineteen years after the battle Charles's son, Pepin the Short, who had succeeded to his father's office, considered it imperative to bring the actual power and the title into conjunction through divine sanction. But how? How indeed, if not through the papacy, the institution that ministered the sanction of the divine in the name of that saint to whom had been given the power to bind and to loose? But Peter's successor was at some distance removed. However, an emissary happened to be at hand in the person of Boniface, by whom the crown was conferred on Pepin with papal approval in 752. The rite was later repeated by Pope Stephen II. In all this there was no claim that the pope conferred authority. He was really only recognizing authority. But he did convey something that was evidently worth having, and the inference that the monarchy would be invalid without such sanction was easily made.

Pepin repaid his debt. Journeying to Rome, he disciplined the Lombards and brought order to the capital. In 754 he conferred upon the pope political authority over a strip of Italy that ran from Rome over the Apennines to Ravenna, the seat of the exarch of the eastern emperor. To confer the latter city upon the pope was tantamount to declaring independence from the Second Rome. Pepin's act, called the Donation of Pepin, is commonly regarded as the beginning of the temporal power of the papacy. But this can be regarded as correct only in a formal sense, inasmuch as the popes, as we have noted, had long been exercising essentially political functions.

The principle underlying the mutual relations of the pope and the king was not made explicit. Centuries earlier, in 494, Pope Gelasius, concerned to ward off any interference in the affairs of the Church by the Byzantine emperors, had made a pronouncement regarding the relation of spiritual and civil powers. Gelasius insisted upon their mutual independence. At the same time, however, he stressed the superiority of the spiritual power to the degree that the things of the spirit and the life to come are superior to the things of the body and the life terrestrial. Yet however little Stephen and Pepin were disposed to theorize, an anonymous forger at this time perpetrated a document, the so-called Donation of Constantine, destined for centuries to buttress the Church's authority. According to this spurious treatise, in his heathen days Constantine, suffering from leprosy, was advised by his priests to bathe in the blood of babies. The humane sovereign shrank from the cruelty. In consequence, Peter and Paul appeared to him in a vision and instructed him to seek out Sylvester, the bishop of Rome, who was in hiding. Sylvester baptized the emperor, who was thereby completely cured and who then withdrew to Constantinople, saying that the imperial dignity should not detract by its presence from the papal. He conferred upon the pope primacy over Antioch, Constantinople, Alexandria, and Jerusalem and temporal jurisdiction over the whole of the West.

Not until the Renaissance was it shown that Constantine had done nothing of the kind. The document was a forgery. In considering the ethical standards of this forger and of others like him in the next century we should realize that in antiquity men sought to gain authority for their convictions by attaching them to a great name, rather than prestige for themselves by avowing their authorship. Thus the Jews attributed their laws to Moses and their psalms to David, and the earlier Christians sometimes ascribed to the apostles books that modern scholarship considers of uncertain authorship.

A more dramatic encounter between the papacy and a king of the Franks had as its principals Pope Leo III and Pepin's son and successor Charles, known as Charlemagne. In spite of Pepin's forceful actions the Lombards had continued to threaten Rome. The emperor in the East tried to reassert his control over Italy, whenever able, and endeavored to subordinate the popes as he had done the patriarchs of Constantinople, but he exercised little control over the Lombards. Stephen's successor, Pope Hadrian, appealed to Charlemagne, who twice descended upon Italy and the second time was finally able to put an end to the Lombard kingdom.

Then, in 799, Pope Leo III was beaten by a Roman mob, accused of numerous crimes and vices, and imprisoned. Again Charlemagne swept into Italy and this time imposed order on Rome and restored Leo to the papacy. On Christmas Day of the year 800, when Charlemagne was kneeling in the Basilica of St. Peter, the pope placed a crown upon his head, and the congregation hailed him by simultaneously chanting the words: "To Charles, the most pious Augustus, crowned of God, to the great and peace-giving emperor, be life and victory," and Charlemagne was "chosen by all to be emperor of the Romans."

Charlemagne's biographer, Einhard, said that had the emperor known this was going to happen, he would never have gone into the church that day. Why should he have objected? Possibly because his assuming the title "emperor of the Romans" would have affronted the eastern emperor or empress, whose subjects still called themselves Romans. Apparently Charlemagne desired a system, like that instituted by Diocletian, of two Augusti, one for the East and one for the West. Therefore he preferred to be called the emperor of the Roman domain, by which he meant not simply the city of Rome or the lands of the old Roman Empire in the West, but the entire territory under his sway.

Before his death in 814 Charlemagne's empire extended from the Mediterranean and the Spanish marches south of the Pyrenees to the Elbe and Danube. Upon the territories he conquered Charlemagne imposed Christianity by force where necessary. In one notable instance eighteen campaigns were required to bring the Saxons to baptism and to submission. His victories over the Avars restored Christianity to the Danubian provinces. In ten years of campaigning he established a base in northern Spain from which the subsequent Christian reconquest of the Peninsula would be launched. His coronation did not alter the manner of his life or the character of his government; but it symbolized and cemented the alliance between the Franks and the spiritual head of Rome. By it Charlemagne's authority in the West received the sanction of Roman tradition; anointed by the pope, he became the leader of western Christendom.

The Carolingian empire was a royal theocracy. In his relations with the Church Charlemagne was devout, concerned, and commanding. Every morning he went to Mass and every evening to Vespers. He took an active share in the life of the Church, summoning councils and interfering with their decisions. He instructed priests how to baptize and he was concerned with the liturgy. In his administration he used churchmen who, by reason of their numerous holdings of land in a society based upon land, were not only prelates, but also magnates. Bishops and abbots were appointed and controlled by patrons. The emperor, himself a patron, saw to it that the patrons did not arouse his displeasure. The Church was virtually a department of state.

Charlemagne promoted the revival of the classical Christian culture. He understood Latin, even though he could not train his clumsy fingers to write. To his court at Aix-la-Chapelle he invited learned men of many extractions: Goth and Frank, Anglo-Saxon and Celt, Lombard and Spaniard. Einhard, his biographer, was a Swabian, Warnefrid (known as Paul the Deacon) was a Lombard, and Alcuin was an Anglo-Saxon. Alcuin, who had earlier headed the famous cathedral school at York, became Charlemagne's adviser in educational and religious matters and the principal intellect of the Carolingian Renaissance. It was his hope, he told Charlemagne, that in the land of the Franks might be reared "a new Athens enriched by the sevenfold fullness of the Holy Spirit." Alcuin revived the ancient disciplines of grammar, rhetoric, and dialectic as tools of the teacher, whom he regarded as a better propagator of Christianity than the warrior. In protest against Charlemagne's imposition of baptism by force on the Saxons, Alcuin asked of what avail baptism had been to these wretched folk: "A man can be driven to baptism, but not to belief," he observed. It was he who first used the figure of the two swords with reference to the roles of Church and state, and Charlemagne was informed that he was not to use his sword— the political power of the state—to impose religion. Charlemagne admired his great adviser, but did not always heed his counsel. When the emperor listened with relish to the reading of Augustine's *City of God*, he was attracted more by the denunciations of paganism than by the excoriation of empire.

The attachment of the Frankish empire to Rome was evidenced by the standardization of ecclesiastical practices in conformity with Roman and Italian models. With the encouragement of the emperor the Rule of St. Benedict supplanted other rules, notably those of Irish provenance, in Frankish monasteries. The canon law, compiled in the age of Justinian by Dionysius Exiguus in Italy and enshrining the principal of papal centralization, was accepted by the Frankish Church in 802. Since the liturgy was of inestimable importance in the formation of a Christian culture, Charlemagne desired uniform practice throughout his domains and commissioned Alcuin to prepare a standardized version based on the Roman rather than the Gallican form. However, Alcuin enriched the Roman version by introducing certain prayers from the Gallican recension, and his revision was then adopted by Rome. Similarly, the Apostles' Creed, emanating from Rome, received its present form among the Franks in the Carolingian era and then became standard at Rome. There was thus, at times, a two-way process toward conformity between Rome and the Frankish world.

The unity and order that Charlemagne had imposed on the western world did not long survive the emperor's death in 814. The Franks were drained by prolonged warfare. Counts and dukes, bishops and abbots had achieved a semi-independence in the management of empire, which they asserted with increasing freedom under Charlemagne's successors. There were divisions within the empire arising from problems of succession and resulting in internal wars. And, even more grave, a new wave of barbarian invasions was sweeping over Europe.

The Vikings came swooping down on their neighbors' northern coasts and invaded the watercourses. Those who dwelt by the rivers feared almost less the fires of hell than the cold light of a clear moon. There is a revealing prayer in the Gallican liturgy: "Let not our own malice within us, but the sense of thy long-suffering be ever before us, that it may ceaselessly keep us from evil delights and graciously guard us from the disasters of this night." By 835 a Scandinavian kingdom had been established in Ireland. In 845 the Danes sacked Hamburg and Paris. Again in 850 there were raids along the Loire and the Seine. In 865 the east coast of England was occupied by the Danes, and they almost succeeded in seizing control of the whole country. In February of the year 880 an entire Saxon army was routed by these same Danes. Two bishops and eleven counts, among others, were slain. By 900 the Viking raids were subsiding, only to be succeeded by Magyar pressures from the east. Meanwhile the raids in the West had wiped out monastic culture in the east of England. Many churches and monasteries in France were wrecked. The Carolingian empire was a shambles.

The disruptions caused by these invasions were made the more possible and serious by the political divisions of Charlemagne's state. These in turn were caused at least partly by the application of the Germanic principle of divided inheritance. In 843 the empire of Charlemagne's son and successor, Louis the Pious, was divided among his three sons: Charles the Bald received western Francia, the future France; Louis the German, eastern Francia, the future Germany; and Lothair, a middle strip that included what later became the Netherlands, Belgium, Luxembourg, Alsace, Lorraine, Switzerland, Burgundy, and northern Italy—much of which area had remained a buffer zone ever since.

None of these governments was strong enough to repel the invaders. When raiders glided up the watercourses, struck, burned, pillaged, captured, and fled, the inhabitants of the assaulted areas had no recourse but self-help. Bridges had to be fortified, fords protected. Small forces of militia had to be constantly ready. Arms were necessary, but arms were costly. How could a peasant afford to exchange six oxen or twelve cows for a breastplate, seven cows for a sword, and three for a sword belt? Nor was he in a position to construct a stockade. He was forced to request protection from a richer, stronger man and to pay for this with service.

Thus grew up a complex series of interrelationships, with everyone, except a slave, over someone else, and everyone, except the emperor, under someone else. The one below swore fealty and service, the one above swore to provide protection. The whole structure rested on good faith. This, in essence, was feudalism, which was to be the basis of the medieval world and which carried within it the seeds of constitutional government, since it involved contractual relationships with mutual obligations. Such localized social organization, however necessary, led to further disorder within the land because the small feudal lords warred with each other. Everyone who was attacked, including bishops, priests, monks, and nuns, took care of himself. "Every man does what seems good in his own eyes," it was reported in 909, "despising laws human and divine and the commands of the Church. The strong oppress the weak, the world is full of violence against the poor and of the plunder of ecclesiastic goods."

The attempt to recover order after the debacle of the Viking invasions occupied both Church and state. The more the menace receded the more these two forces began to clash as to who should take the lead in the ordering of society. As each assumed greater authority over the same persons in the same territories, ambiguities as to their separate jurisdictions produced conflicts.

These developments were intimately related to centralizing and decentralizing tendencies in the structure of the state and of the Church. The ideas of centralization and decentralization, of unity and variety, of authority and autonomy were in perpetual tension throughout the Middle Ages. The splendor of Rome's single empire never ceased to enthrall the imagination of the West; at the same time the local attachments to Germanic tradition were also cherished and retained. When state and Church were in conflict, each sought to integrate its own authority and disintegrate that of the other. Any element of the state at variance with the emperor received papal support; when a bishop of any region defied the pope, the disaffection was encouraged by the emperor.

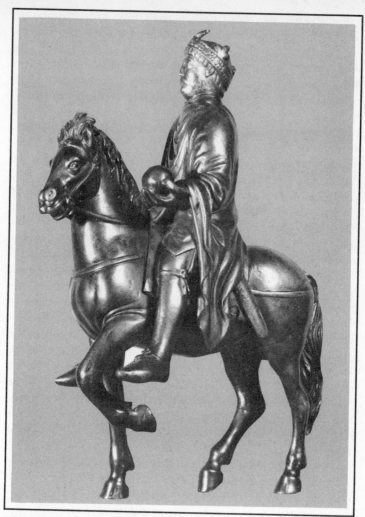

This ninth-century bronze statuette probably represents Charlemagne. His sudden coronation by Pope Leo III took place on Christmas Day, 800, while he was on an expedition to Rome. The event restored the Roman Empire in the West.

In the period just after Charlemagne's death a theoretical justification for centralized authority within the Church under the pope and within society under the Church was introduced to the West. It was contained in writing attributed to Dionysius the Areopagite, who is mentioned in the New Testament as one who listened to the apostle Paul at Athens and believed his account of Christ's resurrection. He had been erroneously equated with the patron saint of France, the martyr Saint Denis, whose name is the French form of "Dionysius." The Christian Neoplatonic writings to which his name was attached, called the Pseudo-Dionysian treatises, were actually composed in the East in the early sixth century. It is believed that a copy of these works had been sent by the Byzantine emperor to Louis the Pious, who gave it to the Abbey of St. Denis. The abbot, Hilduin, promptly ascribed these writings to his patron saint and thereby invested them with an enormous prestige in France.

The Pseudo-Dionysian treatises were translated from Greek into Latin in 860 by John Scotus Erigena. In these writings the structure of the heavenly and the earthly societies is viewed as hierarchical. From the ultimate intelligence the hierarchies descend. The divine afflatus is transmitted from the heavenly to the earthly society and within the earthly from the sacraments to the clergy and from the clergy to the laity. Within the Church the heavenly hierarchy descends from the emperor or king to the serf. The hierarchies themselves are hierarchically structured, with the ecclesiastical above the civil. The Pseudo-Dionysian treatises thus provided theological grounds for the papal theocracy.

Actual practice was moving in that direction at that time, notably during the pontificate of Nicholas I (858–867). One of the controversies in which he was involved illustrates the development of papal supremacy over local autonomy. Hincmar, the archbishop of Reims and metropolitan of France, claimed complete jurisdiction over his own clergy and inflicted discipline upon a bishop, who thereupon appealed to Rome. Nicholas responded to this appeal, claiming for himself jurisdiction, and took the case out of the hands of Hincmar. This was a reassertion of the principle of centralization that had been enshrined in the canon law.

At about the same time further theoretical support for the papalist trend was provided by another forgery called the False or

Pseudo-Isidorian Decretals. Actually compiled by a Frankish clerk, they were attributed to Isidore, the bishop of Seville under the Visigoths and the author of an encyclopedic work of learning. This collection included both forged and genuine letters of earlier popes interspersed with spurious documents making pretentious claims, such as that the Roman church in the second century had exercised authority over all other churches. The forger introduced provision for the creation of a body of churchmen beneath the pope but above the metropolitans—in other words, the college of cardinals, which actually did not come into being until the eleventh century. The purpose of this provision was to establish the absolute and universal supremacy of the pope and to downgrade the metropolitans. The Decretals strongly supported the right of appeal to Rome and further required that civil rulers should not interfere with the internal life and property of the Church. The most interesting point about this collection is that it did not emanate from the papacy but from the lower clergy in France, who were seeking to protect themselves against the exaction of overlords, lay and clerical, by building up the power of the pope at Rome.

Another controversy, between Nicholas and Lothair II, ruler of the middle region of Charlemagne's empire, illustrates the power that the Church had come to exercise through the sacraments. Lothair had repudiated his wife, whom he accused of incest, and had made his concubine queen. The pope commanded him to restore his proper spouse or suffer excommunication. Although Lothair's brother, Emperor Louis II, marched on Rome, Nicholas refused to be intimidated. Lothair was excommunicated. After some tergiversation he capitulated. Nicholas thus reaffirmed the fact that the king as a Christian was subject to the judgment of the Church. Excommunication was for centuries the dread weapon of the Christian Church.

In 875 Pope John VIII bestowed the imperial crown on Charles the Bald, descendant of Charlemagne. There was no question that the pope was the more exalted power. However, in the century to come the power of the monarchy in the North was strongly developed by the rulers of Saxony. In 919 the Saxon duke Henry was elected king of Germany, to be succeeded by his son Otto. When the empire of Charlemagne was reconstructed by Henry, its center was in Germany. In 962 at Rome Otto was recognized as emperor. His domain included

Germany and that middle area once assigned to Lothair, including Italy but not France.

But in the tenth century, whereas the empire revived, the Church declined. The reason for the decay was that the papacy had become again the preserve of Italian families. Among the most influential of the nobles were two domineering women of ill repute, Theodora and Marozia, who dictated papal appointments. In consequence this era in papal history has been called the Pornocracy.

However, the papacy was not the entire Church. Christian missions had been advancing independently of the pope. Newly converted lands passed on the Gospel to their neighbors. As the Vikings continued their raids on the islands and the mainland, the Church started the Christian offensive. In the ninth century Harold of Denmark, having been expelled from his kingdom, sought restoration through the help of France and was informed that assistance would be more readily forthcoming if he were a Christian. He accepted baptism and encouraged the missionary activity of the Frankish monk Anschar, who is remembered as the apostle of the North for his work in Denmark, Norway, and Sweden. Early in the eleventh century there was a real possibility that England might be brought into the Scandinavian confederation by Canute, who then ruled over Denmark, England, and, for a short time, Norway. This was prevented by the Normans, the residue of an earlier Viking invasion that had been assimilated into northern France, who realigned England once more with the Continent as a result of the Norman conquest. The populace of Norway had become nominally Christianized late in the tenth and early in the eleventh centuries under her kings Olaf I and Olaf II, rival of Canute. Together they brought their land into the orbit of Christendom, unhappily not without coercing their subjects. The pagans in Sweden were not fully converted until about 1100.

Contemporary with Anschar's endeavors in the West, the Church in the East was Christianizing the people of the Balkans. Two missionaries of Slavic origin, Cyril (baptized Constantine) and Methodius, adapted the Greek alphabet and translated both the Bible and the liturgy into the Slavic tongue. This Old Slavonic liturgy has been able to serve as a focus for pan-Slavic movements, even after the rise of a variety of Slavic languages. But the Slavs have not been ecclesiastically united. The Serbs, the Bulgarians, and later the Russians have been oriented toward Constantinople, even though they became ecclesiastically independent of the patriarchate; whereas the northern Slavs, the Croats, the Slovenes, the Czechs, the Slovaks, and the Poles, whose conversion emanated from contact with Germany, have been incorporated into western Christendom under Rome.

At the very time when the papacy was a scandal a great movement of reform had been initiated in a monastery. In the year 910 William, duke of Aquitaine, and his wife, Ingelborga, in honor of the blessed Mother of God and of Saint Peter, made over to the apostles Peter and Paul the town and manor of Cluny for the erection of a Benedictine monastery. The donation stipulated that the monks should "ardently pursue celestial converse and sedulously offer prayers and petitions," alike for the donors and for all mankind. Along with the lands, waters, and revenues went the workers on the land—serfs, male and female. The monks, declared the grant, should be free in perpetuity to retain their possessions without alienation and to elect their own abbot without any interference from the patron or his successors or the king, under penalty of the wrath of Peter and Paul. These provisions were of high significance. The independence of the monastery from secular and ecclesiastical authorities, except protection by the pope, meant that it was free from all feudal obligations, including the control of kings and emperors. Cluny added a new feature to monasticism whereby all monasteries founded from Cluny became parts of a congregation; they were subject to the abbot at Cluny and were regularly visited by him.

The program of Cluny differed from that of other Benedictine monasteries. It envisaged a Christian reordering of the whole social order, monastic, civil, and ecclesiastical. The role of the monastery in the world was no longer directed to conversions, often so nominal, but to the permeation of society by Christian ideals. Therefore, the monks, now largely free from manual labor, were expected to dedicate themselves to prayer, to the transmission of even pagan learning, to prayers for the world, and to hospitality toward the world. Whereas Saint Benedict had sought to segregate his monks from society, the Cluniacs tried to integrate monasticism and society.

The monasteries thus served as the inns of the Middle Ages. Cluny had a guest house that accommodated forty men and thirty women, and a guest-master to look after the visitors. In the course of centuries the Benedictines also became integrated into society, largely because they too began to offer hospitality to visitors. The Benedictine monastery of St. Albans, for example, had stabling for three hundred horses, and Abingdon even shod the steeds of the guests. The duties of the hosteler were to provide clean towels, uncracked cups, spoons of silver, blankets, and sheets of full width, of pleasing color, and untorn. In winter he should supply candles and candlesticks, a fire that did not smoke, and writing materials. The guest house should be free from spider's webs and strewn with rushes under foot. On departure the guests should be checked to see that no one left a sword and that no one carried off the linen or the silver of the house, either inadvertently or otherwise. Guests were expected to make some contribution, but the cost of their entertainment was often greater than the cost of maintaining the monastery.

The abbot was burdened with many cares. Abbot Samson at Bury St. Edmonds in the course of twelve years pulled his house out of monstrous debt, but his hair turned white in the process. These examples of the monastery's growing involvement with society are, to be sure, centuries apart, but they indicate a continuous process that brought the world to the monastery and helped to spread monastic ideals throughout the community, though reintroducing the danger that worldly values would infiltrate and corrupt the monastery.

The Cluny reform made a particular point of seeking to eliminate feudal warfare. It wished the nobles to be at peace among themselves and use their arms only to vindicate the weak and protect the Church. Cluny supported the Truce of God and the Peace of God, later to be described. Cluny envisaged also the reform of the Church, demanding among other things that the clergy be celibate. It also forbade the clergy to buy benefices from their ecclesiastical superiors, from lay patrons, or from civil rulers—a practice called simony, from Simon Magus, who, in the Book of Acts, sought to buy the gift of the Holy Spirit from the apostles. But for the implementation of these reforms Cluny did not object to assistance from civil rulers, nor even to initiative on their part. They, too, were ordained of God. They constituted the temporal arm of a Christian society and had the responsibility for the purity of the spiritual arm. There was no valid reason why good emperors should not depose bad popes.

This role the Ottos of the newly reconstituted empire were

ready to assume. They looked upon themselves as the temporal arm of a Christian society with authority directly from God to administer justice, protect religion, and even to discipline the Church. If popes misbehaved, they should be removed by the civil authority and replaced by candidates worthy of their calling. In 963 Otto I deposed John XII and had a council select his successor. For about forty years thereafter the emperors determined the choice of popes. Otto III appointed first a German, then a Frenchman to the papacy. The latter, Gerbert, had studied in Spain and Italy and was the most learned churchman of his day. As pope he took the name Sylvester II in honor of Sylvester I, who, according to the Donation of Constantine, had baptized the first Christian Roman emperor. The very choice of the name witnessed to his intent to restore the glories of the more primitive Church. However, the reform instituted by Sylvester was short-lived; the papacy was again dominated by the Italian counts and once more became disreputable.

A second time reform emanated from the empire, when Henry III intervened to install men of good repute in the Holy See. He deposed three claimants to the papacy and had his own choice consecrated. However, when his son Henry IV tried to depose Pope Gregory VII in 1076, he met with determined resistance from churchmen of a new type, who were themselves bent on reforming the Church. Gregory himself had been chosen neither by the emperor nor the Roman nobles, but by the cardinals, with the approval of the population of Rome.

The so-called Gregorian reformers endorsed Cluny's program, but they did not agree that reforms should be instituted by civil rulers or that emperors should depose popes. Reform should come from within the Church. The leaders of this party were not Italians but northerners from Lorraine, who sought to build up the papacy in order to correct practices prevalent especially in the North. In the Germany of the eleventh century the Church controlled somewhat more than one-third of the land. As in Merovingian and Carolingian times, ownership of the land involved the Church in the political structure. In a feudal society the owner of land provided the resources of government and supplied military contingents. Bishops and abbots who owned land consequently had to be princes as well. To insure their loyalty the king or the emperor controlled their appointment and himself, as patron, would bestow churches on them with the

In this scene of Jerusalem's capture, a
fourteenth-century miniaturist depicted the
city as a Gothic town. Heavily armed
Christians scale a ladder to reach the
battlements while their comrades below
use a trebuchet to catapult stones at the
defenders. Within the city, above, are
scenes from Jesus' life.

formula *Accipe ecclesiam*, "Accept the church." If popes interfered with such appointments, popes themselves might be removed.

Often enough, however, emperors were not interested in reforms, but used ecclesiastical appointments simply as plums with which to reward retainers devoid of spiritual qualifications. Nobles were permitted to use ecclesiastical posts to provide for younger sons, and families built up their power by obtaining several sees in the name of one incumbent. A certain bishop flippantly justified such pluralism on the ground that if one man held several bishoprics fewer men would be damned. A further evil was that bishops of this type had sons who succeeded to their posts. The cure for all these ills, according to the Gregorian reformers, was that no ecclesiastical appointment should be made by laymen, not even by an emperor, whether for a fee or without a fee. The term *simony* was extended to describe lay appointments even if no payment was involved. So that the sons of the clergy should not inherit sees, it was felt that clerical celibacy had to be enforced. Finally, the Gregorian reformers stipulated that the Church should assume direction over the world and that rulers should wield the sword at her behest.

The demands of the reformers understandably met intense opposition. Civil administration would be disrupted if the rulers could not control the clerical landowners, whose holdings were dispersed throughout the empire. But the conflict involved more than a matter of administration. The question of the source of power was involved, and the conflict was sharpened by two opposing views: one, that the state was instituted directly by God, and the other, that the civil power was derived from the spiritual. Churchmen appealed to the hierarchical theories of Dionysius the Areopagite, and imperialists looked to the words of the apostle Paul, who said that rulers are ordained by God but who never mentioned the Church of St. Peter. Thus the debate was pursued in a series of tracts.

The conflict became overt in a disagreement between Emperor Henry IV and Pope Gregory VII shortly after the latter was elevated to the papacy. The struggle illustrates how in the rivalry between Church and state each attempted to reduce the centralized authority of the other. The papal offensive began about 1074 by the prohibition of clerical marriage, simony, and any lay investiture of ecclesiastical posts. The laity was exhorted to refuse to receive the sacraments at the hands of married priests. This was a most dangerous provision, for the inference was very easy that at the hands of the unworthy the sacraments would be invalid, precisely the view of the ancient Donatist heretics. The German clergy in Henry's entourage declared that they would rather give up their lives than their wives. The emperor retaliated against Gregory's decree by making an appointment to the archbishopric of Milan. Milan was the chief see of Lombardy, where the populace was strongly opposed to clerical celibacy; in focusing his defiance to the pope first on a city in that region Henry sought to undermine papal authority at its weak spot.

On the other hand, during the course of the struggle the pope abetted the Saxons in their rebellion against Henry, who was a member of the Franconian ruling house. Furthermore, Gregory could lean on two important allies. The countess Matilda in Tuscany was a warm adherent of his policies; and the Normans, who had recently broken into the Mediterranean world, had been enlisted as allies. A previous pope had, by force of arms, resisted their encroachment on papal lands in southern Italy, but before he became pope Gregory had had the discretion to help one of his predecessors win their allegiance.

To the pope Henry sent a defiance, accusing him of innovation in regard to papal powers. Had not Henry's father, the emperor Henry III, deposed and appointed popes with the full consent of a pope and council? To this Gregory replied that his own program was indeed an innovation with reference to the immediate past; but the immediate past was a corruption of a more primitive past, to which he was seeking to return. The emperor made a further charge that the pope was stepping out of bounds by fomenting war, in that he incited the Saxons to take arms against the emperor. Henry therefore summoned Gregory to come down from the throne of Saint Peter, which he had usurped by the sword, that it might be filled by another more worthy of the holy apostle.

The pope replied with an apostrophe to the blessed Peter, the Mother of God, the blessed Paul, and all the saints, calling upon them to witness that he had not seized his holy office for the glory of the world. He declared Henry to be deposed from the governance of Germany and Italy and to be bound in the bonds of anathema, so that all people might know that on Peter, the

Rock, the Church was founded and that no man would prevail against it. Like Lothair before him, Henry found himself completely undone. His political enemies of the Saxon house could, of course, be expected to exploit the anathema. But even his own party withdrew support, and the German bishops, so opposed to clerical celibacy, interpreted the sudden death of their leader, William of Utrecht, as God's corroboration of the pope's curse. A diet of princes, meeting in October of the year 1076 in Tribur on the Rhine, decreed that Henry must resign all royal insignia and that only if he made his peace with the pope would his status as emperor be reviewed at a council to be held the following February in Augsburg.

Henry had no recourse save to stoop to conquer. With his wife, infant son, and a few retainers he set out for Rome. Christmas was approaching and even the swift Rhine was frozen. Yet with guides he made his way over the Alps. In the meantime the pope had started north to attend a council called by Henry's German enemies. Fearing violence, Gregory took refuge at Canossa, a fortress of the countess Matilda, the emperor's cousin but the pope's supporter. It was now January of the year 1077. The emperor, learning of the pope's location, there sought him out. Clad as a suppliant in white wool, Henry stood barefoot in the snow in the castle enclosure, seeking admission. For a day he stood, and the gate did not open; for a second day likewise, and for a third. Then the emperor requested the mediation of the countess, and the obdurate pope was softened by the entreaty of a woman. Abbot Hugh of Cluny supported Matilda in her plea. But what could the pope do? Would Saint Peter ever reject a penitent? The emperor was admitted, but strict conditions of obedience to the Church were imposed on him, which he accepted; and he was then received to communion. This appeared to be a papal victory.

Immediately Henry's subjects returned to obedience. However, his opponents in Germany, supported by Saxony, elected an anti-king. Rallying his forces, Henry bore down on the Saxons without waiting for any diet to decide whether or not he should be emperor. The Saxons appealed to the pope, who at length excommunicated Henry again, this time for impeding the meeting of the diet. But the second excommunication did not work; the pope had overstepped his limits. Henry marched on Rome, imprisoned the pope in the Castel Sant' Angelo, and set up another pope, who crowned him emperor. Gregory was liberated by the Normans. With them he withdrew from Rome to die, saying, "I have loved justice and hated iniquity. Therefore I die in exile." Some years later Henry was forced by civil wars to abdicate and died soon after.

After long negotiations between new principals the dispute between emperor and pope resulted in a compromise. The Concordat of Worms in 1122 stated that bishops were to be appointed solely by the Church. After having been installed, they should swear fealty to the emperor. Essentially the Church had won. The system of lay investiture was at an end.

The clash had been between the papacy and the German empire. The great conflict between France and the papacy was postponed until the beginning of the fourteenth century. In Normandy there was no rupture, despite the lack of any concession on the part of the kings. Among the Normans the concept of sacral kingship had always prevailed, and their kings had completely controlled the Church. When William the Conqueror took England he continued this practice without opposition from Archbishop Lanfranc of Canterbury. The reason for Gregory's toleration of the Normans in Normandy and England may have been that he did not wish to alienate his Norman allies in Italy. Conflict ensured in England under William Rufus and later under the first two Henrys, with the Church increasing her leadership of Christian society.

Another step in that direction was taken by the launching of the crusades. The crusades were a compound of Viking lust for conquest and a zeal for the faith. They were also the culmination of a great effort to eradicate war between Christians in Europe. We have noted that the Cluny movement had sought to arrest feudal warfare by the imposition of restraints through the Peace of God and the Truce of God. The Truce restricted the times for fighting, allowing no hostilities from sunset Wednesday to Monday morning or on holy days, of which there were so many that warfare would have been reduced to a summer sport were the restrictions enforced. The Peace of God restricted the range of the combatants. There should be no attacks upon priests, nuns, or pilgrims or upon merchants or farmers, their animals, tools, or properties. Princes were called upon to vow to observe the rules, which were not too rigorously phrased. Robert the Pious, for example, swore that he would not attack women traveling without their husbands, unless they were found to be in the wrong. Such concession, however, meant little. Princes took the vows and broke the vows. Then bishops organized armies to punish the oathbreakers, and the Church's armies got out of hand and ravaged the country, so that kings raised armies to suppress the Church's armies.

Then in the year 1095 Pope Urban II, a former monk of Cluny, convoked the Council of Clermont. The eastern emperor, Alexius Comnenus, had appealed to the pope for help against the Seljuk Turks, who had recently irrupted into the Levant. It was a period of unrest and strife within Europe itself. The investiture struggle was still dragging on; but Urban was on strong ground when he addressed the council in terms reminiscent of the great peace speeches in the councils of the preceding fifty years. Let Christians allay their feuds, he urged. Let them unite. Let them take to heart the atrocities practiced by the accursed Turks. Let them deliver the holy places from these infidels, and all the assembly cried, "*Dieu le veult* (God wills it)."

A new concept of war was involved here. Augustine had required that war should be conducted under the auspices of the state. Now it was under the auspices of the Church. Kings, to be sure, took the cross, but at the behest of the pope. According to Augustine the common soldier simply obeyed his prince. Now he volunteered by taking the cross, though, of course, a prince might summon his retainers. The object of the just war, according to Augustine, had been the vindication of justice, meaning primarily the defense of life and property. Now war was for the defense of the faith, or at any rate for the right of the faithful to exercise their faith. The code of the just war called for good faith with the enemy, regard for non-combatants, respect for hostages and prisoners. But all such restraints were abandoned in dealing with the infidel. The warrant for this view of warfare was found in the biblical account of the conquest of Canaan by Joshua.

The first crusade was primarily French. The Council of Clermont had been attended only by the French, among whom there were four groups of participants: the northern French, under Godfrey and Baldwin of Bouillon; the Provençals, under Raymond of Toulouse and Bishop Adhemar of Puy; the Normans of the North, under Robert of Normandy—the son of the Conqueror—and Robert of Flanders; and the Normans of Sicily, under Bohemund and Tancred. The Provençal group, which included a bishop, chosen as papal representative, was the most loyal to the pope.

Urban's hope would seem to have been that the holy places should be delivered from the Turks and then turned over to the eastern empire, but the crusaders were not so disinterested and soon were at odds with the eastern emperor and with each other. The emperor distrusted them at the outset; this was partly because the Greek and Latin Churches had broken decisively in 1054, when the Orthodox Church sharply rebuffed the demand of the Gregorian reformers that it recognize their claims for the papacy. A deeper reason may have been that these reformers, as we have observed, were northerners from Lorraine who had no sense of belonging to the Mediterranean world and no feeling for the Byzantine heritage. Another difference between the eastern emperors and the Franks lay in their attitudes toward the Moslems. The Byzantines, of course, considered themselves to be the guardians of the true faith. But they had relaxed sufficiently to permit a mosque in Constantinople, and they received emissaries from Moslem courts with ceremonial deference. To the easterners the crude zeal of these Franks was obnoxious and the participation of their clergy in fighting was shocking. Their motives also were suspect, for had not the Normans in 1082 tried to capture Durazzo from the Byzantines for no better reason than plunder?

But the emperor could not well turn back the crusaders when they arrived at Constantinople, and they could not go on without him. His solution was to demand oaths of fealty, after the manner of western feudalism. The resistance to taking the oath was most persistent on the part of the Provençals, who thought of themselves as the pope's men. But all, in the end, had to swear in order to secure support. After the host had crossed the Bosporus an initial victory over the Turks at Nicaea opened the way through Asia Minor, where the native Christian population regarded the crusaders as liberators. The struggle with the Moslems was resumed when the Christian forces reached Syria.

Then the divergence in aims among the crusaders became apparent. Baldwin, who was supposed to protect the flank, withdrew and ensconced himself in Edessa with every intention of setting up there an independent, feudal kingdom. Bohemund and Raymond of Toulouse quarreled as to who should have a kingdom in Antioch. The city resisted siege. Bohemund secured from the allies the promise that if he took Antioch he might keep it. Through a traitor he succeeded, but once inside the city the crusaders in turn were besieged by a newly arrived Turkish force. Famine threatened. Peter Bartholomew, one of Raymond's men, received a revelation that the holy lance that had pierced the side of Christ was buried in Antioch. Excavation produced what appeared to be a lance. The crusaders then, in joyous confidence, marched out of the city. The Turks were surprised and routed. Once more the question arose: who should have Antioch? Bohemund claimed it because he had taken the city; Raymond claimed it because his man Peter had found a way out of it. The solution was to give Bohemund Antioch and Raymond Tripoli. The leaders appeared more interested in carving kingdoms than in reaching the Holy City. Only the pressures from the papal party and the common soldiers held the crusaders together until they reached the walls of Jerusalem. The city succumbed in 1099. The crusaders waded to their ankles in the blood of the infidel, then proceeded to the Church of the Holy Sepulcher, singing in jubilation that Christ had conquered. His followers had returned to the city where he had been crucified. Now, once more, pilgrims flocked freely to the East, and with them came knights and traders, and an increase in contacts between the West and the Arabs and Greeks. Christian Europe had begun its first great expansion across the seas.

VII
Medieval Christendom

Abbot Suger, the administrative and
financial genius of the early twelfth century,
appears at the feet of the Virgin in this
window from the abbey of St. Denis.

Jerusalem fell to the Crusaders in the year 1099, on the threshold of a new century that saw such an upsurge of intellectual activity and creative enterprise that the period has been called the medieval renaissance. During the twelfth and the thirteenth centuries, in fact, in virtually every phase of European culture the Middle Ages reached its highest achievements. It was during this period that the first European universities were founded and that scholastic philosophy—scholasticism—reached its most developed form. Chivalry flourished, and with it the new ideal of romantic love contributed to a greater refinement of life.

Especially in the thirteenth century the papacy possessed more power than any other institution and directed even the political affairs of Europe. The ideals of the Church had an impact on every aspect of culture. An increased ethical sensitivity issued in a sense of guilt that sought redemption through the passion of Christ, a sensitivity that found transcendent expression in the flowering of Gothic art. A new type of monasticism that resisted the materialism of society evolved to minister to an increasingly urban and commercial world.

The empire of Charlemagne had been a web of villages. If the old Roman centers of population had not been entirely deserted, it was because they remained the seats of bishops, who administered both the spiritual and the temporal affairs of the dioceses. The late tenth century saw the beginning of the resumption of urban life, together with the renewal of commerce and a monied economy; even the Vikings had come to prefer trading to raiding. The cities in the West, to be sure, were never large during the Middle Ages, in comparison, for example, with Constantinople, which in medieval times had about a million inhabitants. Even at the beginning of the fourteenth century the largest European cities rarely exceeded a population of between fifty and one hundred thousand people. Most, probably, had a population of less than ten thousand.

Economic life within the new little cities early came under the control of the guilds, voluntary commercial associations of individual merchants or craftsmen formed for mutual advantage. The guilds were essentially monopolistic and protectionist: they regulated the quantity and quality of goods produced, set fixed prices for goods and fixed wages for guild members, and rigorously guarded trade secrets. Quarrels were frequent between guilds in related crafts: between harness makers and saddlers, between cooks and mustard makers, between menders of old shoes and makers of new ones. The guilds of one town forbade competing goods to enter from another town. But although they were organized in self-interest the guilds were not without regard for the ethical restraints imposed by the Church. The Church condemned usury—interest in almost every form was called usury—and possible censure by the Church served as a constant reminder to those concerned with credit. The Church distrusted the merchants because they lusted for money; however, it encouraged them to expiate their avarice by contributions to the Church. Guilty consciences thus helped to build cathedrals and to succor the poor.

Within themselves the guilds were charitable organizations, supporting their own needy, building and maintaining hospitals, as well as contributing to public works of various sorts. They were prominent in the religious life of the community: they excluded heretics from their membership; they celebrated the numerous holy days; they assumed the responsibility for the performance of miracle plays when these were moved from the cathedral to the market place; and they contributed stained-glass windows to the cathedrals, such as those at Chartres, where the crafts are depicted. Each guild had its own patron saint; for as there were saints to ward off particular diseases, so there were others to protect particular crafts: Saint Eloi for the goldsmiths, Saint Vincent for the wine growers, Saint Fiacre for the gardeners, Saint Blaise for the masons, Saint Crispin for the shoemakers, and Saint Julian for the village fiddlers.

Besides being trading centers, the cities became the seats of universities. During the Middle Ages some eighty universities were founded, many of which have had an unbroken, distinguished history to our own day: for example, Paris, Montpellier, Bologna, Padua, Oxford, Cambridge, Vienna, Prague, Leipzig, Heidelberg, Basel, Coimbra, Salamanca, Cracow, and Louvain. The oldest of these schools were in operation before the year 1200, although they were not chartered until about that year or slightly later. Salerno, in southern Italy, whose medical school dates back at least to the eleventh century, early achieved distinction, although it did not become a true university until the thirteenth. It was a great medical center for two centuries, but then declined, probably because other universities had instituted medical faculties. Paris, for example, had four faculties: arts (which included philosophy), canon law, theology, and medicine; the outstanding studies were philosophy and theology. Bologna was preeminent in law, both canon and civil. (The degree of LL.D. stands for Doctor of Laws, with "laws" in the plural, signifying the two varieties.) In the twelfth century a new compilation of the canon law was made by Gratian, a monk of Bologna. For centuries to come his work had a vast influence on the administration of the Church and on the rendering of justice throughout the Christian world. The civil law was the old Roman law, which in the centuries of disorder had been partially supplanted by Germanic codes but which, following the rediscovery of the Justinian Code, was now revived. Other centers of legal studies were the universities of Padua and Orleans.

The universities' interest in theology stemmed in part from the fact that some of them had developed from church schools. With the rise of the cities, monastic schools were supplanted by educational centers attached to cathedral chapters, some of which in turn developed into universities; as, for example, the cathedral school of Notre Dame at Paris. Everywhere throughout the Middle Ages theology was considered the queen of the sciences, with philosophy and other disciplines as her handmaidens. The intense preoccupation with the problems of theology and philosophy marked the revival of a spirit of enquiry and of confidence in the power of human reason such as the world had not known since the great age of Greece. The later Middle Ages might well be called the Age of Logic.

The problem that agitated philosophers and theologians concerned the ultimate nature of reality: does reality cohere—that is, is it a unity of immaterial and material things bound by an essential universal relationship—or does it consist simply in the sum of independent and unrelated individual elements? The advocates of coherence were called realists, because they believed in the reality of universals: that universals were the only reality and that individual things had no reality except as they partook of the nature of universals. Thus, the concept of humanity is a reality, a universal in which all individuals cohere.

Those with opposing views were called nominalists, because they held that humanity, for instance, has no reality but is just a name (in Latin, *nomen*) for a set of common characteristics shared by all human beings; that is, mankind has no reality, only individual men do. The realists were divided into extremists and moderates. The first maintained that universals exist as entities conceived in the mind of God before becoming concrete, so that there is humanity apart from human beings. The moderate realists said that universals do exist but only as they comprise concrete particulars. Humanity is a reality, but does not exist apart from individual men.

Such views had far-reaching implications for theology, ethics, science, and institutions. In theology the doctrine of the Trinity was supported by the view called realism, for if *deity* is a universal, then the Father, the Son, and the Spirit are held in unity by deity; in the nominalist view, on the other hand, reality consists only of individuals, the three persons become three individual gods, and the concept of the Trinity becomes tritheism—in short, heresy. In ethics the concept of natural law was affected. In the one case law is the expression of universal principles grounded in the very structure of the universe; in the other it is simply the common element in the ways in which people actually behave. In science the realistic view led to a quest for universal law; the nominalist centered attention upon the examination of individual phenomena, collecting data and constructing categories mainly for purposes of convenience, without claiming for them any objective reality.

On the realist basis the Church, the state, and the family cohere within themselves because they are the concretions of transcendent reality, whereas on the nominalist assumption the Church is an assemblage brought into being by a covenant between individuals; the state is an association made by contract, and, similarly, marriage is a contractual union. In the Middle Ages the great conflicting tendencies of centralization and decentralization receive from these divergent views a philosophical undergirding. The realist view subordinates the individual and can rationalize even a totalitarian degree of centralization, but the nominalist view, with its individualism, encourages decentralization, conceivably even to the point of anarchism.

A more vexing and most fundamental problem for the theologians was whether it could be proved that God exists. There has never been an age of such unquestioning faith that men have not experienced difficulty in believing the claims of the Christian religion. From the Middle Ages we have the confessions of the monk Othlo, who was driven to desperation by his inability to believe in God. To assuage the torment of such a spirit Saint Anselm, the archbishop of Canterbury from 1093 to 1109, sought to discover an irrefragably logical proof for God's existence. Rumination on the subject so disturbed his devotions that he was about to abandon the attempt as presumptuous when, in the night watches, a flash of illumination presented the solution.

Anselm argued that the existence of the idea of God necessarily implies the very existence of God. Thus: by the notion of God we mean something so great that nothing greater can be conceived. Something so great must exist, because that which does not exist, but which in other respects is greater than anything else which can be conceived, can never be as great as something than which nothing greater can be conceived and which also exists. Therefore, something than which nothing greater can be conceived exists. God, being that something, consequently must exist. This is called the ontological argument for God's existence. It did not satisfy all theologians even in the Middle Ages but in variant form it has never ceased to attract religious thinkers.

This method of applying philosophical speculation toward a better understanding of Christian faith and doctrine is called scholasticism. Strictly speaking the term means "that which is taught in the schools"; but in a more restricted sense it signifies a form of Christian theology that commences with an affirmation, or thesis, sets against it a critical doubt, or antithesis, and then by logical ratiocination seeks to achieve a resolution, or synthesis. While recognizing a realm of truths transcending human reason, scholasticism sought to demonstrate and elucidate these truths to the limit of human reason. By such means it sought, moreover, to harmonize the many disparate and often contradictory elements within the Christian tradition.

During the course of the twelfth and the thirteenth centuries the students and scholars and teachers of the western world were confronted by an influx of new knowledge and new ideas for their logic to feed upon. By way of the schools and courts of southern Europe, principally the school at Toledo in Spain, western Christendom was introduced to the portions of the legacy of ancient Greece that had been long lost to the West and to the scientific writings of the Islamic East. Thus the bulk of

Aristotle's writings on science and metaphysics was again available to western Europe, and it became the task of schoolmen and churchmen to reconcile such pagan knowledge with the established truths of Christianity.

Out of the increasing prosperity that accompanied the resumption of urban culture emerged new refinements of life, among them the development of chivalry. The essential figure in chivalry was the armored knight on horseback. In the earlier Middle Ages he had been an anarchic figure, avenging his own wrongs by unbridled private warfare. Chivalry imposed on him a code of honor, which the Church could sanction while seeking to enlist his arms for the succoring of the oppressed. The tournament, as a training or a substitute for war, could receive only the qualified approval of the Church. Chivalry long outlasted the crusading movement, to which it had given its best and worst endeavors. The concept of *noblesse oblige* could easily be sanctioned, but the continued glorification of the martial spirit evoked the qualms of churchmen.

Among those whom the knight undertook to protect were ladies, especially those in distress. His interest was often more than a concern for their distress. In courtly circles in the south of France arose the cult of romantic love, celebrated in the poems of the troubadours. The romantic view of love was something new in history. In classical antiquity love was either a joke, as with Ovid, or a sickness, as with Virgil in his description of Dido's passion for Aeneas. But courtly love as it was conceived in the Midi idealized woman, from whom, it was believed, nobility was transmitted to the worshipful lover. To his lady he owed undeviating devotion.

But courtly love was not associated with marriage. Commonly the lover addressed himself to a woman already married. The languishing in the poetry of the troubadours reflected his constant frustration. Romantic love was held to be incompatible with marriage because such love must be free, a gift of grace, not something that could be claimed as due. Eleanor of Aquitaine declared that ideal love and marriage are incompatible. She had had experience enough of loveless marriage, having been wed for political reasons first to Louis VII, king of France, and then to Henry II, king of England.

Romantic love was a rebellion against the prevalent medieval view of marriage, in accordance with which unions were ar-

Commentaries on Aristotle by the Moslem
Averroës won a wide audience, but they were
condemned by the Church. It remained
for Albertus Magnus and his pupil Thomas
Aquinas to acclimate Aristotle to orthodox
Christian theology. Here, Averroës lies
vanquished as a ray of truth from Aquinas's
Summa Theologica strikes him.

ranged by landowners with an eye to consolidating properties and by royalty in order to enlarge kingdoms. Property married property. Children were betrothed in infancy. Henry II of England, for example, arranged to marry his six-year-old son John to the heiress of Maurienne, a territory that commanded the passes of the Alps. In all this there was almost no regard for personal feeling. However, the system made for stability in the institution of marriage; infidelities were tolerated and did not disrupt marriages. And in some instances, to be sure, a tender mutual affection developed out of such arrangements.

The romantic view of love and marriage also contrasted with the attitude of the Church, for whom marriage was numbered among the seven sacraments, which were first formulated by Peter Lombard about the middle of the twelfth century. Yet the campaign for clerical celibacy had been waged with a general disparagement of marriage and of woman, who was portrayed as the gateway to hell. In any case the sacrament was not contingent on love between the partners, and the union might in certain circumstances be dissolved, without regard for personal attachments. For example, the Church was strict in applying the rules of consanguinity: these forbade the marriage of cousins to the seventh degree of relationship, corresponding to the number of days in the week. (The degree was reduced to the fourth by the thirteenth century.) If after marriage even a remote blood relationship was discovered, the couple, no matter how devoted, had to be separated. The godparent also was considered to be related to the godchild, and his children to the godchildren, and they were subject to the same marriage restrictions as were those related by actual blood ties.

Romantic love was a passionate rebellion against loveless marriage and an affirmation of the dignity of the relation between the sexes. So long as it was extra-matrimonial the Church looked upon it as heresy, but in time marriage was considered proper only if it was the consummation of a romantic attachment.

The nature of romantic love and the intellectual ferment of scholasticism were both exemplified in the life of Peter Abelard (1079–1142), one of the outstanding figures of the age. When he was twenty he became a student at the cathedral school of Notre Dame in Paris, and he later became a teacher there. His generation was dazzled by the brilliance of his dialectic and the acumen of his conclusions. On the great problem of universals he took the position of moderate realism, a view called conceptualism. The universals conceived by man, he said, are not intangible realities, as the extreme realists believed, nor are they mere names, as the nominalists claimed; but they are clues to reality. His view became the common scholastic assumption in the thirteenth century.

Abelard did much to develop the scholastic method of reasoning by his book *Sic et Non* (*Yes and No*), in which he compiled real or apparent contradictions in the writings of the Scriptures and of the Church Fathers. His purpose was not to discredit the faith but to resolve the problems he had raised. When his writings were challenged, Abelard accepted the authority of the Church, but he sought always to understand that he might believe. In this respect, also, he was an architect of the scholastic method.

When he was about forty and she about eighteen, Abelard was attracted by the intellectual precocity and the comeliness of Héloïse, niece of Fulbert, a canon of the Cathedral of Notre Dame. Abelard became her tutor, with the consent of her uncle, who lodged him in his own dwelling, where Héloïse also lived. Abelard faithfully discharged his assignment in instruction, but, as he later recalled, soon there were more kisses than syllogisms and he was singing to her the songs of the troubadours. When she informed him that she was pregnant he took her to his sister's home in Brittany, where they were together until the birth of their son.

Then Abelard proposed that they marry, but she demurred. Her objections reveal the various crosscurrents of the age. First of all she told him that he should continue in a churchly career that would call for celibacy. He might have pursued an academic career as a married layman, but a teacher's fees would not support a family. She pointed out that he would have to take on extra employ to the detriment of his studies. She was not willing to ruin his career in Church and school. But if they were to continue their relationship she preferred to remain unwed, because marriage had been so demeaned by subordination to the interests of property; "I desire," she said, "not yours, but you." The tragic sequel has often been related with sensitivity in modern times and need not be recounted here, save to note that they did marry and yet ended their lives in monasticism, she as an abbess, he as a monk of Cluny.

The age that conceived the ideal of courtly love also witnessed a resurgence of ascetic monasticism. Most important of the several new orders that were founded around the turn of the twelfth century was the Cistercian. Like the others, the Cistercians originated out of a discontent with the Cluniacs, who were criticized for having accommodated their system too much to worldly considerations. They were reproached because of their wealth, because they left manual labor to servants, and because as extraordinary entertainers they fraternized too much with the world. The Cluniacs, it was claimed, were not spiritual even in their prayers, for they rattled off interminable petitions for the souls of others while making no provision for solitude that they might cultivate their own souls. The Cluniac churches were regarded as vast monuments to the pride of man, decorated with grotesque hybrid forms, as in the sculptured capitals of their cloisters and chapter houses, that distracted rather than aided devotion. The Cistercians returned to unadorned simplicity in such matters; they would not even tolerate stained-glass windows.

The Cistercians called for a withdrawal from the world with its wealth, complexity, clutter, and bustle, and a return to a literal observance of Benedict's rule, especially in its emphasis on manual labor in the fields. They were resolved to accept no gift of rich, cultivated land with retainers to do the manual labor. Instead they took waste land and broke it in. They reduced forests to fields and turned swamps into "golden meadows." They had experimental greenhouses and devoted themselves to animal husbandry, intensive agriculture, milling, and weaving. Such activities had a marked effect upon the economic advance of Europe, especially of the northern lands.

Much of the ground that the Cistercians took over, however, was untillable, and they used it to pasture sheep. In time they produced more wool than the monks could wear and took the surplus to the market; the wool of the Cistercians became famous. They then became involved in the world that they had eschewed. Moreover, although they would have no serfs, they did accept lay brothers called *conversi*, who, having taken vows, would not tend to secularize the monastery, but who nevertheless did relieve the monks of manual labor. Within two centuries, in matters of discipline and austerity the Cistercians were scarcely to be distinguished from other orders. For a century or more after their founding, however, the Cistercians had a profound effect upon the culture of Europe, partly inadvertently through the impact of their improved and highly successful husbandry, partly because they constituted the most important monastic order and the chief religious influence in the West.

The degree and nature of this influence is well illustrated in the career of the great Cistercian abbot, Bernard of Clairvaux, who was more powerful than any pope of the twelfth century. Bernard was born of a noble family in southern France in 1090. He was deeply religious from an early age and devoted to the Virgin Mary. With irresistible zeal he gathered a band of thirty companions, including his brothers, relations, and friends, who with him joined the Cistercians at Cîteaux. In 1115 Bernard was appointed abbot of a daughter monastery in a desolate and forbidding valley that he christened Clairvaux, the beautiful valley. He remained the abbot of Clairvaux until his death. Subjecting himself to hard labor and great privation, he was so abstracted from the things of the sense that when he drank he did not distinguish oil from water. But he was also such a marvelous preacher and a person of such great moral force that the world would not leave him alone. He was constantly called away from his cell to adjudicate disputes in the Church, rebuke the mighty, and vindicate the Church and God.

Following the death of Pope Honorius II in 1130, for example, a disputed election left two contenders for the papacy, Anacletus II and Innocent II. Bernard considered the latter the better man and decided in his favor, without concern about which of the two elections conformed more to canonical rules. The next and greater task was to persuade those sovereigns of Europe who supported Anacletus II to transfer their allegiance to Innocent II. A further complication was that in every diocese, when the bishop declared for one pope, a rival, in the name of the other pope, would lay claim to the see, and the king might be willing to accept the right pope without being willing to renounce the wrong bishop.

Bernard ensured the allegiance of all the rulers of Europe but two: William of Aquitaine and Roger, the Norman, of Sicily. William would not repudiate the wrong local bishop. Bernard placed him under excommunication, then proceeded to celebrate the Mass. William, being excluded, stood outside the door.

The courtly-love convention that flourished in feudal society encouraged romantic love but found it to be incompatible with marriage. The choice of marriage partner was governed by other considerations, including this consanguinity table, which cites the relatives between whom marriage was forbidden by the Church.

After consecrating the elements Bernard strode down the aisle, and with the host in his hands addressed him: "We have besought you and you have spurned us. The company of God's servants has implored you and these also you have spurned. See before you now the Virgin's Son, the head and master of the Church which you persecute, comes to you. Before you is your judge, the judge of heaven, earth, and hell in whose presence every knee shall bow. Before you is the judge into whose hands your soul will fall. Dare you spurn and disdain him as you have done his servants?" At these words William became rigid with terror and fell as if dead. His knights lifted him, but he fell again, salivating over his beard like an epileptic. Bernard pushed him with his foot, told him to get up and kiss the right bishop of Poitiers, and William complied.

Roger was more obdurate but finally capitulated. Against him and Anacletus Bernard built up a coalition that was joined by the kings of France and England and the emperor, among others, and that temporarily expelled Roger from southern Italy. When Anacletus died and his successor, persuaded by Bernard, resigned after two months, Roger accepted Innocent in return for that pope's confirmation of his royal title. In 1145 one of Bernard's own monks was elected pope as Eugenius III, and Bernard continued to advise and chide him as if he were still Eugenius's abbot.

Bernard looked upon his withdrawal from the world as vocational and did not expect or wish all men to take the cowl. Some should be monks, some should be soldiers, and soldiers should devote their swords to the vindication of justice and the service of the Church. Obeying Eugenius's command, one year after the pope's consecration Bernard preached the ill-fated second crusade with such extraordinary eloquence that, as he wrote the pope, "villages and towns are now deserted." Writing to the crusading Knights Templars, Bernard said: "The soldier may securely kill, kill for Christ and more securely die. He benefits himself if he dies and Christ if he kills. To kill a malefactor is not homicide but malicide [the killing of the bad]. In the death of the pagan the Christian is glorified because Christ is glorified."

The Knights Templars, so named because they occupied a house in Jerusalem that adjoined a building presumed to be Solomon's Temple, adopted a form of the Cistercian rule that Bernard is said to have drawn up. The order was, in any case, both monastic and military and was devoted to the defense of Christianity and the Holy Land. Such a conjunction of monasticism and militarism would have seemed to earlier ages a defection from the ideal of monasticism. Unable to eradicate militarism, the Church now sought to direct it to Christian ends.

The great impact of Bernard on the centuries to come lay in his mysticism and particularly in his insistence that love is superior to knowledge and goes beyond all knowledge; that is, not carnal love, but love of God. To Bernard, Abelard's quest for knowledge was arrogant probing into mysteries that are beyond the reach of man's mind. Bernard's sermons on the Song of Solomon remain the best known of many monastic commentaries on these Canticles. He interpreted them allegorically as nuptial songs or poems on the mystical marriage between the human soul and Christ. He likened the bride addressing the bridegroom in the verse "Let him kiss me with the kiss of his mouth," to the soul thirsting for God, breathing a sacred flame.

During the lifetimes of Abelard and Bernard there re-emerged in the western world a fundamentally personal view of sin. Centuries earlier Saint Augustine had acutely experienced such a sense of sin, but in subsequent years it had been virtually unrecognized. The early barbarian converts had been uninhibited in their behavior and untormented by any pangs of remorse. The development of the penitential system in feudal society had led to a more objective view, at least in some quarters, that regarded a specified amount of penance as proper satisfaction paid for each sinful act. Monks, to be sure, included the penitential psalms in their weekly devotions, but how deep was their sorrow over their offenses? Only with a developed sensitivity does a sense of unworthiness emerge.

In this period men turned to the suffering Christ for their protection. For Constantine and for Clovis, Christ had been the victor over death rather than the suffering Redeemer. But with a deeper sense of sin came an emphasis upon the passion of Christ and the expiation of sin. This may explain why Saint Anselm in the last years of the eleventh century wrote his *Cur Deus Homo* (*Why God Became Man*). His answer was not that of the Greek Fathers of the Church, that God became man in order that man might become God, but rather in order that man might be forgiven. Anselm's views were based on the feudal view of sin, which rated its enormity in terms of the rank of the person against whom it was committed. Since God is infinite in his greatness, a sin against him is infinite. Such a sin requires infinite satisfaction, or atonement; and since it is man who commits such sin, it must also be man who suffers in atonement for it. But man, a finite being, is not capable of infinite suffering. Only a being who is both human and divine, and thus infinite, can offer adequate satisfaction as expiation; that being is Christ, in whom God became incarnate and who offered himself in death as atonement for the sins of man. That Anselm who devised the ontological argument for the existence of God here wrestled with the excruciating question of the redemption of man, the infinite sinner.

A poignant expression of this view of atonement is found in a letter of Abelard to Héloïse, written after the calamity that terminated their carnal relation, when he was seeking to divert her passion from himself to the heavenly Bridegroom. He wrote: "Dearest sister, are you not moved to compunction by the sight of the only begotten of God who, although he was innocent, yet for you and for all men was taken by the impious, was scourged, mocked, spat upon, crowned with thorns, and executed between thieves by so frightful and shameful a death? Look upon him, your bridegroom and the bridegroom of the Church. See him on the way, staggering beneath his cross. Take your place with the throng and the women who wept as he passed by. He bought you not with his own but with himself. With his own blood he bought you and redeemed you. What, I ask, did he, who lacked nothing, see in you that he should do battle for you in the agonies of death so ignominious? What did he seek in you except yourself? He is the true lover who seeks not yours but you."

The religious ardor that pervaded every area of life in the eleventh, twelfth, and thirteenth centuries found its tangible expression in a veritable fever of church building. Between 1050 and 1350 in France alone several million tons of stone were quarried and carted to construct eighty cathedrals, five hundred large churches, and thousands of smaller edifices. The great monastic establishments that developed so abundantly and importantly in the eleventh and twelfth centuries were mostly built in what has become known as the Romanesque style, a bold, strong style of architecture that with its round arches and thick walls supporting barrel vaults recalls—as the name implies—the monumental structures built by the ancient Romans.

Appearing first in the Ile-de-France about the middle of the twelfth century and then spreading throughout much of northern Europe, the Gothic style emerged from and replaced the Romanesque. In its most typical form the new architecture was an architecture of the cathedral rather than of the monastery, an architecture that was also primarily of the city and the public square. The cathedral was more than a church, it was a community house and the seat of municipal government. For a time, at least, the cities with cathedrals did not build city halls, because business was conducted in the church; the only sacred portion of the building was the sanctuary, whereas the nave could be put to mundane uses. The cathedral was often large enough to accommodate the entire populace of the bishopric. Amiens Cathedral could hold nearly ten thousand persons, the total population of the city when the structure was built.

The building of a cathedral did much to unite the community. During the construction of the cathedral at Chartres, for example, the town's inhabitants, from nobles to children, harnessed themselves to carts like beasts to haul the stones, and, it is said, tugged in silence, save for penitential prayers when they paused for rest. Even mortal foes competed in the common purpose of beautifying the house of God. At Chartres the rose window of the south transept was given by Pierre de Dreux, and the rose window of the north transept bears the fleurs-de-lis of France and the castles of Castile, showing that it was given by King Louis and the queen mother Blanche. Although Pierre, with other French barons, had at one point conspired to kidnap Louis and incarcerate Blanche, the rose windows face each other across the transepts, and the colored light from each is blended in the glow upon the stones beneath.

With its massive walls, its relatively low vaults, and its enclosed, dark interiors, Romanesque architecture suggests enduring stability and austerity. The Gothic cathedral expressed new concepts in terms of height and light. Cathedral builders strove to achieve the utmost height that they could reach with their materials, and their accomplishments were astonishing. The spire of Chartres Cathedral rises over three hundred feet; its nave is over one hundred feet high. At Beauvais the cathedral's spire rose to five hundred feet before it collapsed; the roof also fell, but then stronger supports were erected and the vaulted interior finally reached to more than one hundred fifty-seven feet. Flying buttresses made possible thinner walls, slenderer piers, and the opening of walls into spacious windows with myriad pieces of jewel-like colored glass.

Unlike the Byzantine church, the Gothic cathedral did not convey a sense of composure but rather one of precarious balance. Thrust was met by counterthrust, as in scholastic theology thesis was confronted by antithesis. The capitals of the columns and the borders of the windows set forth the glory of creation with accurate delineations of the flowers and the foliage of the burgeoning spring; the water spouts take the form of leering gargoyles, sardonic minions of the Prince of Darkness, who could insinuate himself into the very house of God. The cathedral expresses all those forces battling for the soul of man, to whom tranquility is not granted on his earthly pilgrimage. He can but walk in hope and faith that he who was slain has conquered and "the Lord God Omnipotent reigneth."

Gothic architecture enshrines the torment and the tension, the sense of guilt and the joy of redemption, the struggle of man to scale the battlements of heaven and the outstretched arm of God reaching down to assist his ascent. To instruct and edify the congregation, painted and carved images and stories told in stained glass were incorporated in the architecture and adorned the walls of cathedrals as graphic adjuncts to the written word. Chartres alone includes more than eight thousand images in various mediums; it was virtually a pictorial encyclopedia encased in a stone binding. Here, as elsewhere, was portrayed the whole drama of the Redemption, from the Creation to the Last Judgment. Here were the patriarchs and the prophets, the apostles and the evangelists, the doctors and the saints, and above all the blessed Redeemer, especially in his birth and passion. The Passion received a prominent place as the focus of the piety of the age. The separate episodes of the Passion were depicted on the walls of the church in the stations of the cross, among which were the trial before Pilate; Christ, with the crown of thorns, receiving the cross; the several scenes of the *via dolorosa*, with Christ stumbling and Simon of Cyrene being given the cross to carry; the Crucifixion; the descent from the cross; and the entombment of Christ. Whether in stone or glass there were also portrayals of the Resurrection and Ascension, of the Last Judgment, the enthronement of Christ, the coronation of the Virgin, and presiding over all, God the Almighty and Beneficent Father surrounded by the company of the heavenly host singing the praises of the Lamb that was slain. And here, too, were scenes from the lives of the saints depicted in anecdotal detail that in some cases is otherwise not recorded, as well as themes from the apocryphal gospels and other popular religious literature.

That the Gothic style spread as rapidly as it did, first within France and then to neighboring countries, reflects not only the predominance of French culture but an essential unity within the international Church organization. The Gregorian reform that envisioned a Christian theocracy governing the world through the Roman pontiff underwent further developments in the late twelfth and the thirteenth centuries. Struggles had increased between Church and state over the source of authority and the hegemony of power.

One aspect of this persistent controversy was the dispute over the administration of justice. Both Church and king had their separate courts and systems of law. The canon law of the Church applied to a wide variety of circumstances, which often brought it into direct conflict with the claims of the secular law under civil authorities. The Church defended the right of women to inherit property; it first introduced the making of wills; it denied that possession is nine-tenths of the law and prohibited usury. The Church claimed jurisdiction over all cases involving clerics, and this meant a vast number of property disputes, because the Church held so much property vested in the names of abbots and bishops. Since it claimed jurisdiction over all cases involving the sacraments, and since marriage was a sacrament, all matrimonial cases were supposed to be referred to Church courts. Usury and perjury were sins in her eyes, rather than simply civil crimes, and where the state did not act in such matters the Church presumed to judge and sentence.

The greatest clash came over the application of penalties. The Church was scarcely more humanitarian than the state, although when the punishment involved the shedding of blood, the carrying out of the sentence was delegated to the secular power. For example, Saint Dunstan, the abbot of Glastonbury in the tenth century, refused on one occasion to say Mass until justice had been executed on some counterfeiters. The justice consisted in chopping off their hands. In the twelfth century Saint Bernard sent a letter of reproof to Theobald, the count of Champagne,

The crusader castle of Krak des Chevaliers,
shown here, guarded the northern approaches
to the Holy Land. After Saladin recaptured
Jerusalem from the Christians, successive
crusades all failed to regain control of the
Holy Land. With little evidence of the
religious devotion that had charged earlier
efforts, the later crusaders were more often
marching for their own political gain.

on whose orders a man defeated in a duel had had his eyes put out and his goods confiscated. Bernard protested against the confiscation of his goods because this impinged upon the rights of his innocent family, but had no word of remonstrance over his being blinded.

But the Church would not suffer capital punishment or bodily mutilation to be inflicted on clerics, although clerics were quite as capable as laymen of any crime. In England the crown maintained that a criminal should not be treated more leniently because of clerical status. This was part of the conflict between King Henry II of England and Thomas à Becket, the archbishop of Canterbury. Henry was struggling valiantly to organize the judicial administration in his realm. He did not demand that the Church's courts be disbanded. He was quite willing that clerics be tried by the Church, but if they were pronounced guilty, Henry wished that they then be committed to the secular arm for the same punishment accorded to laymen. Becket had been made archbishop by the king because he had been his majesty's chancellor and the king wanted strong support in his reforms; but after his consecration Becket transferred his homage from the king to the Church, and he would not suffer the rights of the Church to be abrogated. The outcome of the subsequent conflict between the two is well known. Henry, being at the time in France, muttered in the presence of some knights, "Is there no one to rid me of this priest?" The knights made off for England. Henry surmised their intent too late to intervene. Becket fell in 1170, Henry in his contrition did penance at his tomb, and the elimination of clerical immunities in England was postponed to a later age.

At the same time on the Continent Pope Alexander III came into conflict with Frederick Barbarossa, the first to be called Holy Roman emperor. The emperor was seeking to regain the control of the Italian territories that his predecessors had possessed and lost. In the attempt the liberties of the newly risen Italian towns of Lombardy were threatened, as was the independence of the papacy itself. After a struggle of many years the emperor was defeated in 1176 by the towns that had united in the Lombard League; he was forced to submit to the pope, and some years thereafter he was drowned while on the third crusade. The papacy had been victorious and was ready to enter upon its most dazzling century of power.

In terms of papal supremacy the thirteenth is the greatest of centuries, and the greatest pope in that century was Innocent III, who served as pontiff at the dawn of the century, from 1198 to 1216. Innocent was a trained canon lawyer; a marvelous administrator; an indefatigable champion of justice; a drastic foe of corruption; a mystic to whom could be attributed the authorship of the *Stabat Mater Dolorosa*, a hymn describing the sorrows of the Virgin at the cross; and the author of the treatise *De Contemptu Mundi (On Contempt of the World)*. Innocent has been called the greatest of medieval popes, and in his pontificate the Gregorian ideal of Church leadership was most nearly approximated.

Innocent's most spectacular achievements appear in his dealings with Europe's crowned heads. He asserted his authority in the elections and investiture of the Holy Roman emperor, by dint of adroit and continual manipulation seeking always to keep in power the party most favorable to the papacy. There were two parties striving for the imperial dignity, the Guelphs and Ghibellines. These parties had adherents in the Italian cities as well as in Germany, and their names were Italian corruptions of German words: *Guelph* was derived from the German family named Welf; *Ghibelline* from Waiblingen, the name of a fortress belonging to the House of Hohenstaufen, the family of Frederick Barbarossa. The Guelphs became identified as supporters of the papacy, the Ghibellines as the imperial, anti-papal party. By playing the one off against the other in a series of maneuvers, Innocent succeeded, in 1212, in placing his candidate on the throne in the person of Frederick II. In the struggle for authority the papal victory was assured.

In France Innocent had trouble with Philip Augustus, who had set aside his Danish wife, Ingeborg, and married the daughter of a Bavarian duke. The pope laid France under an interdict, an excommunication that applied not merely to the king but to all those within his realm. Within the interdicted area the rites of the Church were forbidden. No incense was burned, Mass was not said, and corpses were denied Christian burial. Whether marriage was invalidated is not altogether clear, but the prudent went beyond the interdicted territory to cement their vows. When Philip capitulated and the ban was lifted in 1200, so great was the rejoicing that three hundred persons were killed in the celebrations.

In the Iberian Peninsula Innocent annulled the marriage of Alfonso IX of Leon and Berengaria of Castile on grounds of consanguinity. They resisted for five years, but then Berengaria went into a convent. The king of Navarre was deposed for making a treaty with the Moors. The king of Aragon was crowned in Rome and gave his kingdom as a fief to Saint Peter, with the promise of a yearly tribute. In 1212, by his approval of a crusade against the Moors, Innocent encouraged the kingdoms of Aragon, Navarre, and Castile in a common action, which culminated in a victory for the Christians at the battle of Las Navas de Tolosa; this was a major step in their long-drawn-out reconquest of Spain.

In a quarrel over an appointment to the archbishopric of Canterbury Innocent forced King John of England to submit and to recognize the pope as his feudal overlord. Innocent also had dealings with all the outlying regions of Europe and with the kingdoms of the East. He aided Sweden in the establishment of a legitimate line of sovereigns. In Norway he protected the clergy from being brought before lay tribunals. In Denmark he resisted an ambitious bastard aspiring to the crown. In Hungary he supported the king against his brother and the bishop against the king. In Ireland the king of Connaught was made to respect the right of asylum. In Poland the bishops were incited to reform. The churches of Bulgaria, Serbia, and Armenia were induced to join the Roman fold, though these unions were only temporary. The Jews were protected against violence and intimidation.

In 1215 Innocent summoned the great Fourth Lateran Council, which was attended by the patriarchs of Jerusalem and Constantinople; twenty-nine archbishops, four hundred twelve bishops, and eight hundred abbots and priors; plus the envoys of the major rulers of Europe and the Levant, including the Holy Roman emperor, the emperor of the eastern empire, and the kings of England, France, Aragon, Hungary, and Jerusalem. Among other enactments of far-reaching importance, this council officially formulated the doctrine of transubstantiation, which teaches that when the priest at the altar pronounces the words "*hoc est corpus meum* (This is my body)," the substance of bread and wine is changed into the substance of the body and blood of Christ.

During the pontificate of Innocent III the introduction of a new type of monasticism strengthened the Church's leadership and influence in the changing medieval society. The members of the new orders were called not monks but brothers—in Italian *fratello*, or simply *fra*, in French *frère*, in English friar. The leaders of the new movement, Saint Francis and Saint Dominic, were partly opposed to and partly in accord with the spirit of their age. Both men, particularly Francis, rejected the rising commercialism. However, intensely spiritual though they were, they did not withdraw from the world as had earlier monks, but rather went out into it to perform their mission.

Francis was the son of a merchant of Assisi and of a French woman from the land of troubadours, the Midi. He had little sympathy for the acquisitiveness of his father and adored the blithe insouciance of his mother. He was a gay spirit who preferred larks to ledgers. However, as a result of serious illness he underwent a psychological change. Revelry began to pall and disquiet invaded his spirit. One night, when he had been singing in the streets following a party, a companion discovered him sitting in dejection, staring into space, and inquired, "What's the matter, Francis? Have you gotten married?" "Yes," he replied, "to the fairest of all brides, to the Lady Poverty." As his decision took form Francis—the Poverello, as he was called—dedicated his life to absolute poverty and to preaching and teaching among the poor, the outcasts, and the sick, whose number had grown with the changing conditions of the new urban society. The intensity of his dedication soon attracted a band of followers.

Franciscan poverty was not Cynic poverty. The object was not to secure peace of mind by divesting oneself in advance of all that might be taken away. It was not the poverty of the early Christians, who anticipated the imminent return of Christ. The poverty of Francis was indeed an emancipation from care, but basically it was in the very spirit of Christ himself. The renunciation of any claim to worldly goods removed all distraction from the service of God and the love of one's fellows. It was a more effective way to achieve peace among men than was the Peace of God, the Truce of God, or the building of a cathedral.

Francis' poverty bears no trace of despising the created world. Possessing nothing, he possessed everything, and rejoiced in wonder at God's creations. The saint composed the first recorded poem in the Italian language, "The Canticle of the Sun," in which the Most High is praised: for the sun, who is called a brother; for the moon and stars, "precious, bright, and fair"; for wind and fire; for water, flower, and fruit; and for the love of those who meekly suffer woe.

This very song expresses the thrust and counterthrust of joy in

In the late thirteenth century, men revered the Virgin passionately, depicting her in sculpture, stained glass, and painting. The illuminations above illustrate in part one of the hundreds of legends about Mary. Here, she saves the cleric Theophilus from damnation by getting his pact with the devil back for him and presenting it to him on his deathbed.

salvation and pain at the thought of Christ's passion, as does more markedly a legend from *The Mirror of Perfection*: "Inebriated with the love and compassion of Christ, the blessed Francis would betimes voice in the French tongue the most sweet melodies that welled up within him. . . . He would pick up a stick from the ground and lay it across his left arm and then in his right hand would draw another across it like a bow, as if he were playing on a viol or some other stringed instrument, and making appropriate gestures, he would sing in French of the Lord Jesus. But all this pantomime ended in tears, and his exuberance was dissolved in passion for Christ.

Francis so fervently meditated upon the passion of Christ that, it is recorded, before his death marks suggesting the wounds of the crucified Christ appeared on his hands and feet and side. The impact of Franciscan piety was attended by a change in the portrayal of the Crucifixion. Instead of the draped figure, composed and passionless, appeared the almost nude figure writhing in pain. An innovation, for some time resisted, was the crossing of the legs and the use of only one nail, so that one knee was bent, and the appearance of writhing rendered more realistic.

Francis' followers grew in numbers. Their mission was to bathe the lepers, work with the peasants, preach to the people. They were different from the older monastic orders in that their poverty was more drastic; further, Francis sought to guard it against any mitigation, either through the accumulated fruits of the friars' labor or the acceptance of large donations, lest his order go the way of the older Cluniac and Cistercian orders. The Franciscan friars might work or beg, but only for the needs of the day. The other difference was that for the Franciscans *stabilitas* was to be replaced by *mobilitas*. The brothers might have some rude shelters as a base, but their mission was to go to the people wherever they were congregated and where the need of physical help and spiritual guidance was greatest, and that meant primarily in the cities.

The mission on which Francis and his followers had embarked would not for long be tolerated by the local churchmen, with whom they competed wherever they traveled, unless authorized by the pope. In 1210 Francis sought and obtained approval of his group as a separate order from Innocent III, who, however, laid upon them a restriction in view of their lack of learning. They were not to discuss theology, but were to preach penitence. This meant that they must center on sin, remorse, and forgiveness through the merits of the passion of the Redeemer. The sins against which they most commonly inveighed were sodomy, usury, luxury, vanity, and vengeance. The Franciscans were renowned for the reconciliation of feuds. Into town and hamlet, village and farm, market and leper house these troubadours of God went, preaching and singing.

The order grew and that made for trouble. Society can manage a dozen unpredictable, improvident poets, but five hundred is another matter. How could they survive by begging only for the day? Some days were bound to be lean. When one of the brothers was seen sorting filthy lucre with a stick, he was reproached by another, but he replied, What was to be done with so many bellies to feed? Cardinal Ugolino, the protector of the order, came forward with a happy suggestion. Let the Church assume the burden of ownership (*dominium*), and let the brothers have the use (*usus*). Some of the brothers agreed to this, and they became the Conventuals. Some did not; they became the Spirituals.

Francis was very unhappy over the trend away from the stark simplicity of his original program. After his death the rift among the Franciscans became overt. Brother Elias, who was devoted to Saint Francis, was less enamored of poverty and simplicity than his master had been, and started to build a church in the saint's honor at Assisi. But great churches cannot be built by unskilled troubadours of God. Masons must be engaged and paid. Elias set up a money box which Brother Leo smashed. Sister Clare—an early convert who became the head of a branch order for women—sympathized with Leo. The unity of the order was seriously imperiled by the violence of such discussions, and although this temporarily abated, the Spirituals were subject to persecution. In time the order by and large went the way of the earlier monastic orders, although radical groups repeatedly split off from the parent organization.

The Dominicans, named for Saint Dominic, a Spaniard of noble birth, were in many ways similar to the Franciscans. Late in the twelfth century heretical sects—notably the Albigenses around Albi and the Waldenses around Lyons in southern France—had risen to challenge the papacy. While accompanying his bishop through the Midi, Dominic observed the devoutness of the heretics he saw there, who outdid the monks themselves in their extreme asceticism. He perceived that they would never be reclaimed by bishops riding on luxurious palfreys. The upholders of the true faith would have to commend it by imitation of the Master, "who had nowhere to lay his head." With Dominic poverty was not so much an ideal as a technique, and poverty of itself, he realized, would not suffice. To overcome false teaching there must be true teaching. Dominic founded his order to combat the ignorance of both clergy and laity. Although it was called the Order of Preachers, it was primarily a teaching order composed of friars trained in theology and the vernacular tongues. For a number of years the Dominicans sought to convert the Albigenses, but they met with only very limited success. However, with their zeal for learning the friars of the Dominican order supplied important leadership in the intellectual life of the Church.

It is strange that the period when the Church exercised its greatest control over European society also saw the revival of schisms and heresies. Why, when the ecclesiastical structure was most completely integrated, should these fissures have appeared? The early Church had known many splits, and the period from the twelfth century to the twentieth had been notoriously divisive. But from the barbarian invasions until the 1100's the Church in the West was able to maintain a fairly united structure, perhaps because the low level of general culture during that period militated against theological concern. But men can quarrel without theology, and the divisions of the twelfth and thirteenth centuries were not only theological. The Church in the early Middle Ages was held together by the struggle against paganism and anarchy, while monasticism provided a sufficient outlet for individualism and diversity. When the Church grew more rigid, the cracks began to appear.

Such troubles were apparent before the pontificate of Innocent. The Albigenses, the Waldenses, and other sects that arose in the twelfth century maintained that moral reform was too imperative to wait for ecclesiastical permission. The spirit of the sects was the same as that of the eleventh-century Gregorian reformers and of the monastic reform orders like the Cistercians, but disillusionment with the achievements of previous reformers gave the sects an added impetus. The great "peace" movement had resulted in a crusade against the infidels, but the crusaders, increasingly recruited from the dregs of society, were falling into disrepute; the second and third crusades had been failures. The fourth, which was launched by Innocent III, was a disaster. The crusaders were excommunicated for having destroyed a Christian town to pay off their debt to their Venetian carriers; but, heedless of the pope's curse, they went on to Constantinople, and there, quarreling with the Greeks, captured and looted the city, doing more damage to its sacred shrines than the Turks ever did in the years that followed.

In addition to these failures, the requirement of clerical celibacy had only resulted in widespread concubinage. The efforts of the Church to administer the world had involved her even more in the affairs of the world. The monastic orders, as noted, were forever being undone by their virtues, which created wealth that in turn corrupted virtue. The conclusion to be deduced from the relative failure of such vast endeavors was that if reform could not be achieved on a large scale, it should be undertaken on a small one, and if not by institutions then by convinced individuals who should not wait for the assistance or even the permission of the authorities.

One such individual was Peter Waldo, a twelfth-century merchant of Lyons and the founder of a sect called the Waldenses. Waldo was induced to embrace a life of poverty by hearing the song of a wandering minstrel celebrating not the deeds of a knight but those of a saint, Alexius, who on his wedding day forsook his bride and went on a pilgrimage. Returning too emaciated to be recognized, he lived for years as a beggar in a shed beside his parents' house and was identified only after his death. Impelled by this ideal of renunciation, Waldo gave a portion of his goods to his wife and distributed the rest to the poor, thereby reducing himself to mendicancy. Thus far there was nothing to which the Church could object. His next step was to engage a priest to translate large portions of the Gospel into the vernacular. These he learned by heart and began passing them on to others. He and his followers were thus entering upon the role of teachers and preachers, and here his archbishop intervened and forbade them to continue. Waldo appealed to Pope Alexander III. An examiner reported that the sectaries were utterly unlearned. Nevertheless, the pope granted them permission to preach if they had the consent of their bishop, but they refused to accept such a condition and were finally excommunicated.

The Waldenses were widespread in southern France and were

soon joined by followers in northern Italy. At first they were not heretical but merely anticlerical. But eventually they went so far as to maintain that sacraments administered by unworthy priests were invalid, recalling the ancient heresy of the Donatists. From literal obedience to the command to sell all, they passed to an equally literal observance of the injunction on swearing and resisting evil men. Popular piety was affronted by their unwillingness to do reverence to a crucifix. The rejection of oaths in a society where all agreements were so sealed and the refusal to participate in war caused them to be regarded as a menace to society. Rejected by the community at large, they could no longer live by begging and were forced to develop two classes within their own society, one of which supported the other. Under persecution they survived by withdrawing to the fastnesses of the Italian Alps, and there they continued to live, until the nineteenth-century *Risorgimento*, when they were permitted to expand into Italy and the New World.

The Albigenses, so called because they were numerous in and about the town of Albi in southern France, were another heretical sect that challenged the Church in the twelfth and thirteenth centuries. Commonly known as the Cathari, or the "Pure," these sectaries probably infiltrated into Europe from Bulgaria, where one of their chief branches bore the name of Bogomiles. In line with the Gnostics and Manichaeans of the East the Albigenses shared the dualistic view that there are two basic world principles, of good and evil: spirit was the creation of the good principle, matter of the evil one.

Like the Gnostics before them, the Albigenses rejected the Old Testament because it testified to the goodness of the created world. Since in their eyes matter was evil, nothing material could be used in the service of religion. Also, since they believed that Christ did not have a physical body, they rejected the idea that the bread and wine of the Eucharist were transubstantiated into his body and blood. Their Lord's Supper was merely a commemoration. They would tolerate no images, not even the crucifix, and they derided music.

Plainly the Albigenses were more drastic than the iconoclasts in their effort to spiritualize Christianity. They branded sex as utterly evil and would eat nothing they knew to be a product of sexual reproduction. They held that birth is an imprisonment of the spirit in the flesh, inflicted as punishment for sins committed in a pre-existent state. Sins committed in this life had to be expiated by the transmigration of the soul through further births. Should one attain perfection in this life, the Albigenses believed, it would be better to commit suicide than run the risk of a subsequent lapse. If universally adopted, their ideas would have led to the termination of the human race; but not all their members practiced the full rigors, and a division was made between the *perfecti* (the "perfect") and the *credentes* (the "believers"), of whom less was required. Since for them expiation had to be made in successive reincarnations, the Catholic doctrine of purgation in purgatory was naturally rejected.

In the eyes of the Albigenses the popes who had introduced so many corruptions into the Church were not the successors of Peter but of Constantine. Innocent III, on the other hand, attributed the popular spread of the Albigensian heresy to the dissoluteness of some of the clergy in Provence. No sectary ever denounced the clergy more mercilessly than did the pope. He sent Peter Castelnau as a legate to exhort Count Raymond of Toulouse (a successor of that Count Raymond who had gone on the first crusade) to suppress heresy in his domain; but the count was extremely dilatory, since the sectaries had a great many adherents among the nobility. Then Castelnau was murdered, and the count was suspected of complicity in the crime. Like Thomas à Becket, Castelnau achieved more by dying than by living. In 1179 the pope declared a crusade, offering the northern French the salvation of their souls as well as property in the south in return for forty days of sacking cities and burning heretics. The northern French were eager to reduce the power of the south, but the Albigensian crusade was not actually undertaken until 1209. After twenty years of warfare the heretics were crushed and Provence was wrecked. Eventually the territory was annexed to the crown of France.

Several concepts played a role in the ideology of the medieval sects. One was the effort to recover the past. All Christian groups, of course, appealed to the authority of the past, since for them all the Golden Age was the period of the New Testament. The papal church appealed to the mandate given by Christ to Peter, as the empire appealed to the apostle Paul's endorsement of the state. But these mandates were not construed as constricting the Church and the empire to the pattern of the past, whereas the sects were more disposed to attempt to follow New

The complex architecture of the Gothic
cathedrals is seen in this interior view of
Reims Cathedral. With available materials
and technical resources, medieval builders
showed great skill and boldness in achieving
lofty naves and towering spires of beauty.

Testament precepts, including that of poverty, as closely as they could. Whereas the Church based its authority on the unbroken continuity of Church history and tradition, the sects repudiated the authority of the centuries that had intervened since the earlier Golden Age. For them the supreme mandate was the word of the Master, "Go, sell what you possess and give to the poor . . . and come, follow me."

Another extremely important idea was the doctrine of predestination. The current view was that the Church consisted of those baptized in infancy, but the sectaries frequently said that the true Church was the company of those chosen by God before the very foundation of the world, the company of the elect. Augustine had considered these views compatible, if there were no way of distinguishing the elect. But if, as the sectaries believed, the elect could be discerned by the probity of their lives and the non-elect by the enormity of their behavior, then the sheep could be segregated from the goats and the Church could no longer be considered coterminous with the entire community. Collaboration between Church and state, so characteristic of medieval times, would then be inappropriate. The idea of predestination undercuts the Church on earth by regarding the membership of the true Church as predetermined in the mind of God.

Another view looks upon the true Church as lying in the future, or at least, as the primitive Church had expected, as about to become manifest in the future. In the late twelfth century, a Calabrian abbot, Joachim of Flora, divided history into three ages: one of the Father, one of the Son, and one of the Holy Spirit. Each was subdivided into seven others. His own generation, he claimed, fell in the second age and the sixth period, so that very shortly the advent of the age of the Spirit could be expected. Then the visible Church would be dissolved into the Church invisible and "the eternal Gospel" would be ushered in. The date would be the year 1260, a number taken from an account in the Book of Revelation that tells how a woman clothed with the sun fled from a dragon with seven heads and hid in the wilderness for 1,260 days. Not too far in advance of his own time, then, the mighty papacy would have served its historical purpose and would give way to a nobler successor. The heretics, who put such ideas to their own use, menaced the supremacy of the Church, which held that the only salvation lay within its fold. To deal with them and with the remnants of the Albigenses and Waldenses the Holy Office of the Inquisition was instituted under papal control. In 1233, under Pope Gregory IX, the bishops who had previously dealt with heresy were replaced by papal inquisitors selected largely from the friars.

The Inquisition sought its justification in Augustine's theory that constraint may be exercised on heretics for their salvation, out of love for their souls. As earlier explained, he had in mind only fines and imprisonment, but now the penalty was death by burning. Beheading was avoided because "the Church abhors the shedding of blood." Augustine had also used the analogy of saving the body by amputating the rotten limb. The body was now interpreted as the Church, and the rotten limb, the heretic. Heresy was considered the greatest of all sins because it was an affront to the greatest of all persons, God; it was worse than treason against a king because it was directed against the heavenly sovereign. It was worse than counterfeiting money because it counterfeited the truth of salvation, worse than parricide and matricide, which destroy only the body. Whatever penalties were appropriate for these crimes were all the more fitting for the greatest crime. To burn the heretic was an act of love toward the community, deterring by fear others who were inclined to the same sin. It was an act of love toward the heretic, for he might be recalled by fear of the fire and save his soul.

The inquisitors tried to secure a confession of guilt from the heretic by alternating blandishments and intimidation, solitary confinement and torture. If he recanted, he might be committed to life-long confinement enchained in a dungeon, or he might be granted the mercy of being strangled before being burned at the stake. If after his recantation he relapsed into heresy, he was simply burned. Churchmen themselves did not apply torture, nor did they serve as executioners. The convicted heretic was committed with a plea for mercy to the civil magistrate, who was subject to excommunication if he heeded the plea.

The first emperor to inflict the penalty of death for heresy since the days of the Roman Empire was Frederick II, who was himself suspected of heresy, if not indeed of blasphemy. Both as a man and as a thinker he was one of the most remarkable figures in medieval Christendom. He had been reared in Sicily at a court where Jews and Saracens were welcomed and was reputed to be the author of a work on the three impostors, Moses, Mohammed, and Christ. Frederick may have had nothing to do with any such book; but that one who consorted so freely with infidels should have executed heretics is puzzling. The victims were located in the north Italian cities that were disaffected from his rule, and perhaps Frederick used accusations of heresy to cow political enemies. That churchmen themselves could have condoned such expedients to crush heretics at the very moment when the papacy was at the pinnacle of power excites greater wonder than the anomaly of Frederick. Perhaps, after all, these churchmen did not feel so secure, for men are seldom cruel save when they are afraid. The Inquisition was effective in exterminating the Albigenses and dispersing the Waldenses, but in the fourteenth century sectarianism arose once more, and in a much more redoubtable form, because it was joined with nationalism.

The rise of the universities, the recovery of great areas of ancient learning—particularly the works of Aristotle—and the scholarship of the mendicant orders brought the Middle Ages to their highest intellectual achievements in the thirteenth century. At the peak of this development stood the greatest system of the Dominican friar Saint Thomas Aquinas. In the teachings of Aquinas scholastic theology found its ultimate summation. The distinctive genius of Aquinas was that he effected a new synthesis of Christian and classical traditions by incorporating into his theology arguments from the writings of Aristotle and of ancient and Arabic scholars. Aquinas assumed a middle ground between the extreme positions of contemporary scholastics. In his theology faith and reason were distinct but complementary, rather than antithetical; one believes precisely at the point where one does not understand, but reason can make faith more understandable. He rendered compatible the mysteries of Christian faith and the truths observable from man's natural experience.

Aristotle argued for the existence of God on the grounds that causation calls for a first cause and motion requires a prime mover. This Aquinas accepted, while recognizing that the roles of first cause and prime mover by no means encompass the fullness of the Christian image of God. He agreed with Augustine that unaided human reason can never unfold the mystery of the Trinity, but that the concept may be revealed through faith and then rendered intelligible by analogy. Revelation illumines reason, and reason strives to elucidate revelation.

This system has important implications for politics and ethics, because Church and state, right and wrong, fit into the scheme. The state belongs to the order of nature and reason, which lie within the scope of man endowed with reason, as does the whole realm of natural law. To be sure, man's reason was partly vitiated by the fall of Adam, and that is why natural law has come to endorse property, slavery, and war. Nevertheless, the natural faculties of man are still sufficient to enable him to administer the body politic. This view undercuts the notion that political institutions derive from spiritual and ecclesiastical institutions; it gives theoretical support to the independence of the state from the Church. Aquinas apparently did not see the full implications of his position, for he maintained that every human being must be subject to the Roman pontiff; his statement is, however, ambiguous, because it does not make plain whether the word *subject* applies to political or to spiritual authority.

Aquinas provided an encyclopedic summation of scholastic theology in his many treatises, notably in his *Summa Theologica*, which after the Council of Trent became the accepted basis of Roman Catholic theology. A half century later Dante provided another summation, both in his Latin writings and in his sublime vernacular poem *The Divine Comedy*. In theology he was a Thomist, in politics an imperialist, in piety a Franciscan who portrayed Christ on the cross abandoned by all save Lady Poverty, and in his excoriation of evil popes almost a sectarian.

Dante's supreme contribution is his spiritualization of the medieval picture of hell, purgatory, and paradise. What Augustine did for the concept of sin, Dante did for the concept of the punishment of sin. Augustine moved from the outer to the inner man and found the chief sins to be pride and the lust of domination. Dante rationalized hell. For him the ultimate horror was not that man burned, but that sin froze and in hell man remained forever what he once was. Purgatory introduces the hope of change. Passion is purged, ambition curbed, pride cowed, envy expunged. In paradise the eternal law of justice reigns, and the whole cosmos pulses in the harmony of love. Here at the summit of the Church Militant the poet beholds the spirit of Beatrice, a woman he had once seen in Florence, at the peak of the Church Triumphant the Virgin Mary, who appears in radiant splendor, surrounded by a thousand jubilant angels with outstretched wings. *The Divine Comedy* was an allegory of the destiny of mortal man.

VIII
Decline of the Papacy

The schismatic pope Clement VII, who tried
to return from Avignon to Rome, is shown
with Louis I of Anjou. Another pretender to
power, Louis sought the crown of Naples.

The fourteenth and fifteenth centuries are commonly considered by historians of the Church to be a period of decline. This judgment is shared by Catholic and Protestant scholars alike. Catholics lament the decline of the papacy in prestige and power, the waning quality and influence of the monastic orders, the rise of sectarianism, the popularity of nominalist rather than Thomist theology, and the prevalence of clerical concubinage and financial extortion. Protestant historians have in general been inclined to look upon the decline of the papacy and monasticism and on the rise of the sects with approval, for they were preludes to the Reformation. But despite differing assessments of its value, there is agreement in both camps as to what took place.

A number of factors contributed to the decline of the papacy's power and prestige. The challenge of sectarian movements was certainly one. Another was the rise of nationalism. The shift from Thomist to nominalist theology undercut the theoretical foundations of the hierarchical structure of the Church, and certain secularist tendencies of the age weakened religion's grip on culture. The Church began to impose taxes on the faithful, thus enriching itself and aiding the development of a monied economy; but its demands for money cost the papacy the allegiance of many people. These varied changes did not, of course, commence precisely in the year 1300. Some had been in the process of development for centuries.

Although nationalism had not fully assumed its modern form, by 1300 it had become a serious threat to the papacy. At that time three modern nations—Spain, England, and France—were in the process of formation. In each land a populace with a common tradition and a common language was consolidating contiguous territories under increasingly centralized government. The achievement of political autonomy implied a rejection of the over-all authority of the two great universal powers of the Middle Ages, the empire and the Church. The kings took over the roles of the emperors, and their slogan was, *Rex est imperator in regno suo*, "The king is the emperor in his own domain." Likewise, the sovereigns sought to control the Church in their territories, even in defiance of papal authority, so that by the sixteenth century the king of England came very close to claiming that he was the pope in his own domain.

The degree to which the three young nations exhibited these tendencies varied. Spain, not yet united, was least assertive. The *Reconquista* had gone far enough to include most of the Peninsula, but because of Christian disunity the Moors held the Kingdom of Granada until the end of the fifteenth century. England had moved farther on the road to consolidation. What is now England was then already under a single monarch, but the country was weakened by continual strife with Scotland and, because of its unwillingness to abandon Continental claims, with France. Of the three lands France was beginning to attain the largest measure of consolidation and centralization of authority. Although Aquitaine was not included in her domain, northern and southern France had lately become one through the annexation of the Midi as a result of the Albigensian crusade.

England and France were both to clash with the papacy—particularly France, the very kingdom that in the early Middle Ages had done so much to help build up the papacy. Their quarrel centered not on land, as it had in the investiture controversy, but rather on money. The Church's international operations required extensive outlays, but Rome no longer commanded as much direct income as it had in the days of Gregory I. If the Church was to be an international power, she had to build up an international income. A beginning was made at the end of the eleventh century by the imposition on England and on the Scandinavian countries of a small and ancient monetary levy called Peter's pence. Further steps involved the imposition of tithes on all local churches throughout Europe, with excommunication as a penalty for those who failed to pay. In the collection of these monies the Church forgot its aversion to those tainted with lucre and availed itself of the services of Italian bankers, who delivered the money in Rome on credit and reimbursed themselves by pocketing the tithes at the point of collection. The Church thus promoted the development of international finance.

The rulers of Europe objected to the export of gold beyond their borders, particularly because it was frequently spent to their disadvantage. They objected also to the crusading tax, which continued to be exacted even after the last Christian outpost in Palestine had fallen to the Turks in 1291. Even before the crusades were over it was being spent for wars that were called crusades, but that were waged by Christian princes at the pope's behest to discipline other Christian princes who failed to do the pope's bidding. The nobles were not inclined to pay for their own chastisement. When the papacy backed a crusade of the French ruling House of Anjou to expel the great German imperial House of Hohenstaufen from Sicily, neither the Germans nor the English were disposed to contribute. Kings would finance wars only in their own interest; for such ends they had long been willing to lay hands on the Church's wealth. This had come to mean not the expropriation of land but the sequestering of money.

England's quarrel with the papacy in these centuries principally involved the feudal tribute to which King John had committed the country in perpetuity by making England a fief of the papacy in 1213, and which was no longer being paid. Legacies of land to the Church were forbidden by a statute in 1279, and papal appointments to English sees were made illegal in 1351, to keep foreigners from settling in lucrative English bishoprics. Appeals to the courts of Rome were forbidden by the Statute of Praemunire in 1353.

In France the clash at the outset was also largely over money. King Philip the Fair levied taxes on the French clergy of one-half their annual income. In 1296 Pope Boniface VIII replied with threats of excommunication against any layman who exacted and any churchman who paid such taxes without the pope's permission. Philip in turn forbade the exportation of gold to Rome. The quarrel lingered and eventually became worse, and Boniface finally confronted Philip with the most far-reaching claims ever made by the medieval papacy. They were not invented by Boniface, but were taken over from the statements of Innocent IV, who, when the papacy had already passed the peak of power, compensated for its decline with heightened pretensions; he stated that Christ, being a king as well as a priest, had committed to Peter not one key but two, and not one sword but two—the temporal as well as the spiritual. Peter had renounced for himself the actual use of the temporal sword, but had delegated it to kings to be employed under papal direction. Thus the direct institution of kingship by God was flatly denied. This assertion was now cast at Philip by Boniface, together with the claim that to be saved every human being must be subject to the

Roman pontiff. When this claim had been stated earlier by Thomas Aquinas, the word *subject* was ambiguous; but here the context eliminated any ambiguity. Boniface made this assertion in the bull *Unam sanctam* in the year 1299.

But the previous successes of the papacy in the struggle for power had paradoxically reduced the pope's chances of making good his pretensions. The universal Church had weakened the universal empire by pitting against it the north Italian cities and the rising national power of France. After 1250 the imperial throne was vacant for two decades, and the empire's stability was not recovered until the year 1356, when the empire was reconstituted on an elective basis. The papacy had upset the balance of power, and Boniface could raise no champion to challenge Philip. In 1303 some of Philip's henchmen captured the pope in his summer residence at Anagni in northern Italy. This humiliation disturbed Boniface's health, so that he died shortly thereafter.

Then the papacy was transferred from Rome to Avignon, a little principality in the south of France. This city was to be the papal residence from 1309 to 1377, a span so close to seventy years that in memory of the seventy-year captivity of the Jews in the city of Babylon the period has been called the Babylonian captivity of the papacy.

Although their stay was termed a captivity, the popes during these years remained at Avignon of their own accord. They were all French, and exercised even the spiritual sword at the behest of the kings of France. The shift in their position is well evidenced by the way in which King Philip turned the Inquisition into an organ of the state. His object was to disband the Order of the Temple (the Knights Templars), a body of crusading knights whose wealth he coveted and which stood as an obstacle to the consolidation of monarchical power in France. In Spain similar knightly orders were still needed for the struggle against the Moors, and in Germany the Teutonic Knights had been used to subdue Prussia. There was no comparable task for the Templars in France, and the sensible procedure would have been to demobilize them. But this would have been an admission that the crusades in the Holy Land were over, and that no one was as yet willing to concede.

Philip's dilemma was most felicitously solved when a renegade knight brought charges of heresy against the Templars, claiming that they worshiped the head of a cat, blasphemed the Mass, practiced unnatural vice, and had betrayed the holy places to the infidels. They certainly had not betrayed the holy places, and no cat-headed idol has ever been found in any of their churches. The Templars may have been guilty of blasphemy, but blasphemy was, as a matter of fact, not uncommon in the Middle Ages. Nobody was ever burned for it, however, because blasphemy is, in a sense, an affirmation of faith; one has to believe in something before one can blaspheme it. Unnatural vice is probable enough, but the charge was heresy and not vice. The entire Order of the Temple in France was arrested overnight. The incriminated were confronted with lists of charges that varied somewhat from place to place. Torture was used to extract confessions of exactly what was charged in each locality and nothing more. Even the grand master of the order, Jacques de Molay, was alleged to have confessed. The case was then committed to the Inquisition, whereupon Pope Clement V intervened. When the pope took over, many of those who had confessed repudiated their confessions; but instead of being released they were treated as heretics who had relapsed and were sentenced to death. In 1314 fifty-nine Templars, including Jacques de Molay, were burned in Paris. Such pressures were placed by Philip upon the pope that he offered no remonstrance to the king's use of the Inquisition in order to consolidate the royal power.

The transfer of the papacy to Avignon raised for the popes other financial problems. The Patrimony of St. Peter had been taken over by Italian counts, and the Church could no longer collect its revenues. The popes at Avignon recruited armies of mercenaries to recover their lost domains and imposed levies upon the local churches in France, England, and Germany to defray the costs of the military operations. The wizard who reorganized the papal finances was John XXII, pope from 1316 to 1334. He concocted many new money-raising devices and exploited all the old ones. One was to impound for the papacy all the first-year's income of a newly appointed bishop. When a vacancy in a bishopric occurred the pope might transfer a bishop from another see to fill it, thus creating another vacancy. Or he might refrain from naming any bishop at all and reserve for himself all the revenues, pending an appointment. A fee was exacted for the promise of an appointment to a see when a vacancy should occur, and candidates for certain positions even purchased places on a waiting-list. When the pope visited a bishopric his expenses were paid by the see, but the costs of entertainment ran so high that it was often cheaper to pay him not to come. In that case he was free to accept several invitations. New offices were created and appointees were charged for being installed in them; and other fees were exacted for all manner of petty services performed by the papacy.

Another of the great money-raising devices was the sale of indulgences. The practice went back to the crusades. To one who took the cross the bishop granted an indulgence, which remitted a previously imposed penance. Later the right to dispense indulgences was placed under the control of the papacy. Eventually similar remissions were given to those who stayed at home but helped to finance the crusades. By and by the indulgences were dispensed to those who supported wars in Europe sponsored by the pope or charitable projects such as the construction of a cathedral, a hospital, or even a bridge.

One factor in the theory of the indulgence was the old Germanic practice of commuting a corporal punishment to a money fine. Another was the doctrine of the treasury of the merits of saints, which rested on the assumption that during their lifetime the saints had accumulated more merits than they needed for their own salvation. Their superfluous credits were stored in a celestial deposit called the *thesaurus meritorum sanctorum*; the pope could draw from this treasury and make transfers to those whose accounts were deficient. There was no fear that it would ever be exhausted, because the merits of Christ were included in it. There was a question whether the pope pardoned sinners by his own power, or whether he simply petitioned God to pardon them with full assurance that his request would be honored. Late in the fifteenth century the popes claimed authority to remit penalties in purgatory as well as on earth, and some indulgences absolved not only penalties but also guilt. Strictly speaking, indulgences were not sold, but still the granting of a pardon was timed to coincide with a contribution of money by the sinner. By these many devices the popes and the cardinals together during the period of their residence at Avignon reaped a larger income than did the kings of France.

But the demands of the papacy were to meet with opposition. In 1342 an Italian lawyer and layman, Marsilius of Padua, set

Saint James, with staff, wallet, and symbolic
cockle shell, is depicted here as a pilgrim en
route to Santiago de Compostela. His shrine
still attracts devout Catholics.

forth a theory of Church-state relations that exalted the state even more than had the system of Justinian. Marsilius proposed that the ownership (*dominium*) of all property should reside with the state. The Church should own absolutely nothing but should be allowed revenues determined by the state. All the clergy should receive their stipends from the government, making them in essence civil servants. According to Marsilius supreme authority in the Church belonged not to the pope, but to a general council.

Even more radical views were set forth by some of the Franciscans. The whole company of the followers of Saint Francis—the Spirituals, who owned no property, and the Conventuals, whose property was held for them by the pope—were welded together in common opposition to Pope John XXII. John responded to their opposition by resolving that the Church would no longer assume the burden of owning their property while the Conventuals enjoyed the benefits: let them either own property or starve. Then he decided to suppress the few cells of the Spirituals altogether. Next he alienated all the Franciscans by his pronouncement that contrary to the expressed view of an earlier pope, Christ himself had owned property. The Franciscans branded the pope a heretic. He turned some of the Spirituals over to the Inquisition, and they were imprisoned or burned. The Spirituals as a party then disappeared, only to be succeeded by extremists called the Fraticelli, who placed the Rule of St. Francis above the Church's authority, appropriated the eschatology of Joachim of Flora, and identified the pope with antichrist. Thus one branch of the Franciscans became a sect outside the Church.

Further opposition to the pope came from William of Ockham, an English Franciscan who lived from about 1290 to 1350 and who wrote a hefty tome on the errors of John XXII. In another treatise on the powers of emperors and popes, Ockham reverted to the old imperial theory that insisted on the direct, divine institution of the civil power and maintained that the clergy should confine themselves to reading, preaching, ordaining, and administering the sacraments. Much more radical was Ockham's theory of the Church. His nominalist philosophy led him to think of the Church in terms of its individualistic members rather than as a corporate entity. He divided the Church into its components and inquired whether any was able to err.

He concluded promptly that the pope could err, a general council could err, the laity could err; but if one of these groups did err, then inevitably another portion of the Church at that moment would uphold the truth. Ockham was deterred from concluding that all the parts might err at the same time by Christ's words that the gates of hell should not prevail against the Church. At any given moment, therefore, some part of the Church would be right.

Historically there is much to be said for his position. We have noticed that when the papacy was at its nadir, monastic reform and missionary endeavor were initiated elsewhere. Ockham raised another point: if all the parts save one may be wrong, how is anyone to know which part is right? What is the basis of authority? His answer was an appeal to the Bible. But if there is no authoritative body to interpret the Bible, each individual must interpret it for himself. Ockham's views about the Bible were to influence the Protestant reformers; his theories of Church government were soon to be given voice by the councils convened to end the papacy's captivity.

The Babylonian captivity ended in 1377. Pope Gregory XI perceived that the papacy must cut loose from France if other countries were not to renounce obedience to the Holy See. To the distress of the French Gregory went back to Rome; when he died there in 1378, he was succeeded by Urban VI. The French, dissatisfied with the choice of an Italian pope, chose another pope, who returned to Avignon. This pope took the name Clement VII, but he and his successors at Avignon are not recognized by the Roman Church (indeed, at the time of the Reformation another pope bore the name Clement VII). There were then two popes and two sets of cardinals. Thus began the great papal schism, which was not fully terminated until 1459. All of western Christendom was, in consequence, divided into two camps. France supported the popes at Avignon; Naples, often quarreling with Rome, lined up with France. England, Bohemia, most of Germany, and Flanders, out of opposition to France, sided with Rome. But Scotland, at war with England, sided with France and thus against Rome. Spain wavered and finally adhered to France also. In each country rival bishops arose in the names of rival popes, and monarchs were unable to enforce uniformity within their own domains.

What then was to be done? A group of thinkers in Germany

and in France came forward with the suggestion that the only way out of the impasse would be to revive conciliarism, that system which had obtained during the period of the great ecumenical councils, from the fourth through the eighth century. All the great doctrinal decisions then had been made by councils. To be sure, they had been ratified by the popes, yet the Sixth Ecumenical Council had declared an earlier pope a heretic. More was now involved than heresy, however. Never had councils gone so far as to depose one pope and to choose another, and now conciliarism—making a council equal or superior to the pope—seemed like a terrific innovation, reversing the trend toward centralization of the previous two centuries. Conciliarism meant constitutionalism: authority in the Church could then be lodged in a representative assembly. The councils that were convoked during this period achieved their first objective and ended the schism, but they did not arrest the absolutizing of papal power that was destined to culminate in the pronouncement of papal infallibility by the Vatican Council in 1870. Nor did the councils redress the moral and financial abuses that were widespread in the Church.

The ending of the schism was no light accomplishment. Whenever a pope at Avignon or Rome died, his cardinals promptly elected a successor to keep the dispute from being settled by default. When the conciliar idea was broached, each pope vowed willingness to join in summoning an assembly, but evaded fulfillment by proposing a meeting place far from the territory of the other. The cardinals of both popes were at last so utterly disgusted that without either pope they called a council to meet in Pisa in the year 1409, a full thirty-four years after the outbreak of the schism. The popes at the time were Benedict and Gregory, in Latin *Benedictus* and *Gregorius*. The cardinals dubbed them *Benefictus* and *Errorius* and deposed them both. In their place was elected a new pope, who died shortly and was then succeeded by John XXIII, who so debased the name John that it was not taken again by a pope until it was assumed by the most beloved pontiff of the twentieth century.

The other two popes, however, did not resign; consequently, instead of two, there were now three. What was wrong? The answer given was that the Council of Pisa had been assembled by the cardinals and did not represent the view of the whole Church. If a council was summoned by a pope and an emperor, surely it would mend the schism. The emperor Sigismund, who wanted to be crowned by the universally accepted pope, was glad to extend an invitation. John XXIII had no inclination to join him in calling a council, but when the king of Naples drove John out of Rome, he consented, assuming that he would be able to manipulate the assembly. In the year 1414 a great conclave gathered at the German city of Constance. John tried to swamp it by creating a large number of Italian bishops, but the council thwarted him by organizing itself according to nations; thus all John's Italian bishops put together had only one vote. At this setback he ran away from the council, but he was caught, brought back, deposed, deprived of his fisherman's ring, and incarcerated. His successor made him a cardinal, and he sleeps now in the baptistery at Florence beneath his cardinal's hat. A new pope was elected, who took the name Martin V and in 1420 returned the papacy to Rome. Of the other two popes one resigned and one was deposed. The council, before disbanding, asserted the principle of conciliarism and provided for future meetings.

There might never have been another council had not sectarianism, joined with nationalism in England and Bohemia, presented a new threat to the unity of the Church. In England the heretic was the priest John Wycliffe, an adviser to the king and a staunch upholder of English opposition to financial exploitation by the popes. Wycliffe had extended the doctrine of Marsilius of Padua about *dominium* and *usus*, the ownership and use of property. He maintained that all *dominium* is vested in God and that man has only the right of *usus*. This in effect meant that the state could confiscate the goods of a recreant Church—a very convenient doctrine that justified the expropriation of Church properties by John of Gaunt, who was the vice-regent of the kingdom and practically ruled England at the time.

When the papal schism occurred in 1377, Wycliffe's views became vastly more radical. He revived Augustine's doctrine of predestination, but provided a test for identifying the elect, or, at any rate, the non-elect. The true Church, said Wycliffe, consists only of the predestined and excludes the reprobate, who can be identified, even if they are popes, by behavior that is in glaring contradiction to that of the apostles. Such popes are not successors to the apostles, are not the true Church of the elect, but they are "the damned limbs of Lucifer" and the very Antichrist.

In the hands of such prelates the sacraments lose their efficacy. Wycliffe came to deny the doctrine of transubstantiation. He was a philosophical realist who held that substance is one of the universals. Universals cannot be annihilated; therefore, the host remains bread even after its consecration. This was not to say, however, that Christ is not in the sacrament. He is there, in addition to and along with bread and wine, whose substance remains. This doctrine is called remanence.

If the pope should be unworthy, where in the Church does authority reside? Wycliffe, like Ockham, had recourse to the Bible without perceiving that a problem might arise over varying interpretations of it; in his eyes it needed no interpreter because its meaning seemed self-evident. Wycliffe sponsored a translation of the Bible into English—a language that had only lately taken shape—thus making the Bible more accessible to laymen.

In order to disseminate the Bible and to instruct the people Wycliffe instituted an order of poor priests that came to be called Lollards. He had less than confidence in the older monastic orders, especially in the friars. In his eyes the Franciscans and the other itinerants were interlopers, who made the work of the parish priest more difficult. He no more respected their sincerity than did Chaucer, his contemporary, who treated them derisively in the *Canterbury Tales*; the village priest is Chaucer's most amiable character. The Lollards were priests whose mission was to preach to the people throughout the countryside. Whereas the Franciscans began as laymen and later became priests, the Lollards began as priests, were deprived by the Church of their status, and ended as laymen. Wycliffe enjoyed the patronage of the government and was not burned for heresy, but after his death in 1401 the act *De haeretico comburendo* sent many of his followers to the stake. Wycliffe's critique of the Church was basically theological, but there was also in it an element of English national feeling against foreign exploitation.

National feeling was even more marked in Bohemia. Catholicism had come to that land by way of Germany, and as a consequence anti-church sentiment there inevitably had a tinge of Czech anti-German resentment. But there, as in England, nationalism was not the primary cause of the dissension within the Church. The great reformer John Huss, who lived from 1366 to 1415, subscribed to a movement for preaching in the vernacular, not to make the people more Czech, but to make them more

Christian. His critique of the contemporary Church was at the outset a moral one. He upbraided the prelates for their luxury and license and drew a vivid picture of the contrast between Christ riding on a donkey and the pope on a stallion with the people crowding to kiss his feet. This contrast of Christ and Antichrist became a popular theme, later exploited by the Protestant reformers.

Huss was less radical than Wycliffe. He did not hold to the doctrine of remanence, and he maintained that the sacraments at the hands of an unworthy priest are nevertheless valid and efficacious, although the pastoral usefulness of the priest is utterly vitiated by his unseemly behavior. But he did carry over from Wycliffe, without diminution, the doctrine of the Church as the company of the predestined, who are recognizable in some measure by their deportment. Such a view, as we noted, is disruptive of the whole hierarchical structure of the Church. One point that came to be distinctive of the Hussite movement was its insistence on restoring the laity's right to take the cup during Mass. Not too long before, the Church had restricted the cup to the priest, lest the clumsy laity should spill any of the "blood of God." The Hussites pointed to the words of Christ, "Drink of it, all of you." The Church replied that these words were addressed to the apostles and that the apostles all were priests. This the Hussites denied. They resisted a growing tendency in the Church that accentuated the gulf between the clergy and the laity by requiring a distinctive costume of the clergy, by excluding the laity from the sanctuary of the Church, and by restricting the cup to the priest. The chalice came to be the symbol of the Hussite movement.

Huss's relations with the Bohemian king Wenceslaus were cordial at first, but became more complex as Huss became embroiled in controversy. The archbishop of Prague condemned Huss's views, and the king was alienated when Huss criticized an indulgence whose proceeds were to support the pope's war against the king of Naples. Huss did not want to controvert the entire doctrine of indulgences, as Luther was later to do, but only to deny that indulgences should be used as a device for raising money and that such money should be spent by the popes to finance wars. The students at the University of Prague burned the papal bull of indulgence, and Wenceslaus thereupon executed some of them. Because Huss defended them, the king

Wearing a heretic's hat, the reformer John Huss is shown, at top, burning at the stake. Below, workmen dig up the earth from around the spot where he was killed so his ashes could not be gathered and preserved as a relic by his followers.

sent him into retirement for two years; during that time he composed his work *On the Church*, in which he stated his views.

Then came the Council of Constance. The proposal was made that Huss should be examined by the assembly. He welcomed the suggestion, for he was certain that all instructed theologians would perceive the cogency of his arguments. The emperor Sigismund, who was heir to Bohemia, wanted him to attend, because he did not wish his inheritance to be tainted by heresy, and he promised Huss a safe-conduct to go to and from the council. On his arrival at Constance Huss was profoundly shocked by the blatant immorality of the clerics. Pope John XXIII, who was not yet deposed, had Huss imprisoned and induced the emperor to withdraw his safe-conduct on the ground that the Church is not obligated to keep faith with the faithless.

However, Huss' clash at Constance was not primarily with the disreputables, but rather with the noblest men at the council, among them especially the theologian Pierre d'Ailly. The saints are often the persecutors of the saints because only they care enough to persecute their opponents for the sake of what they consider the truth. Huss' theory of the Church as the company of the predestined was just as subversive to a council as it was to the papacy itself. D'Ailly wanted to end the schism and establish the principle of conciliarism; he was aghast at the prospect of disintegrating the Church, which could happen if Huss' teachings were followed to a logical conclusion. Huss was accused of teaching the doctrine of remanence and of holding that even the sacramental acts of priests depend upon their character. He replied that he had never held these views. Nevertheless, he was asked to repudiate them, but he refused, maintaining that it would be false to take back what he had never held. At the stake he recited the litany, "O Christ, thou Son of the living God, have mercy upon me." After his execution the earth was dug up from around the stake and removed, lest his followers have any relics to take back to Bohemia.

Even without relics Bohemia was aflame. The moderates were called Utraquists, from the Latin phrase *sub utraque specie*, which means "under both kinds," alluding to both the bread and the wine; they were prepared to make peace with Rome if the chalice were conceded to the laity. But they were overruled by a more radical group, called the Taborites, who would have no dealings with Rome, whatever the concessions. Peasant hordes were organized under the leadership of the blind general Zizka; though at times they were armed only with flails, they repulsed the armies of the emperor Sigismund, who tried to crush the Hussites, and they even succeeded in carrying their crusade into Saxony.

The Utraquists finally joined with the Catholics to defeat the Taborite armies, and Catholicism was reintroduced into Bohemia. At the council that had been summoned to the city of Basel in the year 1431 to deal with the situation the Utraquists won the right to be tolerated. This was the first definitive breach in the unity of the medieval Church and a foretaste of religious pluralism. One land now permitted two forms of the Christian religion. The pope refused to recognize the agreement that had been reached at Basel, but the independent Hussite Church survived nevertheless until the sixteenth century, when the majority of its members joined the Protestant Church.

The Council of Basel continued to sit in an attempt to reform the papal financial system. Then came an appeal that might well have engaged the attention of the council. With Constantinople beset by the Turks, the eastern empire asked for help. The West would come to its aid only if the East would accept its creed. There would have to be a theological discussion, and since the council was still in session, Basel was an appropriate place to have it, but it was remote from the East. The pope adroitly invited the Greeks to Ferrara, and they accepted. But the Council of Basel continued to sit. Thus, instead of a papal schism, there was a conciliar schism. Nothing could better have discredited antipapal conciliarism. Basel elected an anti-pope, and both the council and its pope flickered out in 1449. In the meantime the other council, which had moved from Ferrara to Florence, arrived at a compromise formula with the Greeks, but it was promptly repudiated when the Byzantine delegates returned home. The western military support that was sent to Constantinople was negligible, and the city fell to the Turks in 1453.

By that year the Renaissance was well under way in Italy. The Renaissance is most commonly regarded as marking a recession, not only of ecclesiastical control over society but also of a prevailingly Christian view of life. In assessing such a claim one must be clear as to what is meant by *Renaissance*. Some historians use the term simply to describe a chronological period: some would go back for the beginning to 1300 to include Dante, and some would go forward to 1600 to take in Shakespeare. Those who view the question from the standpoint of the Church commonly prefer to start with the pontificate of Nicholas V in 1450 and to end with the sack of Rome in 1527. But most often the term is used to describe an attitude toward life, which valued earth more than heaven; the immortality of fame more than the immortality of the soul; self-cultivation more than self-effacement; the delights of the flesh more than asceticism; the striving for success more than justice; individual and intellectual freedom more than authority; and classical Humanism more than Christianity. If this be the Renaissance, then the historian must ask to what degree such attitudes and behavior are discoverable in this period more than in the preceding, to what extent they were prevalent throughout the entire culture after the fourteenth century, and what bearing they had upon the character and continuance of a Christian society?

It was in the Italian city-states, especially during the last half of the fifteenth century, that the Renaissance ideals achieved their first and most vital expression. During this period the Italian cities enjoyed comparative peace and sufficient affluence to enable their rulers to patronize arts and letters, which flourished splendidly. The genius of that age has rarely been equaled, and never surpassed. The classics were studied fervently and assimilated thoroughly into the culture of the period. Later all Europe, from Spain to Poland, sought to emulate the Italian example. But one must beware of assuming that Renaissance ideas set the tone for the masses of people, aside from those who lived in the Italian cities.

The secularism of the Renaissance is most commonly seen in the age's definition of man's place in the universe. The Renaissance is said to have made man autonomous, self-sufficient, without any need for God; the writings of the scholar-prince Pico della Mirandola are cited as an example. Pico said that man is the molder of his own destiny. By this he meant that man, being located at the center of the great hierarchy of being, has freedom to choose descent to the level of the brute or ascent until he is united with the ineffable One. This is, in effect, Neo-platonic mysticism. It presents a danger for Christianity if it excludes the need for Christ's aid in the ascent. Yet it had been accommodated to Christianity by the early Church Fathers, who had declared that God became man in Christ in order to assist man to become God. And the Renaissance, for all its interest in paganism, never abandoned faith in Christ. Although Pico was suspect in the eyes of the Church, he considered himself a good Christian and even became a monk before he died.

The term *secular* also is used to describe the ideal of the cultivated man whose ambition is to round out his personality by the acquisition of all skills. Leonardo da Vinci was a painter, a mathematician, an engineer, and an inventor; Michelangelo, a sculptor, a painter, an architect, and a poet. The Renaissance man was interested in the development of the body as well as of the mind and prized pulchritude. The ideal was set forth in Castiglione's *The Courtier*, which was to serve as a guide to aristocratic behavior far beyond Italy. The courtier was to learn to run, hunt, and swim, to study Latin, Greek, and music, to dance well, to court his lady with finesse, and to bear himself with grace in all situations. In many ways this was a revival of the Greek ideal that had often disquieted Christians. Yet Christian society has traditionally held self-cultivation and self-renunciation in an uneasy tension.

The individualism of the men of the Renaissance often led them to excess, but men have always been guilty of excess. Certainly there were those in the fifteenth century who demeaned themselves with unscrupulous, lecherous, and frivolous deportment, but how novel were they? The Sforzas, the Visconti, and the Medici scarcely outdid the medieval Plantagenets in disposing of rivals and gratifying the flesh. The levity of Boccaccio's writings does not exceed that of the medieval tale of Aucassin, who preferred hell with Nicolette to paradise with the saints. Perhaps the Renaissance surpassed preceding ages in indecency by making pornography a branch of belles-lettres, but what shall one say then of the Middle Ages, when obscene poetry was freely written?

Nowhere was the age's secularism more manifest than in the papacy. During the fifteenth century few popes were distinguished for their spirituality. Rome was one of the Italian city-states, and the popes had all the splendid vices as well as the dazzling endowments of the secular despots in the other cities. Sixtus IV, who built the Sistine Chapel, engaged in all the machinations of the Renaissance despot. He desired to overthrow the rule of the Medici in Florence and substitute for it that of his own family. But he insisted that the conspiracy should involve no killing. His nephews told him to leave the matter to them and be content. He answered, "*Io sono contento* (I am content)." But of course there had to be bloodshed. Giuliano de' Medici was assassinated by one of the conspirators, a priest, at Mass in the Duomo, but his brother Lorenzo, Florence's ruler, escaped and rallied his men to overcome the conspirators. Among those who were hanged was Archbishop Salviati of Pisa. The pope protested against such treatment for an ecclesiastic, but was advised that he would do well not to say too much.

Alexander VI was the most scandalous of the Renaissance popes. He had four illegitimate children—among them, Cesare Borgia and his less criminal but equally notorious sister Lucrezia—and did not shrink from using the Vatican for his orgies. The best that can be said for Alexander is that he acknowledged his concubines and assumed responsibility for his children. His son Cesare terrorized Italy in an effort to build a domain for himself, with such success for a while that Niccolo Machiavelli was inspired to use him as a model for the unscrupulous despot in *The Prince*.

Pope Julius II was a disciplined person, a reformer at some points, a Titan in energy, a noble patron of Bramante, Raphael, and Michelangelo, but a pope so entranced by war that he donned armor to lead his own troops and himself scaled the walls of Bologna. Erasmus was more shocked by the travesty of a pope in armor than by the extravagant behavior of Alexander Borgia.

Leo X, a Medici, was an elegant dilettante, whose chief distinction was his ability to make impromptu speeches in Latin. He spent more on gambling than on artists, loved the chase, and disliked leaving his hunting lodge to come to Rome and have his toe kissed. He is reported to have said, "The papacy is ours. Let us enjoy it." He was pope when Martin Luther posted his ninety-five theses at Wittenberg.

A classic example of the secular outlook during the period of the Renaissance is *The Prince* of Machiavelli, which makes success rather than justice the standard for a ruler's actions. To be strong a state must have a despot, and a despot must be unscrupulous to remain in power. Machiavelli recommends that the despot be sufficiently moral not to goad his subjects to rebellion and sufficiently immoral to let no one take advantage of him or of the state. Machiavelli definitely recognized that his ideas conflicted with Christianity and that Christian ethics were incongruous with the politics of power. But in his generation how representative was *The Prince*? It was in many ways a valid description of the way rulers acted then, and indeed have always acted; but the prevailing opinion of contemporary political thinkers was voiced rather in the *Education of a Christian Prince* of Desiderius Erasmus and the *Utopia* of Thomas More, both in the tradition of Christian political morality.

In this period the Church was more and more drawn into involvement with the processes and mentality of incipient capitalism. We have already noted the way in which the Church came to rely on the bankers for credit. She was also driven to turn to them for loans when her own revenues, wherever located, proved insufficient. Although the Church exacted no interest when making loans, she was compelled to give it when borrowing. Then even the theoretical condemnation of usury started to break down. Aquinas had approved a contract of mutual risk with no fixed return. He had no objection to profits, but only to the demand for definite payment by a specific date, even though the enterprise for which the loan had been made had failed. But later theologians pointed out that whether or not the enterprise failed, the lender forfeited the gain that might have accrued had he invested the funds, and therefore he was entitled to compensation for the cessation of gain. The doctrine of the just price, which Aquinas had determined in terms of material cost and labor, now began to include market value too.

Skepticism in the sense of the denial of any of the great Christian affirmations can hardly be said to have existed in this period, but what was later to be called fideism—that is to say, faith without rational support—was common. However, this was an inheritance from the Middle Ages. There were two Christian affirmations that still lacked an unassailable philosophical foundation. The first was the doctrine of the Trinity; the second was that of immortality. The nominalist philosophers who dominated contemporary thought did not deny the doctrine of the Trinity, but they recognized that it is philosophically unprovable. There are, they said, two kinds of belief, one derived from logical reasoning and the other from theology; they lead to irreconcilable conclusions. There are not two kinds of truth, however; the philosophical conclusion had to be rejected in favor of the theological, which was derived from revelation. Such a posi-

This fifteenth–century Florentine engraving
portrays the Tiburtine Sibyl, who was said
to have predicted the birth of Christ.
Apocryphal Christian writings done in
imitation of pagan oracles, the Sibylline
oracles were an early synthesis of Christian
and classical thought.

tion can be termed skepticism only if revelation is called into question, which at this time it was not. Early in the sixteenth century Pomponazzi, a philosopher at Padua, wrote a book, *On the Immortality of the Soul*, in which with great acumen he examined the problem of the relation of soul to body. He concluded that no evidence demonstrates and no analogy suggests that the soul can survive dissociated from the body, as the Platonists supposed. Yet he too accepted immortality as the revealed doctrine of the Church.

We do find skepticism of a sort in the form of historical criticism used to expose the spuriousness of famous forgeries and to examine sacred documents critically. Historical criticism was a by-product of studies by the Humanists, whose profound interest in the antique encouraged a pure Latin style. Through their comparison of classical and medieval Latin, there arose an awareness of philological development. The Donation of Constantine, upon which the papacy long based its claims to dominion, was exposed as a forgery by Lorenzo Valla. The language, he pointed out, was not that of the age of Constantine. In the document there were references to the iconoclastic controversy of the eighth century. Documents of the period of Constantine never once mentioned the Donation, and at no time during that emperor's reign did the popes actually exercise the authority Constantine was supposed to have bestowed upon them. Valla disproved also the common assumption that the Apostles' Creed was the work of the twelve apostles. More daring was his application of historical, critical methods to the study of the Bible, even though he came up with no startling conclusions. As far as the Church was concerned, Valla's demonstrations were not especially disturbing. She could survive the exposure of forgery.

The Humanists did not attack the Church as such, and in the most famous instance in which elements within the Church attacked the Humanists, the victory went to the Humanists. This was the Reuchlin controversy, which took place not in Italy, but in Germany in the early sixteenth century, and involved an attempt to suppress Hebrew studies. A converted Jew named Pfefferkorn exhibited his zeal for the Christian faith for clamoring for the destruction of Hebrew books. The emperor Maximilian asked the advice of, among others, the great scholar of Hebrew, Johann Reuchlin, who reported that very little Hebrew literature should be destroyed, and nothing without examination by competent persons; for the training of these examiners he proposed the establishment of chairs in Hebrew in all the German universities. The Dominicans rallied to the cause of Pfefferkorn, and the case went to the pope. Reuchlin was tried for heresy and was saddled with the costs of the trial, but he never paid and continued teaching. The study of Hebrew survived, for the Church had herself appropriated the tools and the methods of Humanist scholarship.

Perhaps the most subversive aspect of the thought of the Humanists was their tendency to discount the uniqueness of Christian religion. One way of so doing was to introduce into Christianity a body of occult oriental lore—the Jewish cabala, the Zoroastrian oracles, the Hermetic literature of Gnostic origin—in the hope of supporting Christian teaching, but with the danger of perverting it. More direct was the effort to find common elements in Judaism, Islam, and Christianity. The great fifteenth-century German cardinal, Nicholas of Cusa, imagined a world parliament of religions in which Christianity obtained universal acceptance because its differences with other religions were minimized. Boccaccio gave a new turn to the ancient fable of the father who called in each of three sons separately and to each gave a ring that would make him his heir. After the father's demise the rings were discovered to be identical. These three rings, said Boccaccio, signified Judaism, Islam, and Christianity.

But it must be remembered that some of the outstanding examples of the Renaissance ideal were themselves divided spirits. Petrarch suffered from despondency and the temptation to destroy his works because they had been conceived in pride. At the height of the Renaissance the city of Florence, its center, was seized by a wave of puritan zeal. Under the influence of the great Dominican friar Girolamo Savonarola the populace built bonfires and burned its musical instruments, playing cards, gaudy clothes, works of art, and other "vanities." The Humanist philosopher Pico della Mirandola went to live in a monastery, and Botticelli, whose earlier work epitomizes classical Humanism, began painting profoundly religious canvases. The Florentines proclaimed Jesus Christ the ruler of their city.

Meanwhile in the north during the fourteenth and fifteenth centuries we meet with a great revival of mysticism and a concern with death even more intense than it had been at the height of the Middle Ages. Particularly after the Black Death in 1348, when about one-fourth of the population of Europe died, there arose a great preoccupation with death. Tombs bore sculptures of corpses with entrails protruding, infested with worms. One of the most notable literary forms, which the introduction of printing made even more popular, was the *Ars Moriendi*, the Art of Dying, with its lurid death scenes showing angels and devils contending for a soul, and its even more lurid portrayals of the fate of those who were unreconciled to the Church. In the course of centuries these ghastly exhibits lost some of their emotional impact, and when corpses were left unburied in order to titillate jaded sensibilities, people would have picnics beside the cadavers. Some of the Humanists began to maintain that he who had clean hands and a pure heart need not worry about the afterlife. Nevertheless, thoughts of purgatorial and infernal pangs must have been very vivid to induce the people to contribute so lavishly to indulgences; without a recognition of the average Christian's profound concern with the afterlife, the spiritual upheavals of Luther and Loyola are inexplicable.

The great revival of mystical religion in the north was exemplified by the Friends of God and the Brethren of the Common Life. The Friends of God originated in the Rhineland early in the fourteenth century. The territory was part of the lands of the emperor Louis of Bavaria that lay under an interdict for approximately a quarter of a century. Devout souls, deprived of the sacraments, came to believe that despite their loss they were not excluded from the presence of God. They joined together to form a loose association with mystical inclinations. It was greatly influenced by the German theologian Meister Eckhart, whose mysticism went beyond that of Neoplatonism in considering man's highest achievement to be union with ultimate Naught. Less extreme was Johannes Tauler, the most outstanding member of the group, who believed man's chief end to be total rapture with the love of God and the love of man.

Toward the end of the fourteenth century the Brethren of the Common Life arose in the Netherlands, with their center at Deventer. They represented a much freer type of monasticism and at first took no life-long vows. Their piety resembled that of the Franciscans, but like the Dominicans they placed their members as teachers in schools and universities throughout Europe. The supreme example of their thought was *The Imitation of Christ*, commonly attributed to Thomas à Kempis (1380–1471). Here emphasis is placed upon walking in the steps of the Saviour and sharing with him the cup of his passion; for the Blessed Trinity, it was believed, is better pleased by adoration than speculation. Representative of the Brethren in the period of the high Renaissance was Wessel Gansfort, who, when visiting Rome, was asked by Pope Sixtus IV what favor he might wish. The pope confidently expected that he would ask for a benefice, but Wessel amazed him by his unwillingness to accept anything but a Greek manuscript. Wessel disparaged indulgences by pointing out that the prodigal son needed no indulgence in order to receive his father's kiss. The sacrament of the altar is of no avail, said Wessel, unless the heart itself is repentant; if it is, then the external rite is not essential. The penitent thief was almost the patron saint of Wessel and his school, because the thief was saved by so little theology. Like many of his contemporaries, Wessel knew and believed only this, that Jesus Christ could get him to paradise. Within a few decades ideas such as those of Wessel were to exert a profound influence on thousands of Christians throughout Europe. Those who were moved by such ideas were ready to listen closely to a German monk of Wittenberg named Martin Luther.

IX

An Age of Reformation

This 1526 portrait of Martin Luther may be the work of Lucas Cranach the Elder.

In the early years of the sixteenth century the Church appeared to have surmounted the forces of dissolution by which she had been menaced during the late Middle Ages. Sectarianism and heresy had largely been crushed. Late in the fifteenth century a great prophet, the Dominican friar Savonarola, had arisen in Florence to castigate the sins of the Church and society (although he was ultimately tortured, hanged, and burned for sedition and heresy by the Spanish pope Alexander VI). The conciliar movement had been subordinated to papal control, and schism had been terminated. Spain, long torn between the crescent and the cross, was now definitely aligned with Christendom; the rigors of the Inquisition could be relaxed. As a consequence Christendom enjoyed a period of relative tranquility and liberalism in the first quarter of the century.

Yet there were unrest and dissatisfaction within the Church, and they were justified. Corruption in the Church was rampant, and many high-minded churchmen throughout Europe bemoaned her derelictions and clamored for reform. Complaints centered on three points: immorality among the clergy, severe financial demands imposed upon the faithful, and neglect of the parishes. As earlier noted, the enforcement of clerical celibacy had led in many instances to clerical concubinage. How widespread the practice was cannot be statistically determined, and figures given by reformers may be exaggerated. But complaints about clerical incontinence were heard in every country of Europe; the papacy itself was among the most notorious offenders. Fortunately society did not discriminate against priests' bastards and some, like Erasmus, became persons of great distinction.

The financial exactions of the Church had long been regarded as a grievance. Although the people gave voluntarily with immense generosity, they acutely resented paying tithes when nonpayment meant excommunication. By various forms of exaction the Church at every level acquired sufficient wealth to arouse criticism by the faithful. The sale of offices was widespread. So, too, was the traffic in indulgences by which the wealthy might purchase from the papacy remission of penalties for their sins. The unpopularity of papal taxes was aggravated by resentment over the way this money was spent. Why should the faithful in Germany or England or France finance the siege of Bologna by

Pope Julius II? And why contribute to the rebuilding of St. Peter's at Rome when one's parish church could not afford to patch its roof?

The most severe strictures were directed against the sorry state of parishes. Many of the lower clergy were almost totally uneducated. Moreover, so much money was drained off for the support of the national Church or the universal Church that priests were unable to live on the revenues from a single parish; hence several parishes were combined (a system called pluralism), to the inevitable neglect of each. Pastors and bishops were often not in residence and committed the cure of souls to vicars living on a pittance. When bishops became cardinals they were withdrawn from their sees to Rome. Catholic reformers in all lands were demanding that celibacy be enforced among the clergy, that the financing of the Church be overhauled, and that the flock be properly tended.

There were two types of Catholic reform, at first not sharply differentiated. One was liberal, undogmatic, ethical, relying on education to achieve its ends. The other was doctrinal and disciplinary, demanding the precise formulation of the faith and rigorous enforcement of the rules, with recourse to the secular arm to do so if need be. Both types were found in all Catholic lands and for some decades supported each other. Yet it may not be too much of an exaggeration to describe the first type of reform as Dutch and the second as Spanish, because their roots were grounded respectively in the Netherlands and in Spain.

The great exponent of liberal reform was the Dutchman Desiderius Erasmus. Erasmus was educated in the Humanist tradition by the Brethren of the Common Life and early developed an interest in the classics. Upon the death of his father his guardians persuaded him to enter a monastery, but the lack of freedom to pursue his studies led him to leave it in 1493, and at the age of about twenty-five he embarked on a scholarly career. From the pagan classics he came to direct his major attention to the Bible and the early Christian Fathers. He was influenced by the neoplatonic Academy at Florence to disparage the sensory and external aspects of religion. Over the ensuing years Erasmus wrote the witty and learned works that won him the reputation of one of the leading intellectuals of the period.

Erasmus was aware of the evils within the Church of his own time. *The Praise of Folly*, written when he was a guest in the

London home of Thomas More, was a bitter satire on monasticism and corruption within the Church. The central note in his piety was his emphasis on inner experience rather than on external devotions and ceremony. "Oh, the folly of those who revere a bone of the apostle Paul encased in glass and feel not the glow of his spirit enshrined in his epistles!" he exclaimed. What, he asked, is the point of fasting? To gain a reputation for piety, or to discipline the body for fruitful endeavor? As for the cult of relics, he scoffed at the miracles allegedly wrought by those of Thomas à Becket, one of whose slippers, he observed with irony, would do more after the saint was dead than his whole body did while still alive. Erasmus inveighed against monasticism, largely because of the system's confidence in celibacy and withdrawal from society. Both were externals, he argued; it is the spirit alone that matters, and this may actually be more manifest in family life. The dietary prescriptions of the Catholic Church appeared to him as a new Pharisaism.

With regard to dogma he was anti-speculative, like the Brethren, maintaining that the essential of religion consists not of ratiocination but of piety and charity. He introduced a distinction between the dogmas essential to salvation and those nonessential. To be necessary for salvation, he insisted, a dogma must be simple enough to be universally understood, for God would surely not damn men for not believing what they cannot grasp; it also must be universally accepted, because that which is controverted cannot be certain. Erasmus reduced the essentials to the Apostles' Creed, though as a matter of fact there were portions even of the Creed that meant very little to him; for example, the clause "suffered under Pontius Pilate." For Erasmus the suffering of Christ was not necessary to appease God's wrath or to satisfy his justice. In his mercy God could have forgiven mankind without having Jesus suffer.

From such a position one might easily infer that Calvary was not a sacrifice and that the Mass was therefore not, as orthodox dogma maintained, a repetition of any sacrifice. In accordance with a tradition of long standing in Holland, Erasmus looked upon the doctrine of transubstantiation as an unwarranted scholastic sophistry, and he interpreted the presence of Christ in the sacrament as spiritual. But Erasmus was not prepared to dogmatize any such matters, and he would not go counter to the consensus of the Church.

However, he was greatly concerned to correct morals, curb ambition, and stimulate piety, not only by ridicule but by the dissemination of learning. Much of his life's work consisted of editing and translating the texts of Christian antiquity. Above all he was eager to make known the Bible; the essence of his reform was a return to the simplicity of the Gospel, especially to the Sermon on the Mount. His greatest contribution in this area lay in the publication for the first time of the Greek text of the New Testament, at the press of Froben at Basel in the year 1516. Erasmus worked hastily, relying on only a few manuscripts and these not the best. Unhappily, his version was for too long the accepted one. Nonetheless, it was a great achievement, the more so because Erasmus accompanied the text by a Latin translation that dared depart from the Vulgate of Saint Jerome. Henceforth, any scholar who could read Greek could study the New Testament for himself at first hand, and anyone acquainted with Latin could perceive errors in the version that had been authoritative throughout the Middle Ages.

Any program of reform by education required harmony in the Church and concord in the state. In tracts, biblical commentaries, and letters, Erasmus constantly preached peace. The new nationalism knew no sturdier foe. Why should Englishmen, Frenchmen, and Spaniards, he argued, consider themselves natural enemies when in fact they are brothers in Christ? Erasmus looked back with nostalgia upon a society comprised within a universal empire and a universal Church, a world that had never in fact existed. How deeply he was grieved in 1521, when the banning of Luther divided the Church and the outbreak of war between the most Christian kings of France and the Holy Roman Empire challenged the universality of the empire itself.

Such evangelical Humanism was not confined to the Netherlands but had exponents throughout Europe. In England there were Colet, the dean of St. Paul's, and More, Henry VIII's lord chancellor and the author of *Utopia*; in France, the great biblical scholar Jacobus Faber—also known as Jacques Lefevre d'Etaples—and John Standonck of the College of Montaigu, a residence for clerical students at the University of Paris where both John Calvin and Ignatius Loyola were to live at different times. For a decade or more during the years the Netherlands were ruled by Spain, Erasmus had a vogue in the latter country.

When Charles, who had been reared in the Low Countries, became the king of Spain in 1516, he brought in his entourage counselors from the Netherlands of an Erasmian temper.

In Italy the great exponent of such Humanism was Juan de Valdés, a Spaniard living in Naples, then a dependency of Spain. Thus via the Iberian Peninsula the currents from Holland flowed to Italy. Valdés, like Erasmus, stressed inwardness and considered the death of Christ more an educational device on the part of God for the sake of man than a propitiation.

Italy had also an indigenous company of reforming churchmen, some of whom were members of an association called the Oratory of Divine Love, which convened in Rome until the sack of the city in 1527. These ardent churchmen included bishops who had reluctantly become cardinals and been drawn away from their sees to Rome. Cardinal Giacomo Sadoleto, for example, who composed the bull against Luther, spent all the time the pope would permit attending his episcopal duties in Provence. There was Gasparo Contarini, a nobleman of Venice, who, because of his integrity, was rapidly advanced from the status of a layman to that of a cardinal. He utilized his high office to seek agreement with the Protestants on justification by faith. There were many more of like temper: Cardinal Giovanni Morone; Pietro Carnesecchi, the papal secretary; Reginald Pole, the English cardinal in exile; and many women of the aristocracy, such as Vittoria Colonna, who inspired some of the sonnets of Michelangelo.

Inspired by the ideals of the Oratory and aided by the influence at the papal court of some of its members, the Italian reform movement in these years of crisis gave birth to several new religious orders, most importantly the Theatines. Living a strict and holy life, preaching in the streets of Italian cities, serving the poor and the sick, the prostitute and the prisoner, the Theatines were a powerful example to the laity and to fellow priests as well. From the ranks of the Theatines in particular the papacy was to draw numerous reforming bishops—more than two hundred in the first century of their existence. Another order, the Capuchins, sought to revive the program of the Spiritual Franciscans. Devoted to utter poverty, the Capuchins were at first averse to learning; but a generation after their founding they introduced a program of study.

Reforms in Spain were attended by a unique combination of

circumstances: the political situation and the appearance at a crucial juncture of Francisco Ximénez de Cisneros, commonly called Ximénez, one of the most remarkable religious leaders in the nation's history. In the fifteenth century Spain was in the last throes of a long struggle for religious and political consolidation, in the course of which the land that had once been the most tolerant on the Continent, religiously speaking, became the very reverse. The old Visigothic pattern of rigid orthodoxy was revived, and a close union of Church and state grew up, characterized by considerable independence from the papacy.

Late in the fifteenth century Church and state in Spain had become convinced that all remnants of non-Christian faiths must be stamped out, not only among the *conversos*—the converted Jews—but as well among the *moriscos*—the converted Moors. The Inquisition was established in Spain in 1480, and three years later a Dominican named Tomás de Torquemada was appointed grand inquisitor. Backed by Ferdinand and Isabella, Torquemada over the next fifteen years put an untold number of heretics to torture and death at the stake. He came to perceive, however, that he would never eradicate all remnants of Judaism from among the *conversos* so long as any unconverted Jews remained in the land to seduce them. Ferdinand was loath to expel the unconverted, who were still sufficiently numerous and wealthy to finance his war against the Moors; but after Granada finally fell in 1492 he could dispense with their help. In the very year in which Columbus sailed westward across the Atlantic all unconverted Spanish Jews were exiled. Ten years later the Moors shared the same fate.

Ximénez, who was to become not only the primate of Spain but a cardinal of Rome and a regent of the realm, was a man of very different stamp. In him we see an amazing combination of the old spirit of orthodoxy and the new Humanism. When he was about fifty, after practicing law in Rome and serving as vicar general of the diocese of Siguenza in Spain, Ximénez became a friar. His extreme austerity attracted large crowds of penitents. In 1492, the same year Ferdinand expelled the Jews, Ximénez was called to the royal court as confessor to Queen Isabella, and three years later he was named the archbishop of Toledo and thus became the primate of all Spain.

In that capacity he launched a thoroughgoing reform of the Spanish clergy, both secular and regular, including the branch of the Franciscans to which he himself had belonged. Yet he was also a patron of the new learning. At Alcalá in 1500 he founded, out of his own income, a new university, to provide for clerical education at all levels. In addition to two colleges of liberal arts there was a school of theology, to promote the study of the Church Fathers (a field that also interested Erasmus) and the Scriptures and of the languages—Greek and Hebrew—necessary to read them in the original. Meanwhile, for the education of the populace great numbers of popular religious books in all the languages of Spain were printed at the university press. And, with the aid of several scholars, Ximénez edited the Complutensian Polyglot, the first edition of the entire Bible in the original texts with accompanying translations. The Old Testament was printed in Hebrew, Greek, and Latin, and the New Testament in Greek and Latin.

The life of this extraordinary man was one of sharp contrasts. He wore a hair shirt beneath his cardinal's robes; but as the primate of Spain he controlled the wealth of the Church, and he did not hesitate to use it to finance a crusade against the Moors on the African side of the Straits of Gibraltar, accompanying the troops in person and haranguing them as Saint Bernard had harangued the earlier crusaders. A strict reformer, he enlisted the best scholarship of the Renaissance in his campaign to renew the life of the Church.

Curiously, the reform that was to convulse Christendom was initiated by a Catholic monk and priest interested only in reforming himself. Martin Luther, the son of a copper miner, was born on November 11, 1483, in the little village of Eisleben in Saxony. He took his Bachelor's degree in 1502 in Erfurt, Germany's greatest university, and three years later his Master's degree. In that same year, when he was returning to the university from a visit with his parents, he was overtaken on the road by a thunderstorm so violent that he feared for his life. Then and there he made a vow: if God preserved him, he would become a monk. Two weeks later he fulfilled the vow by entering the Augustinian monastery at Erfurt. He was not quite twenty-two.

Luther was one of those medieval Christians who took very seriously the "four last things"—death, judgment, heaven, and the eternal fire. He was tormented by terror of the wrath of God, by dread of the judgment of Christ, by panic at the power of Satan. For a time he experienced surcease in the cloister. Then the old torments returned, precipitated by his first saying of the Mass. This was—is—an ordeal for any new priest, for who would not tremble at sacrificing upon the altar the very God and Saviour of the world? All went smoothly until Luther came to the words in the Mass "We offer unto thee the living, the true, the eternal God." He related afterward: "At these words I was utterly stupefied and terror-stricken. I thought to myself, With what tongue shall I address such majesty, seeing that all men ought to tremble in the presence of even an earthly prince? Who am I, that I should lift up my eyes or raise my hands to the divine majesty? The angels surround him. At his nod the earth trembles, and shall I, a miserable little pygmy, say, 'I want this, I ask for that'? For I am dust and ashes and full of sin, and I am speaking to the living, the eternal, and the true God."

The words "dust and ashes and full of sin" convey at once Luther's deep sense of man's creatureliness and unworthiness. How should a worm confront the divine majesty, and how should a sinner stand in the presence of the divine holiness? Only in harmony with the Ultimate can man find peace, but what harmony can there be between the finite and the infinite, between the unclean and the holy?

The first answer offered by the Church was that man should seek to purge himself of sinful inclinations by acts of self-denial. Luther chose the castigation of the flesh. But the thought constantly obsessed him that he could never be hungry enough or poor enough to merit God's favor, and that whatever good works he might do, his thoughts were forever tainted by self-love. This discovery did not leave him hopeless, however; the Church addresses herself as much to sinners as to saints and in the sacrament of penance offers absolution to all who transgress, provided they fulfill the three conditions of contrition, confession, and satisfaction.

Luther had come to feel that no satisfaction man can make is enough, nor can he be sure that his contrition is heartfelt. But confession was open to him, and he set himself to exploit it to the utmost of his memory. He believed, together with the leading theologians of his day, that sins, to be forgiven, must be recalled, confessed, and absolved one by one. Luther proceeded to confess for six hours on end and was utterly disconcerted to find that after leaving the confessional, he recalled some trivial offense he had overlooked. Then he would return again and

Bulla contra errores
Martini Lutheri
z sequacium.

The cover of this papal bull "against the
errors of Martin Luther and his followers"
bears the Medici coat of arms of Leo X. The
bull was issued three years after Luther first
attacked the Church for selling indulgences.

again until his confessor grew impatient and told him to go and do something worthy of being confessed, such as killing his father or his mother. But Luther's problem was not whether his sins were big or little, but whether he had confessed them all.

More devastating to him was the insight that many sins are not even recognized as such. So deep is man's corruption that no scrutiny will ever bring him to recognize all that is amiss. Hence, he must seek not the forgiveness of this sin or that, but the redemption of his nature. But experience shows that in this life nature is never wholly redeemed and remade. Therefore, man can only hope that God in his mercy will treat man as if he were good, although actually he is not.

Luther did not arrive at such uneasy peace by a placid series of deductions. He was distraught by what he found in himself, and even more by what he had come to believe about the nature of God. For him God was a God of terror, who suffers men to be crushed by disasters, racked by fantasies, plagued by doubts, driven to desperation by fears. Do not the Scriptures say that some men God justifies and some he rejects, according to his good pleasure? What justice is there in this? Luther's confessor told him he was making the way of salvation too hard. He need only love God. But Luther answered, "I do not love him. I hate him." His confessor could not understand this. And then came to Luther the severest of all trials, the loneliness of uniqueness. If an experienced confessor did not understand, could it be that Luther alone in all history had been so plagued?

Now, his confessor, perceiving that this monk would destroy himself through introspection, sought to call him out of himself further by assigning him to a chair of biblical studies at Wittenberg; to this task were added preaching assignments as well, and the care of the souls attending the university church, which was also the parish church of the town. In 1512 he took the degree of Doctor of Theology; it was on the basis of this doctorate that he later justified his work as a reformer. Beginning in 1513, he engaged in a series of lectures on the Psalms and the Epistles of Saint Paul to the Romans, the Hebrews, and the Galatians.

In the course of these lectures he was confronted by the passion of Christ, in particular by his words upon the cross, "My God, my God, why hast thou forsaken me?" Christ forsaken by his Father in heaven—this was precisely how Luther felt, and he had thought himself unique. Now he saw that Christ was tempted even as we are, and to the point of utter alienation. But why? Surely not because Christ had sinned. Rather, being without sin, he had taken to himself the sins of us all, nailing them to the cross and thereby manifesting the amazing love of the divine Father. What a different view of Christ this presented! He was not the implacable Judge, but the derelict upon the cross. And what a new picture of God, for the all-terrible was the all-loving, too. On the cross his wrath and his mercy met in the wonder of redeeming love.

What then is required of man? Luther asked himself. Only this, he concluded, that he cease all reliance upon himself, that he come to terms with his continuing unworthiness, that he accept God's goodness with belief, trust, and commitment. This, Luther perceived, was what the apostle Paul meant when he quoted the prophet Habakkuk: "The just shall live by faith." The insight opened for Luther the gates of paradise. This is the meaning of justification by faith, and it is the foundation stone of what came to be known as Lutheranism.

Faith for Luther was above all else objective. Christianity, he believed, is a religion of history resting upon something done by God in time—the Incarnation and the Redemption—and done once and for all. This is known to us solely through the Scriptures as they could be interpreted by any Christian under the guidance of the Holy Spirit. Therefore theological education should concern itself exclusively with the Scriptures. Luther viewed himself as a reformer only in that he exalted biblical studies.

In the next few years Luther's ideas gained considerable currency at the university, then the scene of a great intellectual ferment, in which the traditional scholastic philosophy and the traditional theology were being challenged. "The lectures on scholastic theology are deserted," he wrote to a friend, the Augustinian prior at Erfurt, on May 18, 1517, "and no one can be sure of an audience who does not teach our theology." Still, it is possible that Luther's reforms might have been confined to the theological curriculum had not his additional duties as a parish priest opened his eyes to certain abuses then current in the Church, which actually imperiled the souls of his parishoners. Chief among these was the misuse of indulgences.

The particular case that touched off Luther's protest was the most flagrant abuse of indulgences in all the Middle Ages. Albert of the House of Hohenzollern, though not of canonical age to be a bishop, was already bishop of Magdeburg and of Halberstadt. Now he aspired to be made archbishop of Mainz and primate of Germany. Were he to combine these dignities, the House of Hohenzollern would have an advantage over its political rival, the House of Hapsburg. For whoever held the archbishopric of Mainz had one of the seven votes in the election of the Holy Roman emperor; with the current emperor, Maximilian, nearing his end, that vote might have been crucial. But holding three such ecclesiastical offices was a violation of canon law. Further, the normal fee to the pope for installation to the see of Mainz was enormous; a previous incumbent, in his last illness, had apologized to his constituency that he would die so soon after his appointment and thus involve them in the expense of a successor. Albert would be the fourth archbishop in ten years, and Mainz was nearly bankrupt. Moreover, because of the canonical irregularities involved, he would have to pay more than the usual fee. A price of ten thousand ducats was agreed upon. Albert borrowed the money from the great banking house of Fugger in Augsburg and paid the pope in full.

To enable Albert to reimburse the Fuggers the pope permitted an indulgence to be preached throughout his territories for eight years, half of the proceeds to go via Albert to the Fuggers and the other half to the pope to build a mausoleum for the bones of Peter and Paul, the great Basilica of St. Peter. Albert made unprecedented claims for these indulgences; for example, that they would remit not only the penalties for sins but also the sins themselves and would give preferential treatment to one who sinned in the future. Those who secured indulgences on behalf of deceased relatives in purgatory need not themselves be contrite for their own sins. The Dominican Johann Tetzel, who hawked the indulgences, blithely proclaimed their power to ensure immediate release from purgatory, using the jingle:

> As soon as the coin in the coffer rings,
> The soul from purgatory springs.

This was too much for Martin Luther. On the eve of All Saints' Day, October 31, 1517, he posted on the door of the castle church at Wittenberg a series of propositions for debate; ever since known as the Ninety-Five Theses, they were soon circulating everywhere in Germany. Luther did not know all the sordid details, but he had seen Albert's instructions to Tetzel, and these revealed quite enough. Among other points, he complained about the draining of so much money from Germany to Rome. If the pope knew of the poverty of the German people, he would wish to see St. Peter's in ashes, for he would know it was being built out of the blood and hide of his sheep. To this all Germans would agree. Next Luther claimed that the pope had no power over purgatory, though if he did, he should empty the place gratis. With this assertion many of the theologians would agree. But the final point was that the real treasury of the Church is the Gospel, which first of all brings conviction of sin, and they are damned who try to bargain with God to escape damnation. By implication this statement denied the whole concept of the treasury of merits, for Luther had long since come to believe that no man can accumulate enough merit for himself, let alone anything extra. His critique decried not simply the abuses of indulgences, but the very idea itself.

He sent a copy of his theses to Albert of Mainz, who in turn forwarded it to Pope Leo X. That elegant dilettante at first dubbed Luther a drunken German who would soon be sober, but when his "inebriation" continued, Leo commissioned his censor of literature to draft a reply. This dignitary defended the claim of immediate release from purgatory and then moved to more fundamental assertions. The Church, said he, consists virtually in the pope and representatively in the cardinals, and he who goes counter to what the Church actually does is a heretic. Luther replied that the Church consists virtually in Christ and representatively in a Church council, but that not even a council, let alone a pope, is infallible. Now the ground had been shifted from indulgences to authority, which to this day constitutes the greatest line of division between Protestants and Roman Catholics. The latter commonly say that having rejected the authority of the Church, Luther was left only with private, subjective judgment. This Luther never admitted. For the infallibility of popes and councils he substituted the infallibility of the Scriptures. He did not perceive that interpretation of the Scriptures must be to a degree individual and subjective.

Luther was a heretic according to the pope's spokesman, but to many the case did not appear so clear. There had been no definitive pronouncement about indulgences, nor—prior to the

Vatican Council of 1870—were Catholics required to believe that the pope is infallible. One very crucial person in Germany was not satisfied. This was Frederick the Wise, senior member among the seven electors of the Holy Roman Empire, territorial prince of Saxony, and thus Luther's lord. He had founded the University of Wittenberg, and he was resolved that his professor should not be condemned without a proper hearing, particularly because he had the backing of the entire university. When the pope summoned Luther to Rome, Frederick intervened to secure a hearing on German soil.

This took place at Augsburg in 1518 before Cardinal Cajetan, an upright and learned theologian of the school of Saint Thomas. He confronted Luther with the papal bull *Unigenitus*, issued 175 years earlier by Clement VI, which set forth the doctrine of the treasury of the merits of the saints and the papacy's power to issue indulgences drawn upon it. Luther hesitated to repudiate the bull, particularly because it had been incorporated in the canon law; but when he was pressed, he came out with a flat denial of the doctrine. Thereupon the cardinal told him to leave and not return until he was ready to retract his denial.

Luther had good reason to fear death at the stake and would have suffered, had not the popes at the time been embroiled in politics. No better proof could be adduced for the justice of his strictures of the papacy than its slowness in disposing of him. A pope who took seriously the tenets of the Church should have given him more summary treatment. Instead the Church took almost four years to excommunicate the man who proved to be the most disruptive heretic in her history, because the popes were trying to manipulate the imperial election. The emperor Maximilian died early in 1519, and a successor had to be elected from among the reigning monarchs of Europe. The pope was loath to see any augmentation of power of a ruler already strong, that is, of either Francis I of France or Charles I of Spain. As a Hapsburg, Charles also controlled Austria, the Netherlands, and Naples; if in addition he were to have Bohemia and Germany, he could throw a ring around France and then put a vise on Rome. If Francis, on the other hand, were able to combine France with Germany and Bohemia, he would have such a bloc in the center of Europe that he might easily absorb the fringes, and he would dominate the papacy as France had done when the popes were at

Avignon. Pope Leo X preferred a minor prince, and his choice was Frederick the Wise.

It was therefore hardly the moment to pursue action against Frederick's protégé, although Luther's ideas were rapidly gaining adherents. In the summer of 1519 he was drawn into public debate at the great Catholic university at Leipzig with the distinguished doctor Johann Eck, professor of theology at Ingolstadt. The debate centered not on indulgences, but upon the antiquity, divine institution, and authority of the popes. Luther contended that the papacy, as it was in his day, was not over four hundred years old, that it was the creation not of God but of man, and therefore that it lacked authority, which resides solely in the Scriptures. Eck then drove him to admit his affinity with John Huss, the Bohemian burned for heresy by a Church council. Having rejected the authority of the pope, Luther now proceeded to discard that of councils as well. One might have expected Luther's admission to have brought him quickly to the stake, too. Instead his stature increased, probably because Froben, the great publisher at Basel, brought out at that very time Luther's collected Latin works. No other issue from this press was so speedily sold out, copies going not only all over Germany, but to England, France, Switzerland, and even to Spain and Rome. Luther was becoming an international figure. At home in Germany nationalists rallied to him as the spokesman of their complaint against the pope for treating Germany as his "milk cow." The northern Humanists, on the other hand, saw in Luther another Johann Reuchlin battling for freedom of scholarship. Erasmus insisted that Luther was a man of good life whose arguments should be met by reasoning rather than by brimstone.

Pope Leo delayed action against Luther for a whole year and only then issued from his hunting lodge the bull *Exsurge, Domine*, which begins: "Arise, O Lord, and judge thine own cause. . . . A wild boar has invaded thy vineyard." Luther was ordered to recant within sixty days after the bull was placed in his hands. So great was the obstruction, even from the German bishops, that three months elapsed before the document was delivered to Luther on the tenth day of October 1520.

Luther himself took advantage of the delay in the prosecution to compose that summer several tracts, each more devastating than the preceding. The *Address to the Christian Nobility of the German Nation* was an appeal to the ruling class, including the

This woodcut from a pamphlet by Luther's enemies shows him with seven heads, each of a different character. Movable type and wood-block printing came into widespread use at the time of the Reformation. Both Catholics and dissenters were quick to employ printing to broadcast their views in books, pamphlets, and broadsheets—works illustrated with woodcuts that even the illiterate bought eagerly.

emperor, of whom Luther did not yet despair, to take a hand in redressing primarily the financial and political abuses within the Church. Luther was reverting to the program of the reforming German emperors of the time before the investiture controversy, and like them he believed that the temporal arm of Christendom had a responsibility to reform the spiritual. His claim that temporal affairs should be handled by local churches represented a resurgence of the particularism of the Middle Ages against the universalism of the papacy. His graphic contrast between Christ—the poor and humble—and Antichrist—the pope, luxurious and lofty—savored of the style of Wycliffe and Huss.

But there was something in Luther's tract that went far beyond anything medieval. He proclaimed the priesthood of all believers. The medieval Church had held that the clergy, being alone priests with sacramental power, might by giving or withholding the sacraments compel civil rulers to do the Church's bidding. Luther countered that Christian magistrates are also priests, as are all baptized Christians. Any Christian might administer the sacraments, though some are given this role as a vocation. The magistrate has another vocation, no less spiritual for all that, and should not be impeded by excommunication from administering the government, as Henry IV had been after Canossa; though of course a ruler, like any other Christian, might be excommunicated for immoral behavior. When Luther claimed that no one in a thousand years had so defended the secular power as he, he did not mean that he was advocating political absolutism, but only that the state should be emancipated from clerical control.

An even more revolutionary tract written that same summer was called *The Babylonian Captivity*. It was a treatise on the sacraments—taken captive, according to Luther, by the false teaching of Rome. Luther reduced the sacraments from seven to essentially two, baptism and the Eucharist (or three, if penance were to be included). A sacrament, he said, involves an outward sign of an invisible grace and must have been specifically instituted by Christ. On this basis he rejected extreme unction, that is, anointing with oil one who is one the verge of death. He retained ordination and confirmation as rites of the Church, but not as sacraments: they had not, he claimed, been instituted by Christ. Marriage might be blessed by the Church, but it was essentially a civil matter; it was instituted by God in the Garden of Eden, not specifically for Christians, but for all peoples, including Jews and Turks, whereas a Christian sacrament must be exclusively Christian. The way thus was opened to make marriage a purely civil ceremony and to abolish the whole system of impediments based on spiritual and remote physical relationships. He reduced penance to voluntary confession of one's faults to any other Christian, even a layman. Strictly speaking, he said, this is not the sacrament of penance. Baptism—including that of infants—he retained as a sacrament. Finally, there was the Eucharist, and at this point Luther touched the keystone.

The Mass, he said, is not a repetition of the sacrifice of Christ, which took place on Calvary once and for all. There should be no Masses for the dead with no one present save the priest, because the Mass is a communion of the faithful with each other; the cup, therefore, he believed, as the Hussites had before him, should be given not only to the clergy but to the laity. The doctrine of transubstantiation was rejected; bread and wine, said Luther, retain their substance. At the same time he believed in a real, physical presence because of the words of Christ, "This is my body." How the elements could be Christ's body Luther did not try to explain, other than to say that Christ is present with, in, and under the elements. His presence is the result of no miracle worked by the pronunciation of the words "*Hoc est corpus meum* (This is my body)" at the consecration during the Mass, because Christ is actually present everywhere, just as all matter is pervaded by the spirit of God. What happens in the sacrament is that Christ's presence is disclosed. This happens also in the preaching of the Word, and the minister does no more at the altar than in the pulpit.

When Erasmus read this tract, he said, "The breach is irreparable." Always conciliatory, undogmatic, and concerned for harmony, the great Humanist had been seeking to mediate, believing that the doctrines of indulgences and papal infallibility were open to discussion. But Luther's view of the Mass precluded mediation. As a matter of fact Erasmus did not discontinue his efforts at mediation for another decade. He was himself torn, because he spiritualized the Mass even more than Luther, but would not press a private view to the point of disrupting the Church. Erasmus was concerned for unity, Luther for truth.

When Luther's sixty-day period of grace expired, instead of submitting to Rome he burned the bull *Exsurge, Domine*, together with a copy of the canon law. The Church of Rome now desired that Luther be publicly excommunicated as a heretic and turned over to the secular authorities to be burned at the stake. The newly elected emperor, the Hapsburg Charles I of Spain—as emperor he became Charles V—could not act on his own authority except in his own hereditary domains. In the case of a subject of Frederick the Wise of Saxony he required the consent of the Diet, which was to convene in January 1521, in the city of Worms on the Rhine. The Diet was not disposed to act without giving Luther a hearing, especially since a bull of excommunication against him, signed by the pope in January, was withheld from publication until October.

The papal representative at the Diet, Girolamo Aleander by name, discovered that the bull excommunicated not only Luther but also others, including the leader of the German nationalists, Ulrich von Hutten, who was in a position to swoop upon the Diet with armed forces. In terror, Aleander sent the bull back to Rome with an urgent request for a substitute naming only Luther. But the newly elected pope—Clement VII, a cousin of Leo X—dallied. Now that a Hapsburg had been elected emperor, the pope foresaw the renewal of the old conflict between empire and papacy, and realized that Frederick the Wise might still be a useful ally. At any rate Clement did not hasten to send a new bull with only Luther's name. The Diet thereupon declined to ban without trial one not publicly excommunicated by the Church, and Luther was summoned to come for a hearing.

The moderate Catholics of the party of Erasmus were aghast as they foresaw the tumults that would ensue if Luther were burned; they sought to avert schism and possibly war by persuading Luther to compromise on the question of the sacraments, in which case the other points in his attack might be negotiated. Before the Diet Luther was confronted by a stack of his books and asked whether he had written them all. Had he disclaimed the tract on the sacraments the Erasmians would have achieved their hope; but he acknowledged them all. Would he then stand by everything he had taught in his writings? Luther hesitated and asked for time to reflect. The next day, however, he came out with a ringing statement, centering not on the sacraments but on the principle of authority: "Since then your majesty and your lordships desire a simple reply, I will answer without horns and without teeth. Unless I am convicted by the Scriptures and plain reason—I do not accept the authority of popes and councils, for they have contradicted each other—my conscience is captive to the Word of God. I cannot and I will not recant anything, for to go against conscience is neither right nor safe. God help me. Amen."

An attempt was then made to break Luther down in a committee meeting. He was asked whether he could not compromise on something. If he refused, there would be division, war, and insurrection. His reply was that truth is not open to negotiation. Luther, who was at that time still under a safe-conduct issued by the emperor, then left Worms.

The emperor Charles would have been willing to negotiate, for like Erasmus he treasured the ancient unities and placed concord above dogmatic niceties. But when confronted with intransigence he could reply only with intransigence. A month later Charles issued the Edict of Worms, placing Luther under the ban of the empire as an excommunicated heretic. Yet since Luther was being banned by the empire prior to the publication of the bull of excommunication, the Edict of Worms stressed the menace of his teaching to the state, asserting that his defiance of authority would be more subversive of the civil than of the ecclesiastical order. Luther replied by roundly asserting his political allegiance; in no sense did he mean by doing this to encourage political absolutism.

Meanwhile, Frederick the Wise, not yet convinced that Luther had been fairly heard and rightly condemned, secretly subverted the emperor's intentions by hiding Luther for nearly a year in the castle of the Wartburg. Luther took advantage of this enforced withdrawal to render one of the noblest of his contributions. In the space of three months he translated the whole of the New Testament into a powerful German. There had been eighteen printed German Bibles before his time, but all were pedestrian. Luther's was off the press in September 1522, and nothing did more to make the common man his own interpreter of the Scriptures.

During this time two of Luther's colleagues at the University of Wittenberg took the lead in guiding the Reformation. The first was twenty-five-year-old Philipp Melanchthon, a prodigy of classical learning, the grandnephew of Reuchlin. The other was Andreas Bodenstein, called (from his birthplace) Carlstadt, who had conferred on Luther the Doctor's degree. The less temperate among their followers at Wittenberg began intimidating the priests and monks with threats of violence; Melanchthon was too diffident and Carlstadt too impetuous to quell a tumult. The town council therefore asked Luther to return. The elector warned that he could not protect a man under the ban of Church and empire should he come out into the open. Luther sent word asking only that the elector not turn him over to the emperor; should the emperor come to take him, he advised Frederick not to object. Luther came home and actually was able to live untouched for another twenty-five years, because Charles V was involved either in fighting the French or in resisting a confederation of smaller powers, which, if France were defeated, would rally to her side in order to restore the balance of power. At different times this confederation included England, Venice, the German Protestants, the Turks, and the popes.

With his return to Wittenberg in March 1522, the second phase of Luther's career began. Hitherto he had been the flaming prophet of rebellion. Hereafter he was able to be the harassed builder and administrator of a new Church. His first move was to calm the agitation. He pleaded that abuses, however appalling, should be corrected without violence and with discrimination. "Men can go wrong with wine and women," he said. "Shall we then prohibit wine and abolish women?" Catholic services continued in Wittenberg alongside the Lutheran until 1524, when the saying of Mass was abolished in all the churches of the city.

At the same time the new doctrines were spreading throughout Germany. In part they were carried by word of mouth, notably by graduates of the University of Wittenberg; but the most potent means of dissemination was the popular pamphlet—small, cheap, and pungent. More pamphlets were issued in Germany from the beginning of 1521 to the end of 1524 than in any other four years of her history, and the bulk of them dealt with the Reformation. The printers who issued these manifestos were an intrepid breed, who risked not simply the confiscation of their pamphlets and the closing down of their presses, but also the danger of imprisonment.

Lutheranism was able to achieve status as the established religion only in areas where it was favored by the government. In

Germany government meant either the municipal councils in the free, imperial cities; the bishops or abbots in the ecclesiastical territories; or the princes in the territorial states. The free cities early took a decisive stand for the reform, and among them Nuremberg, Ulm, and Strasbourg were the first. In the early 1520s the new teaching penetrated the northern cities Danzig, Lübeck, and Stralsund. Sometimes the two forms of religion continued side by side longer than at Wittenberg. At Strasbourg for some years Mass was said on the altar and Lutheranism preached from the pulpit. In the cities laymen took a prominent lead in promoting the Reformation. At Nuremberg the city secretary, Lazarus Spengler, published a tract favoring the reform, and Hans Sachs, the meistersinger, celebrated Luther as "the nightingale of Wittenberg."

Among the lay princes the first to espouse the new reforms was, of course, Frederick the Wise of Saxony; his successor, John, even more fervently, came out openly for Luther. The elector of Brandenburg, grand master of the Teutonic Knights in East Prussia, soon followed. The ecclesiastical princes held aloof from the new movement, with the exception of the archbishop of Cologne, who toyed with the prospect of changing over, only to reject it in the end. By 1529 the Protestant territories were Saxony, Hesse, Brandenburg, Anhalt, and Lüneburg. The Palatinate and Württemberg came somewhat later. The princes in these areas did not impose Lutheranism upon their subjects, but called in Lutheran ministers to instruct the people. Where the government was hostile the evangelical cause made slight headway, as in Bavaria. But if one branch of the government opposed another, Protestantism could be insinuated, as in the Netherlands, where the local authorities resisted the Spanish overlords and in Austria where the nobility opposed the crown. Among the national states Denmark came first; Lutheran ministers were invited there in the early 1520s. Denmark and her dependency, Norway, were not officially Protestant till 1536. Sweden moved slowly toward Protestantism, and Finland and Livonia also became Lutheran.

But along with the gains in the cities and territorial states there were disappointments, particularly with the fact that on the whole the liberal Catholic reformers did not line up with the Lutherans. Between 1524 and 1526 Luther and Erasmus aired their differences in a series of pamphlets, each an answer to the one that preceded it. While insisting all along that the Luther who accepted the Apostles' Creed was no heretic, Erasmus at the same time set forth fundamental disagreements with him. The most basic concerned the question whether man can co-operate with God in achieving his own salvation. Erasmus believed that this is possible. God supplies grace to which man can add his own endeavor. Thus, God and man collaborate.

Luther, on the other hand, felt that a man can contribute nothing toward his own salvation good enough to be juxtaposed with any work of God. In faith alone can he find salvation. As for authority in religion, Luther appealed to the Scriptures. Erasmus relied upon reason and the authority of the Church. The Scriptures, he pointed out, are frequently obscure; how could Luther be certain of his interpretation? Through inspiration of the Spirit, Luther answered. Erasmus called this going round in a circle. He saw correctly that Luther's principle would lead to private interpretation. Luther naïvely supposed that the Spirit would lead all responsive hearts to a common judgment. Yet the difference between the two was even deeper than Erasmus perceived. Luther felt that Erasmus took religion too casually and was totally devoid of the sense of wonder. Erasmus felt that the cause of true piety could hardly be advanced by disrupting the Church.

The disapprobation of Erasmus infuriated Luther, though he congratulated his critic for penetrating to the core of the controversy with Rome: it was not primarily about morals or money but about man and his relation with God. Much more disquieting to Luther, as he took up the manifold tasks of building his new Church, was the development within his own circle of viewpoints more extreme than his own. No blow from the papacy, he said, ever hurt so much as this. To his dismay he found himself in the middle between the Catholics to the right and the more extreme Protestant radicals to the left.

The first challenger was his old colleague Carlstadt, whose ideas and practices, first given rein while the master was in hiding at the Wartburg, Luther rejected from the outset. Carlstadt interpreted the doctrine of the priesthood of all believers to mean that ministers should be laymen with no title of doctor—he himself desired to be called simply *Bruder Andreas*—without special dress and without a stipend, supporting themselves by manual labor. In addition to being a pastor, he took a farm. Such egalitarianism appeared to Luther to be an evasion of pastoral labors. "Good God," he ejaculated, "what would I not give to be able to look into the eyes of friendly cows, instead of having to put up with a cantankerous congregation!" Even more objectionable were Carlstadt's rejection of church music and of religious images (even those of Christ) as distractions, and his interpretation of the Lord's Supper as purely spiritual. A single concept unites these three points: disparagement of physical things as an aid to devotion. For Luther, spirit and flesh were never to be disjoined; his piety was aided by the sight of the crucifix, the sound of the anthems, and the partaking of the body of Christ upon the altar.

In consequence, Lutheranism retained the liturgical arts. It gave rise to no new concepts of church architecture—its converts simply took over the Catholic churches and adapted them to their own needs. But it retained the images and the paintings; religious art among the Lutherans became individualistic, rather than devoting itself to institutional purposes. But the inevitable reform of the liturgy afforded ample scope for musical creativity.

Meanwhile, as Luther was seeking to curb the excesses of some of his followers and laboring to give ecclesiastical form to the doctrines of the Reformation, all Germany was shaken by the revolution known to history as the Peasants' War. It was not, in its origins, a religious struggle, though the Reformation with its questioning of the existing order certainly had an effect upon it. Rather the cause of the war was social and economic. Long before Luther broke with the Church of Rome, the peasants had been seeking to throw off the chains of feudalism. In opposing their demands the princes had sought to introduce the principles of Roman law, which deprived the masses of access to communal woods, waters, and meadows. The resulting revolt, which began in the Black Forest in June 1524, within a year spread north, east, and west and came to involve two-thirds of Germany.

Luther agreed that many of the peasants' demands were justified, but he did not approve of violence as the way to achieve them. Like Augustine, he said that the common man must never take the sword, because the use of force by individuals on their own behalf results in anarchy and can never vindicate justice. Luther issued a tract excoriating the lords for their extortion but

This woodcut by Dürer depicts a joyous
peasant couple dancing. But in the 1520s
peasants in many parts of Germany rose in
rebellion against economic inequities.
Religion often stirred them to action; in
Luther's Bible, for instance, peasants read
that Jesus said they would inherit the earth.

pleading with the peasants to exercise patience. Instead they cut loose and began ravaging the land, pillaging, plundering, and guzzling down the wine of the monasteries. Frederick the Wise was of a mind to do nothing and leave the outcome to God. Luther told him that as a prince he was obligated to suppress disorder and came out with a second pamphlet in which he exhorted the rulers to "smite, slay, stab, and kill." Unfortunately, this tract appeared at about the time the peasants were being beaten and butchered, and Luther was unduly credited with inciting the repressive measures—over one hundred thousand peasants lost their lives before the revolt was finally put down— to which the propertied classes had already resorted. Indeed, when those measures were adopted Luther wrote a third tract in which he declared that the devils, having left the peasants, had not returned to hell but had gone into the nobles.

The claim has been made that the peasants, disgruntled by Luther's stand, forsook his Church, and that in consequence Lutheranism became a middle-class movement. This was certainly not true in Wittenberg, where to the end of Luther's day his congregation had manure on their boots. Where it was established Lutheranism retained its hold on the populace until the defection of industrial workers in modern times. The chief effect of the peasant defeat was an increase in the power of the Lutheran territorial princes in all areas, including the affairs of the Church.

In view of such disorders the need was acutely felt for the introduction of some system into the church life of electoral Saxony. When Luther returned from the Wartburg in 1522 the town council was handling affairs in Wittenberg, but as the Reformation came to involve all Saxony, there appeared to be no one with sufficient authority to give it permanent, stable form other than the elector himself. This, after the death of Frederick the Wise in 1525, was his nephew John Frederick, a man much more decisively convinced of Luther's whole position. Luther recognized that the civil government has a responsibility for the maintenance of the true faith but not the right to impede the Gospel. Since, then, the elector was committed to the Gospel, why should he not act as interim bishop in the emergency? John Frederick appointed "visitors," some of them laymen, some clerics, to investigate all the parishes in Saxony. Many priests, deplorably ignorant and immoral, were deposed; those who were reputable but still committed to the old Church were given instruction. Only gradually, therefore, did the territory become uniformly Protestant. Unfortunately, the system of state visitation became institutionalized; the appointment and removal of ministers became a government function, and the ministers became dependent on the state even for their salaries, which the rulers paid out of the income of secularized properties of the Catholic Church. Under such circumstances Luther's dictum that the minister should be the teacher of the magistrate sometimes was difficult to realize.

For the newly constituted churches Luther provided an immense body of aids for religious instruction and worship. There were two catechisms, one for children and one for adults, based on the Ten Commandments, the Apostles' Creed, and the Lord's Prayer. Luther issued two hymn books, writing the words for over half a dozen of the hymns himself and collaborating with the Wittenberg organist on the composition of the tunes. He issued a body of sermons for the Christian year as models for the ministers and twice revised the liturgy, once in Latin and again in German. The latter version provided that the church service should consist very largely of instruction, to increase the understanding of Christianity among the ill-informed masses, whose attachment to religion was largely nominal.

One other great departure from Catholic teaching and practice was inaugurated by Luther after his return to Wittenberg: the abolition of monasticism and clerical celibacy. While still at the Wartburg he had persuaded himself from the Scriptures that monastic vows were not ordained by Christ and therefore were not binding. In the Middle Ages it was held that only priests, monks, and nuns had vocations, that is, only they had been called by God to dedicate themselves to his service. But in Luther's view every occupation was a calling, since all Christians are priests. This view elevated not only the magistrate, but the family man, the wife and the mother, and the housemaid as well. (The abolition of mendicant monasticism made poverty either a misfortune or a crime, never a virtue or a way of salvation. The ordinances of the Protestant towns forbade begging: those who could should work, those who could not should be supported by the community.)

The monks and nuns who in consequence now began leaving their monasteries and convents in large numbers were, Luther said, free to marry. He himself originally had no intention of doing so ("They will never force a wife upon me," he said), but in 1525 he was faced by a dilemma. A whole nunnery had escaped in a cart used to transport empty herring barrels and had come to Wittenberg. "A wagonload of vestal virgins has just come to town," a contemporary said. "God give them husbands lest worse befall." Luther undertook to find homes for them, either as servants or as wives. Finally, all had been placed save one, Katharina von Bora, whose fiancé had withdrawn from the arranged marriage under family pressure. Katharina intimated that she would consider Luther. He reasoned that marriage would please his father and displease the pope; moreover, since Christ would come soon, there might never be another opportunity. He married and thereby established the archetype of the Protestant family parsonage, which has given so many eminent sons to Church, state, and school. Luther did not combine romance with matrimony—he married out of a sense of duty—but he developed tender affections for his "Lord Katie," bantering about her dominance over him while at the same time paying tribute to his need of her.

By 1530 Lutheranism had taken on definitive shape and had achieved considerable geographical expansion, but from the beginning and long thereafter its hope of continuance was tenuous. The emperor demanded the enforcement of the Edict of Worms. But he was in Spain. The Diet of Nuremberg in 1524 had decreed that the Edict should be enforced "in so far as might be possible." The Diet of Speyer in 1526 left the question of enforcement to each ruler, "as he would have to answer to God and the emperor." But the Diet that assembled at Speyer in 1529 took stronger action. Until the meeting of a general council Lutheranism might be tolerated where it could not be suppressed without tumult; but Catholic minorities must be allowed in Lutheran areas, although the same liberty was not extended to Lutheran minorities who wished to practice their faith in Catholic districts.

The Lutheran princes protested this decision and thereupon were called Protestants. The next year, 1530, the emperor was able to come to Germany for the meeting of the Diet of Augsburg. He was resolved to try conciliation and then, if need be, coercion. The Lutherans presented as their statement of faith the Augsburg Confession, drafted by Melanchthon, who headed the theologians, since Luther, being under the ban, could not attend. The Confession was presented by the princes who stood to lose their titles, lands, and lives. It stressed the congruence of Lutheranism with Catholicism but yielded nothing on justification solely by faith and the denial of transubstantiation. The Confession was unacceptable to the Diet, and the emperor then gave the reformers until the following April to return to their old faith.

Several of the Lutheran princes and a number of the free cities thereupon organized at Schmalkalden a league for mutual defense. Faced by a new threat from the Turks, the emperor agreed to a truce with the league. In the years that followed, Lutheranism spread. By 1555 the Protestants were in a position to reach a settlement with the emperor, whereby territories that adhered to the Augsburg Confession in 1552 were granted toleration, but Catholic territories might not change thereafter. Subjects who did not wish to subscribe to the religion that prevailed in their territory could emigrate. Not only in Germany, but also in the Scandinavian countries to which Luther's doctrines had spread, the Protestant state had become an established reality.

Concurrent with the expansion of Lutheranism in Germany and to the north, another variety of Protestantism arose, in German Switzerland. Ulrich Zwingli, its leader, was less indebted to Luther than to Erasmus. Erasmus had remained in the Catholic Church, but once the Church's authority was rejected—as it was by such reformers as Zwingli—the Dutchman's views proved to be highly subversive of Catholicism; for Erasmus so spiritualized Christianity that the structure and forms of the Roman Catholic Church were imperiled.

Zwingli was a Swiss Humanist. He became vicar of the cathedral at Zurich in 1519 and there introduced the Reformation by announcing that he would preach on the entire Gospel of Matthew, rather than on the excerpts designated in the liturgy of the ecclesiastical year; further, he would translate on the spot from the Greek. An auditor said he felt as if he were being pulled by the very hair of his head when he heard passages from the Word of God that had been neglected for over a thousand years.

Zwingli was in some respects more bound to the text of the Scriptures than Luther. He regarded the Bible not simply as proclamation of salvation, but also as a pattern for church organization, whereas for Luther polity and liturgy were nonessential and open to variety. Luther also would allow whatever the Bible did not prohibit, whereas Zwingli would reject whatever the Bible did not enjoin. This meant a much more drastic stripping away of all the remnants of Romanism. Luther would reject only that which conflicted directly or by implication with the gospel of Paul. Zwingli, even more than Erasmus, desired to restore the pattern and even the constitution of the primitive Church.

Strictly speaking, this should have entailed the separation of Church and state, but Zwingli recognized that after the state had become Christian, the Church was not obligated to behave as it had in the first century, when the state was pagan. In a truly Christian community, Church and state could collaborate. At this point Zwingli simply took over the practice that had long prevailed in Swiss cities and elsewhere, whereby town councils exercised supervision over the morals and manners of cloisters and churches. To regard the state as an agency for registering the will of a Christian community was the more plausible in the Swiss city-republics, where important decisions in religious matters were taken only after a town meeting in which the populace could voice its opinions.

First of all Zwingli desired to implement the reform of the Mass. Like Luther, he believed that there should be no private Masses for the dead and that the liturgy should include no adoration of the host, no language of sacrifice, no withholding of the cup from the laity. Like Luther also he rejected the authority of the pope, the invocation of saints, and clerical celibacy. Beyond that Zwingli would also abolish fast days, remove images, and discontinue church music. At the cathedral in Zurich the images were removed and the walls whitewashed. Happily, Zwingli did not feel called upon to smash the stained-glass windows. The organ was dismantled, not because Zwingli objected to music as such—he was in fact an accomplished musician—but because he felt God should be worshipped only in spirit and without sensory aids. He interpreted the sacrament of the Lord's Supper in particular as purely commemorative and spiritual. Luther, in his conflict with Carlstadt at Wittenberg, had already championed art, music, and the physical presence of Christ on the altar. It was Zwingli rather than Carlstadt who was to transmit the rejection of all three to English Puritanism.

But with regard to the concept of the Church, Luther and

Zwingli were completely at odds. For Luther the true Church was so spiritual and intangible that it could not be identified with any particular organization. The Church, he said, consists of the elect, but the elect are known only to God. Zwingli, on the other hand, believed that the elect can be identified by their public adherence to the true faith, which is witnessed by their taking Communion in the presence of the congregation. The Lord's Supper thus symbolized the individual Christian's unity not only with God but with the whole Christian community. It could not be assumed with the same degree of assurance that the children of those who made this public confession were also among the elect, yet they were to be regarded as being so. In Christianity infant baptism was the successor to circumcision, which in ancient Israel had designated a child as spiritually of the seed of Abraham.

For Zwingli the reference to the Old Testament was more than an analogy, because he regarded the Christian Church as the new Israel of God, its people a holy people, the successor to the chosen people of old. Society was a theocracy in which Church, state, and all the people should submit to the will of God as set forth in the Bible—not only the New Testament but also the Old, in which the holy community should find the patterns for its social structure. The prophet should guide the king; the king should support the cultus and cast out the ungodly.

Zwingli's system was well suited to the city of Zurich, where, as already noted, the representative government had already assumed authority over the Church. Since few non-adherents remained in the city, its populace might more plausibly be identified with the elect. Some of the other Swiss cantons soon followed her lead by embracing the evangelical faith, notably Bern, Basel, Schaffhausen, Glarus, and St. Gall. But the original cantons of the Swiss Confederation—Uri, Schwyz, and Aug, along with Lucerne and Unterwalden—were against the new ideas and remained loyal to the Catholic Church. Preparations were made for war, and political alliances were sought that might easily have disrupted the entire confederation, because Zwingli hoped for a military league not only with France and Savoy but also with the German Lutherans. This notion was absolutely abhorrent to Luther, who would use no force to defend the Gospel and who disagreed sharply with Zwingli on theological grounds, especially on the interpretation of the Eu-

The Protestant reforms, later adopted by
five of the Swiss cantons, were first
introduced into Zurich by Ulrich Zwingli.
A detail from a painting of Zurich, showing
the cathedral in which Zwingli preached,
appears here.

charist. At the same time the Catholic cantons looked to the traditional enemy, the House of Hapsburg, for help. The result was the Wars of Kappel in 1529 and 1531. In the second, Zwingli, no longer an Erasmian pacifist but a militant crusader, fell dead on the field of battle. Luther saw in his death the manifest evidence of the wrath of God against ministers who by wielding the sword condoned war.

The Second Peace of Kappel allowed Protestantism to remain where it was already established, but permitted no further expansion; in Catholic cantons Protestant minorities were not to be tolerated. This was in 1531, more than twenty years before the Peace of Augsburg. Switzerland was thus the first land after Bohemia to countenance religious pluralism. The basis, as later at Augsburg, was territorial.

Within Zwingli's circle arose another type of radical reformation that in time came to be known as Anabaptism (that is, rebaptism). Its adherents called themselves simply Baptists, because in their eyes infant baptism was no baptism at all, but merely a "dipping in the Romish bath"; the only real baptism was adult baptism. But at first adult baptism was not the point of division, nor was it ever more than an outward sign of these people's new concept of Church, state, and society. These radicals believed that the Church is a voluntary society of convinced believers, that it should be separate from the state, and that where religion is concerned no man's assent should be won by force.

Although Anabaptism has sometimes been interpreted as the cult of the disinherited, the first leaders in the movement were men of substance, who were disinherited because they became Anabaptists. Conrad Grebel and Felix Manz were men of standing in Zurich. Grebel was a patrician, Humanistically educated, exposed to the views of Erasmus, quite able to debate on equal terms with Zwingli; others of similar stamp began to meet with Grebel to search the Scriptures and thereby recover the pattern of the primitive Church. They discovered that the early Christian churches were not financially supported by tithes collected by the state, but rather by the voluntary contributions of the believers. The demands of the peasants, then, for the abolition of tithes did have a biblical warrant as well as economic justification.

A more fundamental question next arose: Should the reform

of the Church wait for the consent of the magistrate? Zwingli wished to win all Zurich by persuasion and believed that the magistrate, though implementing reform, should await a mandate from the people. For two years in Zurich Protestant and Catholic forms of worship continued side by side. Zwingli was willing to be provisionally associated with such a half-and-half arrangement. But the radical Anabaptists objected that no such compromise was tolerable. Of course the Mass was not to be forcibly suppressed, but those who did not believe in it should have no sort of affiliation with those who did. They should feel themselves in no way bound to wait for the magistrate to register the mind of the community, but instead should set up a separate conventicle of true believers.

The radicals complained further that the conduct of those who confessed the reformed faith fell far short of New Testament standards. Neither Zwingli nor Luther denied this—Luther sometimes called his congregation "Wittenberg swine"—but neither of the two wished to use the ban so drastically as to reduce the Church to a handful of saints. This was precisely what the radicals demanded. The unworthy must be cast out, the tepid and doubting must never be forced to come in. Then came the point that focused the issue: the radicals insisted that the Church cannot admit infants, for to make baptism in infancy the mark of membership in a Christian society is to fill the Church with more tares than wheat. Infants should not be baptized. Nor should any adult whose life is still bogged in the mire be laved in the waters of baptism; first must come conversion and moral regeneration and only thereafter the sign of baptism. There is no sense, one of the radicals said, in washing cabbages while they are still in the dirt.

The little separatist congregation that began to assume shape grew even more radical in its attitude to the state, which, it came to believe, is in no sense a Christian institution. Of course the apostle Paul had said that rulers are ordained by God to punish sinners, which means that if there were no sinners there would be no need for rulers. But since there are sinners, let the sinners be the rulers and punish the other sinners. The saints should have no part in all this. Neither should they take up the sword, either in war or in the enforcement of civil justice.

Such were the views of the Anabaptists. They were for the most part pacifists, who took literally both the injunction of the

Sermon on the Mount to resist not evil and the command to take no oath. Their position resembled that of the earlier Waldenses and appeared quite as subversive of the whole structure of society. Their first congregation was formed in the little town of Zollikon, a suburb of Zurich.

The first move of the authorities was to banish the Anabaptists, but this only spread the infection into the Grisons and beyond. Then a number of converts to the new faith were imprisoned, and finally, Grebel having died of the plague, the Anabaptists' other principal leader, Felix Manz, was drowned in a mock baptism. That was in January 1527, and the town council of Zurich justified the execution on the grounds that Anabaptist beliefs were subversive of the state. They found legal grounds for their action in the Justinian Code, which visited death on the Donatists for rebaptizing heretics.

The Zurichers would have done well to recall that the blood of the martyrs is seed. Anabaptist emissaries, both men and women, spread over the land, evangelizing the populace on the roads and in the homes. Conventicles sprang up in other cantons, and the movement shot its tendrils into northern Germany and down the Rhine into the Low Countries, where the local authorities obstructed the efforts of Spain to impose a pattern of rigid orthodoxy. The people of the Netherlands were hospitable to Anabaptism because its simple piety resembled in a measure that of the Brethren of the Common Life. The dissemination of Anabaptism was so broad that both Catholics and Lutherans feared the established Churches would be displaced.

Fear leads to repression. The Catholics burned the Anabaptists; the Protestants drowned them. At the Diet of Speyer in 1529 both Catholics and Lutherans agreed to subject them to the death penalty throughout the Holy Roman Empire. Luther was slower than others in giving his consent; but by 1531 his fear of anarchy led him to agree to the death penalty, not for heresy, but for blasphemy and sedition. He considered pacifism to be sedition because it would destroy the police power of the state. The only Protestant ruler who refused to apply the penalty of death to the Anabaptists was Philip of Hesse. He took arms to defend Lutheranism, as Luther would not, but would kill no man because of his divergent faith.

For the first decade the Anabaptists were sustained by a magnificent hope: the Lord Jesus was coming. The kingdom of Antichrist would fall, the new Jerusalem would descend, and the saints would reign. The more the heathen Christians raged, the more was their doom sure. Martyrdom was the way the Master had trod, and the saints must tread it too. As Christ had been exalted to the right hand of God, even so would the true Church inherit the kingdoms of the world. But as more and more of the saner leaders were executed the less balanced spirits came to the fore, announcing themselves as Elijahs, Enochs, or Davids returned to earth to usher in the speedy return of Christ. Some forsook their habitual pacifism and clamored for the slaughter of the ungodly. One group introduced polygamy in imitation of Abraham, Isaac, and Jacob.

The effects of the extravagances were twofold: increased persecution by their opponents and on their own part a recoil toward sobriety. Three groups emerged. The Swiss Anabaptists survived, as the Waldenses had done, by retreating to the mountains. From this group came the Amish, who established American colonies in Pennsylvania and the Midwest. In Holland the great leader was Menno Simons, whose followers, the Mennonites, are to be found in Russia and in North and South America, as well as in Holland. Menno repudiated polygamy, revolution, private inspiration through dreams and visions, and the setting of dates for the coming of the Lord. His was the simple Christianity of the Sermon on the Mount, which laid minimal emphasis upon theology, stressed discipline in deportment, and insisted upon separation of the Church from the state.

A third branch of the Anabaptists was called Hutterite, after Jacob Hutter, whose followers established colonies of refugees in Moravia and Transylvania, where the old feudal lords provided an asylum against the encroachments of the emperor. Anabaptists have been able to survive for long only by accommodating their views to prevailing opinion—as the Dutch Mennonites have modified their pacifism—or by isolating themselves in more or less remote communities. They have had intrareligious difficulties; those who can magnificently defy their critics cannot always agree with one another. A German Anabaptist visiting the Hutterite colonies in Moravia found the temper so divisive that he said he could get along more easily with Turks and papists. Yet the lesson of cohesion was finally learned, and these communities have displayed an amazing capacity to hold their children and preserve their identity to this day.

If Lutheranism, Zwinglianism, and Anabaptism are considered three varieties of Protestantism, then Calvinism may be accounted a fourth, though Zwinglianism and Calvinism are commonly grouped together and called the Reformed Churches. Calvinism emerged only after Lutheranism and Zwinglianism had grown rigid in the struggle with the radicals. John Calvin, a French theologian and reformer who left the Catholic Church in 1533 at the age of twenty-four, provided for Protestantism at this stage an integrated doctrinal system. His book, *The Institutes of the Christian Religion*, appeared in 1536 in Basel. Incipient Protestantism had been tolerated in his native France for a time. Marguerite of Navarre, sister of the king, Francis I, inclined to the new ideas, and her daughter, Jeanne d'Albret, was an avowed Protestant. Francis himself vacillated in his policy toward the innovators—depending on whether he desired an alliance with the pope, the Turks, or the German Protestants—but in 1534 he was deeply angered by the publication of the placards, vitriolic posters defaming the Mass. Even the Humanists were alienated by such an indecorous stab at the piety of the ages. The resulting repressions scattered the reformers, Calvin's flight terminating in Basel.

Calvin's *Institutes* begin not with justification by faith but with the knowledge of God. Calvin was in the tradition of those scholastics who declined to make faith and knowledge mutually exclusive, insisting rather that they were simply different modes of apprehension. Faith, Calvin said, could be described as conviction, assurance, certitude. His point was that the heathen philosophers, for all their genius, were blinder than bats and moles, whereas Christians relying on revelation could enjoy unshakable confidence. The God in whom Christians believed was the creator, the sustainer, and the sovereign ruler of the universe, seated in majesty, too high and too holy to share his divinity with humans.

Calvin had no use for the view of the Christian Neoplatonists, or of any of the mystics, that man can be united with God. The chief end of man, according to Calvin, is not to be united with God, but to bow before his inscrutable decrees and to fulfill his evident commands. This rather than man's own personal salvation should be his concern. On that score there is absolutely nothing that man can do, because God, out of time, has already decreed who should be saved and who damned. Calvin's theory of predestination was more sharply drawn than that of Luther or Zwingli, because Calvin confronted boldly not only election but also damnation. Since the fall of Adam, he said, all men have deserved damnation. God punishes the majority according to their deserts to illustrate his justice, but some he saves according to his good pleasure in order to display his grace. Calvin knew this decree to be frightful, but there it was. How a good God can do this we do not understand, but we are not to complain or to worry about our salvation.

Yet Calvin and his early followers felt reasonably sure of their salvation. He posited three tests: profession of the true faith, an upright life, and attendance upon the sacrament of the Lord's Supper. He who could meet these fairly tangible requirements could assume that he was one of the elect. For Zwingli the elect could be identified by their profession of faith and their participation in Communion; and the same was true for Calvin. The Anabaptists added purity of life to the tests, as did Calvin. He did not demand, as did the New England Puritans in later years, anything so thoroughly subjective as the rebirth of the spirit. To the tests of Zwingli and the Anabaptists he added a love of the sacrament of the Lord's Supper, his theory of this sacrament lying between the views of Luther and Zwingli. Calvin believed in the real, though not physical, presence of Christ at the celebration of the Lord's Supper; for him the bread and the wine were signs, but the essence of Christ was present in them.

By these tests a company of the elect could be recognized and assembled to constitute a holy commonwealth. For this society God had a great work to be achieved on earth—the establishment of the kingdom of God, which, said Calvin, is the Church restored; God would allow time for its realization.

When Calvin talked about man's destiny, commonly he had in mind the Last Judgment rather than the second coming of Christ. The apocalyptic hope that was lively for Luther, and that was cardinal for many of the Anabaptists, was attenuated by Calvin through an indefinite extension. Just as Augustine had contributed to the realization of the churchly theocracy in the Middle Ages by dropping the primitive Christian hopes of a speedy denouement, so it was that Calvin opened the way for a social gospel to redeem the fabric of society.

PROMPTE ET SINCERE

IOHANNES · CALVINVS ·
ANNO · ÆTATIS · 53 ·
· B ·

In the city of Geneva, Calvin imposed a theocracy patterned after that of the ancient Hebrews. Although some citizens resented such strict supervision of their lives, Calvin, whose portrait appears here, was supported by the city's Protestant refugees from other countries. The practical realization of his doctrines in Geneva's government led Protestants throughout Europe to look upon the city as the new Jerusalem.

To this end the Calvinists expended colossal energies in the ruling of cities, the converting of kingdoms, the beheading of a king, and the taming of wildernesses. Because they felt themselves to be the elect of God they were fearless and indomitable. They worked with fury because they knew that although history is long, life is short. For them time became a precious commodity.

Calvinism has been credited with giving a great impetus to the spirit of capitalism because it induced men, more than Lutheranism did, to work in their callings for the glory of God—not simply diligently, but relentlessly. Business was not disparaged but was regarded as one of the callings, legitimate alike for workers and for entrepreneurs. Further, Calvinism had an ascetic aspect that endorsed using profits for philanthropy or for building up a business, but not for enjoyment. Calvinism was certainly more hospitable to trade and investment than Lutheranism. Luther lived in a peasant community and had a peasant's economic outlook. Geneva, the seat of Calvinism, was on the Rhone River and had plentiful trade connections with southern France. Further, Calvin was confronted with the problem of finding maintenance for thousands of refugees with funds to invest. However, he imposed the same restrictions as Luther and Aquinas and disparaged the pursuit of gain. Yet, as in the case of medieval monasticism, the industry and thrift of his followers produced wealth and eventually made of Calvinists a prosperous middle class.

Calvin's program for a holy commonwealth found its realization in Geneva. The city at the moment had just thrown off the authority of the bishop and the duke of Savoy with the help of Protestant Bern, but was not yet a member of the Swiss Confederation. Evangelical ministers came in from France, particularly William Farel, who had the populace on the verge of civil war when the magistrates recognized the reform. For all his forcefulness, Farel felt unequal to completing the reform of the city, and when young Calvin was passing through Geneva impressed him into service by threats of hell if he declined. Calvin accepted.

His theory of the relations of Church and state soon led to friction. He believed in a Christian community where Church, state, and citizenry were equally dedicated to the glory of God. They should sustain each other, but their functions were not identical. The Church was to be independent and was to determine the forms of the liturgy and above all else should control excommunication. This demand was resisted by the magistrates, and Calvin, because of his insistence, was briefly banished from Geneva. He was recalled, and after another tussle in 1553 the point was definitely conceded that ecclesiastical discipline is the province of the Church. Thus Calvinism became more independent of the state than Lutheranism or Zwinglianism. Jurisdiction over heresy, however, remained with the magistrates. Calvin won, partly because the constituency came to be almost as select as that of a monastery. The Catholics left the city. Thousands of refugees who came to Geneva because of their religious sympathies were made citizens and stoutly supported Calvin. Those banned from the Church, if not reconciled after a period, were banished from the city. Thus Calvin succeeded in uniting the idea of a Church as coterminous with the community and of a Church as a voluntary society of visible saints.

Calvin gave a great stimulus to education by treating teachers as members of the ministry. An academy was founded in Geneva. Calvin's views on arts and music were more moderate than Zwingli's. He would allow a cross but not a crucifix and permitted the singing of the Psalms in church, but no other music. Psalm-singing actually became a distinctive feature of Calvinist services in France, Scotland, and New England.

Calvinism was to become the most international form of Protestantism. The Calvinists refused to respect the previously established territorial principle in religion, and like the Anabaptists they insinuated themselves wherever they could, thus spreading into France, the Netherlands, England, Scotland, and New England, into Lithuania, Poland, and Hungary. In these countries the Genevan pattern of Church, state, and community could not be reproduced, because at first Calvinism was a minority movement. Even later when it became dominant, as in Scotland, there was never such a purging of the populace nor such a control over its behavior as there was at Geneva, where the Consistory governed with relentless rigor.

Calvinism was ultimately to exert a great influence in England, where the Reformation began in the year 1534, two years prior to the appearance of the *Institutes*. The English Reformation is the supreme example of the fusion of nationalism and religious upheaval. It could never have happened if the Tudors had not terminated the wars of succession and established political absolutism. The quarrel with Rome was not over doctrine and not primarily over morality or finances, but over a point at which religion impinged upon politics, the matter of a royal marriage. As a sacrament of the Church, marriage was subject to ecclesiastical jurisdiction; but royal marriages were affairs of state, emphatically so because kings were expected to ensure the succession by producing progeny.

England required a male heir of King Henry VIII. But after sixteen years of marriage to his first wife, Queen Catherine, only one child survived—and a girl at that, the princess Mary. The simplest solution would have been to annul the marriage and leave Henry free to marry another woman. There appeared to be good grounds for an annulment. Catherine had been first the wife of Henry's elder brother Arthur, and her subsequent marriage to Henry had violated the provision in Leviticus forbidding a union with a deceased husband's brother. Pope Julius II had given a dispensation to cover that irregularity. That dispensation could now be declared invalid because it contravened the law of God, the marriage could be annulled, and Henry would be free to take another queen.

Henry took his case before the pope, Clement VII, without expectation of difficulties, since two of his sisters had been able to secure annulments.

One may well suppose that the matter would have been speedily settled had there not been so many political angles. Catherine was a Spanish princess, the daughter of Ferdinand and Isabella and the aunt of the emperor, Charles V, who intervened on her behalf. However, Charles did not wish to push the case too strenuously, for trouble with England would provide France with advantages. The pope feared offending the emperor, whose troops had sacked Rome in 1527 and captured the pope. On the other hand, if England were not obliged, it might renounce papal obedience. The pope instructed his representative to stall to the uttermost, and the case dragged on for four years. Catherine maintained that her marriage with Arthur had not been consummated and that there had never been any impediment to her marriage with Henry. If only she had been willing to concede Henry's point and retire on a pension, she might have saved the unity of the Catholic Church in England, but she would not compromise in the realm of truth.

Henry decided that what he could not get from the pope he could and would secure from the archbishop of Canterbury, Thomas Cranmer, who had been elevated to the primacy because he believed so unreservedly in the royal supremacy. Therefore, in 1534 Henry broke with the papacy and set up an independent national English Church, the *Ecclesia Anglicana*, with the king as the supreme head. The king did not become a priest, nor did he directly administer the church, but Cranmer declared that the king held the two keys, both temporal and spiritual, in a Christian society. The king was most proud of his title, *defensor fidei*—defender of the faith—even though he vacillated not a little as to which faith he would defend. (The title was conferred on Henry as a consequence of a treatise he wrote against Luther.)

Significantly, Henry ordered the translation into English of the tract of Marsilius of Padua, which proposed that all the goods of the Church should be vested in the state. This doctrine, appropriated earlier by Wycliffe, had served to justify confiscation of Church goods by John of Gaunt. It could serve equally well to justify the suppression of the monasteries by Henry VIII. Cardinal Thomas Wolsey, Henry's minister, had suppressed a number even earlier in order to use their revenues to build colleges. Henry pursued this example piecemeal for five years until every monastic house in England had been dissolved. Whenever the time came to confiscate the glebes of a monastic house, its monks were charged with gross immorality and then were pensioned as if they had been altogether reputable. The monasteries were stripped and their goods sold at auction. Many a chalice turned up as a tankard in an ale house. Resentment was acute in the north, where feudal lords resisted interference in local affairs; a brief rebellion occurred there, but it was speedily quelled. However, there was amazingly little opposition to Henry's program on the part of the clergy, the monks, and the laity.

A Catholic historian has said there never has been a major revolution carried through with so little bloodshed. One reason was that in the two hundred years prior to the Reformation, the English monasteries had been distinguished only for mediocrity. Another reason was undoubtedly the popularity of the Tudor monarchy, though another may have been the assumption that the changes would not last. In the Middle Ages kings demanded of the pope more than they expected to get, weathered excommunication for a few years, and then submitted on terms which gave them most of that which they desired. The bishops who acknowledged Henry as the supreme head may have expected him before long to return to obedience to the papacy.

Under Henry only one change affected the practice of religion: the Bible was introduced in an English translation into all the churches. In 1539 Henry commissioned Bishop Miles Coverdale to produce such a version. For the most part he availed himself of an earlier translation, tinged with Protestantism, that had been made by William Tyndale; it had been printed on the Continent and for some time had been smuggled into England.

Toward the end of his reign Henry pursued a religious policy midway between Catholicism and Protestantism. After his death in 1547 the duke of Somerset, regent for Henry's young son Edward VI, sought to introduce a more radical type of Protestantism, including the Mass in English. Somerset was unseated by Warwick, the future duke of Northumberland. The English Reformation moved toward Lutheranism, then toward Zwinglianism, and again toward Calvinism.

The great achievement of this period was the revision and translation of the liturgy into the English tongue, the work of Archbishop Cranmer, who was preeminently qualified for the task. The stately cadences of the Book of Common Prayer, which he compiled, have for centuries carried the petitions of Englishmen to the throne of grace, and more than all else have endeared the English Church to the English people. Cranmer was assisted by a number of eminent Protestant refugees from the Continent with Zwinglian or Calvinist leanings. Their influence may be seen in the Book of Common Prayer, where the priest is termed minister, the communion a commemoration.

When Edward died in 1553 the succession went to his half-sister Mary Tudor, the daughter of Catherine of Aragon, who all along had refused to give up the Mass. In July 1554, she was married to her cousin Philip of Spain, the son of the emperor Charles. The couple had a coin minted in 1555 showing their faces closely adjacent, which gave rise to the jingle:

Amorous, fond, and billing,
Like Philip and Mary on a shilling.

Mary brought England into conformity with Rome. One

marvels that the English, if they loved Rome, should have permitted the Protestant Reformation, and if they loved the Protestant Reformation, should have been willing to return to Rome. Evidently they did not greatly care what happened to monks, whether priests were married or celibate, and whether the Mass was in Latin or in English. Rather than incur civil disorder, they were ready to return to the old ways.

But Mary actually could not restore all the old ways. The monastic lands had been alienated beyond recovery. Cardinal Reginald Pole, son of the martyred duchess of Salisbury, came back from Italy to assist in the restoration of Catholicism, and Cardinal Bartolomé de Carranza came from Spain. The chief Protestant clergy went to the stake, among them Archbishop Cranmer. He went through a frightful ordeal of conscience, because he had been the most forward in asserting the right of the king to be the head of the Church. If the authority of the sovereign were absolute and the sovereign decided to return to Rome, should not the subject submit to Roman authority? But thus to submit was to deny the absolute sovereignty of the king. Cranmer repeatedly recanted and abjured his recantations. He was nevertheless condemned to be burned. Before the execution he was called upon to read his final recantation in St. Mary's Church at Oxford. The audience came to see a reed shaken by the wind, but Cranmer startled them by confessing his shame in having renounced his Protestant faith and then strode smiling to the stake. The archbishop's execution was but one of the many persecutions that alone made Mary's brief reign memorable.

X
Wars of Religion

This representation of the crucified Christ, decorated with Indian carvings, was made in Mexico during the seventeenth century.

As Protestantism spread, Emperor Charles V made repeated efforts to have the popes convene a council that would consider the reform of abuses within the Church, and that thereby might lead toward the restoration of some religious unity among the elements of the empire in Germany and the Netherlands. The popes, fearing a resurgence of conciliarism and a consequent challenge to papal authority, long resisted such proposals. However, in face of the increasing menace of Lutheranism the popes finally yielded; a great council was convened at Trent in 1545 and sat intermittently until 1563, with the dual purpose of instituting moral and administrative reforms and of defining Church doctrine.

The council did not reduce tensions between Protestants and Catholics; rather it confirmed Erasmus' statement that the breach was irreparable. But it had other impressive results. In spite of earlier doubts, the council remained under papal control, thus assuring the centralization of the Church. And it ended by stating the Catholic position in matters of dogma and doctrine with admirable lucidity. The doctrine of justification by faith was so defined that a Christian could still cooperate in his salvation through the accumulation of merits, contrary to the Protestant belief in justification by faith alone. The belief in purgatory was maintained, and tradition was placed on a par with the Scriptures as authority for the teachings of the Church. The Vulgate translation of the Scriptures was declared to be the only authentic version, to be used in all disputations and not to be called into question (a position no longer held by the Catholic Church today).

The council insisted that the rules of the Church regarding clerical celibacy were to be enforced. The clergy were to be in residence in their parishes, with only one parish to a man; plural holdings were forbidden. Provisions were made for better education of the clergy, and bishops were given greater control of their own dioceses. The doctrine of indulgences was upheld, but abuses that had grown up in connection with the sale of them were eliminated. Further, specifically Protestant doctrines were rejected. Humanist scholarship was restrained in that scholarly principles could not be applied to biblical translation. The condemnation of certain works of Erasmus excluded the liberal type of Catholicism that had prevailed earlier in the century. (Indeed, the pope, Paul IV, went so far as to ban the entire body of Erasmus' writings in 1559; his decree was renewed by Pope Sixtus V in 1590.) Catholicism thus became entrenched against liberal, and later against scientific and democratic, tendencies until the latter part of the nineteenth century. In contradiction to the Protestant stand, the council reaffirmed the seven sacraments and the doctrine of transubstantiation; and to further confront the challenge of Protestantism the Church in many ways tightened the efficiency of its administrative machinery.

The Council of Trent manifestly accentuated the breach with the Protestants, and attempts on the part of the emperor to achieve a compromise did not provide any solution. There was none, in fact, save to recognize the heretics. This was done in Germany by the Peace of Augsburg of 1555, through which Lutheranism received recognition in those areas where it had been established by 1552. By this agreement the Catholics admitted the end of the system of one empire and one religion. Charles V would not accept responsibility for such an admission; he left the onus of promulgating the Peace to his brother, Ferdinand of Austria, stipulated that its terms would not apply to his hereditary domains in the Netherlands, and abdicated. The Lutherans, for their part, had to relinquish the ideal of a Protestant Germany, especially because the Peace required that the ecclesiastical states should never embrace the reform. The Lutherans had also to give up their initial attempt to include the other Reformed Churches in the Peace. This exclusion of the Calvinists intensified confessional strife among the Protestants.

The conflict between Catholics and Protestants led each to purge its own moderates. The earlier reforms of Ximénez had fortified the Church in Spain against intrusions of Protestantism and imposed a zealous orthodoxy. All the machinery of the Inquisition was brought into action not only against any traces of Lutheranism but against Erasmian mystics as well. To celebrate the return from the Netherlands of Philip II, son of Charles V, a great auto-da-fé was held in 1559, in which large numbers of heretics were strangled and burned. In that same year Bartolomé de Carranza, archbishop of Toledo and primate of the Spanish Church, returning from his position as confessor to Mary Tudor in England, was imprisoned by the Inquisition because of his

Erasmian leanings; he was kept incarcerated for the remaining seventeen years of his life.

The Spanish spirit of reform had been spread beyond the Peninsula through the founding of the Society of Jesus by Ignatius Loyola. Loyola was a Spaniard of noble birth who had been nurtured on romances of chivalry and who, dedicated to the service of his queen, became a soldier in the Spanish army. In commanding the defense of a fort against an overpowering French force, he quixotically refused to surrender until he was struck in the leg by a cannon ball and left in a pool of blood. His French captors treated him with courtesy and removed him to his own estate, where the young aristocrat made desperate efforts to regain his former grace and prowess. To correct a first, faulty operation he had his leg rebroken and reset. When a bone protruded he had it sawed flush; when the injured leg proved too short he stretched it by weights. But it was all in vain. However, during his convalescence he underwent a conversion and determined to devote his life to the Church. His career as a knight of the queen of Spain was ended, and he resolved to become a knight of the Queen of Heaven.

To this end the pen was mightier than the sword, and therefore, though a grown man, Loyola determined to go to school in order that he might, through learning, correct the evils of his day. At school he engaged in pastoral work among students and others, and was several times investigated and twice imprisoned by the Inquisition for this unauthorized activity. From Spain he repaired to the University of Paris for further study. There he gathered a band of fellow students, including Francis Xavier, who vowed to devote their lives to Church and pope. In 1540 Pope Paul III approved the formation of this group as the Society of Jesus; it was given an autocratic and military constitution and was led by an elected general with absolute authority, subject only to the pope. The Jesuits, as members of the group were called, became the new militia of the papacy for the recovery of Europe from heresy and for the conversion of the New World. Like the Calvinists, they were to justify revolution and even tyrannicide in the interests of religion. The high standards of Jesuit scholarship and learning, as was witnessed at the Council of Trent, made them invaluable advocates of papal authority.

One of the greatest expressions of the new, reforming zeal of

Catholicism was to be found in the spread of missionary work about the globe, a work in which the Jesuits, Franciscans, and other orders played an extraordinary role. In 1541, obeying the command of Loyola, Francis Xavier left on a day's notice for a decade of heroic Christian labor in India and Japan; others who followed penetrated to China. But the major fields of expansion were in the New World. Franciscans and Dominicans followed hard on the heels of the conquistadors, and after them came Jesuits, who were very active in Paraguay. Conversions by the millions were made among the native Indians. The Jesuits and others also advanced via Quebec into the wild heartland of North America. The published records of their intrepidity in the face of great perils constituted the most exciting reading of the French court.

Under missionary auspices the culture of Mexico in the sixteenth century was remarkably advanced. It was there that the first university in the American hemisphere was founded and that fine books were printed which surpassed those printed in New England in the seventeenth century. The missionaries to America were confronted with the awkward fact that when converts are received into Christianity en masse with little prior preparation, they tend to carry their paganism into their Christian worship. The cult of the Virgin of Guadalupe began in this fashion. An Indian painted an image of the Virgin in the garb of the Mexican goddess Toxantzin, and miracles were attributed to the portrait. The Franciscan bishop, Zumarraga, was an Erasmian who disparaged the popular enthusiasm, saying, "Seek not miracles. The greatest miracle on earth is a Christian life." But miracles multiplied. The legend grew, and popular piety at last received ecclesiastical recognition.

The method of teaching the Indians centered on the system of the *encomienda*, a large estate with a central village clustering around a school and a church. The missionaries cultivated apartheid in order to preserve the Indians from the corruption of the whites. The Jesuit colony in Paraguay became so renowned for kindly treatment of the Indians that escapees from other areas flocked in. The resentment of Spaniards and Portuguese against this asylum led to its suppression.

Meanwhile, in Italy the Humanistic approach to reform gave way to sterner procedures. The Inquisition was reestablished in Rome in 1542 by Giampietro Caraffa as a special tribunal to deal with heresy. Many of the liberal reformers went to prison or to the stake. After Caraffa became Pope Paul IV in 1555 the liberal cardinal Giovanni Morone was immured in the chambers of the Inquisition until Paul died in 1559. When Paul's inquisitor general, Michele Ghislieri, became Pope Pius V in 1566, the turn came for Pietro Carnesecchi, a Humanist and one-time secretary of Clement VII. Carnesecchi was a man of singular attractiveness, engaging incaution, and grand illusions about the possibilities of reform by liberal means. For some time he was saved from the Inquisition by the protection of the Medici, but when this failed he was incarcerated and tried. Under torture he would neither incriminate the dead nor accuse the living. He was ambiguous about his own views until he was given the choice of recanting or going to the block. Then he did not waver. The pope required the whole body of cardinals to attend the public reading of the long indictment of Carnesecchi and the pronouncement of the death sentence. On a subsequent morning, as the cardinals came from a conclave, they saw on the Ponte di Sant'Angelo the charred remains of the reformer.

Some of the liberal Italian reformers escaped into exile. They were small in number, but they were a colorful, highly stimulating group who disquieted the Lutherans and, especially, the Calvinists with whom they took refuge and whose rigid theology they were not often willing to accept. One group of such Italian exiles, the so-called Socinians, found a haven in Transylvania and in Poland, where they converted some of the feudal magnates. The Socinians questioned the propitiatory death of Christ and, because they subordinated God the Son to God the Father, were known as anti-Trinitarians.

At the same time the Protestants ruthlessly conducted their own purge. They did not burn Catholics, but they drowned Anabaptists and they beheaded and burned anti-Trinitarians, whose beliefs were repugnant to most Protestants as well as to Catholics. One victim was the Spaniard Michael Servetus, who had abandoned the dogma of the Trinity. He rejected the orthodox view that the second person in the Trinity, the Son, was eternal. Rather, Servetus maintained, the Son came into being when the pre-existent Christ was united by God with the man Jesus. Christ the Word, the Light of the World, was eternal, but the Son was not. For his heresy Servetus was burned in effigy in Catholic France and in actuality in Protestant Geneva. While he was passing through the Swiss city in 1553 he was recognized and indicted by John Calvin, with whom he had earlier corresponded but who had repudiated the Spaniard's anti-Trinitarianism. The town council of Geneva conducted a trial and pronounced the sentence that because of his errors, Michael Servetus should be burned at the stake, "in the name of the Father, the Son, and the Holy Ghost."

The execution of Servetus touched off a controversy over toleration within Protestantism. In 1554 Sebastian Castellio, a Protestant Humanist and a professor of Greek at the University of Basel, issued a treatise with the title *De Haereticis* (*Concerning Heretics*). In this he claimed that Christians do not know enough to justify persecuting others for differing opinions. The tenets which men are burned for denying are still being disputed, and as Erasmus had observed, are by that very token uncertain. In any case, Castellio stated, the sincerity of a conviction matters more to God than the correctness of an opinion; he defined conscience as loyalty to that which one believes to be right, whatever the objective truth.

An Italian, Jacobus Acontius by name, in the same period insisted that there should be persecution only over points declared in the Scriptures to be necessary for salvation. Of these, he said, there are only two: belief in justification by faith and belief in the Lord Jesus Christ. The failure to accept the first might be taken to exclude Catholics, and the second to debar the Socinians. But even in dealing with these Acontius advocated only persuasion; and the way to persuade, he said, is to treat the dissenter with respect and make plain that not victory in debate but verity is the issue. Very few appeals had been made on behalf of liberty of conscience, and Castellio's and Acontius' were like voices crying in the wilderness. Yet the issues these men raised and the arguments they provoked resulted in an agitation that runs in a direct line to the English Act of Toleration, which was promulgated more than a century later.

As the sixteenth century advanced resurgent Catholicism and militant Protestantism confronted each other, each purged and girt for the conflict. In April 1559, Spain and France foreswore their long rivalry and by the Treaty of Cateau-Cambrésis cemented an alliance that included a mutual commitment to extirpate heresy in their respective domains. Spain had already largely done so by the great auto-da-fé already mentioned (there

In 1587 Queen Elizabeth, above, eliminated the threat of Catholic overthrow in England when she ordered the execution of Mary, queen of Scots. Mary was never persuaded by the stern reformer John Knox to adopt Calvinism. Having fled to England from her own country, she encouraged Catholic plots to place her on the English throne. Fearing for her own life, Elizabeth ordered the death of the exiled queen.

would be others), although heresy was still rife in her dependency, the Netherlands. In France the Protestants—Huguenots, as they were there called—were a strong minority. In the year the Treaty was signed they formed a national organization, Calvinist in persuasion, through the meeting of a synod in Paris. The execution of the Treaty meant civil war.

The religious struggle in France was made more intense because the issue also involved political and social divisions within the realm. In its efforts to centralize authority the crown was impeded by rivalry on the part of the nobility and disaffection in the towns. The ruling House of Valois was dominated after the middle of the century by the queen mother, Catherine de Médicis, who, although she was a Catholic, was too politically minded to put the interests of the Church above those of her house and her country. The Bourbons, the family next in line for the throne, were partly Protestant. Their ablest member was the prince de Condé, who adopted Protestantism for political reasons. The powerful House of Guise, represented by Duke Francis, his brother the cardinal of Lorraine, and their sister Mary, queen regent of Scotland, was intransigently Catholic. The House of Chatillon, whose most distinguished member was Gaspard de Coligny, the admiral of France, was intensely Protestant and saw its religious claims as an opportunity to oppose the crown. The Huguenots were primarily artisans in the towns who had economic as well as religious grievances. Quite possibly there would have been civil war even if the religious issue had not been injected.

In 1562, by the so-called Edict of January, Catherine had, in the interest of tranquility, granted Huguenots the right to worship in certain localities. When in March of that year the duc de Guise attacked a congregation of Huguenots at Vassy, claiming it was beyond the bounds stipulated by the Edict, war broke out. In the course of the next nine years three conflicts followed, each ending inconclusively.

By 1572 the people were sick of carnage, and Catherine thought the time propitious to try again for pacification of the warring elements. Peace between the religions might be cemented by the marriage of her daughter Margaret to Henry of Navarre of the House of Bourbon, a Huguenot and heir to the crown after the Valois. Leaders of all parties came to Paris for the wedding, among them Coligny, a Calvinist. Catherine considered his influence over her son, King Charles IX, dangerously strong. Further distressed because Coligny was meditating an alliance with Elizabeth of England, Catherine appears to have plotted with the duc de Guise to have him murdered. Coligny was wounded, but not killed. Panicking at the thought of the religious strife that would follow, Catherine and her son Charles apparently determined to murder all the Huguenots who had gathered for the wedding. In the ensuing chaos, remembered as the massacre of St. Bartholomew's Day, thousands of Huguenots were slaughtered in Paris and other large French cities.

When the last male of the Valois died without issue, the Protestant Henry of Navarre became heir to the throne. To pacify the land he joined the Catholic Church and also, in 1598, issued the Edict of Nantes, which allowed the Huguenots freedom of worship in certain cities, which were garrisoned with troops at state expense as a guarantee of this freedom. The Huguenots were to have full rights to public office. Thus peace was restored.

In the Netherlands the Protestant struggle for religious freedom was joined with a revolt against Spanish domination. Emperor Charles V had always favored the Netherlands, where he had been reared. But in 1555, when he abdicated to spend the remainder of his days in a monastery, his son and successor Philip II subjected the Low Countries to the Spanish Inquisition. The central figure in the resistance was William of Orange, who had been a favorite of Charles, but who became the implacable enemy of Philip. William had passed from Catholicism to Lutheranism and from Lutheranism to Calvinism; toward all he counseled tolerance, particularly since a religious war would wreck the economic prosperity of the Netherlands. He led the resistance to check Spanish persecution and restore tranquility to the land.

William's resources were small. When told that he must seek the aid of a foreign potentate he replied, "We are aided by the greatest of all potentates, the Lord of Hosts." Nevertheless, he did not disdain clandestine help from Queen Elizabeth and was looking for aid from the Huguenots under Coligny when word came that the French admiral had been slain in the massacre of St. Bartholomew. However, in the end William's forces were able to secure the northern provinces of the Low Countries, which declared their independence in 1581, with religious liberty assured for Catholics, Lutherans, Calvinists, and even Mennonites.

The struggle of Protestantism in Scotland was also complicated by political relations, with France and England. Mary, the queen regent and widow of James V, was of the rabidly Catholic House of Guise. Her daughter Mary was the queen of France until 1561, when, following the death of her mother and her husband, she became Mary, queen of Scots. Herself a Catholic, she arrived to confront a sternly Protestant country.

Shortly before, the impassioned reformer John Knox had returned to Scotland. Knox was an extreme Calvinist who had earlier lived in exile at Geneva, which he considered to be "the most perfect school of Christ since the days of the apostles." There were in Scotland those who were rabidly anti-Roman and, among the nobility, those who were staunchly anti-French and pro-English. Knox was able to unite the two factions and, in 1560, to obtain the acceptance of Calvinism by the Scottish Parliament. He had arrived enflamed with the conviction that a celebration of the Mass was more deadly than a draught of poison, and Parliament issued a decree that prescribed the death penalty for anyone who attended Mass more than twice.

Mary blatantly defied the decree, although she did nothing to interfere with the Protestant settlement. She even made several attempts to soften Knox's attitude toward her, but he continued to berate the young queen because her conscience was tied to "that harlot, the kirk of Rome." He was quite right that Mary, if she could, would impose on Scotland obedience to the Roman Church.

Had Mary been discreet and upright, she might have detached the moderates from the intransigent Knox, but her indiscretions and crimes played into his hands. Knox inveighed against the saying of Mass in her private chapel and railed against the prospect of her remarriage with a Catholic. She summoned him to her presence and argued with him as if he represented Scotland, which indeed he did more than any lord of the realm. She was sufficiently politic not to marry a Spanish or a French Catholic, but she did marry Darnley, a Scottish Catholic who had a claim to the throne of England that she hoped would strengthen her own. When after a series of sordid intrigues she was accused of having Darnley murdered, Protestants and Catholics alike turned against her and she was forced to seek asylum in England. As she continually plotted with English, French, and Spanish Catholics to gain the English crown for herself, Queen Elizabeth felt obliged to have her executed. In the meantime, under the leadership of Knox and his followers, Presbyterianism became the established religion in Scotland, with an emergent church polity that in its final form consisted of a series of representative assemblies, from presbyteries through synods to the General Assembly of the entire Church at the top.

England was the country least affected by religious strife in the late sixteenth century. Her turn was yet to come. In 1559, the same year as the Treaty of Cateau-Cambrésis, Queen Elizabeth had been declared by act of Parliament to be the supreme governor of the Church of England. She sought to include as many Englishmen as possible within a single national Church. Marking a return to her father's solution of religious problems, she severed relations with Rome. The queen herself was not interested in doctrinal differences. On the other hand, she was not indifferent to religion or to Protestantism. With a Catholic coalition on the Continent and, at the time of her accession, a Catholic Scotland to the north, she was involved in risks that made her stand seem one of strong conviction. However, her settlement was definitely not belligerently Protestant. A reference to the "detestable enormities" of the bishop of Rome in an earlier draft of the Act of Supremacy was deleted. The doctrinal position of the Anglican Church was set forth in the Thirty-Nine Articles and was broad enough in its doctrines and definitions to have proved acceptable to all but the confirmed Catholics and the rigorous Calvinists.

Though the temper of the Anglican settlement was not inquisitorial, at one point it left no room for individual predilections. Englishmen might believe as they would, but must worship as Parliament required, which meant that they must accept episcopacy, the royal supremacy, and the Book of Common Prayer. Richard Hooker set forth the rationale in his *Treatise on the Laws of Ecclesiastical Polity*. Hooker contended therein that the attempt of the Calvinists to make the outward forms of the Church conform to the Scriptures is, in view of the Scriptures' ambiguities, to "torment weak consciences with infinite perplexities." It is better to regulate such matters by "the light of nature and common discretion." Most English Protestants were satisfied to have it so during the reign of Elizabeth, though a Puritan party was in the making that would convulse the land in the next century.

The Catholics, of course, could not acquiesce, and their position was rendered frightfully difficult when in 1570 the pope excommunicated the queen and absolved her subjects of allegiance. Thus Catholics loyal to the pope were traitors to the crown. Jesuit missionaries entered England, and the situation was further complicated by plots against the crown by Mary, queen of Scots, and Philip II of Spain. To protect her government Elizabeth undertook the persecution of Catholics. Although executions were relatively few, the hostility of both France and Spain was aroused. By diplomacy Elizabeth averted war with France, but not with Spain. The dramatic sequel culminating in the defeat of the Spanish Armada, dispatched by Philip II to restore England to the Catholic faith, is well known. England remained Protestant.

By the close of the sixteenth century the religious confessions had become fairly stabilized in Europe. Several different religions were tolerated on a territorial basis in Switzerland, Germany, and Poland. Catholicism, Lutheranism, Calvinism, and Anabaptism were all permitted in Holland, while in France Catholicism and Calvinism coexisted in separate areas. Religious liberty for individuals was not yet envisaged. Catholicism was proscribed in Scotland and England. In Spain and Italy Protestantism was banned. Although Catholicism largely prevailed in the South and Protestantism in the North, it would grossly oversimplify matters to claim that the former was suited to the temperament of the Latin peoples and the latter to that of the descendants of the northern invaders of the ancient Roman Empire. Also, in all lands there would have been much larger minorities had more liberal circumstances prevailed. But in any event the lines had come to be drawn, and the scene was set for greater conflicts in the century to come.

The seventeenth century had hardly begun when in 1618 a war broke out that was to embroil all Europe and that was to last thirty years. The issues were complex, for never have religion, economics, and politics been more closely interwoven. Yet the Thirty Years' War was at the outset a religious war; the behavior of many of the participants frequently makes no sense unless one realizes that military considerations were overridden by religious convictions. The war dragged on as long as it did because neither the Catholics nor the Protestants presented a united front.

The struggle was so complicated that only the barest outline can be offered here. It began in Bohemia, essentially because the Peace of Augsburg no longer corresponded to the facts. That settlement had granted toleration only to the Lutherans among the Protestants and had excluded Calvinists, who subsequently declined to accept this territorial solution and who continued their propaganda at the expense of both Catholics and Lutherans. Many areas covered by the settlement had become Calvinist, including Brandenburg and particularly the Palatinate. There were Calvinist infiltrations also into Württemberg and Hesse. Hungary was strongly Calvinist, and Bohemia had, in addition to the various Hussite groups, both Lutherans and Calvinists.

Shortly before he was elected Holy Roman emperor, the Hapsburg Catholic Ferdinand II was made the king of Bohemia. By rigidly applying the principle of the Augsburg settlement he attempted to root out Protestantism from this domain and to impose Catholicism. Thus the long conflict was precipitated. The Bohemians would not submit and in a revival of medieval particularism challenged the very constitution of the empire. Claiming the right to choose their own king, they invited the elector of the Palatinate, an ardent Calvinist, to serve as sovereign, and he accepted. Such flagrant disregard for the structure of the empire, coupled with the establishment in Bohemia of a form of Protestantism not countenanced by the Peace of Augsburg, caused Bavaria to line up with the Austrian Hapsburg, whereas Lutheran Saxony maintained neutrality. The Bohemians were crushed, and the estates of the insurgents were widely confiscated. Thereupon Lutheran Denmark, appalled by this Catholic advance, imprudently intervened. The Danes were repulsed and retreated within their own borders.

The Catholic forces swept up to the Baltic. Then the Swedes interposed under their great king Gustavus Adolphus, a brilliant administrator and tactician who had built up centralized government and created a professional army. Like William of Orange, he was a man of profound but not narrow religious conviction, and though Lutheran, he did not scruple to assist Calvinists. Catholic France, abetted by the pope, actually gave support to

An Anglican service in St. Paul's Cathedral,
with James I in the balcony of the church,
is shown in this engraving. The Puritans
detested the ritual of such services. Like
other Calvinists, they sought to purify the
Church of forms not based on the Scriptures.

the Swedes in order to curb the Spanish Hapsburg imperialists. Electoral Saxony still held aloof from an alliance with Sweden to the north and Calvinists to the south, until the Catholic coalition had the indiscretion to sack Magdeburg in Saxony. Then Saxons, Swedes, German Lutherans, and Calvinists, assisted by the French and the pope, confronted the Catholics, and Gustavus Adolphus registered a smashing victory. However, the Catholic forces rallied and at the Battle of Lützen in 1632 the valor of Gustavus outran his prudence. He rode into a band of the foe and was cut down.

Had Gustavus lived, he might have been able to construct a great northern, Protestant confederation consisting of Sweden, Germany, Denmark, Holland, and probably England and Scotland. After his death, however, religious issues were displaced by secular concerns. For another sixteen years a desultory conflict dragged on, largely as a struggle between France and Spain for control of the Rhineland. Faced by the opposition of France, Bavaria, and the pope, the empire was unable to unify Europe under the dynasty of the Hapsburgs. At the same time a deep attachment to the idea of the empire impeded the German states from the realization of national unity. Their lands were left ravaged.

Though religious questions played a diminishing role in the further course of the war, the issues that had precipitated the conflict could not be disregarded. When the struggle finally ceased, the Treaty of Westphalia in 1648 provided a religious settlement, albeit an unimaginative one. The territorial principle still prevailed, but the lines were more realistically drawn. Calvinism was accorded the same status as Lutheranism and Catholicism; the territorial status was stabilized according to the prevailing conditions of January 1, 1624. (After that date there had actually been little change.) The Treaty precluded interference from the Church of Rome in religious matters in Germany, and it was therefore condemned by Innocent X, which only highlighted the point that thereafter the Church was no longer regarded either as an overlord or even as a partner in the arranging of political settlements.

The period following the war saw the growth of political absolutism on the Continent. France was the most notable example, but Spain, though diminished in prestige abroad, became even more absolutist at home. And the German states, although they were incapable of political unification, built up despotic regimes within their own territories.

France emerged from the Thirty Years' War as the most brilliant, powerful, and absolutist of the European states. Late in the previous century the Edict of Nantes had solved the problem of religious duality by a kind of territorialism within the state. The Huguenots, to be sure, were not separated from the Catholics in the schools, the markets, or the courts, but their temples—they were not called churches—were restricted to fortified and garrisoned citadels. Thus the guarantee of religious freedom entailed political decentralization; Huguenot cities corresponded to the baronial castles of the Middle Ages.

This system, of course, conflicted with monarchial absolutism. Cardinal Richelieu, who became actual ruler of France early in the course of the Thirty Years' War, saw very plainly that the Huguenots constituted a state within the state and a menace to the authority of the crown. He therefore resolved to take away from them their fortified cities. The strongest of these was La Rochelle, since it was open to the sea and to succor by allies, who that moment were the English. Richelieu determined to reduce the city. After a year of incredible effort, he succeeded in blocking its harbor with sunken ships, thus cutting off help from the English, and the city was called upon to surrender. The mayor, one Jean Guiton, placed his dagger on the table, declaring that he would stab anyone who entertained the thought of yielding, and reminded the people that it was better to die than suffer the ravages of the soldiery. As hunger and disease took over, the city several times might nonetheless have surrendered had not the white sails of the English fleet appeared beyond the harbor bar. But each time the would-be rescuers were halted by the barricade, and the people on shore watched the sails disappear beyond the horizon.

When La Rochelle at last surrendered, after heroic resistance, Richelieu and the king rode into the city at the head of perfectly disciplined troops, followed by food trains for the famished. The cardinal allowed a meeting of the Protestant assembly. The religious clauses of the Edict of Nantes were confirmed, but all the Protestant fortresses were to be razed. Tolerance for the Huguenots was to depend henceforth on the good will of the crown, and there was every reason why the crown should have continued to extend that good will, because the Huguenots, when their religion was confirmed, became utterly loyal. When later there were insurrections against the crown on political grounds—the Fronde in the time of Louis XIV was an attempt by the nobles to recover their independence—the Huguenots would have nothing to do with them. Mazarin, the successor of Richelieu, expressed to them the gratitude of the throne.

Nevertheless, before the century had ended the Edict of Nantes was revoked. To understand why, one must consider Louis XIV's concept of monarchy and the trends of thought within the French Church in the seventeenth century. In this period French Catholicism produced great minds and great spirits, profoundly exercised for the faith. There was the philosopher René Descartes. His philosophical problem was at the same time a religious problem. How can a man be sure of the existence of God? Let man start, Descartes counseled, by stripping his knowledge down to the bare assumption of his own existence. This he may assume because he cannot even doubt unless he exists. Thus the departure is to be made from the capacity for logical thought: "I think; therefore, I am."

But how now do I move from myself to God? asked Descartes. The passage from my mind to God is really easier, he answered himself, than from my mind to matter because mind and matter are different, but God is mind. There is still a difficulty, because God has characteristics that cannot be predicated of man. God is eternal, omniscient, omnipotent, immutable. Man, in order to perceive that he lacks these characteristics, must be able to conceive of them. But how can he conceive of them if they do not exist? The idea of a being more perfect than man could have proceeded only from the existence of a being more perfect than man. Here we have again the ontological demonstration. Whether or not this reasoning is convincing, the significant point is that it preoccupied a French philosopher of the seventeenth century as urgently as it did Saint Anselm in the twelfth.

The argument was, however, not at all convincing to another great philosopher of the period, Blaise Pascal, who devoted more time to problems of religion. He was the great proponent of the Jansenists, who might be called Calvinist Catholics, because of the rigor of their deportment and their acceptance of the doctrine of predestination. Pascal held that man arrives at his belief in God by no processes of ratiocination, but only by seeing him disclosed in Jesus Christ. "The God of the Christians is not a God who is simply the theory of geometric truths," Pascal wrote. "This is the God of the pagans. He is not a God who crowns with blessings those who serve him. This is the God of the Jews. The God of the Christians is a God of love and consecration, a God who makes them feel their utter misery and his infinite mercy, who unites himself with the ground of their being and fills them with humility, joy, confidence, and love. He makes the soul feel that its peace lies wholly in him, and that it has no joy save to love him. To know God after this fashion one must know first one's own misery and worthlessness and the need of a mediator in order to approach God and be united with him. The knowledge of God without the recognition of our misery engenders pride. The recognition of our misery without the knowledge of Jesus Christ produces despair. But the knowledge of Christ frees us alike from pride and despair, because here we find conjoined God and our misery and the only way in which it can be repaired."

To these philosophers, preoccupied with religion, one must add as exemplars of a revived Catholicism the great mystic François de la Mothe Fénelon and the eloquent preacher Jacques Bénigne Bossuet. It was Bossuet who in 1682, with the support of the clergy, drew up the Four Gallican Articles, which proclaimed that the king of France was not subject to the pope in temporal and civil matters, that Church councils held authority over the pope, that the liberties of the Gallican Church were inviolable, and that the decisions of the pope were subject to the approval of the Church. Louis XIV believed that he ruled by divine right; he had greater pretensions to absolute authority than any other reigning monarch. His personal piety steadily developed under the influence of that remarkable woman Madame de Maintenon, a convert to strict Catholic orthodoxy who pressed upon the king the old ideal of a single Catholic religion for all France.

The Revocation of the Edict of Nantes was accomplished by degrees, and with brutality. Prior to the actual Revocation, troops were quartered on Huguenots with license to pillage, violate, and bludgeon. Thousands of conversions to Catholicism were reported. Yet when the Edict was revoked in 1685, and the Huguenots were confronted with submission or banishment, some of those who had previously submitted now elected to go into exile. Some two hundred thousand persons were expelled from France, leaving behind an absolutist, religiously unified state. A contemporary estimated that the king thereby lost nine thousand soldiers, and six hundred of his best officers, not to mention thousands of the finest artisans of France. The refugees were received in Switzerland, in Prussia (the greatness of Berlin as a city dates from their arrival), in England and Holland, in the English colonies of North America, and in the Dutch colonies of South Africa. France was again the land of one king, one law, and one faith.

The course in England was very different. While France moved toward absolutism, England moved toward constitutionalism. England had had her chaos in the Wars of the Roses in the fifteenth century. The despotism that restored order came with the Tudors in the sixteenth century. With order restored, the cry for emancipation from despotism came during Stuart rule, in the seventeenth century.

There were particular circumstances that enabled England to stage a moderate revolution. One was her isolation from the Continent and her comparative non-involvement in the Thirty Years' War. Another was the union with Scotland, which occurred n 1603 when James VI of Scotland—the son of Mary, queen of Scots, and Darnley—became James I of England. This union was, to be sure, a decisive factor in the outbreak of the civil war, but still the conflict was not primarily between the two kingdoms but between parties in both; and those parties were all Protestant, less bitterly opposed to each other than all of them were to Rome. Another important consideration was the convergence of economic, political, and religious interests in resistance to the crown and the established Church.

The first Stuarts, James I and his successor Charles I, were in dire need of funds. They were loath to appeal for Parliamentary grants, for this would have subjected them to Parliamentary control. Instead, they had recourse to levies by royal decree. Two sources that could be tapped were land and trade. But to touch them involved the religious issue indirectly, since many of the landed gentry and the London merchants from whom such revenues might be raised were of the Puritan party. These interests also were all well represented in Parliament, where economic, political, and religious opposition to the crown was centered.

The Puritans, who were essentially Calvinists in their doctrine, had deep grievances against the established Church. For them the Elizabethan settlement had not gone far enough. They wished to abolish all religious ceremonies not expressly called for by the Scriptures. They attacked the Anglican Church for its "popery," preferring a simplified service with emphasis on the sermon. A petition enumerating the changes they desired was presented to James I in 1603, but none of their requests was granted except for the revision of the Bible. In 1611 the "authorized," or King James, version made its appearance. James aggravated their grievances by a number of measures, especially by recommending sports and games as Sunday pastimes in violation of their own emphasis on a strict observance of the Sabbath. The Puritans were further alienated by James' restoration of episcopacy in Scotland and by his forcing on the Scottish Parliament the Articles of Perth, which legally instituted such Anglican practices as kneeling for Communion and the observance of Easter and Christmas.

The widespread fear of a Catholic restoration should the king's party prevail accentuated the conflict. The slogan "No Popery" gathered up memories of the persecutions under Mary, of the plots to assassinate Elizabeth, of the Armada, and of the Guy Fawkes plot of 1605 to blow up the Houses of Parliament. James' negotiations to marry his son Charles to a Spanish Catholic princess and his failure to aid the German Protestants in the opening years of the Thirty Years' War were resented not only by Puritans but by all those with anti-Catholic sentiments.

Under Charles, who succeeded to the throne in 1625, the monarchy became increasingly associated with the Catholic cause in the minds of many Englishmen. Charles' marriage to the Catholic princess Henrietta Maria, sister of Louis XIII of France, was unpopular, as was his refusal to help his own sister's husband, the Calvinist elector of the Palatinate, now the exiled king of Bohemia. The uneasiness was great when Charles's deputy in Ireland, Thomas Wentworth (later the earl of Strafford), by efficient and upright administration increased the prosperity of Ireland and built up an army consisting mainly of Roman Catholics.

The figure on whom Puritan disaffection focused was William Laud, whom Charles appointed archbishop of Canterbury in 1633. Laud was himself a reformer. He lamented the low quality of the clergy, but perceived that its roots lay partly in their ex-

This painting is one of several portraits of
Oliver Cromwell by Robert Walker. It shows
the lord protector in steel armor, holding a
baton, while a page ties a white sash around
him. In his rise to power Cromwell was
driven to win freedom for "all species of
Protestants, to worship God according to
their own light and consciences." He
believed that his successes were due to the
fact that he carried out God's will.

treme poverty. The Tudors had not turned over the confiscated monastic lands to the Church of England. For the sake of ready cash the Church had leased its own lands for long terms on condition that the lessee collect the tithes and support the clergy on these estates. But the lessee pocketed the bulk and left the starveling curate to eke out a living by tending his own glebe or by taking several charges to the inevitable neglect of all. Laud wanted direct grants from Parliament to relieve the need of the clergy, but these were never conferred.

Laud's program differed fundamentally from the Puritans'. Following the theory of the Elizabethan settlement, Laud believed there should be latitude in doctrine but uniformity in polity and liturgy. The liturgy was set forth in the Book of Common Prayer, which required that the Communion table should always be at the east end of the church and not in the nave as if, said Laud, the church were a tavern. He also believed that the clergy should be attired in the vestments prescribed by the changing seasons of the Christian year. Laud cared more that every Englishman should eat the same kind of wafer at the Lord's Supper than that all should have the same theory as to the real Presence.

Laud punished non-compliance with his measures by mutilation and imprisonment. The Star Chamber, which had been instituted to force compliance to the state, and the Court of High Commission, which since Elizabeth's day had been employed against non-conformists to the established Church, were both called into use against the Puritans. An individual might suffer at the hands of both. Alexander Leighton, for example, who had issued *Sions Plea Against the Prelacie*, was defrocked by the Court of High Commission and then was sentenced by the Star Chamber to be whipped, his ears cropped, his nose slit, and his forehead branded, and, in addition, to be fined and imprisoned. The like treatment of other dedicated Puritans, such as William Prynne, John Bastwick, and Henry Burton, provoked intense resentment. Despite the outcry against barbarous penalties, Laud would grant no concessions and no relief. In 1640 an oath was imposed on all members of the learned professions, "Never to consent to alter the government of this Church by archbishops, bishops, deans, and archdeacons, etc., as it stands now established." That *et cetera* was derided as a cover behind which might lurk the Mass, the pope, and the Church of Rome.

The opposition to the king and to Laud was not united in its own programs, save in antagonism to the government and the established Church. Religious pluralism combined with religious intensity threatened to nullify not only Laud's program but any other. After a century of placidity in England, the fire of religious enthusiasm had leaped across the Channel from France. Englishmen who under King Hal and Queen Bess had accepted religious changes with docility had become dogmatic about their own increasingly various religious beliefs and practices. England had become a welter of sects: there were Presbyterians, Independents (Congregationalists), Baptists, and Unitarians, to name those that have survived; and besides there were a number now extinct: Familists, Ranters, Seekers, Fifth Monarchy Men, not to mention political parties with a strong religious cast, such as the Levelers. In the near future still others, such as the Quakers, the Muggletonians, and the Diggers, would be added to the list. The very existence of these different groups enormously complicated the problem of religious settlement.

Of the main groups one of the most important was the Presbyterian, including both the Scottish Calvinists who objected to the Stuarts' imposition of episcopacy and the Book of Common Prayer, and a strong contingent in England. Politically they favored constitutional monarchy. Their great proponent, Samuel Rutherford, wrote a book called *Lex Rex*, which means "the law is king," as opposed to *rex lex*, "the king is law."

The Independents had as their central idea the concept of "the gathered Church," espoused a century earlier by the Anabaptists. The Church, they claimed, consists not of those baptized in infancy, although they did baptize their children, but only of visible saints; that is, those who in reasonable charity may be adjudged to be saints. For New England Puritans a heartfelt experience of regeneration was the most crucial mark of election and the necessary condition for membership in the Church and for admission to the sacrament. There is no evidence that the English Independents had set up this condition in any formal way, but they surely sympathized with the stipulations of their American cousins, that to be accounted members of a gathered Church people must have been "wounded in their hearts for their original sin and actual transgressions and able to pitch upon some promise of free grace in the Scriptures for the ground of their faith, and must find their hearts drawn to believe in Jesus

Christ for their justification and salvation." Those who could thus testify made a covenant with God and with each other, namely, "a solemn and public promise before the Lord, whereby a company of Christians, called by the power and mercy of God and fellowship with Christ, and by his providence to live together and by his grace to cleave together in the unity of faith, in brotherly love . . . do bind themselves to the Lord and to one another, to walk together in all such ways of holy worship and edification one towards another as the Gospel of Christ requires."

The polity of the Independents was congregational. Above the local congregation stood no bishop, no general assembly, no synod or presbytery. The governing of each church was essentially democratic. Within the congregation there was disagreement as to whether Church discipline should be exercised by elders or by the congregation as a whole, but one point was clear: discipline should be rigorously exercised and the unworthy disowned. Those who at the time suggested that the congregationalism of the sectaries would lead to democracy in the state were refuted, but they may have been right.

The Baptists sprang from a group of Independents living in exile in Holland. Contact with Mennonites convinced them that infant baptism was incompatible with their theory of the Church. Thomas Helwys, a member of the Baptist Church of Amsterdam, having reached this conclusion, decided that to remain in exile conflicted with the command of the Lord to bear witness before kings. Therefore he returned to London, where he founded the Baptist Church of England.

The Quakers, called by their own preference the Society of Friends, had their origin in the north of England. In 1646 their founder, George Fox, had a profound religious experience that he felt he must communicate. He was led to believe that within each man resides a portion of God's light, through which the individual can himself find truth. Fox began traveling about gathering an elect group, to whom he preached that there was no need for ministers, liturgy, sacraments, music, or sanctuary. His program may be regarded as the ultimate reduction of the Puritan rejection of Romanism. He solved the bitter contention over the wafer, the Communion table, vestments, liturgy, episcopacy, and presbyteries by simply abolishing them all. But despite his ability to cite Scriptures in support of such measures, his emphasis was upon the Spirit, which transcends the letter. The very Quaker meeting was led by the Spirit, silently, until someone, whether man or woman, was driven to utterance. The Quaker rejection of war and oaths recalls the Anabaptist position; but, unlike the Anabaptists, the Quakers did not withdraw from the framework of society. They retained the hope for a Christian world and addressed their pleas not simply to the Friends but to all England.

The Unitarians in this period were few. They gained strength in England in the eighteenth century and in New England in the late eighteenth and early nineteenth, in each case by deviation from Calvinism. By its emphasis upon the monarchical absolutism of God, Calvinism tends to exclude the concept of pluralism within deity. Unitarians affirmed the unity of deity by subordinating Christ to God. They differed from the Calvinists also in their concept of the character of God and the abilities of man. The importance of the group in seventeenth-century England lies primarily in its relation to the problem of religious liberty. Even one Unitarian was enough to pose that problem, because denial of the Trinity was the offense for which the last heretic in England had been burned.

The existence of all these groups—Presbyterians, Independents, Baptists, Quakers, and Unitarians, not to mention all the smaller ones—confronted any ruler in England with a grave dilemma. Although the disagreement among the sects was in one respect a boon to Charles, who hoped to conquer by dividing them, he was unable to solve the problem of dealing with increasing religious pluralism. Corporal punishment and imprisonment were proving of benefit to the nonconformists by advertising their claims, as in the case of John Lilburne, leader of the Levelers, who made a career of going to jail as a protest against unconstitutional procedures on the part of every government. On the other hand, if the government were to remove all restrictions on religious dissent, what would the sects then do to each other?

That depended upon their views of Church, state, and liberty. The Presbyterians would not have been more tolerant than the Anglicans. They were actually more illiberal than Laud, because their insistence upon uniformity applied not only to liturgy and polity, but also to doctrine. Among the so-called Separatists, the Baptists and the Quakers, with their demand for the complete separation of Church and state, were most unequivocally in favor of religious liberty. The Independents were not altogether of one mind. Some among them believed in a thoroughgoing separation of Church and state with full religious freedom. But others were willing to continue the union of Church and state, provided both were fashioned according to their model. That policy was followed in early New England, but at home, in England, the Independents were never other than dissenters. Until quite recent years they have continued to agitate for the disestablishment of the Church of England, and indeed of any Church in any country.

In championing freedom in religion some of the Independents and many Baptists frankly repudiated the ideal of uniformity. They declared that variety is the law of creation, and that competition is the life blood not only of trade but also of religion, because truth emerges only in the battle of free minds. The effect of constraint, they claimed, is to make martyrs of the stalwart and hypocrites of the weak. They redefined conscience as loyalty to what one believes to be true, even though it may actually be false, because only by the path of sincerity can truth be attained. So said John Milton, fully confident that truth would vindicate itself. "Let truth and falsehood grapple; whoever knew truth put to the worst in free and open encounter? . . . For who knows not that truth is strong next to the Almighty. She needs no policies nor stratagems nor licensings to make her victorious . . . Give her but room, and do not bind her when she sleeps. . . ." Such a position left Christendom intact only as a state of mind, without a corporate structure to bind it together.

Such divergent viewpoints may have encouraged the pursuit of truth but certainly did not help the cause of the dissenters. There was good reason to doubt whether the sects could hold together long enough to deal with Charles and Laud. Their strategy allowed for only two possibilities. Either they would have to leave England or dominate England. They could emigrate separately, but if they were to dominate, they would have to hold together. They tried everything. Emigration and agitation with a view to domination went on concurrently. The fortunes of the émigrés will engage us later. Suffice it here to point out that they continued to participate in the English struggle by printing tracts in Holland for English consumption and by constant comings and goings between America and England.

Neither the inquisitorial procedures of the High Commission, nor the brutal sentences of the Star Chamber, nor Wentworth's Catholic army in Ireland, nor Charles's demands for money and monopolies precipitated civil war in England. It remained for Laud's handling of the religious controversies in Scotland to accomplish that. Laud believed, as most men still commonly believed, that one kingdom should have one religion, or at any rate, one Church. England and Scotland were now the United Kingdom and should have a uniform religion. Each wished to impose its form of Protestantism upon the other. Laud took the initiative. There was no need to enforce episcopacy on the Scots, for James had already done that. There had been deep resentment to his acts, but no rebellion. Laud was not interested in requiring subscription to the Thirty-Nine Articles; he was willing to let the Scots believe as they would. But he insisted that they conduct their services from the Book of Common Prayer.

To the Presbyterians the Book of Common Prayer was objectionable, despite its stately cadences and noble piety, because it was "an unperfect book culled and picked out of that popish dunghill, the Mass book, full of abominations." It called for the use of a wafer instead of ordinary bread in the Lord's Supper and for kneeling at Communion, which might be taken to imply belief in the physical presence of Christ. It called for a ring in the marriage ceremony as the visible sign of a sacrament, whereas the Presbyterians, like Luther, did not include marriage among the sacraments. The Prayer Book, furthermore, was built around the Christian year, which the Presbyterians and Puritans as a whole rejected. Christmas, they said, is "Christ-Mass, the devil with the sting in his tail." Away with Ash Wednesday, Lent, and Easter and all the holy days of Rome, which withdraw men from their godly callings! The Sabbath only, they insisted, was instituted by God and should be scrupulously observed on penalty of divine displeasure. When, then, Archbishop Laud in 1637 issued the order to the clergy of Scotland that they must use the Book of Common Prayer, a riot broke out in Edinburgh.

In 1638 the Scots drafted the National Covenant, which read: "From the knowledge and conscience of our duty to God, to our king and country, without any worldly respect or inducement, we promise and swear by the great name of the Lord our God to continue in the profession and obedience of our religion; that we shall defend the same and resist all those contrary errors and corruptions according to our vocation, and to the utmost of that

Unrest caused by religious wars and reformers' exaggerated concern with the devil stirred up renewed fear of witches among both Protestants and Catholics. In seventeenth-century England even the highly educated believed in the powers of sorcery. The witch-hunter Matthew Hopkins was largely responsible for the deaths of almost three hundred victims. Above, the frontispiece of his book shows him with two witches and their spirits.

power which God has put into our hands, all the days of our life."

Through hamlet and kirk all over the lowlands—there were still Catholics in the highlands—men set their hands to the marriage contract of this nation with God. The reference in the Covenant to the "utmost of that power" meant war. The clans were mustered to the singing of psalms. The good wives of Edinburgh sacrificed three thousand sheets to make tents for the soldiers.

Charles called out his troops, but in the face of the Scots' strength he could not risk a battle. A treaty was signed before any fighting took place. The king then summoned Wentworth from Ireland, making him earl of Strafford, to raise an effective fighting force. To pay for troops money was necessary. In order to raise it Charles had to convene Parliament, which was soon to be dubbed the Short Parliament. But he could not count on a united England. The Puritans in England would not fight the Presbyterians of Scotland. Instead of granting funds for an army, Parliament began discussing its political and religious grievances, and Charles was soon obliged to dissolve it.

That summer the king's forces were defeated by the Scots, who crossed the Tweed, and Charles again had to negotiate. As the Scots refused to quit England until Charles paid their troops the king, now desperately in need of money, again convened Parliament. This, the so-called Long Parliament, consisted principally of Puritans. It was ready neither to fight the Scots nor to allow the king money to pay them. It imprisoned Laud, who was later executed, and it brought the earl of Strafford to trial for treason. A letter had been discovered that Strafford had written to the king, stating, "You have an army in Ireland you may imploy here to reduce this kingdom." The word *this* was taken by John Pym, a leading member of Parliament, and his party to refer to England. Strafford averred that "*this* kingdom" meant Scotland. Both sides were right. When he wrote, Strafford surely was thinking only of Scotland, but had Scotland been reduced, the royal will would certainly have been imposed upon England. Yet since the charge could not be proved, Pym dropped the accusation of treason and introduced a bill of attainder, by which a man could be put to death "for the safety of the state." The vote carried. Its execution required the signature of the king. Charles protested and wept, but when he was told that he must distinguish between his duty as a man and his duty as a king, he signed. Subsequently he looked upon this as the greatest sin of his life. He did not see that it was also a blunder, since thereby he conceded that the king is a constitutional monarch whose function it is to implement the will of Parliament.

Meanwhile, the removal of the strong hand of Strafford in Ireland led to an uprising there in October and November 1641, during which, it was reported, probably with some exaggeration, thousands of Protestants were massacred. Parliament, excited by this murderous display of religious feeling, carried through the Root and Branch Petition for the eradication of episcopacy. The Grand Remonstrance enumerating the whole gamut of grievances, constitutional as well as ecclesiastical, followed by suggestions for reform, was presented to the king. To suppress this devastating ultimatum Charles, with armed force, attempted to arrest the five leading members of Parliament. They escaped, the king left London, and the war was on.

In general the North and West aligned themselves with the king, the South and East with Parliament. The first battles were indecisive, largely because there were many in Parliament itself—notably the Presbyterians—who had grave misgivings about fighting the Lord's anointed. As one of them said, "If you beat the king ninety-nine times, yet he is king still . . . but if the king beat us once, we shall all be hanged. . . ." The answer to that was not let the king win once. In order to secure the aid of the Scots, Parliament signed with Scotland the Solemn League and Covenant, promising to work toward uniformity of religion in the British Isles and toward the abolition in England of both "popery" and episcopacy. Scottish commissioners joined the Westminster Assembly, whose duty it was to reform the English Church. The Westminster Confession, a confession of faith for the British Isles issued by the Assembly, was an exposition of Calvinist doctrine. It was accepted by Parliament in slightly modified form in 1648.

Meanwhile, the increasing successes of the Parliamentary forces was largely due to the extraordinary abilities of Oliver Cromwell, who had risen to leadership of the Parliamentary armies. He was resolved to have an army of saints, "men of spirit." Only such could stand against the sons of gentlemen, who fought for the king. Social status was not to be regarded. "I had rather have a plain russet-coated captain that knows what he fights for and loves what he knows, than that which you call a 'gentleman' and is nothing else. I honor a gentleman that is so indeed." Nor did religious affiliation matter within the general framework of Puritan Protestantism. The charge was leveled against Cromwell that his men were "a company of Brownists, Anabaptists, factious inferior persons, etc." However, when a Presbyterian officer wished to discharge a fellow officer as an Anabaptist, Cromwell rejoined: "Sir, the state, in choosing men to serve it, takes no notice of their opinions; if they be willing faithfully to serve it, that suffices." Cromwell was an Independent imbued with Milton's ideal of variety. Cromwell compared the several sects to the trees mentioned by the prophet Isaiah, the myrrh and the olive, the cypress and the plantains of Israel, all different and all alike affording shade.

Cromwell was not fatuous in looking upon the regiments that he thus recruited as Congregational churches; their chaplains were Congregational ministers. A meeting of officers was conducted alternately as a debate and a prayer meeting. Cromwell would sum up the sense of the meeting as if he were the clerk of the Society of Friends. When he was not in accord with the general will, he would offer to resign. Colonel William Goffe, one of Cromwell's commanders, would then remonstrate that although Moses was not permitted by God to cross over into the Land of Promise, nevertheless he did not resign. The reference to the Old Testament was not lost on Cromwell, for the whole concept of the Holy Commonwealth was deeply rooted in the pattern of ancient Israel. The Old Testament supplied the ethic for the holy war. *The Souldiers Pocket Bible* disposed of the Sermon on the Mount by setting up texts in this manner:

Matthew 5:44   I say unto you, love your enemies.
II Chronicles 19:2   Wouldst thou help the wicked and love them that hate the Lord?
Psalm 139:21–22   Do not I hate them, O Lord, that hate thee? . . . I hate them with an unfeigned hatred.

All Cromwell's victories were ascribed to the Lord. God gave the enemy "as stubble to our swords," he wrote to his brother-in-law after one battle. The Battle of Dunbar, occurring late in the war when Cromwell was fighting the Scottish royalists, might well have been considered a miracle, for Cromwell had been outgeneraled and outnumbered. He called his officers to a day of prayer. The leaders in the other camp, against the counsel of their general, forsook advantageous ground. Cromwell, singing the 68th Psalm, drove them into a wedge. Three thousand Scots fell, ten thousand were captured, and Cromwell lost less than thirty men. His army started in pursuit, but he halted them to sing the 117th Psalm. It has only two verses, but these were enough to praise the Lord and hold the ranks. To Parliament Cromwell wrote, "We that serve you beg you not to own us, but God alone"; and to his wife, "The Lord has showed us an exceeding mercy; who can tell how great it is? My weak faith has been upheld. I have been in my inward man marvelously supported." The victories were described by Cromwell as providences, and providences were the proof of divine favor. "My dear friend," he wrote, "let us look unto providences; surely they mean somewhat. They hang so together; have been so constant, so clear and unclouded. . . . What think you of Providence disposing the hearts of so many of God's people this way, especially in this poor army, wherein the great God has vouchsafed to appear. . . . we [desire] only to fear our great God, that we do nothing against his will."

Three years before that battle the king had surrendered to the Scots. Unable to come to terms with him, the Scots turned Charles over to the English. The king continued to negotiate with the Presbyterians, who controlled Parliament, against the Independents, who largely made up the army; with Independents against Presbyterians; and separately with Scotland and with France. Cromwell favored the king's restoration and tried to come to terms with him. But the king and Cromwell could not fathom each other. The king could not understand a man with no ambition and no point of corruptibility. Cromwell could not comprehend a man of undeviating intent but devious strategy. The king was of no other mind than to restore absolute monarchy and the Church of England. By pretending to support Presbyterianism he induced a Scottish army to invade England on his behalf. This force Cromwell defeated in August 1648. The king's deviousness came to light when his courier was intercepted carrying correspondence with the queen in which Charles made plain that he had no intention of keeping the promises he had been making.

Now convinced that a restoration was impossible, Cromwell's army of Independents purged the Presbyterians from Parliament. The rump body was declared to be a Supreme Court of Judicature, with authority to sit in judgment on the king's life. The charge against the king was really war guilt. He was responsible "for unnatural wars" by which "much innocent blood of the free people of this nation hath been spilt." The king refused to recognize the jurisdiction of the court, saying that "the king cannot be tried by any superior jurisdiction on earth" and to violate this principle was to violate the "freedom and liberty of the people of England." Cromwell replied that the king had been guilty "of a breach of trust," which "in a king ought to be punished more than any crime whatsoever." On January 30, 1649, the king was beheaded.

The war did not end with his execution. The ultimate victory posed all the problems of a settlement. Cromwell still had to suppress royalism in Ireland and Scotland. The treatment of Ireland was brutal. Cromwell was reminded that eight years previously the Irish "unprovoked had put the English to the most unheard of and most barbarous massacre (without respect to sex) that ever the sun beheld." When, then, Drogheda fell, the whole garrison was massacred. Cromwell's justification was that this slaughter would "tend to prevent the effusion of blood for the future," the current justification of those who extenuate the incineration of cities to shorten war. Even greater resentment was occasioned in Ireland by the deportation of priests, the confiscation of estates and the establishment of English Protestant landlords, and the prohibition of the public exercise of Catholicism. Then Cromwell turned to Scotland. Charles II had been crowned by the Scots, who, never having approved of the execution of a king of Scottish blood, now undertook to place the son upon his father's throne. Cromwell's last battles were with the Scottish Presbyterians, whom he defeated in 1651, thus reuniting Great Britain. The settlement in Scotland was generous. Presbyterianism was not suppressed, and the Scots were granted representation in Parliament.

And now came the question of England. Cromwell was able to rule under a constitution called the Instrument of Government. But Cromwell had as hard a time trying to be constitutional as Charles I had trying not to be. It was suggested that Cromwell should be made king, but he declined the bauble of a crown, and wisely, for in that case he would have been a pretender pitted against the legitimate aspirant. He chose rather the title used by the duke of Somerset during the minority of Edward VI, and was called the lord protector. Among his other difficulties, a conservative element in Parliament wished to retain property qualifications for the franchise. The more radical Levelers pointed out that not a few had lost their property through supporting the Parliamentary cause and ought not on that account to lose their votes. Some even asserted that "any he is as good as any other he in England." That was too much for Cromwell, who believed in the reign of the saints.

But who were the saints, and what was to be done with regard to the whole question of Church, state, and freedom of conscience? What Cromwell actually did was to abandon a state Church in favor of a national religion resting on three pillars: Presbyterian, Independent, and Baptist. They enjoyed full liberty, and to them he looked for full support. A remnant of the Long Parliament having been dismissed because it would not dissolve itself, Cromwell called a second Parliament, consisting of nominees from the Independent congregations and called the Barebones Parliament, from the name of one of its members. At its first session Cromwell delivered a commission that sounded like a sermon of ordination. The protector was tolerant and believed in disestablished Churches, as did the other Independents, including John Milton. Catholics, Episcopalians, and Unitarians were not allowed to worship publicly, but they were not persecuted. The Quakers were to enjoy freedom of worship. Cromwell had great respect for George Fox, saying to him, "If thou and I were but an hour of a day together we should be nearer one to the other." But the Quakers were imprisoned for refusal to pay tithes, which Cromwell had not abolished. Whether to allow the Anglicans to make public use of the Prayer Book was a question that divided Cromwell and Parliament. He favored liberty, but could ensure it only by flouting democracy. Rather than override his own Parliament he suffered the Book of Common Prayer to be suppressed.

Two notorious cases of blasphemy came up during the Protectorate. Blasphemy was deemed more serious than heresy because it was a public affront to the faith of the community. Because of a heated public defense of his position, John Biddle, a Unitarian, was arrested under the Blasphemy Act. He was not put to death, but banished to the Scilly Isles, where Cromwell

Shown here is a decorated German hymn
sheet from Maryland. German Pietists in
search of religious freedom and Lutherans
seeking the peace and prosperity that the
colonies enjoyed emigrated in great
numbers to Pennsylvania and Maryland.

saw to it that he received an allowance. He subsequently returned to England where, in the end, he died in prison.

More exasperating was the case of a Quaker, James Nayler. Distraught by long imprisonment, on his release he had not the strength to silence some enthusiastic women who, as he was riding into Bristol, marched alongside him singing, "Hosanna! Blessed is he who comes in the name of the Lord!" Nayler was arrested on the charge that he had staged a triumphal entry in imitation of Christ. This was deemed manifest blasphemy. His case was tried before Parliament, which spent days wrangling over this instead of getting on with the business of government. The upshot was that he was subjected to barbarous penalties but his life was spared. Neither heresy nor even blasphemy was any longer to be subject to the penalty of death. All in all, under Cromwell's Protectorate England was nearer to religious toleration and liberty than it ever had been in the past.

The reign of the saints was little more successful than that of the Stuarts at many points. To raise money for maintaining the army and for foreign wars more Church lands and crown lands were sold and the estates of royalists confiscated. Direct taxation, also to support continuous war, caused acute discontent. For a time many Englishmen feared a military despotism. In 1655 uprisings and conspiracies drove Cromwell to impose a system of military rule; England was divided into districts, each under the charge of a major general who exercised stern control in the name of moral welfare and social security. This meant an even more centralized administration than under the Stuarts. Attacks on the government became so irritating that censorship had to be introduced, and John Milton, proponent of free speech, became the licenser of books. Cromwell had never meant that the warfare for truth should include scurrility. A tone of disillusionment is heard in the prayer ascribed to the dying lord protector: "Lord, though I am a miserable and wretched creature, I am in covenant with thee through grace. . . . Teach those who look too much on thy instruments to depend more upon thyself. Pardon such as desire to trample upon the dust of a poor worm, for they are thy people too. And pardon the folly of this short prayer:—even for Jesus Christ's sake. And give us a good night, if it be thy pleasure. Amen."

Cromwell died in 1658 and was succeeded by his son Richard, who was dismissed after a brief time in office. With the approval of Cromwell's general, George Monck, and even of that rabid clipped-eared Puritan William Prynne, Charles II was summoned to England with almost universal consent. He came to London as a constitutional monarch, operating with a Parliament that provided his revenue. Furthermore, he came promising to extend "a liberty to tender consciences and that no man shall be disquieted or called into question for differences of opinion in matters of religion which do not disturb the peace of the kingdom."

Yet the reigns of Charles II and his successor James II were marked by the last important resurgence of persecution. Curiously, the reason was in large part a fear of persecution. Englishmen would not tolerate Catholics because they did not trust Catholics to be tolerant of Protestants. Charles himself had strong leanings toward Catholicism. Every move on his party to fulfill his promise of indulgence, if it included any relaxation for Catholics, was looked upon askance by Parliament lest the Catholics gain control. Such misgiving was not without warrant, for Charles did entertain a vast plan whereby England should be made Catholic in religion and absolutist in government. Charles did not avow his plan, but his brother James, duke of York, openly declared himself to be a Catholic—and he was the heir to the throne. Protestant England responded by passing the Test Act of 1673, which excluded from public office any who did not disclaim the doctrine of transubstantiation. Yet the succession to the throne was not altered, and James the Catholic followed his brother.

But if the hostility against Rome was motivated by distrust and fear of Roman intolerance, Charles had indicated he would be tolerant toward the sectaries. However, his promises were of little substance. Furthermore, the Parliament elected in 1661, known as the Cavalier Parliament, was not only strictly royalist but strictly Anglican in temper; and it sat for seventeen years. Fear of disorder and a refusal to relinquish the ideal of one state and one Church, embracing one people born and baptized into a commonwealth both of earth and of heaven, led to repressive steps.

The actual measures against the nonconformists were enacted under Charles II in the Clarendon Code. As a result of these laws, the Puritans, instead of remaining nonconformists, now became dissenters. The most drastic stroke was the Uniformity

Act of 1662, which required all the clergy to give unfeigned assent to the Book of Common Prayer, newly revised. They must also renounce the Solemn League and Covenant and profess the unlawfulness of taking up arms against the king. Those who refused to comply by the feast of St. Bartholomew were to be deposed from the ministry of the Church of England. The number of evictions approximated two thousand. The Uniformity Act was followed by others, including the Conventicle Act, forbidding unauthorized meetings of more than four persons at a time, and the Five Mile Act, which forbade ministers of the sects to come within five miles of cities unless they took an oath of nonresistance. For disobedience to these, clergy and laity alike suffered distraint of goods and prolonged imprisonments. In the course of twenty years some eight ministers died in prison. The last persecution—which kept John Bunyan in Bedford jail, where he began to write *Pilgrim's Progress*, and so many Quakers in durance—is not by any means to be minimized. Neither is it to be exaggerated, for the treatment of dissent had been greatly modified since the days of Torquemada or Calvin.

When in 1685 James II succeeded his brother, he felt that the time had come for toleration, not the least because he sought to reintroduce Catholicism to England. He therefore issued in 1687 a Declaration of Indulgence, in which he candidly avowed his own adherence to the Church of Rome and his wish that all his subjects might be members of this communion. "Yet we humbly thank Almighty God, it is and has of long time been our constant sense and opinion that conscience ought not to be constrained nor people forced in matters of mere religion. It has ever been contrary to our inclination, as we think it is to the interest of government, which it destroys by spoiling trade, depopulating countries, and discouraging strangers, and finally, that it never obtained the end for which it was employed."

The king's behavior, however, rendered dubious his sincerity, since in Scotland he demanded of the estates a sanguinary law against Protestants. He appointed Catholics to high offices and attempted a military despotism. He sired a son and heir, born to Catholicism. It became evident that the menace of Catholicism would not end with his reign. England had had enough. The king must be a Protestant. An invitation was therefore issued to the king's son-in-law, William, prince of Orange, to come over from Holland to England and assume the crown. Thus came to pass the Glorious Revolution of 1688.

The religious question had now to be settled. William, a Calvinist, would have been glad to make the Church of England more comprehensive by reducing its demands, and would have granted toleration to those who still would not subscribe. He would exact no religious test for public office. But Parliament was not willing to accept such a program. Instead of comprehension within the established Church, it favored toleration of those who would not conform. The Act of Toleration, passed in 1689, is commonly regarded as one of the milestones in the struggle for religious liberty. It marked a great gain over the past, though the liberty it accorded was distinctly limited. The Presbyterians and the Independents, in order to be tolerated, had to subscribe to all the Thirty-Nine Articles save those bearing on polity and liturgy. The Baptists were excused from the article on infant baptism. Quakers received a special exemption from the obligation to take an oath. But Catholics and Unitarians were left still entirely outside the pale, and disabilities as to public office and university degrees continued to apply to all dissenters.

The significance of the Act of Toleration is to be found less in its actual enactments than in its position on the boundary between two eras. Behind lay the Inquisition, the wars of religion, the persecution of the Huguenots, imprisonments, and exiles. The sixteenth century had been marked by extensive use of the death penalty for heresy, and the seventeenth, in England, by incarceration or exile, plus many social distraints. The eighteenth century would be the age of the Enlightenment, with its war upon superstition, fanaticism, and bigotry, even to the point of extinguishing all religious enthusiasm. The Act of Toleration stands at the threshold of this change. Its ambiguity lies in its effort to combine religious liberty with a national establishment, to bring together the union of Church and state with freedom of religion. The concept of a Christian society, if only on a national scale, was still not abandoned, though its outward structure was relinquished when the sects were conceded an independent existence alongside the established Church.

In the meantime Puritanism had made an attempt in the New World to realize more perfectly than was possible in the old the erection of God's Holy Commonwealth. The migrations had not begun with so lofty a plan, but simply with the intent to escape persecution, and the first asylum early in the seventeenth century was found in Holland. At first the refugees had difficulty in getting away from the homeland and had to elude the officers of the crown. Some families in their efforts to escape were separated, to be reunited only after long periods of time.

Holland proved to be only a transitory haven; the arm of Archbishop Laud reached across the Channel. He informed the Dutch government that unless surveillance were exercised over the refugees in Amsterdam and Leyden—who printed in Holland books and pamphlets filled with their nefarious notions and smuggled them into England—he would curtail the religious freedom of Dutch merchants in London. This threat may have helped to precipitate the refugees' move to the New World.

William Bradford, however, an early governor of Plymouth, stated in his *History of the Plymouth Plantation* that the Pilgrims left Holland not out of "newfangledness or giddy humor," but lest their children be seduced by the licentiousness of evil company and lest they be absorbed into the Dutch community and cease to be Englishmen. Those who journeyed overseas insisted that they had not abandoned "dear England." They regarded themselves still as participants in the struggle in the homeland and believed that their "hazardous and voluntary banishment into this remote wilderness" would light a candle whose rays would span the ocean and enlighten old England. There was constant going back and forth across the Atlantic, and those in the old home watched in high hope the raising across the seas of the model of that godly commonwealth to which they aspired.

The oddest and most troublesome feature of the venture was that at the outset the constituency was not homogeneous. The *Mayflower* carried fewer saints than strangers, "profane men, who, being but seeming Christians, have made Christ and Christianity stink in the nostrils of the poor infidels [the Indians]." These were servants, craftsmen, and representatives of the merchant company that financed the expedition and that was to be repaid out of their labors of the next seven years. There were also "sundry elder and younger persons who came over hither not out of respect to conscience or spiritual ends, but out of respect to friends or outward enlargements." There was near mutiny on the *Mayflower* when strangers announced that upon landing they would have their liberty. The saints then assembled the strangers and by "wisdom, patience, and a just and equal carriage" quelled their mutinous speeches and induced them to drop their talk of liberty and submit to the reign of the saints in a Civil Body Politic.

The Mayflower Compact was both a church covenant and a civil contract. It provided for the temporary government of the colony in accordance with the will of the majority. After all, the critics of Puritanism were right; there was a connection between the theory of the Church and the constitution of the state. But there was no democracy in Plymouth, save within the coterie of the saints. Church and state were one, but were not identical with the community. Only those who had tasted the sweetness of the Lord were qualified to come to Communion, and only those thus qualified could be members of the Church. Only members of the Church could hold office or vote for the highest offices. Only saints were full citizens; others were inhabitants. This system instituted in Massachusetts in the 1620's was unlike anything else in the old world.

Yet there was still some regard for the feelings of divergent conscience. On a Christmas Day, for example, Governor William Bradford, in order to show contempt for this Romish festival, summoned the men to work in the woods, and when some protested on grounds of scruple he excused them "till they were better informed." Again, when a Jesuit visited the colony to discuss Indian affairs, Bradford took pains to serve him only fish on Friday.

But schism in the colony could not be tolerated. The Pilgrims, and later the Puritans of the Massachusetts Bay Colony, operated on the territorial principle. They had staked out an area for their holy experiment. Let those who joined, conform. If they would not conform, let them stake out another claim for themselves. There was room in such abundance that John Cotton could say, "Banishment in this country is not counted so much a confinement as an enlargement." Thus the principle of territorialism was vastly more liberal in the New World than in the old because here there was always some place else to go. This situation explains why Massachusetts later was far more reactionary than England when, for example, it reverted to the death penalty in hanging four Quakers on Boston Common. These Quakers had been repeatedly expelled and were hanged because they refused to stay out of Massachusetts. They were offered their lives if they would leave and promise not to come back. They died for their rejection of territorialism in religion. Later in the century the Quakers, led by William Penn, established their own colony, Pennsylvania, which became for all the world a model of religious toleration.

XI
A Century of Enlightenment

In an age marked by apathy John Wesley led
a religious revival in the British Isles.

The age of Enlightenment was in many respects a revolt against the seventeenth century. By the time that century was reaching its close there was an intense revulsion against the religious fanaticism that had marked most of its course. Men came to scorn what they called enthusiasm, by which they meant fanaticism, and to mock "the petulant capricious sects" and their quarrelsome and noisy members—"those spider-saints, that hang by threads spun out of the entrails of their heads." But such sectaries had been chiefly responsible for creating the toleration that the eighteenth century so prized and that gave it a name as an era of enlightenment.

Comparatively speaking, the century was an age of toleration. In England the dissenters suffered only from legal disabilities. They were excluded from public life, but could obviate the rule by the compromise of taking Communion once in their lives in the Anglican Church. They could not take degrees at the universities, but the academies, which they themselves founded, so excelled the universities that Anglicans sent their sons to them to be educated. In the German lands there was a considerable degree of tolerance. Under the terms of the Treaty of Westphalia, which was based on the territorial principle, the archbishop of Salzburg banished fifteen thousand Protestants, but such action was very rare. In Prussia Frederick the Great tolerated all religions, in part because he believed in none, and in Austria Joseph II, a devout Catholic sovereign, asserted that the state is not a cloister and that coercing of conscience is an arrogant flouting of the patience of God. There were still Protestants in France, despite the revocation of the Edict of Nantes. In the Cévennes they had rebelled rather than turn Catholic or go into exile; the insurrection was suppressed, but thereafter survivors enjoyed the tolerance of indifference.

Pope Benedict XIV was ready to let the thunders of the Vatican rest, for Christ had refused to call down fire from heaven. To be sure, the Inquisition continued in Spain and in South America until the early decades of the nineteenth century, but the Jesuits, the great arm of the Counter-Reformation, were expelled from Portugal, Spain, and France. In 1773 Pope Clement IV dissolved the Society, which was not reconstituted until 1814.

In comparison with previous centuries, the eighteenth was an age of religious liberty.

The age was also one of relative peace. Men of the seventeenth century had fought so much that the desire for war disappeared for some time to come. War is commonly followed by revulsion against war, and antiwar literature generally flourishes in the first flush of peace. In the eighteenth century Voltaire had his hero Candide pass from a village of the Avars, fired by the Bulgars, to a village of the Bulgars, fired by the Avars. He found both sights equally appalling. And in Jonathan Swift's *Gulliver's Travels* the Houyhnhnms, a race of horses, marveled when Gulliver told them how humans fought over such questions as "Whether flesh be bread or bread be flesh, and whether the juice of a certain berry be blood or wine." The Houyhnhnms were not greatly disturbed, because the humans could do each other little damage, having no claws. Then Gulliver, to set forth the valor of his own countrymen, described their weapons of carnage and told how he had seen them blow up a hundred enemies at once while besieging a town or attacking a ship, and how the dead bodies had come down in pieces from the clouds to the great diversion of the spectators. The Enlightenment revived the old Stoic theme that beasts of the same species are not so deadly to each other as men are to men. Voltaire concluded his history with the query, "Is this history which I have finished the history of serpents and tigers? No . . . tigers and serpents would never treat their fellows so."

But satire is generally born of hope, and the men of this era were profoundly hopeful that they could achieve universal peace, not by conquest, but by a federation of the world. This was the age of peace plans: by the Quaker William Penn in England; by the abbé de Saint Pierre, Emeric Crucé, and Jean Jacques Rousseau, two Catholics and a deist, in France; by Immanuel Kant in Germany; and by John Comenius in Moravia. Their hopes did not appear illusory, because a relative degree of peace had already been achieved. This was because the nation-states shared a community of culture and had achieved a balance of power in which none desired the extermination of any other.

When wars did occur they were fought by mercenaries and with relative moderation. Monarchs had enough money to pay their troops regularly and restrain them from living by pillage.

Mercenaries are not crusaders; they prefer to serve their paymaster by wearing down the enemy with maneuvers rather than with bloodshed. Daniel Defoe wrote that in his day it was customary for armies of fifty thousand to spend the whole campaign dodging each other. The art of war, said another, consists less of knowing how to defend a fortress than of knowing how to surrender it honorably. The code of honor of the age of chivalry was revived. When battles did occur, they were costly. But when hostilities ended, the peace would be magnanimous.

The doctrine of natural law had long enabled Christians to believe that they could deal with Jews and Turks on the basis of a common moral code. Early in the sixteenth century the Spanish theologian Francisco de Vitoria had extended this doctrine to include the American Indians. But could natural law provide a common morality for Christians if they were split into warring confessional groups? To ensure that it should, Hugo Grotius, a devout Hollander of the seventeenth century, dechristianized natural law by treating it as an ethic valid "even if there were no God (which God forbid)."

This secularized natural law was further developed in the seventeenth century, to become a commonplace in the eighteenth. Such natural law is not anti-Christian but sub-Christian, an ethic of justice that the age commonly interpreted in conservative rather than revolutionary terms. But if political morality rests on a base broader than Christianity, then there is no ground for the Church's direction of governmental affairs. Such a conclusion was already implicit in the view of Aquinas that political principles are discernible by reason without revelation. The Enlightenment went still further by disclaiming the need for divine guidance in reaching political decisions. That was why Benjamin Franklin's proposal of recourse to prayer to resolve a deadlock in the Constitutional Convention was rejected. Cromwell's officers would have taken a day out to seek the mind of the Lord, but the American founding fathers felt that politics lies within the domain of man's natural reason, which should not be abdicated. Prayer begins where reason ends. This does not mean that the state is emancipated from the will of God, but that in matters of state man need seek no special illumination from God. This point of view, widely prevalent in the age of the Enlightenment, allowed for diversity in religion and unity in ethics. Thereby a new garb was tailored for Christendom.

In an atmosphere of tolerance and peace the spirit of inquiry revived. Men began to grapple afresh with the perennial difficulties of religious faith. In their aversion to all the bickering of the previous age, they reverted to the cardinal tenets of Erasmus: charity, modesty, and a minimum of dogma couched in terms of simplicity and universality. They spoke much of reason, and to them reason meant primarily common sense—as Swift unkindly said, "that which any fool can get through his noodle." But in many ways the credo of these rationalists was not so simple. They were intellectuals. The Puritan elect had become the enlightened elite, which was not, like Erasmus, content with unquestioning faith. With their inquiring spirit the men of the Enlightenment engaged in a new war, against superstition on the one hand and skepticism on the other. Against superstition they could be vitriolic; confronted by skepticism they wistfully and earnestly sought grounds for maintaining their faith. Their religious problem cut deeper than Luther's, who had asked, "How can I get right with God?" Their question was, "How do I know there is a God to get right with?"

The type of religion through which they found their answer is called deism, to be distinguished from theism and atheism. The atheists, and there were a few, were scornful of deists, saying that they were not weak enough to be Christians nor strong enough to be atheists. The deists nevertheless considered themselves Christians. Their God was not the personal God of the theists, a God who operated through history and concerned himself continually with the affairs of men. Their God was the Great Artificer of the universe, who, with a thrust of his almighty hand, had set rolling the myriad spheres and had established the celestial harmony that preserved them in their courses without collision. The Mighty Architect had done his work so well that he could withdraw into the vast silences and leave men rightly to order their own affairs guided by reason, that "candle of the Lord." In all this scheme there is little need for Christ, save that in him man's ignorance of the ultimate was once relieved.

Deism became a widespread phenomenon throughout Europe and in the English colonies. It developed national varieties, and it was no more able than were the sects to achieve universal concord. The deists, to be sure, did not start wars of opinion. They were reasonable men; but during the French Revolution the goddess of reason became a Fury. English deism was mild and relatively timorous and thus it was enabled to find a place even among the divines of the establishment. Matthew Tindal, in his *Christianity as Old as Creation* (1730), a book that is often called the deists' Bible, penned these lines:

> The Builder of this universe was wise;
>   He planned all souls, all systems,
>   planets, particles:
> The plan he shaped all worlds and
>   aeons by
> Was—heavens!—was thy small nine-
>   and-thirty articles!

But to imply that the Thirty-Nine Articles, the tenets of the Church of England, had not been God's blueprint in the creation of the universe was not to deny the validity of any one of the articles. John Toland, in his *Christianity Not Mysterious* (1696), after an imposing proclamation of the supremacy of reason, denied no more of the traditional faith than transubstantiation and consubstantiation. He became really radical only when he denied the fall of Adam and impugned the character of Old Testament worthies. David Hume, the Scottish philosopher, was much more subversive in his criticism than Toland, but he put his manuscript back into his drawer lest it be too disconcerting.

The French deists had no such inhibitions, because they were avowedly assaulting established religious authority. They were infuriated men, akin in their temper to the Jansenists and the Puritans. Voltaire, for all his persiflage, was one of their prophets. In the North American English colonies deism had the French complexion. Thomas Paine scoffed that if the devil had taken Jesus to the top of a mountain whence he could see all the kingdoms of the earth, he ought to have discovered America; Franklin and Jefferson imbibed also from France the slogans of nature and equality, and reasonableness of temper. In Germany the Prussian king, Frederick the Great, adopted some of the liberal ideas of the French, and the critic Gotthold Lessing, who believed that mankind might advance beyond the need for revelation, started a course of rigorous historical investigation of Christian documents. The first serious impact of the West on Russia came precisely at the time when deism was widespread on the Continent. Peter the Great was influenced by the English deists, and later Catherine the Great looked to the French thinkers. Voltaire visited St. Petersburg, and some of his manuscripts are still preserved there. In a number of countries, under the influence of liberal thought, monastic lands were confiscated, but the Church remained rich. Throughout Europe and even in Catholic lands the Church became more subservient to the state.

All varieties of deism were engaged in a mighty quest, first to demolish superstition and then to replace it by a rational religion, lest man be left a creature in the void. Basically the question was, is there any God at all? The ontological argument, revived by Descartes, was no longer convincing. If one may infer the existence of God from the idea of God, why might not one infer the existence of a hippogriff from the idea of a hippogriff, asked one of the scoffers. In the Middle Ages a similar question had been addressed to Saint Anselm, who had answered that this form of argument is valid only with regard to God. But the Enlightenment distrusted subjective reasoning that proceeds from that which is within to that which is without. Because both God and nature are outside man, they believed that man had to study nature and thence proceed to nature's God. Such was the view of John Locke, who insisted that we are not to start from our own existence but from our own experience, which results from the impact made upon us by that which is without. We can grasp externals only through sensation. Without it we get nowhere because the mind is a clean slate; there are no innate ideas. But given sensations, the reasoning faculty of man can deduce the unknown from the known.

By the eighteenth century the range of sensations by which man could come to know God had been enormously enlarged. The new natural science had exerted a profound impact upon general thinking. In 1609, when Galileo Galilei trained his "optic glass" upon the moon, one of his friends refused to look through it, lest he suffer the shattering of his presuppositions. But after Galileo no one hesitated any longer; and then came Sir Isaac Newton.

> *Nature and Nature's laws lay hid in night:*
> *God said, "Let Newton be!" and all was*
>   *light.*

wrote Alexander Pope. The Milky Way was proved to be a galaxy of stars held in their respective courses by the force of gravity.

The vast universe which thus swam before the eye filled some with dismay. Pascal recoiled before "the terrifying expanses which engulf us as a fleeting atom"; but the prevailing mood was that of the Englishman Joseph Addison, who wrote:

The spacious firmament on high
With all the blue ethereal sky
And spangled heavens, a shining frame,
Their great Original proclaim.

Kant was moved by the starry heavens, and Voltaire was awed by them. He wrote: "Last night, I was meditating, absorbed in the contemplation of nature. I was filled with wonder at its immensity, at the stars in their courses, at the mutual interaction of those countless orbs, one upon another, which people look upon unmoved. And I marveled still more at the Mind which governs the whole mighty scheme. A man must be blind, I said to myself, not to be dazzled by such a spectacle, a fool not to acknowledge its Author, a madman not to adore him. What tribute of adoration can I pay him? Must it not be the same, wherever it is offered? Whatever thinking being inhabits the Milky Way owes him the like homage. The light shines for Sirius, even as it shines for us." This enlarging of the universe did not create a conflict between science and religion, but only added force to the old Aristotelian arguments for the existence of God as the First Cause and the Prime Mover of the universe.

Another argument for the existence of God depended on analogy; that is, if we can draw conclusions about man's mind from the work of man, we can also draw conclusions about the mind of God from the work of God. The classic illustration used for the argument was a watch. Suppose, said William Paley, I kick my foot against a stone. If I were asked how it came to be there, I might reply that, for all I knew, it had been there forever. But should I find a watch, I would not give the same answer, because the watch has manifestly been contrived for a purpose. Such a contrivance, so marvelously designed, must surely be the work of an artificer. But suppose I discover that the watch is able to produce another watch. I may say that the one watch is the cause of the other, but still I have to account for the first. Similarly, when I behold the ordering of the universe, I have to infer the mind of the First Artificer, an intelligence vastly greater than our own, but yet not wholly dissimilar.

This argumentation involves the difficulty that what we experience is not the artificer but the artifact; and if the latter is material, but the former immaterial, how do we bridge the gap? The English philosopher Bishop George Berkeley solved that problem by claiming that matter itself is spirit or idea, capable of direct apprehension by the mind. And since God is spirit, he can be directly apprehended without any recourse to interference from sensation.

But however we arrive at God, a more difficult question is, what do we then find? We discover a Great Artificer who sits enthroned above the Milky Way and lets his worlds go reeling on, apparently heedless of the lives that come and go. Has he any concern for us? The age of Enlightenment sought to explain that apparent unconcern and to "justify the ways of God and man." A philosophy that sets such a goal for itself is called a theodicy. Theodicies did not originate, of course, in the eighteenth century; every great religious system has sought an explanation for the ruthlessness of nature and for the suffering of the just. Such was the ancient quest of Job. In the seventeenth century John Milton was tormented by the fact that God had permitted the English saints to suffer after the collapse of the Puritan revolution. The answer he gave in *Samson Agonistes* was that England would recover its strength as had Samson after he had been shorn, blinded, and mocked by the Philistines. Vastly more troublesome was the problem of God's judgments upon all mankind. In *Paradise Lost* Milton described man's plight as chastisement for his pride and disobedience.

In the eighteenth century Alexander Pope substituted for the myth of Adam and his fall the philosophical myth of "the great chain of being," according to which all reality consists of parts linked in a harmonious whole, in which man, be he stationed high or low, is merely one link. Man should not complain, wrote Pope, if nature does not devote to him her exclusive care, for she must look also after the other links. Nor should man grumble that he has not been endowed with all the excellencies of other links: "Why has not man a microscopic eye? For this plain reason, man is not a fly." God has established the chain and "whatever is, is right." Man is under obligation to fulfill his role as a link. To protest against his assigned place is to commit the

This title page of one of Galileo's works
shows him, at left, discussing the structure
of the universe with the great astronomers
Ptolemy and Copernicus. It was Copernicus
who suggested that the earth revolves
around the sun, not the sun around the
earth, as Ptolemy had maintained. Galileo's
advocacy of the Copernican theory, displacing
man from the center of the universe,
brought him the enmity of the Inquisition.

sin of pride, and to fall out of place invites the doom of disorder. Pope's theodicy recalls both the Stoics' acquiescence in fate and Milton's submission to the divine decrees.

The German philosopher Gottfried Leibnitz had a similar view; he held that of all possible worlds, this one is the best that God could have contrived. At first Voltaire also thought so. Then in 1755 came the Lisbon earthquake, and he was forced to change his mind. In a poem about the disaster he wrote:

> Come, ye philosophers, who cry, "All's
> well,"
> And contemplate this ruin of a world.
> Behold these shreds and cinders of your
> race,
> This child and mother heaped in common
> wreck,
> These scattered limbs beneath the marble
> shafts—
> A hundred thousand whom the earth
> devours,
> Who, torn and bloody, palpitating yet,
> Entombed beneath their hospitable roofs,
> In racking torment end their stricken
> lives. . . .
> O wondrous mingling of diversities!
> A God came down to lift our stricken
> race:
> He visited the earth, and changed it not!
> One sophist says he had not power to
> change;
> "He had," another cries, "but willed it
> not:
> In time he will, no doubt." And, while
> they prate,
> The hidden thunders, belched from
> underground,
> Fling wide the ruins of a hundred towns
> Across the smiling face of Portugal.

In *Candide* Voltaire wrote a savage satire on this "best of all possible worlds." He had no answer save that of Job, to bow before the inscrutable and then to tend one's garden. Pope had no other answer but to admit that man is unable to find an explanation.

If the goodness of God cannot be demonstrated, but only believed, can one in any case take solace in the goodness of man? The eighteenth century began with optimism about man, imagining him as untainted by the fall of Adam, capable of enthroning reason and with its help of mastering his environment and ordering his affairs in wisdom, charity, and peace. Plainly this was not a verdict about man but a vote of confidence in him. Man had never yet displayed such capacity and was still far from it. Eighteenth-century writers pointed this out in a series of satires modeled on the work of Sir Thomas More, who had rebuked Tudor England by contrasting its society disparagingly with that of a fictional land, Utopia (derived from the Greek word meaning "nowhere"). In *Gulliver's Travels* Swift invented Lilliput, which Gulliver contrasted with England. The Far East served the same end for Oliver Goldsmith, who brought a Chinese traveler to London to laugh at wigs. Voyagers who had actually visited foreign parts were so imbued with consciousness of Europe's vices and follies, that when abroad they saw only what they had gone out to see and came home to Europe corroborating the tales of the superiority of other lands.

And then came the myth of the noble savage, the primitive such as the American Indian whose natural goodness was undefiled by the civilization. In comparison to this innocent creature what should be said of the contemporary European? Frederick the Great talked about "this damned human race." Voltaire's Zadig spoke of men as "a lot of insects, devouring one another on a drop of mud." How similar this sounds to the indictment of mankind by Celsus, the pagan, in the second century of our era! But if primitive man was so excellent, and contemporary man so depraved, how can one explain the discrepancy? Obviously only by recourse again to the myth of a fall, not of Adam any longer, but of mankind, which degenerated as ages of silver, bronze, and iron succeeded the age of gold. The pagan myth supplanted the Christian myth; one finds it in Pope's *Essay on Man*. In the seventeenth century Thomas Hobbes rejected the myth of man's fall, but not to the advantage of man, for Hobbes felt that man from the very outset had preyed upon his fellows as wolf upon wolf.

No picture of human depravity drawn by Luther or Calvin could exceed the revulsion against man of those who lifted him out of the context of Christianity.

If this is the universe, if this is man, experience and reason do not demonstrate the goodness of God or the redeemability of man. These are teachings of the Christian religion, and to the Christian religion one must turn for confirmation of the teachings. Christianity confirms them on the basis of revelation. But how is one to know that revelation is trustworthy? The initial response of the eighteenth century was that the revelation had been validated by miracles. But how can one know that the miracles actually occurred? Throughout the age of Enlightenment this was a question of deep concern among the English Protestants. John Locke said that we can know only through sensation, our own or that of another. The problem then comes to rest on the credibility of those who claim to have witnessed the miracles, their good faith, and the accuracy of their observation.

The problem of miracles was the only point at which the eighteenth century found a conflict between science and religion. The new science taught the uniformity of nature's procedures, and that a natural law gave order to the physical world. A miracle involved a breach in the established order. It was by definition a divine intervention. If one assumed an omnipotent God, one could not deny the possibility of intervention, but to be convinced that it had actually occurred one had to be supplied with very exceptional evidence.

In 1729 Thomas Sherlock, in the *Trial of the Witnesses of the Resurrection*, soberly imitated courtroom procedure to demonstrate the credibility and the reliability of the authors of the Gospels. His contemporary Thomas Woolston maintained that miracles simply have to be taken on faith; to reinforce his point he magnified the difficulties that are encountered in believing them. The only witness to the resurrection of Lazarus, said he, was the apostle John, who wrote sixty years after the event. Lazarus, of course, was actually dead, if it were true that he stank, but the only witness to that was his sister.

Others were even less accepting of the miraculous. Voltaire and the French rationalists treated miracles with scorn. One of the miracles of Jesus, said Voltaire, was to turn water into wine at a wedding where the peasants were already drunk. Jesus withered a fig tree that did not even belong to him because it bore no fruit out of season. He sent devils into a drove of pigs and caused them to jump into a lake and drown, and this supposedly took place in a country where pigs are not even raised! David Hume, the Scot, earnestly argued that no miracle could ever be proved, because a miracle involves the concept of causation, and causation can never be experienced. If one billiard ball hits another, we see a succession of movements. This happens every time the balls collide, but all that we see is succession. We do not and we cannot experience and prove that one motion is caused by the other. This line of reasoning is not so much a disproof of miracles as it is a flight into skepticism, since by it we can neither prove nor disprove.

The Germans were to wrestle with the problem more earnestly and more persistently than any others. Hermann Reimarus accused the apostles of fraud and claimed that the Resurrection was a trick. Reimarus had adopted the procedure, sound within limits, of interpreting a historical movement in terms of its antecedents. But he explained Christianity as so completely Jewish that nothing new remained, and fraud was the only way in which he could account for the emergence of a new religion. Reimarus never dared to publish his manuscript, which appeared only following his death, when it was brought out by Gotthold Lessing in the hope that it might be refuted. After Reimarus's work was published other advocates of truth tackled the problem. Heinrich Paulus, a professor at Heidelberg, set himself to refute the charge of fraud by substituting for it an accusation of error. The disciples were not deceivers but deceived, for they had misunderstood what they saw and had interpreted natural events as miracles. Paulus then undertook to discover what really had happened to give rise to the stories of miracles. Jesus, he explained, when supposedly walking on water, was actually standing upon the shore and was barely visible through a mist. The Resurrection never actually occurred; Jesus had been entombed when he was still alive but unconscious, and an earthquake had revived him.

The explanations were often more incredible than the miracles; and in any case, the integrity of the disciples was saved only at the expense of their intelligence. Still more serious was the uselessness of the whole system for validating revelation, for if the miracles were simply natural events misunderstood, they could prove nothing whatever. Thus the Protestants and rationalists of the eighteenth and nineteenth centuries struggled with the problem. The Catholics did not come to grips with these questions until early in the twentieth.

The coldness of the rationalists inevitably provoked a revolt against them. The Scottish revivalist Thomas Chalmers said, "Moonlight preaching ripens no harvest." And the Wesleys—founders of Methodism—felt that England would never be revitalized by those who modestly defended revelation as actually no more obscure than nature. In the Enlightenment, as in the Puritan revolution, and indeed in every vital new venture, achievement had failed to catch up with aspiration. The lyrical hope with which the eighteenth century began gave way, as the decades succeeded each other, to chastened resignation.

Yet despite its failures the Enlightenment bequeathed many positive gains. The campaign against superstition did terminate the trials for witchcraft, which had taken place during the seventeenth century, particularly in Protestant lands. The Enlightenment's ideal of natural law as a universal ethic serves to this day to distinguish the western democracies from the totalitarian states. The age's slogan—liberty, equality, fraternity—gave impetus, as did Christian compassion, to the emancipation of serfs and slaves. The Christian hope for the coming of the Lord was reshaped into the idea of progress. When the age came to perceive the limitations of reason, Kant, who pointed them out in his book *Critique of Pure Reason*, proceeded to make a new start by basing righteous behavior on moral consciousness instead of on reason. The reformatory urge was still that of Christian reformers—of men like Gregory VII, Luther, Loyola, or Cromwell.

During the age of the Enlightenment deism was by no means the only religious movement. At the same time and in many places where the advocates of reason dominated intellectual life there were revivals of the most profound religious feeling. The revivalist movements had a wide spread. In England Methodism arose in the middle of the eighteenth century and eventually separated from the established Church. Within the Anglican Church the goals of the Clapham sect paralleled certain ideals of the Methodist revivalists. The Pietist movement in Germany and Scandinavia worked for the most part within the established Protestant Churches and strengthened their hold on the populace. In America the preacher Jonathan Edwards led what was called the Great Awakening, which revitalized the religion of the New England colonies. These movements were in part a reaction against the arid intellectualism and the lax moral standards of the Enlightenment and against the rigid conservatism and ritualism of much contemporary Protestantism. But primarily they were in effort to reach back to earlier roots of experiential religion.

In Germany the ideals of the revivalists can be traced back to the German mystics of the late Middle Ages, to Eckhart and Tauler and to Luther in one of his phases. But a more direct precursor was Kaspar Schwenckfeld, a sixteenth-century Silesian nobleman of courtly carriage and gracious demeanor. He was alienated by the acrimony of the religious controversies and by the emphasis on dogma rather than on inner religious experience. Banished from his own domains, he became a wanderer over Europe, seeking not to form a following but to fan among all confessions the sacred flame. Despite his desires, a following gathered that later migrated to Pennsylvania, where some Schwenckfeldian churches still exist. Another influence was the great seventeenth-century mystic Jakob Boehme, a shoemaker, who asked what it would profit a man to know the Bible by heart if he knew not the Spirit that inspired the book?

Steeped in this tradition, several figures arose within German Lutheranism whose intent was not to create a secession, but to establish cells of fervor within the larger Church. The leaders appealed to the peasants, but were not of the peasants. Philipp Jacob Spener, whose work was instrumental in the rise of German Pietism, was a preacher; his follower August Francke was a professor; Ludwig von Zinzendorf, Francke's pupil and Spener's godson, was a count. With the work of Zinzendorf, a mystic of the most ardent nature, Pietist sects did begin to leave the established Churches. Zinzendorf's religion cut across both class and creed. He consorted with kings and fraternized with peasants. However much it roughed his aristocratic grain, he insisted that peasants address him with the familiar *du* and *dich*, and after the death of his wife he married a peasant woman. Although he himself had no intent to separate from the Lutherans, he nevertheless received on his estate non-Lutherans, Hussite refugees from Moravia, and Schwenckfeldians from Silesia, and was even on close terms with a French Roman Catholic cardinal.

This was too much for the Lutheran establishment. The count was banished and thereupon became an itinerant evangelist. But he did not take his expulsion meekly. He agitated for the vindication of his orthodoxy and got it, even to the point that he

There was no bishop in America, so Anglicans
in the colonies had to go to England to be
ordained as ministers. An attempt to send a
bishop to the colonies was fiercely opposed.
Most Americans saw the move as an effort
to establish the Church of England's supremacy.
In this engraving, colonists are shown
hurling books, among them works of Locke
and Calvin, at an English prelate, who climbs
the rigging of his ship to escape assault.

was ordained a Lutheran bishop. His followers, the Herrnhuters—named after their village on his estate, which they called Herrnhut, or Lord's Hill—received recognition as a group within the Lutheran Church. Yet their communities tended to become separated from the established Church. Under the leadership of Zinzendorf some of the group, chiefly Moravians, migrated to Pennsylvania and there founded the city of Bethlehem. The Church they established is called the Unity of the Brethren, or more commonly, the Moravian Church.

The effects of Pietism on the religious and social life of Germany can be approximately discerned. Pietism may have contributed to the rise of German nationalism. The suggestion has been made that when Pietism kindled the emotions of many in the nation and the Enlightenment diminished the intensity of faith, emotion was transferred from God the Father to the fatherland. It is at least plain that the romanticists who saw a special divine afflatus in the German soul had been reared in the Pietist tradition.

In conjunction with the Enlightenment Pietism introduced a new way of viewing the history of the Church. From the time of the Reformation, Church history had been written with a confessional intent. In the sixteenth century the *Magdeburg Centuries* (a history divided into centuries and printed at Magdeburg) amassed evidence to support Protestant claims. Caesar Baronius, a Roman Catholic scholar, countered in his *Annals*. The eighteenth century, however, strove for impartiality. This could be achieved in one of two ways. The first was equal detachment from all movements. The men of the Enlightenment, who felt that Catholics and Protestants alike were addicted to superstitions, sometimes treated all with scarcely veiled hostility, as did Gibbon, who reserved warmth only for such figures as Julian the Apostate. Others, most notably Johann Lorenz von Mosheim in the early eighteenth century, endeavored to depict all the varieties of Christianity with judicial impartiality. His history, translated as the *Institutes of the Christian Religion*, enjoyed a wide vogue in England and America up to the end of the nineteenth century.

Another way, that of the Pietists, was to approach all systems with equal empathy. The Pietists fastened upon signs of fervor in the Christian past, whether among the orthodox or the heretics, but more frequently among the heretics. Such was the point of view of Gottfried Arnold in his epic-making *History of the Church and the Heretics*. This type of liberalism fostered Church unity among all those who like the Pietists felt themselves kindled by a profound religious spirit, although at the same time it produced divisions between them and other less fervent Christians.

In domestic relations Pietists subordinated the romantic element in marriage to the concept of partnership in the vineyard of the Lord. Marriages at Herrnhut were sometimes determined by lot—it was not that any with distinct antipathies were forcibly mated, but merely that religious obligation overrode personal predilection. The attitude of the Pietists toward marital relations was even more ascetic than was the attitude of the earlier Puritans.

From its inception the Pietist movement generated humanitarian endeavors. Francke founded an orphanage; Zinzendorf received refugees. In the nineteenth century Johann Wichern organized in Germany the so-called Inner Mission, composed of numerous agencies that cared for the halt, the maimed, and the blind; for epileptics, lepers, unwanted children, unwed mothers; the deranged, prisoners, seamen, the unemployed; and all those deficient in body and in mind. In its charitable endeavors Pietism joined Christian compassion with the humanitarianism of the Enlightenment. The Enlightenment stressed the reasonable, decried the irrationality of war, and opposed as superstition the hanging of witches and the treatment of the insane as demoniacs. Pietism stressed love and compassion, opposed the murder of war, and took care of the victims of fate, fault, and folly.

Wichern would have gone further in the remodeling of society, but his followers confined themselves to measures of relief. This may be the reason why Pietism warmed the hearts of the peasants and the aristocracy but did not win the industrial proletariat, who later were swept into the currents of Marxist socialism. But the Pietist movement did stimulate popular education through the development of the *volksschulen*, not only in Germany but also in the Scandinavian lands.

The Methodist revival in England was also a protest against the abuses prevalent in the established Church. The lamentable state of the clergy in the seventeenth century had never been redressed. Poverty, pluralism, and absenteeism were rife; of eleven thousand parishes in the early eighteenth century about six thousand are estimated to have been without resident incumbents. Ecclesiastical sinecures provided refuge for the younger sons of the gentry, who all too often lacked dedication to their calling. The Methodists reacted against the frigidity of clergymen like Bishop Butler, who told John Wesley to his face that "pretending to extraordinary revelations and gifts of the Holy Spirit is a horrid thing; a very horrid thing!" But even more serious was the indifference of the Church of England toward the growing proletariat, which had been created by the incipient industrial revolution; those who worked in the coal mines were especially neglected. "The Church, like the ark of Noah, is worth saving," one bishop declared; "not for the sake of the unclean beasts and vermin that almost filled it, and probably made most noise and clamor in it, but for the little corner of rationality that was as much distressed by the stink within as by the tempest without." Wesley's mission was, so to speak, to the unclean beasts.

But we must not overstate the deplorable condition of English religious life in his day. Had there been no spark of religious fervor there would have been no Wesley. In 1701 the Anglican Church founded the Society for the Propagation of the Gospel in Foreign Parts, whose endeavors spread far beyond the British colonies. And in 1728 a devout churchman, William Law, an opponent of deism, published his *Serious Call to a Devout and Holy Life*, which was to influence Wesley profoundly.

The home into which John Wesley was born in the year 1703 combined the finest strains of Anglican and dissenting piety. His father was an Anglican priest, his mother the daughter of a dissenting minister. She was a remarkable woman who bore nineteen children, of whom John was the fifteenth. She taught them "to fear the rod and cry softly." During each week she set aside time for the separate religious instruction of each of her children. John looked to her for guidance to the day of her death.

The Methodist movement was a youth movement which had its beginnings among a group of students at Oxford. Their ascetic deportment and addiction to prayer occasioned derision, and they were mocked even more for their visits to the jails to minister to prisoners. The missionary impulse seized Wesley. He went to America to preach in Georgia both to the colonists and to the Indians, whom he glorified as "noble savages." On his way over there was a storm at sea. Wesley, badly frightened, was profoundly impressed by the composure of some Moravians—men, women, and children, followers of Zinzendorf—who sang in the tempest. Once in Georgia he was dismayed to find that the savages were less noble than he had imagined. He experience further disappointment over an unhappy romance.

In the year 1738, thoroughly dispirited, Wesley returned to England and sought out a chapel of the Moravians in London. There, on the twenty-fourth day of May, at a quarter before nine, Wesley experienced a new birth. In one of his sermons he compared the birth in the spirit to the birth in the flesh. Prior to physical birth one is not dead, but the unborn babe, having eyes sees not, having ears hears not. Similarly, before the new birth there is no knowledge of the things of God. "But," Wesley wrote, "the 'eyes of his understanding are opened.' . . . He feels 'the love of God shed abroad in his heart.' . . . And now he may be properly said to live. . . . From hence it manifestly appears, what is the nature of the new birth. It is a great change . . . wrought in the whole soul by the almighty Spirit of God, when it is 'created anew in Christ Jesus' . . . when the love of the world is changed into the love of God; pride into humility; passion into meekness; hatred, envy, malice into a sincere, tender, disinterested love for all mankind. In a word, it is that change whereby the earthly, sensual, devilish mind is turned into the 'mind which was in Jesus Christ.' This is the nature of the new birth: 'so is every one that is born of the Spirit.'"

Three weeks after his conversion Wesley preached in the Church of St. Mary the Virgin at Oxford. The subject was justification by faith. There are some, said the preacher, who think it is a council of despair to say that we cannot be saved by what we do. True, to those who rely on what they can do. This doctrine is very comforting to all "self-condemned sinners. That 'whosoever believeth in him shall not be ashamed' . . . here is comfort, high as heaven, stronger than death! What! Mercy for all? For Zacchaeus, a public robber? For Mary Magdalene, a common harlot? Methinks I hear one say, 'Then I, even I, may hope for mercy!' . . . O! glad tidings! . . . Whatsoever your sins be, 'though red like crimson' . . . 'return unto the Lord and he will have mercy upon you . . . for he will abundantly pardon.' Nothing but this can give a check to that immorality which has 'overspread the land like a flood.' Can you empty the great deep, drop by drop? Then you may reform us by dissuasives from particular vices. But 'let the righteousness which is of God by faith' be brought in, and so shall its proud waves be stayed.''

Here was a manifesto of social regeneration through individual conversions; with it Wesley did more to make England Puritan by conversion than the Puritan movement had ever done by force of arms. To reach the people he depended on his preaching, but soon the churches were closed to him, for he was not soothing when he told Christians that he wished they could be converted into honest heathen. When Wesley, barred from the pulpit, visited his father's parish at Epworth, he preached to the large congregation in the churchyard as he stood upon his father's tomb.

He and his followers revived the practice of field preaching. The medieval friars had preached in the fields and so had some of the Protestant reformers, and in the seventeenth century the Quakers did also. On horseback Wesley set out for the hamlets and the mines. The mobs regarded a field preacher as fair game, and when crowds assembled to hear him the town crier would bellow, horns would blow, a cow or a bull would be driven into the crowd, and stones would be thrown. But sometimes the attackers recoiled. Wesley records that when one man raised his hand to throw a stone at him, another, from the rear, hit the assailant and forced him to drop the stone. One spectator, who had large pockets bulging with rotten eggs, found himself being clapped from behind by one of the preacher's supporters. "He savored not of balsam," Wesley recalled in his diary. Another time, when Wesley was riding in a coach and the mob began pelting him with stones, a large gentlewoman sat in his lap to shield him. Frequently he was able to quiet mobs by his sheer intrepidity. Many toughs were so moved by Wesley's composure that they turned suddenly on his assailants and defied anyone to touch him. And not a few of these bullies became the captains of the great crusade. Wesley relates how he confronted a hostile crowd: "My heart was filled with love, my eyes with tears, and my mouth with arguments. They were amazed, they were ashamed, they were melted down, they devoured every word. What a turn was this!"

From village to village Wesley rode, between stops giving free rein to his horse while he read the ancient classics and contemporary poets—across England and Scotland, across the Irish bogs and the Welsh mountains. No one in his century knew the British Isles so intimately, and his journal is one of the great social documents of the period. Toward the end of his long career, when he returned to places where once he had been mobbed, the crowds hailed him as if he were King George.

Wesley sought to help the miners in particular. At five in the morning, as they went down into the pits, he was there to preach to them, and when after incredible hours they came up from the bowels of the earth, he was there again at their side. As they heard the word of redemption, tears made gutters down their blackened cheeks. For them the new birth meant hard work. They were called upon to mend their ways, to be sober, chaste, and humane. Drunkenness had grown more prevalent after the industrial revolution had introduced distilled liquors, and beer and wine were replaced by gin. Those who spent most of their waking hours in the pits, not only men, but women and little children too, guzzled their weeks' wages in the pub. To make a clean break with their former life was difficult, and to suffer all week the jibes of unregenerated fellow workers even worse. There was no better prank than to get a Methodist drunk; witness the sport in *The Pickwick Papers* over "the red-nosed Mr. Stiggins of the Brick Lane Branch of the United Grand Junction Ebenezer Temperance Association."

Those who took the path of rectitude needed mutual support. Classes were formed, meeting weekly to recount trials, failures, and support from the Lord. These classes became the nucleus of an organization. By and by, in London, an abandoned cannon factory with the roof blown off was re-roofed and made into a tabernacle. Lay preaching was introduced. Wesley oversaw Methodist meetings that had been formed throughout the land, and thus he became, in effect, a pope without a tiara. He did not dream that he was founding a new Church; but separation was inevitable so long as the establishment continued to ignore the working classes.

The decisive step in separating from the Church of England came with Wesley's appointment of Thomas Coke to serve as superintendent of North America. Wesley believed that in the early Church bishop and presbyter, or priest, were synonymous. He was a priest and therefore a bishop, with the power to ordain others. By the same token, Coke, who was a priest, was also already a bishop. What Wesley conferred on him was really only an administrative authority; but to claim, as later happened, that Coke was being consecrated as a bishop conflicted with the doctrine of the Anglican Church. Wesley himself never left the established Church and was never disowned by it, but the Methodists, in time, came to recognize themselves as dissenters. A new denomination had come into being.

Yet the separation was in a sense unifying; since the Methodists had some points in common with the establishment and some with the dissenters, they bridged the gap between the two. Like the establishment the Methodists were generally Tory and opposed Catholic emancipation. Like the evangelicals in the Church of England they agitated against slavery. To the other dissenters they transmitted their itinerant ministry and, in Church government, a measure of their "connectionalism" among congregations, rather than sheer autonomy for each. On the social life of England their influence was unparalleled. Wesley was a Tory in economics as well as in politics and had nothing more drastic to propose for social reform than the abolition of distilling and of the excessive breeding of horses for the aristocracy, both of which used up grain needed to feed the poor. To his own alarm he was making the poor prosperous through sobriety, industry, and thrift, and thereby introducing them to the danger of indolence. But Wesley knew the poor and was concerned for them. By converting them he brought the proletariat within the orbit of the Gospel, which the Pietists in Germany had failed to do. Herein may lie one factor in the vast difference between German and English society in the centuries to come.

In America the revivalist movement was called the Great Awakening. The First Great Awakening took place during the first half of the eighteenth century; the Second came at the turn of the century, but there were a number of lesser revivals in between. The American movements were in touch with those of England and the Continent (Cotton Mather was lyrical over German Pietism) and a little later were associated even more closely with Methodism. Wesley's colleague, George Whitefield, the ex-actor who could pronounce the word *Mesopotamia* so as to bring tears to the eyes, came to America and swept up and down the Atlantic seaboard, leaving behind a train of faithful converts with wounded hearts. But revivalism in the colonies needed no impetus from abroad. It had been a feature of

American Protestantism from the time of its plantation in the wilderness.

At the very outset the Church in New England consisted only of the awakened. The ability to claim evidences of grace was a prerequisite of church membership, and church membership was a prerequisite of full citizenship. Church and state were one, yet together they embraced only a minority of the community. At first this caused no restiveness; the so-called strangers had never enjoyed the franchise in England anyway, because they failed to meet the property qualification. But when in the second generation the sons of the saints could not produce the proper spiritual credentials, and when, consequently, even a minister's son could not vote for an officer in the militia, there was murmuring in the new Israel. One solution was to extend the franchise, and by 1700 this had come to pass. But it did not suffice, because there were many devout and upright folk who wanted not merely a vote in the state but a share in the life of the Church, even though they could not claim an emotional conversion. To accommodate them a second level of Church membership was devised through the creation of ecclesiastical societies to handle certain Church affairs. Solomon Stoddard, the grandfather of Jonathan Edwards, was ready to go so far as to admit the unconverted to Communion in the hope of their conversion. But it would be vastly better to convert the entire community. In that case, Church, state, and community would be bound in the bond of grace, and the Holy Commonwealth would become such a reality as it had never been. This was the hope of Jonathan Edwards.

It must not be thought that Edwards's primary concern was for the Holy Commonwealth. His intent was to warn souls to flee from the wrath to come, so that they might enjoy the blessedness of life in God. He wished for them what he had himself known. "The sense I had of divine things would often of a sudden kindle up, as it were, a sweet burning in my heart; an ardor of soul . . . I walked abroad alone, in a solitary place in my father's pasture, for contemplation. And as I was walking there and looking up on the sky and clouds, there came into my mind so sweet a sense of the glorious *majesty* and *grace* of God, that I know not how to express. . . . The appearance of everything was altered; there seemed to be, as it were, a calm, sweet cast, or appearance of divine glory, in almost everything. God's excellence, his wisdom, his purity and love, seemed to appear in everything; in the sun, moon . . . and all nature . . . I often used to sit and view the moon for continuance; and in the day, spent much time in viewing the clouds and sky, to behold the sweet glory of God in these things; in the meantime, singing forth, with a low voice, my contemplations of the Creator and Redeemer." Edwards was a poet in prose. He was attuned to the Enlightenment and was influenced by the writings of Locke and Newton. He was a theologian in the tradition of Calvin and an experiential Christian in the tradition of the mystics.

Edwards set out to convert the entire community. That he should ever have supposed he could may well appear fatuous, seeing that he believed in predestination. Roger Williams had long since pointed out that if God has already chosen some to be saved and some to be damned, there is no possibility of converting an entire community; since all live in the community and are governed by the state, all should share in the state, while the Church should be confined to the elect. Edwards would have only the elect in the Church, but he wanted everyone to be elect. At any rate, the preacher must proffer God's grace to everyone, for God has ordained preaching as the way in which to disclose the elect. And who was the preacher to assume that any in his congregation were not? Edwards's sermon "Sinners in the Hands of an Angry God" was a summons to awake. God is indeed an angry God, said the preacher, and he has fully as much reason to drop rebellious men in the flames of hell as men have to fling a venomous spider into the fire. But God is holding back to give men another chance. Only his hand prevents them from falling into the flames at any moment. "O sinner! Consider the fearful danger you are in. . . . It would be no wonder if some persons, that now sit here in some seats of this meetinghouse in health, and in quiet and secure, should be in hell before tomorrow morning." Before the close of that sermon, it was reported, "there was a great moaning and crying out through the whole house. The shrieks and crys were piercing and amazing. Several souls were hopefully wrought upon that night, and oh, the cheerfulness and pleasantness of their countenances that received comfort!" The Great Awakening was on the way.

It revivified the churches, that is to say, some of them, but it did not restore the outward fabric of the Holy Commonwealth of Massachusetts. Instead it caused a split among the churches. To this day in New England, villages sometimes have two Congregational churches on the green, reminiscent of the schism.

XII

Christianity in The Modern Age

A cross formed by charred beams stands in
the midst of the ruins of Coventry Cathedral
in England. Behind it rises the cathedral
tower, which survived World War II.

The history of Christianity during the last century and a half has been marked by unparalleled gains and by unprecedented losses, by expansion of the faith into areas previously untouched and by recession in other areas where it had been solidly entrenched. In modern times the Churches have profoundly affected the structure of societies. Yet for the most part they have been impotent to direct the behavior of nations. The forms of Christian activity are in constant flux and fraught with anomalies. To suggest the varied nature of these circumstances down to our own day within a single chapter requires more schematic treatment than was followed in earlier sections of this book.

In the last decade of the eighteenth century a new wave of revivalism swept New England. This Second Great Awakening sought to avoid the excesses of the first, earlier in the century, when members of Jonathan Edwards's congregation had swooned in their fervor—and one had even taken his life. When reproaches against the excesses of that revival reached Edwards from Boston, he had replied that physical manifestations neither proved nor disproved the reality of religious experience; the test lay in the fruits of the spirit.

Some of his successors were not so discriminating, and therefore the architects of the later revival advised restraint. Nevertheless, when the awakening struck his congregation in Boston, Lyman Beecher, the father of Henry Ward Beecher and Harriet Beecher Stowe, described it as "fire in the leaves." Such fire easily gets out of hand. At first Beecher thought that it had when in the 1820s the revivalist preacher Charles Finney undertook his evangelical work in western New York State. That region experienced such repeated waves of revivalist excitement that it has been referred to as "burned-over ground," where religious emotion had finally been spent. It was here that, among millennialism and other manifestations, Mormonism arose in response to the visions of Joseph Smith. Smith related how an angel, Moroni, had disclosed to him the link between the old dispensation and the new, for the ten lost tribes of Israel had migrated to South America and there had had the series of adventures that are described in the Book of Mormon.

In the 1790s and early 1800s a separate wave of revivalism

swept the Kentucky frontier. The camp meeting, typical of the early West but by no means peculiar to it, was a uniquely American form of religious demonstration that brought together people of many different denominations. It also brought together people of many different types, from the hard-drinking, rough-and-tumble frontiersman to families of earnest, pioneering homeseekers. In areas where life was hard and where loneliness could be a desperate thing, such meetings provided occasions for companionship and outlets for pent-up spirits. As well, they carried the Gospel with enthusiasm to places on the western frontier that were beyond the reach of ordinary church practices.

The Methodists were particularly successful with camp meetings. Circuit-riding, a practice originated by John Wesley to further his missionary work in England, proved especially well suited to conditions along the American frontier. The itinerant preachers—at first principally laymen—rode their circuit, or districts, visiting in succession a large number of communities scattered over a wide area of sparsely settled country.

The expression "spiritual inebriation" that was applied to the temper of their camp meetings was more than a metaphor. James Finley, who himself subsequently became a famous backwoods evangelist, wrote of the meeting at which he was converted: "The noise was like the roar of Niagara. The vast sea of human beings seemed to be agitated as if by a storm. . . . Some of the people were singing, others praying, some crying for mercy in the most piteous accents, while others were shouting most vociferously. . . . A strange supernatural power seemed to pervade the entire mass of mind there collected. . . . At one time I saw at least five hundred swept down in a moment, as if a battery of a thousand guns had been opened upon them, and then immediately followed shrieks that rent the very heavens." The turbulence of those demonstrations went far to channel emotions that might have found more violent outlets. The camp meeting helped to tame the unruly frontier.

England also experienced revivals in the late eighteenth and early nineteenth centuries. An evangelical wing of the Anglican Church, composed of wealthy enthusiasts and called the Clapham Sect from the village where it centered, was imbued with a pietistic religious fervor combined with an intense concern for bettering social conditions. The revival called the Oxford Movement, which was especially active from 1833 to 1841, more profoundly affected the future not only of Anglicanism but of Protestantism in general. The Oxford Movement aimed at stirring new life in the old Anglican parishes and restoring the ideals that had given the established Church such vigor in the early centuries of its existence.

The chief architect of the revival was John Keble, professor of poetry at Oxford, who, however, spent his days chiefly in a secluded country parish. His circle included notable men—among them, Edward Pusey, Wilfred Ward, and above all, John Henry Newman—who perceived that if there were to be a revival in the parishes, there must be changes in the structure and outlook of the Church as a whole. One grievous obstacle to their intentions was the dependence of the Church upon the state. The prime minister appointed the bishops, not always exercising serious responsibility in making the choice. He might be as flippant as Lord Melbourne, who swore that the bishops died to annoy him. The Church could not even revise the Prayer Book without the consent of Parliament, which was filled with rabid "No-popery" dissenters.

The proponents of the Oxford Movement were prepared to go to the length of disestablishment for the sake of strengthening and invigorating the Church; but where then would authority be found? Not in the pew, said they, for such torpid congregations as they observed would not represent the Church of Jesus Christ. Not in the whole people of England, for the ideal of a more catholic Church that would include everyone could be achieved only by reducing Christianity to an unexciting minimum. No, the Church must proclaim the maximum; and abide by the ancient creeds. The Church must recover her heritage as it had been transmitted to later generations by the successors of the apostles.

To discover successors of the apostles among the English bishops of that day might seem a trifle anomalous, but the real concern was not to make a shibboleth of the external succession; it was rather to revive reverence, piety, prayer, and commitment. John Henry Newman, in one of his university sermons, declared that the real religion of nature is not the abstraction devised by the philosophy of the Enlightenment; it is not to be found in the optimistic platitudes of deism, but in the dark and bloody superstitions of the heathen. "Doubtless these desperate and dark struggles are to be called superstition when viewed by the side of true religion," he wrote, "and it is easy enough to speak of them as superstition, when we have been informed of the gracious and joyful result in which the scheme of Divine Governance issues. But it is man's truest and best religion, *before* the Gospel shines on him."

The way to recapture the sense of the numinous, these men believed, was through the worship in the parish churches, and this should be restored to its pristine splendor. Not only had the dissenters abandoned the Christian year; the Anglicans had neglected it too. Keble wrote *The Christian Year*, a devotional book of poems for each Sunday, feast day, and saint's day of the Anglican year. A verse for Good Friday reads:

> *Lord of my heart, by Thy last cry,*
> *Let not Thy blood on earth be spent.*
> *Now at Thy feet I fainting lie,*
> *Mine eyes upon Thy wounds are bent;*
> *Upon Thy streaming wounds my weary*
>   *eyes*
> *Wait like the parched earth on April skies.*

The architecture of old English churches and the liturgy that was anciently practiced in them cast a nostalgic spell on the revivalists at a time when the romanticism of the period was rebelling at the ugly new factories that were covering the countryside with a pall of soot. How fair, in contrast, appeared the ruins of a long-forsaken cloister to Isaac Williams, the poet of the group, who wrote:

> *I seem to walk through angel-haunted*
>   *caves,*
> *Lit by celestial light, not of the sun,*
> *That leadeth to a kingdom far away.*

Basing their work on principles of the Oxford reformers, a Cambridge group commenced a great architectural and liturgical revival. Its chief figure was John Mason Neale, who inaugurated a revival of interest in Gothic architecture by detailed studies of medieval parish churches, revealing what they once were and the desecrations to which they had been prey. Neale translated a great many Christian hymns from the Greek and

Latin. Fully fifteen of his renderings are common in current hymnbooks. Among them are "Good Christian Men, Rejoice"; "All Glory, Laud, and Honor"; "Art Thou Weary?"; "Christian, Dost Thou See Them?"; and "Jerusalem, the Golden."

Perchance the most fertile spirit of the Oxford group, while he was in the Church of England and after he went over to the Church of Rome, was John Henry Newman. Even those who differed from him radically in their views—like his two most prominent pupils, the historian James Anthony Froude and the author Matthew Arnold—fell under the spell of this wise, earnest, and eloquent man and paid tribute to his inspiring genius. Newman came to believe that the Thirty-Nine Articles of the Anglican Church were amenable to a Catholic interpretation, and that the "superstitions" were popular exaggerations and not the essence of Catholicism. He then became convinced that the apostolic succession was not represented in the Anglican Church, that the ultimate authority emanated only from Rome. Some of his disciples followed him when he joined the Roman Catholic Church. But the reasons that moved Newman to submit to Rome could not induce such men as Keble and Pusey to sever themselves from their English parish churches.

The evangelical revivals gave impetus to the great Protestant missionary crusade, as a result of which Christianity was to achieve a geographical expansion unparalleled in all the previous centuries—"from Greenland's icy mountains to India's coral strands," from the Ganges to the Limpopo, from the fiords to the jungles, from the Eskimos to the Zulus. In the late eighteenth and nineteenth centuries numbers of Protestant missionary societies were founded to carry the Gospel to areas about the globe where it had never before been preached. In the Roman Catholic Church there was also a revival of missionary fervor, which has not abated since.

In the missionary endeavor the Protestants were in the lead by the nineteenth century. In the earlier centuries they had been far behind the Catholics. In the age of the Reformation and during the wars of religion the Protestants had been too busy converting the Catholics and fighting for their own existence to be concerned about the heathen. One of the Protestants consoled himself that God would use an angel to convert the Indians. As a matter of fact, the angels used by God to that end were mainly the Franciscans and the Jesuits. Although in the colonial period in New England John Eliot, David Brainerd, Roger Williams, and Jonathan Edwards labored among the Indians, by and large the Protestants awoke to their missionary labors only in the latter part of the eighteenth century and under the impact of the evangelical revivals.

A secular factor contributed to the shift of preponderance from the Catholic to the Protestant missions. The decline of the one is associated with the waning of the Spanish and Portuguese colonial empires, and the rise of the other with the emergence of the great imperialist powers in northern Europe, notably Britain and Holland. This fact raises the question whether the frequent allegation may not be correct that Christian missions were simply an adjunct of western imperialism, that the missionary would call upon the natives to shut their eyes in prayer, only to discover, when they opened them, the Union Jack waving over their heads. The charge is rendered plausible by the fact that at a particular juncture in the nineteenth century Christian missionaries would not have been able to enter China and Japan had not the western powers forced the "open door." But such particular instances do not warrant a generalization. Against this case may be set the wide following gained by Catholic missions in the sixteenth century in Japan, without political assistance.

Undeniably the missionaries accompanied the flag, and it often became one of their necessary burdens to mitigate the asperities of the colonialism by which they had gained access to remote lands. The missionaries, of course, could not engage in persistent criticism of their own governments without being sent home. But not a few emulated Bartolomeo de las Casas, who blazed out against the barbarities practiced on the natives in the Caribbean in the first flush of Spanish conquest. Far from constituting a department of the colonial office, the missionaries were at times restricted by western authorities lest they put ideas that would prove troublesome into the heads of the natives. On the other hand, colonial governors and missionaries were often able to collaborate. In India the British fostered education, and to a degree industrialization, with which measures the missionaries were in sympathy; wherever they went the missionaries themselves founded schools, a contribution particularly welcomed by the native population. Many government officials engaged in missionary work, and missionaries were not unwilling to enter government service, though they usually resigned from

From time to time certain Christians had
decried the evils of slavery, but it was not
until the late eighteenth century that
English and American groups were
organized to abolish the practice. This
Wedgwood medallion was made in 1768
for England's Slave Emancipation Society.

the mission in this case. Not a few missionaries have served as government ambassadors.

A subtler criticism of the missionaries is that they have sought to westernize their converts and have destroyed the fiber of primitive people by introducing the corruptions of western civilization. Unquestionably the missionaries have sought to introduce whatever they deemed to be good in their own culture—medicine, sanitation, education, transportation, and technology, especially in agriculture—even though this at times has uprooted and disrupted ancient and valued cultural patterns and traditions. Of course missionaries in India have opposed suttee, the burning of widows, which was suppressed by the British government. They have opposed child murder, prostitution, polygamy, cannibalism, and headhunting, but native literature, native drama, native music, native architecture they have sought to learn, conserve, and revive. The missionaries have put hundreds of languages in writing and have provided these tongues with dictionaries and grammars, the main purpose, of course, being to translate the Scriptures.

Of especial significance was the introduction of the printing press. William Carey, at Serampore in Bengal, working in a Baptist mission under the Danish flag, established the first press in the land; by 1832 it had issued translations of portions of the Scriptures in almost forty languages and dialects. He and his associates also translated into English a great Indian epic poem. Beyond such endeavors, by instilling ideals of dignity and equality of opportunity the missionary movement has been indirectly responsible for the rise of self-government and nationhood among many erstwhile primitive peoples.

With regard to the accommodation to native cultures there has been a difference of approach between the Catholics and the Protestants. The Catholics have continued the tradition that won Europe by conversions en masse, whereas since Protestant missions began under the impact of the great revivals, the emphasis with them has generally been upon an individual experience of conversion followed by a period of training and testing before admission to the Church (although there were instances of mass conversions in India). The unhappy concomitant is that the convert entering the Church by himself is cut off from his own people. His family disowns him; his wife divorces him. He has no recourse but to enter a European enclave. This problem has plagued the Protestants.

The Catholics, who have striven to bring whole communities into the Church, have felt this difficulty less acutely. However, in modern, as in ancient, times, they have been confronted with another dilemma, because the masses bring with them pagan beliefs and practices that are incompatible with Christian ideals. In India this means caste; in Africa, polygamy; in China, the cult of ancestors; in Japan, until recently, the worship of the emperor. The question once more arises as to what is the inalienable core of Christianity that cannot be compromised, and what the flexible periphery that can assimilate the innocuous elements of paganism. Among the Catholic missions there have been two great examples of Christian accommodation to native ways. In the late sixteenth century in China Matteo Ricci, an Italian Jesuit, attempted to win converts from Confucianism without insisting on a complete break with that religion's practices. He used Confucian words for God, regarded the cult of ancestors as harmless, and encouraged the pagoda type of architecture for churches. Rome first approved but later banned certain Confucian expressions for God and the ancestral cult. In the next century in India Robert de Nobili, also an Italian Jesuit, tried to win the leaders by living like a Brahmin and by accepting caste. He felt there should be one branch of the Church for the Brahmins and a separate branch for the pariahs. Rome gave its approval, which, however, was retracted more than a century later.

Protestants have not been altogether immune to these problems. The Presbyterians in Korea ruled against participation in the cult of the emperor, whereas other denominations considered it merely a civil rite. Often the question of what is innocuous in these matters can be a very difficult one.

Christianity has naturally confronted different situations in the various areas into which it has penetrated. In India the Hindus are tolerant of other religions and ideas and are willing to borrow from them; but they are extremely loath to forsake their Hindu affiliation for that of another faith. In approaching them missions have largely adopted the strategy of promulgating Christian ideals. Mahatma Gandhi, for example, expressed great reverence for Jesus and exemplified more of his spirit than many a Christian, but he was of no mind to join the Christian Church.

In some lands, such as Turkey, the Church for political reasons can make no other approach than this one, since the government forbids open proselytizing. Roberts College at Constantinople, though manned by Christians, cannot teach Christianity. Conversions to Christianity in India have been chiefly from among the lower castes, for whom a change in religion has meant a gain in social status. Since the Church itself was popularly regarded as constituting another caste, the outcastes, by joining, acquired at least the status of caste. In China likewise converts have been largely from the lower social strata. The cultivated Buddhists recoiled from Christian activism, and the cultivated Confucianists from Christian religious affirmations. In Japan, however, in recent times the chief gains have been among the intelligentsia, and the masses have not been affected by the Christian teaching of the missionaries.

Despite the impressiveness of the geographical spread of Christianity, it cannot be said that the world has been won for Christ in our generation. No serious dent has been made on the other major religions of the world—Judaism, Islam, Hinduism, Buddhism, and Confucianism. The great gains have been at the expense of primitive religions, notably animism. In lands where there has been prodigious missionary endeavor the percentage of Christians remains small. It is estimated that before the Second World War the Christians in India numbered two per cent of the total population; in China it was only one per cent, and in Japan a mere one-half per cent. Christianity is a minority religion in the world at large, as it always has been.

The work of Christian missions is not ultimately to be assessed in terms of numerical gains, nor even in terms of their material and cultural contributions. The dedication of the missionaries is an undying witness to the strength of their faith. One thinks of Henry Martyn, who started his missionary labor saying, "I will burn myself out for God," and who died at the age of thirty-one. One thinks of David Livingstone, who penetrated Africa, not in order to discover the Falls of Victoria, but because he saw the smoke rising from a thousand villages that had not heard of Christ. One thinks of Stanley, who when Livingstone was deemed lost was commissioned by the British government to find him and did. Though Stanley hated Africa, after Livingstone died he went back to carry on his work. Continents have not been gained, but converts to whom Christianity has come as a blinding flash have often better exemplified the spirit of the Gospel than those who have enjoyed the light of Christianity all their lives.

During the century of comparative peace, from the end of the Napoleonic Wars to the beginning of the First World War, the concern of the Churches, both Protestant and Catholic, for justice in the social order received a new impetus. In this setting the humanitarianism of the Enlightenment, the ethical sensitivity of Pietism, and the traditional Catholic preoccupation with the social order combined to launch numerous crusades for the amelioration of the ills that plagued society.

Protestants in England and America have espoused many and various reformatory movements. Anglican bishops of the early nineteenth century were generally conservative in such matters; but dissenters fought for relief from the disabilities which barred them from political offices, they favored home rule for the Irish, and they sought to impose ethical restraints on British imperialism. In other directions societies were organized that drew their membership from all faiths to pursue with Christian conscience such specific objectives as anti-slavery and anti-vivisection legislation.

In the English-speaking world in the nineteenth century one of the greatest evils to be overcome with the help of such organized activity was slavery. The campaign against the slave trade in England was instigated by the Methodist and Anglican evangelicals. John Wesley blazed against the traffic. When told that only black men could work in the climate of the American South, he gave that statement the lie on the basis of what he himself had seen in Georgia. Another reformer, the Anglican evangelical William Wilberforce, agitated for thirty years in the British Parliament for the suppression of the slave trade and then for the abolition of slavery in the British dominions. He was a man of a single cause, which put a great strain upon the friendship with William Pitt, the prime minister. Pitt was occasionally willing to postpone the program for abolition in order not to jeopardize his broader imperial plans; but Wilberforce was adamant. He appealed always to the conscience of England. Slavery, he told the House of Commons in 1789, battens upon vices. A delegate from Liverpool, one of the centers of the slave trade, had said that the apartments of slaves in transit were perfumed with frankincense and lime juice, "when the surgeons tell you the slaves are stowed so close that there is not room to tread among them and . . . the stench is intolerable. . . . Death, at least, is a sure ground of proof and . . . upon the whole there is a mortality of about 50 per cent. . . . Many persons [argue] that if we relinquish slave trade France will take it up. . . . we cannot wish a greater mischief to France. . . . For the sake of France, however, and for the sake of humanity, I trust—nay, I am sure—she will not."

The French Revolution engendered a great revulsion in England toward social innovation. England did not renounce the slave trade until 1808 (the same year it was banned by the United States). Then came the second great crusade for the abolition of slavery itself in the British colonies. Victory came only in 1833 with the passage of the emancipation law. Slave owners were indemnified to the amount of twenty million pounds sterling. "Thank God," said the dying Wilberforce, and as his body was being laid in Westminster Abbey, eight hundred thousand slaves received the proclamation of their freedom.

In colonial America there had been slaves, Negro and Indian, in North and South alike. Because of the plantation system more were held in the South, supplied principally by New England traders who acquired this human commodity from the ruthless slave merchants of the African coast. Protests against the evil were strongest among the Quakers. The first American anti-slavery tract was written by the Quaker George Keith in 1693. A New Jersey Quaker, John Woolman, visiting Friends in the South in 1757, left money with his hosts to pay for the unre-quited labor of the slaves, whereby many a conscience was quickened. In 1776 the Quakers declared that any of their own sect who did not free their slaves would be expelled. On the eve of the Revolution Samuel Hopkins, pastor of an opulent Congregational church in Newport, Rhode Island, whose wealth was derived from the slave trade, shocked his parishioners by asking how they would feel if their own sons were among the European slaves in Algiers. In the Middle Atlantic and New England states there were many others who cried out in protest. In Connecticut, for example, there had been no free Blacks and 3,634 slaves in 1756; in 1850 there were 7,693 free Blacks and no slaves at all.

This does not mean that the Christian conscience in the South was unaroused. In his first draft of the Declaration of Independence Thomas Jefferson mentioned slavery, but others struck out his words. To George Washington his slaves were an embarrassment, and he provided for their manumission in his will. In 1789 the Baptists in Virginia combined evangelical fervor with Jeffersonian tenets in a resolution that condemned slavery as "a violent deprivation of the rights of nature and inconsistent with a republican government." How, then, did the South come to be so solidified behind slavery in the decades that followed? It was partly because of the fear of insurrection, partly by reason of the death or emigration of southern leaders with anti-slavery sentiments, partly in reaction to the diatribes of northern abolitionists, who, it was said, "united the South and divided the North." But most of all the South developed a solid front because the Yankee Eli Whitney invented the cotton gin, which vastly accelerated the production of cotton fiber to feed the new mills of the North. Slaves to gather raw material for this booming industry became an immense economic asset to the South.

With its culture and economy dependent upon slavery the South prepared the defense of its peculiar institution. Among other reasons in support of slavery, it was claimed that human bondage was condoned by the Bible. Three of the major religious denominations—the Methodists, the Presbyterians, and the Baptists—were split into northern and southern branches by the issue. Loyalty to the unity of their Churches preserved the Catholics and Episcopalians from rupture, and the Quakers did not divide because they were all against slavery; nor did the Congregationalists, whose terrain was solely in the North.

The anti-slavery agitation in that area stemmed from the spirit of the Second Great Awakening. It was in this spirit that William Lloyd Garrison wrote John Greenleaf Whittier, "The cause is worthy of Gabriel—Yea, and the God of Hosts places himself at its head." Slaveholders were reviled as sinners. The "crusader in crinoline" who aroused the land with *Uncle Tom's Cabin*, Harriet Beecher Stowe, was the daughter of the revivalist Lyman Beecher. The New England abolitionists were divided as to strategy between the advocates of gradual and of immediate emancipation. Northern abolitionists helped slaves to escape from the South through the Underground Railroad, a maneuver that was forbidden by the Fugitive Slave Law of 1850, which required the return of runaways. Some of the moderates, like

Charles Darwin is portrayed in the sketch
above. In an age when scientific discovery
was making religion increasingly difficult
for educated people to accept, Darwin's *On
the Origin of Species* may have delivered the
greatest blow. Most Christians have since
reconciled the Bible with the theories of
Darwin, but some fundamentalists still
claim that his ideas on evolution conflict
with Christian thought.

Daniel Webster, pointed out that to connive in the escape of a few would only rivet the chains on the many. In the interests of ultimate emancipation, he pointed out, the fugitives must be returned. A large number of northern abolitionists repudiated the law, among them the Quaker Whittier. Then in 1854 came the Kansas-Nebraska Act, which many in the North protested as a means of extending slavery to the West. Seven years later the South seceded, and the war ensued; God had "loosed the fateful lightning of his terrible swift sword." The nation ultimately survived its worst agony: the union was preserved, and slavery was abolished; but the problems underlying that bloody dispute have remained to plague us today.

Other great social problems of the nineteenth century were connected with the increase of population, the growth of cities, and the effects of industrialization. In England, for example, the population increased between 1811 and 1851 from twelve to twenty-one million; the larger cities doubled and trebled their numbers. Great cities engendered slums, filled, in part, by artisans, whose work could not compete with machine-made goods. The changes wrought by the rapid growth of industrialization are not to be exaggerated. At the time of the accession of Victoria to the throne of England in 1837 there were more women and girls in domestic service than in the mills, and more tailors and bootmakers in London than miners in Northumbria. But still thousands of people suffered from technological unemployment; those who worked in the factories were employed at low wages, for long hours, under miserable conditions—not only men and women, but small children. A bill passed in 1833 seemed to many very radical when it proposed that children under nine should be excluded from factories, that those under thirteen should not work more than nine hours a day, and those under eighteen no more than twelve. The conditions of labor were unsanitary. Employers who may have considered improving them had to compete with others who had no compunction about driving their workers. Only government could deal with a situation so widespread, but the working class in England did not have the right to vote and was not represented in Parliament. In the meantime such conditions engendered crime, punishable by imprisonment or death. Of the two, death was almost to be preferred, for prisoners were exploited by jailers whose only pay was what they could extort. The accused and the condemned, the sick and the well, were housed together without proper sanitary facilites.

In dealing with this complex of problems the Churches, as Churches, usually took no stand, although individual members were active—frequently one man to a single cause after the manner of Wilberforce. Richard Oastler, an Anglican and the administrator of a Yorkshire estate, was greatly concerned about slavery in Africa, when he was made aware of a slavery as dark in the factories of his own area. He then became the champion of the workers, demanding shorter hours and better conditions. The Christian Socialists, a group active in England around the middle of the century, opposed the prevailing utilitarian ethics, claiming that the industrial competition it countenanced was unchristian. Charles Kingsley, a leader in this movement and also an Anglican, upbraided consumers who wore "Cheap Clothes and Nasty"; this was the title of one of his tracts against the product of sweated labor. The Ten Hours Bill went through in 1846, its chief proponent in Parliament being the earl of Shaftesbury. A man of more than a single cause, Shaftesbury sponsored care for underground workers, child laborers, chimney sweeps, and lunatics, and worked for the abolition of slavery, the protection of animals, the reformation of juvenile delinquents, the education of poor children, and improved housing.

If for the most part social reform in England was the work of individuals, one Church constitutes an exception—a branch of the Methodist Church whose members are called the Primitive Methodists. Shortly after Wesley died the Wesleyan movement became subject to the splintering process, which proved to the advantage of social reform. Unlike the more conservative parent group, the Primitive Methodists had profound sympathy for those displaced by the loom, which included many of their own members. In the second decade of the century the so-called Luddites tried to recover their jobs by smashing the looms. The Methodists eschewed violence, but they were willing to join working-men's associations. Labor unions were, however, illegal, and the Methodist leaders forbade their members to join, whereupon one-third of the Methodists left the Church around the middle of the century and did join unions. They did not thereby cease to be evangelicals. Rather, they brought to the labor movement their zeal, their Christian ideology, and their experience as lay preachers. Many a labor leader had his apprenticeship as a Methodist lay preacher. Methodism gave to the labor movement men of the stamp of Arthur Henderson, Ramsay MacDonald, and Philip Snowden.

But the regulation of hours and wages was not enough. There needed to be provision for periods when there were no wages: insurance against sickness, accidents, old age, and incapacity. The pioneering welfare state was Germany, where Lutheranism had always encouraged paternalistic government and Pietism quickened concern for social welfare. In accord with these traditions, Bismarck in the 1880s set an example in social legislation with a policy he termed Christian socialism.

In England recourse to the state meant a reversal of the trend inaugurated by the Puritan Revolution to curb the role of the state, a trend that had resulted in a *laissez-faire* policy in economics. The welfare state had its beginnings on the local level when Joseph Chamberlain, as mayor of Birmingham in the 1870s, municipalized gas and water utilities and cleared slums. Himself a Unitarian, he was warmly supported on the public platform by the Congregational minister in Birmingham, Robert William Dale. Among the Catholics Leo XIII in his great encyclical on labor problems, *Rerum Novarum*, in 1891, endorsed the welfare state and labor organizations. The encyclical evinced a new concern on the part of the Catholic Church for the lot of the workers, and it has been hailed for its important influence in furthering social justice.

In the United States the struggle with the problems of industrialization was retarded because industrialization was itself retarded. The traditional assumption, encouraged by persistent optimism, that America's was a classless society, favored by boundless opportunities for all, tended to hide the plight of the working man, which worsened late in the nineteenth century with the wide development of industrialization. However, there were those who protested the grim facts, among them the Baptist Walter Rauschenbush, who about the turn of the century sounded the clarion of the "Social Gospel," an appeal to Christians to join in social reform. His program has subsequently been largely realized, and labor has become a power scarcely needing any longer to be championed by the Churches.

The ancient plague of war continued to concern the Churches. As earlier noted, the eighteenth century had seen peace plans in abundance. An opportunity to implement such plans was afforded by the Quakers' Holy Experiment in Pennsylvania, which attracted like-minded Moravians, Schwenckfelders, and Mennonites. As a colony under the British crown, however, Pennsylvania could not be permitted by its pacifism to become a breach in the colonial defense against the French. Others with different ideals, notably Scotch-Irish Presbyterians, were permitted to settle in Pennsylvania and soon outnumbered the Quakers, who in 1756 withdrew from the legislature rather than take part in the French and Indian Wars.

The Puritans of New England were not tinctured by any pacifism. Although they established some missions to the Indians, they treated them in general as Joshua did the Canaanites, and resisted the French as the minions of the Catholic antichrist. What may well have been the first peace society in the world, the New York Peace Society, was formed in New York in 1815, admitting as members only those in good standing in their churches. Agitation for peace also developed in New England after the War of 1812, which had been very unpopular in that section because of the disruption of New England's vital commerce with Britain. The New England Non-Resistance Society, founded in 1838, was thoroughly pacifist. Under the leadership of William Ladd, a Congregationalist, the American Peace Society sought to restrain war by a congress of Christian nations. The Civil War, of course, caused a drastic setback to such movements. For the Churches in the Calvinist tradition—Congregationalists, Unitarians, Presbyterians, Baptists, and Methodists—the war was a crusade to abolish slavery. For the successors of the old, established Churches of Europe—Catholics, Anglicans, and Lutherans—it was the suppression of a rebellion.

After the war the peace societies revived and became international. Their congresses did prompt disarmament conferences between governments, in which, for a time, Russia took the lead. When the First World War began, however, the shelves of peace literature became irrelevant. In the United States all save the historic peace Churches rallied to a crusade to make the world safe for democracy and to end wars. The failure of victory to achieve these ideals caused great revulsion, and the Churches then embarked on a crusade to outlaw war. This was implemented in 1928 by the Kellogg-Briand Pact to renounce war as an instrument of national policy. The Second World War, though the evil to be resisted was more monstrous, was fought in a mood of chastened sobriety. In the ensuing Cold War the dove of peace has been caged, to be released on occasion by either side in the interests of propaganda. The preservation of peace by the balance of terror elicits protests from those Christians who recoil from the use and the threat of massive retaliation and from humanists who think the universe would be impoverished by the extinction of the human race.

Another social problem that engaged especially the Churches of the United States and England was alcoholism. The evil had been accentuated, as we have observed, by the introduction of distilled liquors. Greater evils calls for more drastic remedies. Prior to the nineteenth century most Christian Churches did not require members to abstain from strong drink. Monastic orders—such as the Benedictine and the Carthusian—even became famous for their cordials. Methodism was the first to call for thorough-going renunciation on the part of hard-drinking miners. In the late eighteenth century Methodists in America discountenanced the making and drinking of distilled liquor. In Pennsylvania Benjamin Rush, a Quaker physician who advocated temperance, recorded with scientific precision the effects of alcohol on the soldiers in the Revolutionary War. Lyman Beecher, the revivalist, was outraged by the tippling that took place at an ordination he attended.

Advocacy of temperance in some quarters developed into a demand for abstinence. First it was for abstinence from hard liquors, but with the realization that alcoholics could as readily lapse on wines and beer, a t for "total" was added to the pledge: hence the term *teetotal*. An appeal to the state to regulate the sale and manufacture of liquor stemmed from the Churches of the Calvinist tradition, with their ideal of the Holy Commonwealth. State-wide prohibition began in Maine in 1846 under the impetus supplied by the Quaker Neal Dow. Catholics, Episcopalians, and Lutherans supported prohibition because it was the law, not because it met with their approval. Catholic ethical rigorism does not apply to drink, although there have been numerous anti-alcoholic campaigns by Catholic groups. Episcopalians have always felt that if wine could be used as a sacrament, it was not wholly to be eschewed, and German Lutherans have felt no scruples about accepting contributions to their Church from wealthy brewers. Prohibition began with local option, and before the eighteenth amendment to the Constitution was passed nearly two-thirds of the American people already lived under prohibitory laws. But after 1919, when the constitutional amendment establishing national prohibition was ratified, violations of the law by otherwise respectable people of virtually all persuasions soon reduced it to a mockery.

The settling of disputes by law and the humane treatment of criminals has constantly advanced over the past century and a half. Dueling was vigorously attacked by Lyman Beecher when Aaron Burr shot Alexander Hamilton. Prison reform was initiated in the late eighteenth century by an Anglican layman in England, John Howard. Having been made a sheriff, he acquainted himself with the appalling conditions in the jails of his own jurisdiction, then moved on to investigate those of all England and eventually of all the Continent. During his lifetime he traveled fifty thousand miles and expended from his own funds thirty thousand pounds in his efforts to promote penal reforms. Early in the nineteenth century Elizabeth Fry, a Quaker, devoted herself to the care of women prisoners. In 1823 Robert Peel, the prime minister, exempted one hundred offenses from the death penalty, and in 1841 deportation for crime was abolished. In America, thanks in good measure to the humanitarian principles of the Quakers, the hospitals and prisons of Philadelphia were early among the most advanced institutions of their kind in the world and attracted wide interest. When Alexis de Tocqueville visited America in the 1830s to study penal institutions, he was amazed at the encouragement given to the moral reform of prisoners.

As was the Church in Europe in the Middle Ages, the Churches in the New World have been the promoters of education, the Catholics to the south, the Protestants to the north. Prior to the establishment of state universities nearly all the educational foundations on the Atlantic seaboard were Church-sponsored. Because of the desire of the various sects to keep learning close to the people, wherever they scattered, even the early frontier had its sprinkling of little denominational institutions offering schooling at various levels and competing for prestige.

These definite gains in so many areas have not by any means created a perfect social order. The attempt to prevent war by preparation for war entails grave risks and dissipates resources that might be better used to feed the hungry and clothe the naked. The emancipation of slaves has not ensured civil rights. Neither prohibition nor repeal has eliminated alcoholism. But enough in these areas has been gained to prove that the social problems that have beset man are not altogether without solution.

Yet the very centuries that have witnessed the greatest missionary outreach of Christianity, and the most striking social reforms under the impact of Christian motivation, have seen also the greatest recessions from the Church and from Christianity, not because of any conquests of Christian lands by unbelievers, but because of corrosive influences within established Christian societies. Those lands that once gloried in their orthodoxy suffer from the recession caused by indifference and hostility. Catholics and Protestants are both affected in varying degrees. France, nominally Catholic, is accounted missionary territory by the Church despite the eminence of many of the French clergy. The popes lament over South America, where in Buenos Aires one may see a sign reading, "You are a Catholic. Go to Mass once a year." There is said to be less religious vitality in Protestant Sweden with an established Church than there is in Russia under persecution; and it has also been remarked that "the Englishman likes the Church of England to be there for him to stay away from." In the established Churches in Germany the active participation of the nominal membership is placed at about six percent. The United States is the most church-going country in the world, yet even here for many the country club rates greater interest on Sunday.

Manifestly, in some once-Christian lands the Church is subject to savage attack by a movement that some consider to be itself equivalent to a religion. In theory, Communism believes mankind to be moving with an ineluctable dynamic toward a classless society. Just as Christians believing in predestination have been most active, so those espousing a determinist theory of history have felt bound to hasten the processes by revolution; they have demanded of their followers a complete devotion and have ruthlessly crushed all opposition to their programs.

The opposition to Christianity had a long gestation in Russia. Since the time of Peter the Great the intelligentsia had been in touch with the West. Along with literature, dress, music, and social customs they borrowed the anti-clericalism of Voltaire and, in the nineteenth century, the evolutionary theory of Darwin as applied to human society and the anti-capitalist theories of Karl Marx. Many Russian intellectuals were atheists who looked upon religion as "the opium of the people" that enervated the will for emancipation. True, some Slavophiles would have revived the ancient mission of "Holy Russia" to the world. But the Church remained reactionary and was used in the interest of an autocratic government. Common folk, largely illiterate and beyond the reach of theological refinements, were devoted to the liturgy, loved the icons, and revered the saints. They did not particularly resent the immense wealth of the Church, because they saw little of opulent ecclesiastics and much of parish priests, who were as impoverished as themselves and who, though not uneducated, were versed only in the theological and devotional literature of the Orthodox Russian and Byzantine traditions. They were not abreast of the currents of western thought and were unable to contend with the polemics of the anti-Christian intellectuals.

Through expansion Russia had come to embrace territories inhabited by Roman Catholics, Lutherans, Moslems, Jews, and Armenians, sects she tolerated in varying degrees. Mennonites and Baptists came from without. There were also native Russian sects outside the Orthodox Church that suffered some legal disabilities. One schismatic group, the Old Believers, alternately tolerated and persecuted, numbered around thirteen million at the time of the 1917 Revolution. Among the lesser sects were the Stundists, the Dukhobors, and the Molokans; the last were so pacifist that they would not even coerce the earth by plowing. These splinter groups, which exerted an attraction on the lower classes principally, altered neither the piety of the great masses of peasants nor the impiety of the intellectuals.

The first Russian revolution, in 1905, was moderate. The czar issued an edict of toleration to all faiths, but this was soon modified to limit the rights of Roman Catholics. Reforms of the established Church were urged but never realized under czarist government. The Bolshevik government that followed was blatantly "godless." Bishops and priests were slaughtered and one-half the monasteries were liquidated. An attempt was made to destroy the Church by fomenting divisions within it. Tikhon, the patriarch of the Orthodox Church, was imprisoned and maltreated. Thousands of priests and laymen who might have saved themselves by recantation went to concentration camps. The

Kaethe Kollwitz's drawing of a tortured
man reflects a concern with the inevitability
of human suffering. The twentieth-century
angst that succeeded centuries of relative
optimism owes much to Freud, the
existentialists, and the discoveries of modern
science. Men and women have been forced
to reassess their place in the universe.

Church was actually purified by fire, for only those of deep conviction resisted persecution. The rites of religion were carried on with such secrecy that husband and wife often did not dare let each other know that they were both practicing believers. Religious instruction for those under eighteen years of age in groups of more than four was forbidden. Yet a census taken in 1927 in six schools near Moscow revealed that over a fifth of the boys and a little more than half of the girls avowed themselves as believers.

After the relative failure of such rigorous and sometimes bloody measures, the government took a new line in 1929 and sought to eradicate religion by intense propaganda. Measures of repression were launched, purportedly as responses to popular demand. Petitions from the people were stimulated for the removal of church bells and the burning of icons. Rents for the use of church buildings were increased 120 percent. In consequence, many thousands of places of worship were closed. Heavier pressures were placed upon the sects and upon the Catholics. Yet this policy also fell far short of its goal. After a census in 1937 the head of the Militant Atheists' League stated that one-third of the adults among the industrial workers in the cities and probably two-thirds of the village population were believers. Since the rural areas constituted 67 percent of the population, these figures meant that nearly half the population were Christians. In 1940 an atheist journal conceded that in the cities at least half the workers were believers and that in the villages hardly an atheist was to be found.

In 1939 the government relaxed some of its repressive measures. Among other things, the excessive rents were dropped, religious celebrations were permitted, and the clergy was granted civil rights. Christianity was recognized as having been a great cultural force in the formation of old Russia. The icons were to be prized as art, and the cathedrals preserved as monuments. The loyal support given to the state by the churches during the war has diminished the rift. The remaining Orthodox churches today are said to be crowded; the sects are all now classified together as Baptists, though the Roman Catholics and the Lutherans hardly fit this category. These Baptist churches are also thronged, and the preaching is powerful, but one must not forget the many churches that have been closed. In the Communist satellite countries the Church survives, although it is under constant harassment.

Although Christianity was never a major religion in China, it has survived there under a Communist regime. The considerable investments on the part of the foreign missionary boards in schools, colleges, and hospitals have passed into the hands of the Communists. The saddest aspect of the revolution is that those Christians who refused injunctions to denounce all "foreign imperialism" have been branded as traitors by fellow Christians who have in conscience complied with those demands. Yet the latter are not to be accused of abject subservience, for they could have escaped great pressures had they simply repudiated Christianity altogether. The situation is parallel to the imprisonment of Quakers in seventeenth-century England during the reign of that devout Puritan, Oliver Cromwell.

The other great movements that have sought at least to curb and if possible to crush Christianity have been Fascism and Nazism. Many of their methods were taken over from Communism, but Fascism and Nazism have had less in common with Christianity than has Communism. They have been racist, nationalistic, and built upon class structure. If less overtly, they have been no less averse to Christianity, even though their activities have occasionally enjoyed the support or approval of the Church.

Hitler began his efforts to control the Church by signing a concordat with the pope in 1933; he also consolidated the many territorially organized Protestant Churches into one national Church, by which means he hoped to be better able to manipulate the people in the interest of Nazi aims. At the outset these Churches saw no objection to uniting at the behest of the state. Such a union might well have been consummated earlier on grounds of religious principle. They expected that the Church would be free to determine its own inner life, but Hitler ousted the bishop of their choice in favor of one of his own. Not only were the Protestant Churches made a department of state, but the attempt was made to revamp Christianity as a Germanic religion, with no Semitic admixtures; those of Jewish blood, even though members of Christian Churches, were to be expunged. The Catholic Center Party in the Reichstag was liquidated, and the Catholic youth organizations were absorbed into the Hitler Youth.

The only organized opposition to Hitler's program was offered by the Churches. Albert Einstein testified that he had expected resistance on the part of the universities, editors, and independent authors, but all remained mute: "Only the churches stood squarely across the path of Hitler's campaign for suppressing truth." The Catholic cardinal Michael von Faulhaber denounced the Nazis for unscrupulously disregarding the Concordat in 1935 and 1936, and Bishop von Gallen in broader terms said that no nation that thus violated justice could long endure. Some four thousand Protestant ministers, led by Karl Barth and Hans Asmussen, formed the Confessing Church, which at Barmen in 1934 declared that no human *Führer* could stand above the Word of God. The Confessing Church lost its properties, its seminary was suppressed, its journals were prohibited, and when war came the members of its clergy of military age and not in prison were assigned to positions of greatest danger, while the older leaders were sent to concentration camps. Among them was Martin Niemöller, a Lutheran pastor who after more than half a year in solitary confinement was brought to trial under Hitler's law against "treacherous attacks upon state and party." His refusal to capitulate and his persistent resistance to Nazism made him the symbolic figure of the Protestant opposition until the downfall of the Nazis.

After the war Catholicism emerged with great strength in West Germany; the heavily Protestant area was now the East Zone, under Communist rule. The Protestant groups have formed a loose federation that spans the iron curtain, and the *Kirchentag*, the annual convocation, is attended by representatives of the Churches of the east sector as well as of the west. The assembly has acquired more than religious significance as a symbol of the unity of the divided German nation.

The separation of Church and state has had an ambivalent effect on the influence of Christianity, because the separation has come about from diverse motives, has been sometimes friendly and sometimes unfriendly; it has been initiated now by one partner, now by the other, and on occasion, though opposed by the Church, in the sequel it has proved of benefit to the Church. No more beneficent calamity ever overtook the papacy than the loss of temporal sovereignty. Never in centuries have the popes enjoyed such prestige as in the years since 1870. The concordat with Mussolini in 1929 nominally restored the papacy to complete political independence but did not materially alter its status; the papacy thereby acquired little more than the right to issue its own postage stamps. But although the popes have been divested of political power, they have not ceased to exercise an influence upon political regimes. The Catholic Church is able to come to terms with any government that will grant freedom for the sacraments, religious education, monastic orders, and the holding of property. This is why the popes could make concordats with Mussolini and, at first, even with Hitler.

But naturally the Church prefers a Catholic government, and can deal more readily with one that is highly centralized like the papacy itself. Hence, throughout the nineteenth century in many lands the Catholic Church gave support to legitimism—specifically to monarchic and royal claimants, even though they may have been out of power. This has meant in Spain, the Carlists; in France, the Bourbons; in Austria, the Hapsburgs; and in Germany, the Hanoverians. Yet the Church supported republicanism in Belgium in order to aid that largely Catholic country win independence from Protestant Holland. And in Poland, at that time divided between Germany and Russia, it did not look askance upon revolutionary movements that would curb the intrusion of Lutheranism and of Russian Orthodoxy. Centralization of government, however, has been opposed if it would prove inimical to the Church, as in Germany, where the domination of Protestant Prussia in the imperial government threatened Catholic interests, and in Italy where the *Risorgimento* stripped the Church of most of its territory.

The motivation for the separation of Church and state, as just remarked, was quite diverse in the many lands in which it came to pass in the nineteenth century. Aversion to the substance of Christianity was evident in some cases, whereas in others there was merely anti-clericalism. In still others, where various religions enjoyed strong popular support, there was no practical alternative to the separation of Church and state. In Scotland a section of the Presbyterian Church objected not to establishment as such, but to the power, authorized by Parliament, of a lay patron to force his nominee upon an unwilling congregation. Against this system a protest was led by Thomas Chalmers in 1843, and 451 ministers out of 1,203 seceded and set up the Free

Church, having first renounced their parish churches, their manses, and their endowments.

In Latin countries the separation was almost invariably caused by hostility on the part of the state to the strong influence of the Church. In South America the separations were an aspect of the overthrow of Spanish and Portuguese colonialism. Only in Chile was the separation friendly. In France the rift came early in the twentieth century and also entailed the expulsion of the monastic orders. In Germany Hitler intensified the association of Church and state only in order to control the Church. Complete separation came only after his collapse, although there is still a connection of a sort, because the state, having expropriated Church lands to finance the Napoleonic Wars, promised the Church revenue in perpetuity, which is still being paid. The Bolshevik Revolution, of course, left the state in virtual control of the Church in Russia. In England and Sweden established Churches survive.

The situation in the United States is unique and calls for a further historical explanation. As already noted, in the Puritan colonies of New England Congregationalism was the established Church and dissenters were not tolerated, except in Rhode Island, where Roger Williams offered settlers complete religious liberty. In the other colonial settlements, conforming to the pattern of a single, authorized state Church, one denomination was privileged and dominant, at least in the beginning—the Dutch Reformed Church in New Netherland, the Presbyterian in New Jersey, the Swedish Lutheran in Delaware, and the Quaker in Pennsylvania. The Anglican Church became established in Virginia and the Carolinas. Maryland, founded by a Catholic under a charter from an Anglican king, was the first colony to separate Church and state and to offer complete religious freedom to all settlers.

Actually, in order to promote settlement, the proprietary governments of Pennsylvania, Georgia, and the Carolinas—like Maryland—invited persecuted religious groups to come to those colonies. The system of established Churches gradually broke down. Sometimes shifts in political jurisdiction created untenable anomalies. For example, the Dutch Reformed, being Calvinists, would not at first tolerate Lutherans in New York, but when these Dutch gained control of Delaware in 1655, they were constrained by treaty not to interfere with the Swedish

Lutherans. Thereafter to keep Lutherans out of New York itself was hardly defensible. When, in turn, the English took New York and established the Anglican Church, the treaty accorded toleration to the Dutch Calvinists. The attempt to suppress the American Presbyterian Calvinists in New York then speedily collapsed.

A very important factor in the disestablishment of colonial Churches was continuous immigration. Along with German sectarians, the Scotch-Irish, staunch Presbyterians, settled Pennsylvania in such numbers that they came to control the colony. In Virginia they were welcomed to the western frontier as a bulwark against the Indians, even though they weakened Anglican dominance in the colony. The need for joint defense tended to draw the colonies together, and intercolonial trade helped to develop common interests; and as traffic in goods and people increased, more people of different religious persuasions mingled throughout the colonies. The imposition of England's Act of Toleration in 1689 gave colonial dissenters the right of appeal.

Coincidently the differences between the denominations were reduced. All tended to become congregational in polity—even the Anglicans and the Roman Catholics—because with the distance between settlements and the much greater distance of all from Europe, no central authority could be effectively exercised over individual congregations. Then the great revivals shifted interest from the religion of the head with formally prescribed doctrine to the religion of the heart, regardless of creed. In consequence the "revived" were drawn together. But as we noted, the Holy Commonwealth was not restored by the revivals, and the Congregational churches were split. In the meantime the Methodists established themselves in all the seaboard colonies, thus challenging whichever Church was established.

The logic of the revivals called for the separation of Church and state, since it called for a Church consisting only of the converted; and since the entire populace was obviously not to be converted, the revivalists ran the risk of interference at the hands of others in the state administration. Coincidently the concepts of the Enlightenment gained a great vogue among the Anglicans in Virginia, notably Jefferson, who believed that the state, which belongs to the order of nature, should not be confused with the Church, which depends on revelation. Led by Jefferson and Madison, supported principally by Baptists and Presbyterians,

In the pronounced upward thrust of their
designs, many Protestant churches freshly
interpret an age-old symbol of aspiration. In
Eero Saarinen's interdenominational chapel
in Cambridge, Massachusetts, Harry
Bertoia's metal sculpture cascades to the
floor from grillwork set in the ceiling.

Virginia disestablished the Anglican Church just before the Revolution. Thus the growing religious pluralism and the logic of the revivals, coalescing with the impact of the Enlightenment, caused the framers of the American Constitution to forbid any national establishment of religion. The Constitution left religious questions to the individual states, and among them the separation of Church and state was not completed until the 1830s.

Thereafter a unique situation developed. The distinction between Church and sect disappeared. *Church* had commonly signified the established religion, and *sect* a non-established one, but now in the United States none of the groups was established. From that point on the American Churches have been generally called denominations rather than sects. Again, the sect has frequently been outside the main cultural pattern of the state, but the denominations have contributed substantially to the cultural pattern of America—as the Congregationalists did in New England, the Anglicans in Virginia and the Carolinas, the Methodists in the West, and the Baptists in the South, with, of course, some overlapping. In early New England Church and state were one but not identical with the community at large. Now Church and state are separate, but the denominational Churches may be identified with the cultures they have helped fashion.

Amid all these changes the concept of the Holy Commonwealth, however, did not vanish. Its external contours disintegrated, but the idea was transferred from the Puritan colonies to the nation at large, the New Israel of God with a destiny to fulfill on this continent for the benefit of the world. The nation came to be regarded as the arm of the Churches to implement the social reforms and the ideals they advocated. The Churches have been all too disposed to envisage their role simply as that of agitators to create sufficient public sentiment to secure legislation, and then to withdraw and leave its implementation to the state. The nation has replaced the Church as the symbol of unity, and whereas secession from the Church has been regarded as unexceptionable, secession from the nation was prevented by war. Indeed, faith in America's mission itself took on the fervor of a state religion. To this day the rite of induction into United States citizenship includes a little homily on American ideals with the tacit assumption that those who do not subscribe to them should be merely inhabitants of the country, not citizens.

The separation of Church and state, however diverse the causes, has benefited Christianity; relieved from state interference and thrown upon their own resources, the Churches have displayed great vitality. The proliferation of small religious groups, still commonly called sects, is but one evidence of that vitality. The United States is dotted with such movements, which by no means represent merely the impoverished and submerged elements of the population. They have made their appeal not only in the United States but to a degree in Europe and in South America as well.

Alongside this phenomenal formation of new sects there have been extensive movements throughout the world toward the integration of the older branches of Protestantism and, particularly in recent years, toward a *rapprochement* between the Protestant and the Catholic Churches. Some of the initial impulse came from the missionary activity, which from the beginning, in societies and conferences, drew support across denominational lines. The revival movement also cut across the old confessional lines and tended to unite all those who had experienced the new birth in the spirit, though often at the same time to separate them from the unconverted. The theological movements of the nineteenth century drew together the liberals from all camps, though again, sometimes occasioning breaches with the conservatives. In the United States the tendency of the Protestant denominations to stress the claims of the heart in religion rather than of the mind enables them to work together toward religious objectives even though they do not always believe alike.

In this country also divisions of Churches arising from diverse European origins of the population are diminishing. For example, Danish, Swedish, Norwegian, Finnish, and German Lutherans are in the process of forming unions. Churches of the same family, such as the varieties of Methodists, have been reunited, healing the breach caused by the Civil War. The Northern and Southern Baptists have not yet come together, but the reason for the continuing separation has become theological rather than sociological; the issue now is not slavery but fundamentalism. In Canada, Methodists, Congregationalists, and Presbyterians have formed the United Church of Canada; in North India, Presbyterians and Congregationalists have been brought together in a single Church; and Anglicans, Methodists, Presbyterians, and Congregationalists have joined to form the

Church of South India. In the United States two previously united bodies have formed a further union: the Evangelical (Lutheran) and Reformed (Zwinglian) Church united with the Congregational Christian Churches. The National Council of Churches gathers many Protestant groups into a federation for the coordination of numerous activities; so does the World Council, which includes also the Greek and Russian Orthodox. The Russian Protestant sects may soon be admitted.

Recently the initiative of Pope John XXIII in convening the Vatican Council has opened the door to *rapprochement* between Catholics and Protestants. The deepest reason for this move is that Christian division is felt to be incompatible with the prayer of Christ that all his disciples might be one. An additional consideration may be the need for a united front against secularism and Communism. The possibility of reunion has become realistic since Protestantism and Catholicism have been moving to a point of convergence. The more radical Protestants of the Puritan tradition have been returning to the liturgical heritage with the observance of certain feast days in the Christian year and the centrality in the church of the altar rather than the pulpit. Coincidently the Catholics have sometimes brought the altar down from the sanctuary close to the congregation and in the shape of a Communion table. The dialogue Mass, in which there is much participation by the congregation, has been favored. Hymn-singing is encouraged, even Protestant hymns such as Luther's "A Mighty Fortress is our God." Large portions of the Mass are being permitted in various vernaculars. As for church music, the Catholics are appropriating Bach, and the Protestants, Palestrina.

Protestants have moved away from the liberalism of the nineteenth century which reduced Christianity to little more than a belief in the fatherhood of God, the brotherhood of man, and the leadership of Christ. The neoorthodox movement has revived the cardinal tenets of biblical Christianity as set forth by the early reformers. In the meantime the Catholic Church has come to terms with the methodology of biblical scholarship, and in this area differences between Protestant and Catholic scholars are scarcely discernible. The attitude of Catholic historians to the Protestant Reformation of the sixteenth century has altered greatly in tone, and the Catholic Church is ready to assume some measure of responsibility for the schism. Catholics no longer refer to Protestants as heretics but as "separated brethren." But though Catholics and Protestants can collaborate in prayer and work, organic union will require also agreement as to the formulation of the faith. The dialogue in that area is yet to come, but when it does, it will be conducted in an ambiance of fraternity.

But however much the intellectualizing of religion has been deprecated in certain Christian quarters, the question of the historical truth of Christianity cannot be for long evaded by any group. The scientific revelations of the nineteenth century shook the Protestant mind even more than the Catholic, because they undermined the great Protestant bulwark of authority, the Bible; in addition, the slowness with which Church leaders accommodated their thinking to scientific discoveries led to the disaffection of many intellectuals. That problem had existed in the sixteenth and seventeenth centuries, when Copernicus and Galileo developed cosmologies that conflicted with that of the Bible; but for churchmen of the time the new astronomy ultimately served to make God seem the more majestic. A more serious problem for the faith was raised by the Newtonian picture of a natural law in the physical world, which excluded the possibility of miracles save by special divine intervention.

The science of the nineteenth century was more shattering because both newly discovered geological evidence and the theory of biological evolution conflicted with the account of the creation in the Book of Genesis. Plainly, the earth was vastly more ancient than indicated by the biblical chronology worked out in the seventeenth century by Archbishop Ussher, who set the creation in 4004 B.C.; and evidently the world was not created in six days. Some scientists themselves attempted to harmonize geology and Genesis by expanding the days to six periods, but rigorously honest biblical scholars insisted that the word used for *day* in Genesis—the Hebrew *yom*—meant to the biblical writers twenty-four hours. Nor did geology give any warrant for the view that the periods were precisely six. The theologians would have to come to terms with the new knowledge of science.

However, the particular explanation of geological formations with which the theologians did first come to terms was not the theory current among scientists today. An English geologist, William Buckland, proposed a theory that a series of catastrophes had wiped out all life on earth, but that each was succeeded by new beginnings and new forms. A New England theologian of the mid-nineteenth century, Horace Bushnell, gave to this theory a religious interpretation as he pictured "Eternal Forethought reaching across the tottering mountains and the boiling seas" to bring into being, by his almighty fiat, the lineaments of his majestic plan. The transiency of this particular scientific theory illustrates the point that religion cannot regard the science of a given day as incontrovertible. Knowledge increases, interpretations must be tentative, and dialogue must be continuous between the religious insights of the past and the accumulating knowledge of the present. Yet, however much the geological process was subject to interpretation, it was definitely established that the story of creation in Genesis was not science but inspired mythology.

This conclusion had already been reached by several scholars when, in 1859, Charles Darwin's *Origin of Species* provided a further demonstration of the inaccuracy of the biblical account, by showing that the species did not originate each by a separate act of creation. Much more disconcerting was the claim elaborated in his *Descent of Man* (1871) that Adam was not fashioned by God out of the dust of the earth but was descended from a progenitor not remote in nature from the ape. The guiding principle in this evolutionary process had been the struggle for existence, resulting in the "survival of the fittest"—those that were most capable of adapting to their environment and able to eliminate rivals.

There were larger problems for religion here than the scientific accuracy of Genesis. What of man? If he is descended from the beasts, is he a beast? Nature is "red in tooth and claw." Must man then devour man? In 1894 Henry Drummond, a Scottish professor of natural science, addressed himself to this question in *The Ascent of Man*, claiming that the great determinative principle in biological evolution is not the survival of the fittest by the elimination of the unfit, but the principle of sacrificial mother love. Another inference drawn from evolution was that advance is the law of life; the principle of progress is written into the very structure of the universe, and man is bound to move ineluctably to a nobler state. In the case of the nineteenth-century English philosopher Herbert Spencer such sublime optimism replaced the traditional Christian apocalyptic dreams.

Linking man organically to the animal kingdom raised the question of immortality. If man is descended from the animals, and the animals are mortal, when did man become immortal; is he also mortal or, perchance, are animals immortal? Luther certainly had expected to find his dog Tölpel in heaven. Henry Drummond moved up the line of demarcation to exclude some men; according to him only those attuned to the life of the spirit can survive when the body is no more. Newman Smyth, a New England divine trained in biology, found in the doctrine of evolution support for belief in immortality, because the emergence of loftier forms is the law of life. Physical evolution having now reached its limit, further development will dispense with the body, and the evolutionary process will reach its consummation beyond the grave.

Catholic thought was much slower than Protestant in confronting the new scientific discoveries and theories, but in the twentieth century a great Catholic biologist, Pierre Teilhard de Chardin, provided in poetic form a synthesis of scientific knowledge and Christian faith. For him, as for Drummond, love rather than strife is the law of life, and its origins have a primordial anticipation in molecular attraction. Like Smyth he visualized the evolutionary process emerging toward ever nobler forms of life. He felt a divine dynamism pulsing through the cosmos, reminiscent of the vitalism often posited by medical humanists of the Renaissance, or again of the *élan vital* of the modern French philosopher Henri Bergson. But that which is distinctive and most significant is that for Teilhard, a devout and faithful Roman Catholic (and a Jesuit priest), the whole universe is sacramental, the visible sign of an invisible grace, enabling him to pray: "Since once again, O Lord, no longer in the forest of the Aisne, but in the Asian steppes, I have neither bread, nor wine, nor an altar, I will lift myself above the symbol to the pure majesty of the Real and I, thy priest, will offer unto thee upon the altar of the entire earth the labor and the suffering of the world. The sun begins to lighten from below the extreme fringe of the east. Once again beneath the curtain of his fire the living surface of the earth awakes, trembles to begin again its appalling labor. I will place upon my paten, O God, the harvest expected from this new endeavor. I will pour into my chalice the juice of all the fruits that shall be pressed this day."

Here the conflict of science and religion has vanished, because the universe is not conceived in mechanistic terms. The Jewish philosopher Martin Buber similarly has protested against the kind of science that views the cosmos simply as an object, an "it" rather than a being, a "thou" with whom the spirit of man can hold converse. The comprehension of the universe, many scientists are coming to see, calls not only for examination of that which meets the senses, but also for interpretation by way of intuition, inner vision, and spiritual illumination. In religious terminology this is revelation.

To say this is to affirm that knowledge of God can be derived from the study of the world without and by illumination from within. This affirmation raises for Christianity again the problem it faced in the first century A.D., of a religion grounded in history and set among religions based on nature or on contemplation. Christianity affirms that the knowledge of God— not simply as Creator, but as the Father and Redeemer of men— came through his own self-disclosure in Christ. This claim was made by those who knew Jesus in the flesh. Ever since then it has rested on their testimony, which is recorded in the Scriptures. For that reason the truth of the Scriptures has been subject to never-ceasing investigation.

We have noticed that the eighteenth century believed the truth to have been validated by miracles and sought to substantiate the miracles by proving the reliability of the witnesses. Then Paulus rationalized the miracles as natural events incorrectly understood. In 1835 the German scholar David Friedrich Strauss mocked Paulus' conjectures about what really happened as being more miraculous than the miracles. Strauss found the key to the Gospels in myth; the supernatural elements in the story of Christ's life were not historical facts but parts of a symbolic story enshrining an eternal truth. The miracles, he said, were myths setting forth the power of Christ, the God incarnate. This did not mean that the whole story of the life of Christ was a myth, but it did divert attention from any particular event to the one central fact of the Incarnation; and even this, as a temporal event, tended for Strauss, under the impact of Hegel's philosophy, to be swallowed up in the timelessness of God.

If a religious anchorage in history becomes insecure, then man, if he is to remain religious, must find his anchorage elsewhere. The romantics looked to feeling. Friedrich Schleiermacher, a German preacher and professor of theology during and after the Napoleonic period, claimed that religion consists in the feeling of absolute dependence. Hegel objected that in this case the dog would be the most religious of all creatures. But Schleiermacher referred solely to man's dependence upon God as revealed in Christ; and the feeling of this dependence was an intuitive grasp of ultimate reality. In other words, history itself is meaningful only when it is thus inwardly appropriated. Actually, Schleiermacher was presenting to the secularized intelligentsia of his time Lutheran theology in the language of the Romantics. Man is dependent, weak in body, weak in spirit, weak and depraved, in need of forgiveness and strength. In contrition and with confession he must acknowledge his utter dependence, that he may be helped. But the emphasis on feeling was not Lutheran, for Luther treated man's dependence and God's grace as objective facts, whether felt or not.

The English Romantics and the American Transcendentalists went further than Schleiermacher in treating feeling as a clue to fact, even historical fact. Samuel Taylor Coleridge said that to enter into religion one must submit oneself "as a many stringed instrument to the fire-tipped fingers of the royal Harper," and then, whatever "finds me" in the Scriptures is true, for "whatever finds me bears witness of itself that it has proceeded from a holy spirit." Bushnell in New England declared that the key to the Bible is not logic but imagination, passion, emotion. The logic-chopping theologians, he said, in the presence of Moses' burning bush would analyze the flame and put out the fire.

This approach was regarded by the nineteenth-century German theologian Albrecht Ritschl as altogether too subjective. Feeling, he said, is an inadequate criterion of ultimate truth. We must lay hold of what has happened, of what God has done for us in Christ. To find that out we are driven back again to history, and history can be recovered only through sources. Under the impact of Ritschl's thought Christian scholars set themselves by analysis of the sources to get back to what Jesus and the apostles actually said and did.

A later German theologian, Adolph Harnack of Berlin, believed that critical acumen would be able to disengage the legendary accretions from the authentic nucleus of early Christian records, and thus reveal the Jesus of history. One principle employed to discover what was valid history in the Gospels was to consider whatever went counter to the assumptions of the evan-

Le Corbusier's commission for the pilgrimage chapel of Notre Dame du Haut, in northeastern France, stipulated only that the structure, shown here, serve for the celebration of Mass. The architect explained that the most important influence on his design was the open countryside where the chapel was to stand, with the horizon visible in all directions. A pulpit on the porch allows for outdoor services.

gelists to be really true. For example, since the early Church was in rivalry with disciples of John the Baptist and disparaged him, all praise of John by Jesus must therefore be authentic, and so on. By this process he recovered what he considered a nucleus of indisputable material that had been obscured and elaborated by the growth of dogma in the early Church. But the character of the argument was disconcerting because among the incontestable words of Jesus was the prophecy, undoubtedly authentic by Harnack's reasoning because it had obviously *not* been fulfilled, that the Son of Man would come on the clouds of heaven within Jesus' own generation. Confronted with this dilemma the school of liberal Christianity tended to emancipate Christianity from history, by reducing Christian faith to a belief in the fatherhood of God, the brotherhood of man, and the example of Christ, inspiring even if not altogether true.

Into this attenuation of historic Christianity the Swiss theologian Karl Barth crashed, with a reaffirmation of the revelation of God in the Christ of history. Barth pictured himself as a man looking out of the window of an upper room beneath the eaves, cut off from the view above. Below in the streets he sees the crowds looking up (this was in the day of the first airplanes). They see what he does not see. Even so, in reading the Bible Barth sensed that all writers had this upward gaze, because something was coming down from above. God was revealing himself in Christ and only in Christ. The world of nature and the non-Christian religions yield no knowledge of God. This was the faith that nerved Barth and his followers to defy Hitler.

Coincidently with Barth another figure arose, the German Rudolf Bultmann, who has seemed to many to have cut completely Christianity's anchorage in history. He has affirmed that what we can know with certainty about Jesus is very slight, because the New Testament, our sole source, presents a picture of Jesus adapted to the religious needs of the early Christian community. Actually, it is a composite of diverse interpretations, cast in the thought mould of a pre-Copernican cosmology, which conceived of the Son of Man coming on the clouds of heaven, as if heaven were up in the clouds. But, as a matter of fact, Bultmann did not cut loose from history. The Christian community that fashioned the New Testament, he said, is historically inconceivable unless it had been brought into being by an unparalleled event, including the death and resurrection of

Christ. This he calls the Christ event. It is an event that, for its very understanding, calls as much now as it did then for an absolute commitment to Christ. Here is the paradox, that to get faith one must first make the venture of committing oneself to faith.

This faith, however, is not belief in the literal truth of angelology, demonology, and supernaturalism, of the sort that marked the outlook of the first century A.D. All this is mythology, of which Christianity must be divested. The question then arises whether, if Christianity be thus peeled away, it will prove to be without a core. This Bultmann would deny, and even more would his disciples, who have grown less skeptical about the historical picture of Jesus.

But there is still the question of what is the core that twentieth-century man can find meaningful in terms of his outlook and his predicament. It is to the predicament first of all that the Christian existentialists address themselves. The term *existentialist* is elusive and is used both by non-Christians and by Christians, among them Bultmann and his school. The existentialists are concerned to know whether man's existence has any meaning at all. The predicament of man lies in his alienation from the cosmos. He is poised between two naughts, between birth, before which he remembers nothing, and death, beyond which he can see nothing, in the midst of a universe whose vastness appalls him. What are his three score years and ten when he looks at a piece of amber imbedding an insect trapped thirty million years ago? Man is oppressed by the callousness of the universe, which will crush him in the end. In his early years Bertrand Russell pictured the human race as men standing on a frozen lake with unscalable banks, awaiting the thaw with unflinching dignity. Man is alienated from man. The totalitarian society tries to break the will of the nonconformist by wracking his body. His dignity consists in enduring torture rather than recant his faith or betray his kind. This is the ultimate for the non-Christian existentialist Jean Paul Sartre. Again, man is alienated by the work of his hands. Science has been prostituted to technology, and technology menaces its creatures with annihilation. Man is further alienated from himself. Probings into the unconscious have documented the Puritan picture of man "with a civil war in his bowels." Under these manifold strains some maintain the pose of heroic defiance, and some break down.

The Christian existentialists accept this picture of the human predicament, but they feel that the answer of the secular existentialists is bleak and not inevitable. As for man's alienation from himself, a solution with which Christianity is in partial accord is given by psychiatry, which seeks to heal the broken by way of self-understanding. Let the distraught achieve emancipation by recognizing the nature of such feelings as guilt, hate, and fear which emerge from the subconscious.

With regard to all these alienations the Christian answer is the old one, that despite all appearances God does have a concern for man and that tragedy, supremely manifest in the cross of Christ, is not the final word, because death is swallowed up in victory. Man's sense of guilt arises in part from subconscious disquiet, to be dispelled by understanding, but even more from genuine guilt, which must be confessed and then can be forgiven by God.

These Christian affirmations need to be stated in terms meaningful to modern man, who frequently is no longer familiar with the older vocabulary. To this task Paul Tillich, formerly of Germany and now of the United States, has particularly addressed himself. He points out that one cannot denude Christianity of mythology. One can only substitute one mythology for another. In this case mythology means the symbolic. Everything we say about God beyond his mere existence has to be conveyed in terms of symbol. Literally he is not Father, Sovereign, Lord, King, or Creator. All these words point to something beyond them. At this point Barth goes further than Tillich and asserts that no analogy has validity until after God has disclosed himself in Christ. Here is another paradox: to comprehend God one must employ analogies, but to comprehend the analogies one must first know God. Christianity calls for a leap of faith; no analogy or experience can demonstrate or validate it enough to ensure that nothing is risked in believing.

But still the practical task remains to find in our day a terminology in which Christian affirmations can be couched. An example is found in the way in which Tillich recasts Luther's doctrine of justification. Luther said that man is at the same time a sinner and justified, because God treats him as if he were not a sinner. Tillich phrases this assertion in the terms that God accepts the unacceptable. Man is unacceptable, but God accepts him and therefore man can accept himself.

The recent developments here described have taken place almost exclusively in Protestant circles. During the nineteenth century the Catholic Church very largely sealed itself off from progressive thought, whether political or theological. The reason may well have been in part that the Church of Rome during this century was too sorely pressed politically to be flexible in its theology. The pressures on the papacy came from Catholic lands, from France and Italy. The French Revolution had stripped the Church of her possessions in France. Napoleon attempted to control the Church through the manipulation of the pope. By the Concordat of 1801 the pope acquiesced to the loss of the properties but retained the right to remove bishops. Since, however, they were paid by the state, they became dependent upon the state. Confronted by so much opposition the popes became less concessive and increasingly disinclined to heed the French Catholic liberals such as Charles Montalembert, Henri Dominique Lacordaire, and Felix Dupanloup, who wished the Church to espouse the cause of political liberty, or those in England and Germany who stressed in particular religious liberty.

In 1864 Pope Pius IX in the Syllabus of Errors condemned them all, rejecting rationalism, socialism, communism, naturalism, the separation of Church and state, and liberty of the press and of religion. In conclusion he stated, "The Roman pontiff cannot and should not be reconciled and come to terms with progress, liberalism, and modern civilization." Dupanloup took the edge off this pronouncement by making a distinction between the *thesis*, which is what ideally should be done, and the *hypothesis*, which is the right thing to do in particular circumstances. In other words, the pope's condemnations ordinarily would not take effect. The pope allowed this interpretation to pass. Modern Catholic interpreters are more disposed to say that the pope had in mind only particular varieties of liberalism, liberty, and so on.

In 1870 came the unification of Italy and the termination of the temporal power of the papacy. Shortly before the troops captured the city of Rome the Vatican Council hurled a defiance against all secularisms by proclaiming the pope's infallibility. This does not mean that he cannot make a mistake, but only that when he speaks on faith and morals *ex cathedra*, that is officially, making his pronouncement binding upon all the faithful on pain of damnation, the Holy Spirit will prevent him from imposing error upon his flock. His pronouncement will not be due to any new revelation, but will be only an explication of that already given.

Around the turn of the twentieth century a group of Catholic scholars adopted the methods of biblical study in vogue among the Protestants. They were called Modernists, and many of them were excommunicated in 1910; they were accused of saying that an article of faith such as the Virgin Birth can be rejected as historical fact and then accepted as myth. They certainly reinterpreted the doctrine of infallibility as no more than the consensus of the faithful. In recent years not so much their conclusions as their methods in biblical studies have been employed by many Catholic scholars.

The deepest difference between Protestantism and Catholicism, despite all the *rapprochement*, lies in the definition of revelation. For Catholics it is objective and can be set forth in propositions. For Protestants, at any rate for Protestants of the existential variety, revelation, if it is to be revealing, must be inwardly appropriated. It must lay hold of the man in the very core of his being. It requires his uttermost commitment. But it will fluctuate, for there are tides of the spirit. Consequently, though revelation is grounded in the objective world of reality, man's grasp of it can never be definitive.

Another aspect of the same point is that revelation as a deposit must always be brought into relation with truth as a quest. The dialogue must be constant between the faith "once and for all delivered to the saints" and the growing body of man's knowledge. Therefore definitions must be tentative. This claim cuts athwart the Catholic view that the pope can make an infallible pronouncement.

This book has been concerned with the impact of Christianity upon the formation of western culture. We end with the query whether Christianity is compatible with culture at all. In the early centuries of our era Celsus and Julian the Apostate, to be echoed later by Machiavelli and Lenin, asserted that Christianity is too much addicted to the gentler virtues to undergird the structure of a state. From the Christian side the Danish philosopher Soren Kierkegaard in the early nineteenth century was savagely scornful of calling any culture Christian. Everything in Denmark, he jibed, has to be called Christian. We even have Christian brother-keepers, he said. But if one considers the rigor of Christ's demands, an entire populace will never meet them.

Christ said, "Narrow is the way, and few are they that find it."
Christianity demands an absolute commitment. It can never be
regarded as a mere item of interest to be reported in the press
between accounts of sports and the theatre. As a religion, Christianity is not simply a matter of curiosity, less fascinating perhaps than the religion of the Aztecs. Christianity is not a cultural
item; it sits in judgment on every culture in every nation of the
world, even on those it has helped fashion.

This conviction, as we have seen, has led some groups to
withdraw from society; but much more prevalent has been the
view of Augustine, who saw no possibility on earth of a perfect
society, yet believed in striving for an approximation of such a
society. In view of man's fallibility Christian rulers, Augustine
said, even if their intentions are unalloyed, cannot avoid inequities. Yet they should not shun the encounter in order to preserve their own purity. On the other hand they are not to make
any and every concession to the exigencies of the present in
order in a given circumstance to get something done. There are
occasions when for the Christian the only possible word is No.

What of the future? No man knows. Historical probabilities
render it very doubtful that Christianity will ever be the religion
of the world. Yet the shadow of the cross is cast across the years,
and faith in the Resurrection has quickened myriad hearts. The
day may never come when "every knee shall bow and every
tongue confess that Christ is Lord of all." Like the Christian
himself, the Church must in faith step forward boldly into darkness, leaving the outcome to God.

Picture Credits
Index

Picture
Credits

INDEX

Italic page numbers refer to illustrations and captions.

A

Apostles, 35–36, *42,* 47, 58, 69, 158, 380
Apostles' Creed, 68, 104, 150, 226, 233, 253, 257
Apostolic succession, 73–74
Aquila and Priscilla, 53
Aquinas, Thomas, Saint, 202–3, 208, 224, 244, 270; *Summa Theologica, 175,* 203
Arabs. *See* Islamic world
Aramaic language, 14, 49
Arch of Titus, 50
Arianism, 95–99, 100, 115, 117, 138, 145; barbarian conversions to, 126–27, 141–42
Aristotle, 21, 22, 174, *174,* 202
Ark of the Covenant, 15, 18, 29
Armenia. *See* Byzantine Church; Orthodox Churches
Arnold, Gottfried, *History of the Church and the Heretics,* 335
Arnold, Matthew, 349
Ars Moriendi (Art of Dying), 228
Artemis, worship of, 53
Articles of Perth, 296
Ascent of Man, by Drummond, 379–80
Asceticism, *98,* 101, 194–95. *See also* Monasticism
Ashtoreth, 76
Asmussen, Hans, 370
Assyria, 7, *11,* 17–19
Astarte, 14, 76
Astrology, 52
Athanasius, bishop of Alexandria, 72, 95–99, 100
Atheism, 322, 365–68
Attis, 76, 77
Aucassin and Nicolette, 222
Augsburg, Germany: confession, 258–59; Diet of, 258–59; Peace of, 263, 278, 289
Augustine, Saint, of Canterbury, 134–35
Augustine, Saint, of Hippo, 63, 111, *114,* 165, 182, 199, 201, 202, 203, 215, 254, 268, 389; *City of God,* 120–24, 150; *Confessions,* 115–19

Augustine, emperor, 94
Augustus, emperor, 7, 29, 57, 75
Aurelian, emperor, 76
Averroës, *175*
Avignon, France, papacy in, *204,* 208–15
Aztecs, 389

B

Baal, 76
Babylon, 7, 9, *11,* 18, 19, 20, 76
Babylonian Captivity, 18–20, 26
"Babylonian Captivity," of papacy. *See* Avignon, France, papacy in
Babylonian Captivity, by Luther, 247–48
Bach, Johann Sebastian, 377
Baldwin of Bouillon, 165, 166
Baptism, 47, 68, 200, 263, 264
Baptists, 263, 299, 300, 301, 302, 310, 315, 352, 357, 362, 366, 368, 373, 375, 376
Barabbas, 44
Barbarian tribes, 21, 103–9, *130,* 131–34, 138–39, 151, 155, 195; conversion, 126–31, 141–42, 182
Bar Kochba, 50
Barnabas, 53
Baronius, Caesar, *Annals,* 335
Barth, Karl, 370, 384, 386
Bartholomew, apostle, 35
Basil, Saint, 102
Bastwick, John, 298
Beauvais, France, cathedral, 184
Becket. *See* Thomas à Becket
Beecher, Henry Ward, 345, 363
Beecher, Lyman, 345, 357, 364
Belgium, 151, 371
Benedict, Saint, 102, 129–32, 157. *See also* Benedictine Rule
Benedict XIII, schismatic pope, 214
Benedict XIV, pope, 319

Church Fathers, 69, 72, 76, 80, 221, 237
Church of England, 273–75, 287–88, 296–302, 308–10, 313–15, 319, 323, *334,* 336–37, 340–41, 346–49, 355, 365, 373. *See also* Book of Common Prayer; Clapham Sect; Episcopal Church, U.S.; Oxford Movement
Church of Rome, 224, 349, 366–67, 368–70; Apostolic succession, 73–74; "Babylonian Captivity" (Avignon papacy), 208–15; Biblical scholarship, 277, 386–88; contemporary, 365, 371, 376–80, 386–88; early doctrinal controversies, 92–100, 104–7, 111–13, 123, 161–62, 196–98, 265; early organization, 59, 73; eastern schism, 166; finances and possessions, 132–34, 140, 170; Gregorian reforms, 159–64, 166, 186, 195; Hellenism, 61, 67, 79, 173–74; Hitler and, 369–72; Humanism and, 226–27, 228; medieval decline, 205–29; pre-Lutheran reformers, 232–37; Protestant *rapprochement* with, 376–77, 387, 388; science and, 278, 378–81, 386–87; social reforms and, 354–56, 361–62, 363–64. *See also* Cardinals, College of; Counter-Reformation; Monasticism; Papacy
Cicero, 115, 116, 122, 124
Cistercians, 178–81, 193, 195
Cities, medieval, 169, 184
City of God, by Saint Augustine, 120–24, 150
Clapham sect, 332, 346
Clarendon Code, 313
Claudius, emperor, 53
Clement I, pope, 73–74
Clement V, pope, 209

Clement VI, pope, 244
Clement VII, pope, 249, 272, 281
Clement VII, schismatic pope, *204,* 213
Clement XIV, pope, 319
Clement of Alexandria, 79, 80
Clotilda, queen, 136
Clovis, king of the Franks, 136–39, 146, 182
Cluniac order, 164–65, 178, 193
Cluny, France, 157–58, 159, 165
Coke, Thomas, 340–41
Coleridge, Samuel Taylor, 382
Colet, John, 234
Coligny, Gaspard de, 284
Colonna, Vittoria, 235
Colossians, Epistle to the. *See* New Testament
Columba, Saint, 135, 136
Columbanus, 141
Columbus, Christopher, 236
Comenius, John, 320
Communism, 24, 365, 387
Conceptualism, 177
Conciliarism, 214, 215, 220, 231, 277
Concordats: of 1801, 387; of 1929, 370; of 1933, 369; of Worms, 164
Condé, prince de, 283
Confessing Church, 370
Confessions, of Saint Augustine, 115–20
Confucianism, 353, 354
Congregational Christian Churches, 376
Congregationalism, 299–301, 307–15, 343, 357, 361, 362, 372, 376; early, 59
Consanguinity table, *180*
Constans I, emperor, 97–98
Constantine I, emperor, 63, 88–94, 95–101, 103, 109, 125–26, 133, 147–48, 182, 226
Constantine II, emperor, 98
Constantinople, 97–112, 147–48, 166, 169, 196, 220; Hagia Sophia, 109, *110. See also* Byzantine Empire

Consubstantiation, 79, 96, 323
Contarini, Gaspard, 235
Conventicle Act, 314
Conventuals, Franciscan sect, 194, 212
Copernicus, *327*, 378
Coptic art, *105*
Copts, 104, 109
Corinthians, Epistle to the. *See* New Testament
Cotton, John, 317
Councils: of Basel, 220; of Chalcedon, 107; of Clermont, 165; of Constance, 215, 219; of Constantinople, 100; of Nicaea, 97, 104; of Pisa, 214; of Trent, 203, 277–79. *See also* Ecumenical Councils
Counter-Reformation, 277–95, 319
Courtier, The, by Castiglione, 222
Court of High Commission, 297, 302–3
Coventry, England, cathedral, *344*
Coverdale, Miles, bishop, 274
Cranach, Lucas, the Elder, drawing of Luther, *230*
Cranmer, Thomas, 272–75
Credentes, 198
Crispin, Saint, 170
Cromwell, Oliver, *297,* 306–12
Cromwell, Richard, 312
Cross, as symbol, *86*
Crucé, Emeric, 320
Crusades, 164–67, 174, 181, *187,* 195–96, 206–7, 208, 210, 237
Cur Deus Homo, by Saint Anselm, 182
Cynics, 24, 64
Cyprian, Saint, 82
Cyril of Alexandria, 104
Cyril and Methodius, 156
Cyrus the Great, 20

D

Dale, Robert William, 361
Damasus I, pope, 102
Daniel, Book of, 30, 40, 58
Dante Alighieri, 220; *Divine Comedy,* 203
Darius, king of Persia, 20
Darnley, Henry Stuart, 286, 295
Darwin, Charles, 365; *Descent of Man,* 379; *Origin of Species, 358,* 379
David, king, 13, 15–17, *16,* 18, 22, 30, 33, 108
Deacons, early, 59
Dead Sea, 61; Scrolls, *23,* 30
Decius, emperor, 75, 81–82, 83, 87, 94
Declaration of Indulgence (1687), 314
De Contemptu Mundi, by Innocent III, 189
Defoe, Daniel, 321
De Haereticis, by Castellio, 282
De Haeretico Comburendo, 216
Deism, 322–31, 347
Denis, Saint, 153
Denmark, 156, 190, 289, 290
Descartes, René, 324
Descent of Man, by Darwin, 379
Devil, tempting Christ, *37*
Diaspora, 25, 61
Dickens, Charles, *Pickwick Papers,* 340
Dido, 174
Diggers, 299
Diocletian, emperor, *55,* 87–89, *93,* 94
Dionysius Exiguus, 150
Dionysius the Areopagite, 153, 160
Divine Comedy, by Dante, 203
Dominic, Saint, 191, 194–95
Dominicans, 194–95, 202, 227, 228
Domitian, emperor, 58, 60
Donation of Constantine, 147–48, 159, 226

Gandhi, Mahatma, 353
Garrison, William Lloyd, 357
Gaul, *71*
Gelasius I, pope, 147
Geneva, *269,* 270–71, 281–82
Genevieve, Saint, 140
George, Saint, 139
Gerbert. *See* Sylvester II
Germanic law, *130*
Germanic tribes. *See* Barbarian tribes
Germany, 155–156, 189, 207, 208, 277, 278, 288–91, 319, 365, 371–72, 387; Christian Socialism in, 361; nationalism, 245, 335; Nazism in, 369–70, 372; Pietism, 332–36, 341. *See also* Holy Roman Empire; Lutheranism; Reformation; individual cities
Gethsemane, 43
Ghibellines, 189
Ghislieri, Michele, 281
Gibbon, Edward, 335
Gnosticism, 66–68, 76, 116, 197, 227
Godfrey of Bouillon, 165
Goffe, William, 307
Goldsmith, Oliver, 329
Golgotha, 44
Gospels. *See* New Testament
Goths, 103, 117, 125, 126, 131, 149. *See also* Barbarian tribes
Grand Remonstrance, 306
Gratian, founder of canon law, 171
Great Awakening: First, 332, 341; Second, 341–43, 345
Grebel, Conrad, 263, 265
Greece, *11*
Greek culture, ancient, 21–26, 52–53; in Christianity, 63, 67, 79, 173–74. *See also* Early Christians
Greek Orthodox Church, 106, 377. *See also* Byzantine Church

Gregory I, pope (Saint Gregory the Great), 133–38, 141
Gregory VII, pope, 159, 161, 162, 164, 166, 186, 195, 332
Gregory IX, pope, 201
Gregory XI, pope, 213
Gregory XII, pope, 214
Gregory of Tours, 136, 139
Grotius, Hugo, 321
Guelphs, 189
Guilds, 169–70
Guise family, 284–86
Guiton, Jean, 292
Gulliver's Travels, by Swift, 320
Gustavus Adolphus, king of Sweden, 289–90

H

Hadrian, emperor, 50, 133
Hadrian I, pope, 148
Hagia Sophia. *See* Constantinople
Hammurabi, Code of, 9, 10
Hanoverians, 371
Hanukkah, *28*
Hapsburgs, 242, 249, 263, 289–91, 371
Harnack, Adolph, 382–84
Harold, king of Denmark, 156
Hebrews. *See* Jews; Old Testament
Hebrews, Epistle to the. *See* New Testament
Hegel, Georg Wilhelm Friedrich, 381
Heliogabalus. *See* Elagabalus
Hellenism. *See* Greek culture
Héloïse, 177, 183
Helwys, Thomas, 300
Henderson, Arthur, 360
Henry III, emperor, 159, 162
Henry IV, emperor, 159–64, 247
Henry II, king of England, 164, 174, 176, 188
Henry VIII, king of England, 272–74, 299

Isaiah, 18–19, 41, 92
Ishtar, 76, 77
Isidore of Seville, 155
Isis, 76
Islamic world, 146, 173, 227, 354. *See also* Moslems
Israel. *See* Jews; Palestine
Italy, 152, 181, 188, 220, 221, 222, 223, 235, 280–84, 370–71, 387. *See also* Roman Empire; individual cities

J

Jacobite Church, Syrian, 106
James the Greater, apostle, 35, 139
James the Less, apostle, 50; Epistle of, *see* New Testament
James, Saint, *211*
James I, king of England, *290,* 295–96, 303
James II, king of England, 313–14
James V, king of Scotland, 286
James VI, king of Scotland. *See* James I, King of England
Jannaeus. *See* Alexander Jannaeus
Jansenists, 293, 323
January, Edict of, 284
Japan, 280, 350–54 *passim*
Jeanne d'Albret, 267
Jefferson, Thomas, 323, 356, 373
Jehovah. *See* Yahweh
Jeremiah, 48
Jericho, 13
Jerome, Saint, 99 (quoted), 102–3, 115; Vulgate, 102, 234, 277
Jerusalem, 15–30 *passim, 16,* 41, 44, 48, 50, 109, *160,* 167, 169, *187;* Church of the Holy Sepulcher, 167; Mount of Olives, 17, 43; Temple of, *28;* Temple of Herod, 39, 41, 50; Temple of Solomon, 17–20 *passim,* 26–27, 112

Jesuits, 279–80, 288, 319, 349, 353, 380
Jesus Christ, *23, 32, 37, 42,* 58–59, *71,* 74, 80, *86, 105,* 136, 140, 233, 240–41, 247–48, 282, 322, 331, 353, 377, 381; Anabaptist belief in, 265–66; Anti-Trinitarians and, 281; baptism, 33; birth, 7, 30–31, 33, *225,* 388; childhood, 34; cleanses the Temple, 41; Crucifixion, 44–45, 70–73, *137, 276;* entry into Jerusalem, 41; Erasmus on, 233; first preachings, 34–35; genealogy, 33, *78;* historical study of, 382–84; incarnation, 96–97, 113, 241; Last Supper, 43, 47; Luther on, 240–41; miracles, 34; Paul's interpretation of, 33, 49; and Pharisees, 36–38; plot against, 41–44; Renaissance view of, 227–28; resurrection, 45, 53, 70, 74, 90; Sermon on the Mount, 124, 234; Servetus on, 281–82; as Son of Man, 39, 40, 47, 384; trial, 43–44
Jews, *6,* 7–31 *passim, 11, 28,* 168, 142, 190, 321, 366, 369; in Rome, 25, 53–57, 61; in Spain, 142, 236. *See also* Judaic tradition
Joachim of Flora, 200, 212
Job, 19, 326, 328
John, apostle, 35, 48, 72, 330; Epistles of, *see* New Testament; Gospel of, *see* New Testament
John, king of England, 176, 190, 207
John VIII, pope, 155
John XII, pope, 159
John XXII, pope, 209–12
John XXIII, Pope, 214, 377
John XXIII, schismatic Pope, 214–15, 219

John Chrysostom, Saint, 102, 115, 125
John Frederick, of Saxony, 252, 256
John of Damascus, 112
John of Gaunt, 215, 273
John the Baptist, *23*, 34, 382
Jordan Valley, *37*
Joseph, 7, 33, 34
Joseph II, emperor of Austria, 319
Josephus, 15
Joshua, 12–13, 26, 362
Judaic tradition, 8–31, 227, 354, 366; circumcision, 49–50; early Christianity and, 48–51; in Gnosticism, 67; Jesus' conflict with, 36–39; Messianism, 30, 33; and Mohammed, 111; Passover festival, 9. *See also* Moses, Law of; Talmud; Torah
Judas Iscariot, 35, 43–44
Jude, Epistle of. *See* New Testament
Julian, Saint, 170
Julian the Apostate, 99–100, 335, 388
Julius II, pope, 223, 231–32, 272
Julius Caesar, 51
Jupiter Heliopolitan, *62*
Justina, empress, 117–18
Justinian, emperor, 107, 109, 125, 132–33, 141, 150, 212
Justinian Code, 107–8, 171, 265
Juvenal, 52

K

Kant, Immanual, 320, 325; *Critique of Pure Reason*, 332
Kappel, Switzerland, 263
Keble, John, 347; *The Christian Year*, 348
Keith, George, 356
Kellogg-Briand Pact (1928), 362
Kierkegaard, Soren, 388

King James Bible, 296
Kingsley, Charles, 360
Kirchentag, 370
Knights Templars, 181–82, 208–9
Knox, John, *283*, 286–87
Koine (Greek dialect), 51
Kollwitz, Kaethe, drawing, *367*
Korea, 353

L

Lacordaire, Henri Dominique, 387
Ladd, William, 362
Lanfranc, archbishop, 164
Las Casas, Bartolomeo de, 350
Last Supper, 43, 47
Lateran Council, Fourth, 190
Laud, William, 296–99, 301–3, 316
Law. *See* Canon law; Judaic tradition; Roman law
Law, William, *Serious Call to a Devout and Holy Life*, 337
Lazarus, 330
Le Corbusier, Notre Dame du Haut, Ronchamps, France, *383*
Lefèvre, Jacques. *See* Faber, Jacobus
Leibnitz, Gottfried, 328
Leighton, Alexander, *Sions Plea Against the Prelacie*, 298
Lenin, Vladimir Ilyich, 388
Leo III, pope, 148, *153*
Leo X, pope, 223, *239*, 243–45; *Exsurge, Domine*, 245, 249
Leo XIII, pope, *Rerum Novarum*, 361
Leonardo da Vinci, 242
Lessing, Gotthold, 323, 331
Levelers, 299, 301, 310
Lex Rex, by Rutherford, 299
Liberian Catalogue, 74
Liberius, pope, 99
Licinius, 88, 89, 90, 92

Lilburne, John, 301
Linus, pope, 73, 74
Lisbon, Portugal, earthquake, 328
Livingstone, David, 354
Locke, John, 324, 330, *334,* 343
Logos, 33
Lollards, 216
Lombard League, 188
Lombards, 109, 132–34, 141–42, 146–49. *See also* Barbarian tribes
Lord's Prayer, 257
Lord's Supper, 59, 66, 70, 260–61. *See also* Consubstantiation; Eucharist; Transubstantiation
Lorenzo the Magnificent. *See* Medici family
Lothair I, emperor, 151
Lothair II, king, 155–56, 163
Louis I the Pious, emperor, 151, 154, *204*
Louis II, emperor, 155
Louis VII, king of France, 174
Louis IX, king of France (Saint Louis), 184
Louis XIII, king of France, 296
Louis XIV, king of France, 293, 294
Louis the German, 151
Loyola, Ignatius, Saint, 228, 234, 279, 332
Luddites, 360
Luke, 72; Gospel of, *see* New Testament
Luther, Martin, 229, *230,* 237, 238, *239,* 240–245, *246,* 247–261, 273, 322, 332, 333, 379, 382, 386; *Address to the Christian Nobility of the German Nation,* 245–47; *Babylonian Captivity,* 247–48; Erasmus and, 245–49, 252–53; "A Mighty Fortress Is Our God," 377; New Testament translation, 250; Ninety-Five Theses, 242–43;

quoted, 238, 249–250; Zwingli and, 259–64
Lutheranism, 251–59, 261–75, *311,* 333, 362–76, 382
Lyons, France, 66
Lystra, Asia Minor, 53

M

Maccabees, 26, 27, 39
MacDonald, Ramsay, 360–61
Machiavelli, Niccolò, *The Prince,* 223–24, 388
Madison, James, 373
Magdeburg Centuries, 335
Magi, 33
Magna Mater, 56, 76, 77
Maintenon, Madame de, 294
Manichaeans, 116–17, 124, 197
Manz, Felix, 263, 265
Marcion, 63, 68–70
Marcus Aurelius, emperor, 65–66; *Meditations,* 116
Marguerite of Navarre, 267
Mark, Saint, 48, 70–71, *78;* Gospel of, *see* New Testament
Marozia, 156
Marsilius of Padua, 210–12, 215, 273
Martel. *See* Charles Martel
Mar Thoma Church, India, 106
Martin V, pope, 215
Martin of Tours, Saint, *71*
Martyn, Henry, 354
Martyrs. *See* Early Christians, persecution of
Marx, Karl, 365
Mary, 7, 33, 68, 104, *160,* 162, 179, 181, 189, *192,* 203, 380, 388; cult of, 100
Mary, queen of England, 272, 274–75, 278
Mary, queen of Scots, *283,* 286–88, 295
Mary, queen regent of Scotland, 286
Mary Magdalene, 36, 45, 84

Erasmian, 278; Neoplatonic, 221; Renaissance, 227, 228

N

Naaman the Syrian, 39
Nantes, France, Edict of (1598), 285, 292–94
Naples, *204*
Napoleon Bonaparte, 387
Napoleonic Wars, 355, 372
Nathanael, apostle, 35
National Council of Churches, 376
National Covenant (1638), 303–5
Nationalism, 234, 247, 271–75, 335
Natural law, 321
Nayler, James, 312
Nazareth, 7, 33, 39, 50
Nazism, 369–70
Neoplatonism, 83, 154, 228, 232, 267; of Augustine, 117, 118–19, 124; mystic, 221
Nero, emperor, 54, 58, 74
Nestorianism, 97, 104–7
Netherlands, 151, 277, 278, 282, 288, 289–91, 350, 371; Anabaptists in, *see* Mennonites; Dutch Reformed Church, 372; Protestant struggles, 285; Puritans in, 295–96, 298–99, 305, 315–17; under Spain, 234–35
New England Colonies. *See* American Colonies
New England Non-Resistance Society, 362
Newman, John Henry, cardinal, 347–48
New Testament, 118–19, 198, 200; Acts of the Apostles, 29, 47, 69, 158; Apocrypha, 72; Colossians, Epistle to the, 96; Corinthians, First Epistle to the, 43; formulation of, 69–73; Gospels, *37*, 38, 40, 43–45, 48, 69–72, *see also* individual gospels; Hebrews, Epistle to the, 69, 72; James, Epistle of, 69; John, Epistles of, 69; John, Gospel of, 33, 36, 69–72, 96; Jude, Epistle of, 69; Luke, Gospel of, 7, 33, 34, 70–72; Luther's translation of, 250; Mark, Gospel of, 33, 45, 70–72, *78;* Matthew, Gospel of, 33, 36, 70, 307; Paul, Epistles of, 69; Philemon, Epistle to, 69; Revelation, Book of, 58, 69, 72; Romans, Epistle to the, 58; Timothy, Epistle to, 69–70; Titus, Epistle to, 69–70. *See also* Bible
Newton, Isaac, 324, 343, 378
New York Peace Society, 362
Nicene Creed, 96–100, 117, 138
Nicholas I, pope, 54
Nicholas V, pope, 221
Nicholas of Cusa, 227
Niemöller, Martin, 370
Ninety-Five Theses, by Luther, 242–43
Noah, 49, 80, 82, 337
Nobili, Robert de, 353
Nominalism, 171–72, 177, 205, 212, 224
North Carolina Colony, 101
Norway, 156
Novatianists, 101
Nuns, 258
Nuremberg, Germany, Diet of, 258

O

Oastler, Richard, 360
Occultism, 227
Olaf I, king of Norway, 156
Olaf II, king of Norway, 156
Old Believers, 366
Old Roman Symbol, 68
Old Testament, 8–20, 25, 40–41,

58, 68–69, 307, 323. *See also* Bible

Omayyad dynasty, 142

On Contempt of the World, by Innocent III, 189

On the Church, by Huss, 219

On the Immortality of the Soul, by Pomponazzi, 226

Oracles, *225*

Oratory of Divine Love, 235

Order of Preachers. *See* Dominicans

Order of the Temple. *See* Knights Templars

Origen, 63–64, 79, 84, 85, 96, 100

Origin of Species, by Darwin, *358,* 379

Orphic cult, 76, 77

Orthodox Churches, 166; Greek, 106, 377; Russian, 366–71, 377. *See also* Byzantine Church

Osiris, 76–77

Ostrogoths, 107, 125, 132

Otto I, emperor, 155–56, 159

Otto III, emperor, 159

Ovid, 174

Oxford Movement, 346–49

Oxford, England, university of, 170; St. Mary's Church, 275

P

Pachomius, Saint, 102

Pacifism, 362; early Christian, 63–64; early Protestant, 263, 265, 266

Paganism, 64, 88—92, 195, 353; influence on early Christianity, 61; influence on Judaism, 20, 22, 26; Justinian Code and, 108; Mystery cults, *62,* 76–77; Phoenician, 56; Roman, 51–58, 61–64

Paine, Thomas, 323

Palestine (Holy Land), 10–31 *passim,* 206. *See also* individual cities

Palestrina, Giovanni Pierluigi da, 377

Paley, William, 325

Papacy, 132–34; "Babylonian Captivity" (Avignon papacy), 208–15; Conciliarism and, 214–220, 231; decline, 205–29 *passim;* Gallican Articles and, 294; Gregorian reforms, 159–62, 186; Jesuits and, 279–80; medieval, 146–67, 169; modern, 370–71, 387; Renaissance secularism, 221–24; schism and, 213–15, 220, 231. *See also* Church of Rome; Counter-Reformation; individual popes

Papal bull, *239*

Papal infallibility, 214, 387

Paradise Lost, by Milton, 326–28

Paraguay, 280

Paris, France, 176; Notre Dame, 171, 176, 177, 284–85; Synod of, 284; University of, 170, 234, 279

Pascal, Blaise, 293–94, 325

Patrick, Saint, 128, 135

Paul, Apostle, 25, 48–56, 69, 72, 73, 74, 83, 119, 124, 147, 154, 157, 161, 233, 264; Epistles of, *see* New Testament; teachings of, 43, 45, 48–49, 72

Paul III, pope, 279

Paul IV, pope, 278, 280

Paul the Deacon, 149

Paulus, Heinrich, 331, 381

Pax romana, 51–52

Peace of God, 158, 164, 191

Peasants' War, 254–56

Peel, Robert, 364

Penance, 82–83, 182, 248

Penn, William, 317, 320

Pennsylvania Colony, *311,* 317, 335, 361–62, 372

Pentateuch, 20

Pentecost, 47

Ptolemy, *327*
Puritans: American, 268, 298–99, 315–17, 322, 361–62, 372, 377; English, 260, 287, *290,* 295–315 *passim,* 326, 339, 369
Pusey, Edward, 347, 349
Pym, John, 305

Q

Quakers, 299–317 *passim,* 339, 356, 362, 364, 369, 372
Quartodeciman Churches, 70
Quirinius, 7, 33
Qumran, 34

R

Ranters, 299
Raphael, 223
Rauschenbush, Walter, 361
Ravenna, Italy, 132; S. Apollinare Nuovo, 125
Raymond IV, count of Toulouse, 165, 167
Raymond VI, count of Toulouse, 198
Realism, 172, 177, 216
Rechabites, 111
Reformation, 205, 213, 231–75, *246,* 335, 349, 377. *See also* Calvin; Luther; Protestantism; Zwingli, Ulrich
Reimarus, Hermann, 331
Reims, France, cathedral, *199*
Relics, *23, 225*
Religious wars, 277–317
Remanence, doctrine of, 216, 219
Renaissance: Carolingian, 149–50; Italian, 220–29 *passim,* 380
Republic, The, by Plato, 24
Rerum Novarum, by Leo XIII, 361
Reuchlin, Johann, 226–27, 245, 250

Revelation, Book of. *See* New Testament
Revivalism, 138–39; American, 345–46, 373–75; English, 346–49. *See also* Great Awakening; Methodism; Pietism
Ricci, Matteo, 353
Richelieu, cardinal, 392–93
Risorgimento, 371
Ritschl, Albrecht, 380
Robert of Flanders, 166
Robert II of Normandy, 165
Robert the Pious, 164–65
Roderick, king, 142
Roger the Norman, 179–81
Roman Empire: under Constantine, 88–94; under Diocletian, 87–89; emperor worship, 25–26, 57–58, 63, 81, 92; fall of, 81, 103–4, 115, 117, 120, 122, 221; gladiatorial contests, 51, 63; Jews and, 21–25, 53–58, 61; paganism in, 52–57, 61, 64, 76–79, 99; Palestine and, 26–30; Paul and, 47, 51, 52–54; *Pax romana,* 51–52; restoration of, *153. See also* Rome, city of
Roman law, 107–8, *130,* 133, 171, 254.
Romans, Epistle to the. *See* New Testament
Romanticism, 382
Rome. *See* Church of Rome; Roman Empire; Rome, city of
Rome, city of, *11, 93,* 97, 117, 132–34, *153;* Castel Sant' Angelo, 133, 164; St. Peter's Basilica, 148, 232, 242; Sistine Chapel, 222. *See also* Church of Rome; Roman Empire
Romulus and Remus, 120
Root and Branch Petition (1640), 306
Rousseau, Jean Jacques, 320
Russell, Bertrand, 385

Russia, 362, 365–68, 372; deism, 323–24

Russian Orthodox Church, 366–71, 377

Rutherford, Samuel, *Lex Rex,* 299

S

Saarinen, Eero, Chapel, Massachusetts Institute of Technology, Cambridge, Mass., *374*

Sabbatarianism, 296

Sabbath, 25, 36–37, 50, 91, 303

Sachs, Hans, 252

Sacraments, 176, 215, 216, 217, 228, 229, 238, 247, 248

Sadducees, 24, 27, 30, 36

St. Bartholomew's Day, massacre of, 385

St. Denis, France, abbey of, 154, *168*

St. Paul's Cathedral, *290*

St. Peter, Patrimony of, 209

St. Peter's Basilica. *See* Rome, St. Peter's Basilica

Saints, cult of, 140. *See also* Martyrs; individual saints

Salvation, 49, 52, 67, 80, 257, 277

Salvian, monk, 126

Salviati, archbishop, 223

Samson Agonistes, by Milton, 326

Samuel, *16*

Sanhedrin, 30, 41, 50, 61

Santiago de Compostela, Spain, *211*

Sarmatians, 125

Sartre, Jean Paul, 385

Saturninus, Saint, 140

Savonarola, Girolamo, 227, 231

Saxons, 103, 135, 145, 149, 159, 162

Scandinavia, 156, 336. *See also* individual countries

Schism, papal, 213–15, 220, 231.

See also Church of Rome, Eastern Schism

Schleiermacher, Friedrich, 381–82

Schmalkaldic League, 259

Scholasticism, 169, 173–77, 202–3, 234, 241

Schwenckfeld, Kaspar, 333, 361

Science, 278, 324–25, 330, 378–81, 384–85

Scotland, 103, 135, 206, 213, 284–308 *passim,* 339, 371

Scotus, John. *See* Erigena

Scythians, 125

Sebastian, Saint, *55*

Seekers, 299

Seneca, 52

Septuagint. *See* Bible

Serious Call to a Devout and Holy Life, by Law, 337

Servetus, Michael, 281–82

Severus, house of, 74–75, 88

Sforza family, 222

Shakespeare, William, 220

Shepherd of Hermas, The, 83

Sherlock, Thomas, *Trial of the Witnesses of the Resurrection,* 330

Sic et Non, by Abelard, 177

Sicily, 133, 166, 201, 207

Sigismund, emperor, 214–15, 219, 220

Simeon Stylites, Saint, *98*

Simon Magus, 73, 158

Simon Peter. *See* Peter, apostle

Simony, 158, 172

Sions Plea Against the Prelacie, by Leighton, 298

Sistine Chapel. *See* Rome, city of

Sixtus I, pope, 73

Sixtus IV, pope, 222, 229

Slave Emancipation Society, *351*

Slavery, 21, 24, 25, 332, 355–60, *351*

Slavic Bible, 156

Smith, Joseph, 345

"Social Gospel," 361

Socialism, 360–61, 387

Society for the Propagation of

the Gospel in Foreign Parts, 337

Society of Friends. *See* Quakers

Society of Jesus. *See* Jesuits

Socinians, 281, 282

Solemn League and Covenant (1643), 306, 313

Solomon, king, 17, 108; Temple of, 17–20 *passim,* 26–27, 112

Son of Man. *See* Jesus Christ

Sorbonne. *See* Paris, University of

Sorcery, belief in, *304,* 332

Soter, pope, 73

The Souldier's Pocket Bible, 307

South Africa, 295

Spain, 149, 213; colonies, 350, 371–72; conversion, 142–143; Humanism and, 234–36; Inquisition, 231, 236; Jews in, 142, 236; Moors in, 113, 142–43, 190, 206, 208, 236; Ximénez reforms, 236–37

Spencer, Herbert, 379

Spener, Philipp Jacob, 333

Spengler, Lazarus, 252

Speyer, Germany, Diet of, 258

Spirituals (sect), 194, 213, 235

Stabat Mater Dolorosa, 189

Standonck, John, 234

Stanley, Henry Morton, 354

Star Chamber, 298, 303

Stephen, Saint, 48

Stephen II, pope, 147

Stoddard, Solomon, 342

Stoicism, 21, 22, 24, 53, 65, 124

Stowe, Harriet Beecher, 345; *Uncle Tom's Cabin,* 357

Strafford, Earl of. *See* Wentworth, Thomas

Strauss, David Friedrich, 381

Stundists, 366

Suger, Abbot, *168*

Summa Theologica, by Aquinas, *175,* 203

Supreme Court of Judicature, 309

Sweden, 156, 289–91, 365, 372

Swedish Lutheran Church, 372

Swift, Jonathan, 322; *Gulliver's Travels,* 320, 329

Switzerland, 141, 151, 259–71 *passim,* 288, 295. *See also* individual cities

Syllabus of Errors, by Pius IX, 387

Sylvester I, pope, 147, 159

Sylvester II, pope, 159

Syria, 13, 26, 27, 65, 73, 76, 102, 104, 106, 107, 109, 111, 166

T

Taborites, 219–20

Tacitus, 54, 58

Talmud, 20. *See also* Judaic tradition

Tamerlane, 106

Tammuz, 76

Tancred, 166

Tarik, 142

Tauler, Johannes, 228, 333

Teilhard de Chardin, Pierre, 380

Telesphorus, pope, 73

Templars. *See* Knights Templars

Temple. *See* Jerusalem

Ten Commandments, 9–10, 49, 257

Ten Hours Bill (1846), 360

Tertullian, 63–64, 66, 79–80, 82, 96, 100

Test Act (1673), 313

Tetzel, Johann, 242–43

Teutonic Knights, 208, 252

Theatines, 235

Theism, 322

Theobald, count of Champagne, 186

Theodora of Rome, 156

Theodosian Code, 100, 108

Theodosius I, 100, 118

Theodosius II, 100

Thirty-Nine Articles, 287, 303, 315, 323, 349

Thirty Years' War, 288–92, 295, 296

Victoria, queen of England, 359
Victorinus, 117, 118
Vigilius, pope, 107
Viking invasions, 151–52, 156, 164
Vincent, Saint, 170
Virgil, 63; *Aeneid,* 103
Virgin Mary. *See* Mary
Visigoths, 103, 107, 109, *121,* 138, 141–42, 155. *See also* Barbarian tribes
Vitoria, Francisco de, 321
Voltaire, 323, 325, 328, 330, 365; *Candide,* 320, 328; *Poem on the Disaster of Lisbon,* 328
Vulgate. *See* Bible

W

Waldenses, 194–97, 201–2, 265–66
Waldo, Peter, 196
Walker, Robert, portrait of Oliver Cromwell, *297*
Ward, Wilfred, 347
Wartburg Castle, Germany, 250, 253, 256
Washington, George, 356
Webster, Daniel, 357
Wentworth, Thomas, earl of Strafford, 296, 303–6
Wesley, John, *318,* 332, 337–41, 346, 355, 360
Wessel Gansfort, 229
Westminster Assembly, 306
Westminster Confession (1648), 306
Westphalia, Germany, Treaty of (1648), 291, 319
Whitby, England, Synod of (664), 136
Whitefield, George, 341
Whittier, John Greenleaf, 357–59
Wichern, Johann, 336
Wilberforce, William, 355–56
William of Aquitaine, 157
William of Ockham, 212–13, 216

William of Orange, 285, 289, 314–15
William of Utrecht, 163
William Rufus of England, 164
William the Conqueror, 164
Williams, Roger, 343, 350, 372
Winfrith. *See* Boniface, Saint
Witches. *See* Sorcery
Wittenberg, Germany, 229, 242, 251–56 *passim;* University of, 240, 244, 250
Wolsey, Thomas, cardinal, 273
Woolman, John, 356
Woolston, Thomas, 330
World Council of Churches, 377
Worms, Germany: Concordat of (1122), 164; Diet of, 249–250; Edict of (1521), 250, 258
Wycliffe, John, 215–17, 247, 273; translation of Bible, 216

X

Xavier. *See* Francis Xavier, Saint
Ximénez de Cisneros, Francisco, 236–37, 278

Y

Yahweh, 12, 14–19 *passim,* 27, 29, 31, 57, 67, 69

Z

Zealots, 29, 36, 40, 41–43
Zechariah, 41
Zinzendorf, Ludwig von, 333, 336–38
Zizka, John, 219–20
Zoroastrianism, 227
Zumarraga, bishop, 280
Zurich, Switzerland, 259–64, *262,* 265
Zwingli, Ulrich, 259–64, *262,* 268, 271
Zwinglianism, 267, 271, 274, 376

416

Roland H. Bainton was born in Ilkeston, Derbyshire, England, in 1894 and educated in the United States. He became Titus Street professor of ecclesiastical history at the Yale Divinity School, where he was a member of the faculty for forty-two years. He wrote thirty-two books, including *Here I Stand: A Life of Martin Luther; Early and Medieval Christianity; The Travail of Religious Liberty; The Age of the Reformation; Christian Attitudes Toward War and Peace;* and *Erasmus of Christendom.*

Roland H. Bainton died in 1984 at the age of eighty-nine.

Jaroslav Pelikan introduced this new edition of *Christianity.* A Sterling Professor of History Emeritus at Yale University, he is the author of numerous works including the best-selling *Jesus Through the Centuries.* He has received honorary degrees from universities all over the world, as well as medals and awards from many scholarly societies and institutions, including the Jefferson Award of the National Endowment for the Humanities, the highest honor conferred by the U.S. government on a scholar in the humanities.